Your
Book
of
Days

YOUR
BOOK OF DAYS

A compendium of history, anecdote, sciences, and curiosities
Asking your insight, your thoughts, your reactions
That make this book a record of your days.

ArLynn Leiber Presser
and
Lynn Schmelzer PE (Ret.)
M.A. Del Rosario

Your Book of Days
Copyright © 2024 by ArLynn Leiber Presser. All rights reserved.

ISBN   9798304784085

Cover Design by M.A. Del Rosario Paper Drawing Studio
Interior Design by Lynn Schmelzer

Printed in the United States of America.
2024 FIRST EDITION

For information, address Paper Drawing Studio,
    WEBSITE: www.paperdrawing.com
    FACEBOOK: paperdrawingstudio
    INSTAGRAM: paperdrawingstudio
    X (nèe TWITTER): paperdrawing

paper
drawing
studio

Dedicated

To
Joseph, Lauren, Remy, Eastman, Frances, David and Crystall

To
Peggy, Chris, Sami, Matt, Mollie, Kevin, Sabrina, & Mimi

To
Morpheus, Nona, lost loves and old promises kept

and of course to
Robert Chambers

Foreword

July 10, 1802 was an auspicious day for the Scots. Born the second son of James and Jean Chambers, Robert Chambers surpassed all the expectations of his middle class family. He was a phrenologist, geologist, publisher, writer, and evolutionary thinker. He was a voracious reader, largely self-taught and didn't narrow his interests. He wrote treatises on geology and even (anonymously) wrote Vestiges of the Natural History of Creation in 1844 which basically beat Charles Darwin to the punch on that evolution thing by fifteen years.

His most ambitious project was his, alas, his final glorious moment of sharing his genius. Robert Chambers' Book of Days investigated history, arcane celebrations, the funny oddities and the significance of each day of the year. He spent a lot of time at the British Museum because he didn't have a laptop and Google hadn't yet been released. The book came out in 1864 in two volumes--each with over 2,000 individual essays and a page count totaling 1,600. It was such an enormous feat, consuming him for four years, that it is said to have hastened his death in 1871.

Oh, wait, this isn't about Chambers! This book is YOURS! Read an essay for each day of the year. Maybe you start on January 1st and maybe you start on March 3rd. Read, reflect, and then get out your pencil or pen. They still can be found on Amazon or at your local drugstore. Write what you think about the day.

Just as every person and every winter snowflake is unique, so is every day.

And so are you!

Bestest,

ArLynn Leiber Presser

Lynn Schmelzer

M.A. del Rosario

January is the time for plans and projects; a time to set the course of the year.

–Leo Tolstoy

Happy New Year to you and your family and friends! A great year to reflect, celebrate, renew day by day and I think we should start right here—

On January 1, 1509 at 1:30 a.m. there was perhaps no happier of a New Year's reveler than the newly crowned nineteen year old Henry VIII. His wife and former sister-in-law Katherine of Aragon had just brought forth a son, to be named Henry IX. The new heir was also bestowed with the title Duke of Cornwall. He was given forty servants for his own household to be stationed at Richmond Castle where he had come into the world. Henry VIII handed out money to his counselors and courtiers, servants, the wet nurse and midwife, and set up committees to plan parades, jousts, street parties and free wine for the peasants.

On January 5th, Henry IX was baptized at the Church of the Observant Friars in Greenwich. As tradition dictated, neither parent was present and as this was 1509 it wasn't like someone sent a text to the two godparents. So there were a couple of proxies who did their parts and then vanished in history. The potentates who slowly got word of the birth sent lavish gifts, including Louis XII of France who sent a 48.5 pound cup of pure gold to hold the precious 51 ounces of salt he gifted the boy with.

After an elaborate baptism, diplomats and courtiers elbowed each other into Katherine's chambers even though, quelle horreur!, She hadn't been churched yet. Churching was an ancient tradition where new mothers couldn't go out in public until forty days after the birth of their child. There was a special blessing and ceremony to make sure they were "pure" enough. New mom peasants just got up the next day and slapped the baby on their back with swaddling and went back to work.

On the 12th Henry VIII went on a pilgrimage to Our Lady of Walsingham to give thanks. He had a lot to be thankful for. He had been but a spare. A spare, at that time, had the usual Miss Runner Up America role but there was more. A spare was expected to take over military aspects of the kingdom. If a king were so lucky as to have three sons, that one got sent to the church as a bishop if not a cardinal and was expected to get everyone in the family into heaven. Girls were like pokemon cards to be traded for foreign marital alliances. Henry was a loyal and courageous spare and he served as pageboy at his brother Arthur's wedding. He had a massive crush on Katherine. Arthur died only months into the wedding and there was a tussle about what to do with Katherine. Still, after Henry married her

Young Henry VIII and Katherine of Aragon
Married 1509

(special Papal dispensation) and she bore a son, Henry VIII gave thanks for having married the love of his life, of becoming king, and of fulfilling his dynastic duty by bringing forth Henry IX. He sent back two doves from Walsingham to Katherine to symbolize their eternal love.

And that's sort of the end of the story that began on January 1, 1509. Katherine and Henry had a happy marriage, even if Henry stepped out occasionally. He died of old age and Henry IX who had had tutors added to his household, took over or maybe if he was too young, Katherine took over as regent until he reached his majority. Henry IX married a suitable foreign princess, maybe French or Spanish and there were no more European wars. Divorced, beheaded, died, divorced, beheaded, died—nobody knows what you're talking about.

Oh, wait, that's not what happened. On February 22, 1509 at just seven and a half weeks of age, Henry who would be the nineth died at Richmond. After a lavish funeral on the 27th Henry's small coffin was buried on the north side of Westminster Abbey near King Edward the Confessor. Presents from the city of Venice with "congratulations on the birth of your son" arrived March 5th.

In reality, all of English history was changed. Lots of wives for Henry VIII, religious persecutions, beheadings (LOTS of those), and later, that pesky Spanish Armada.

Count your blessings when you can. Hand out coins with a cheerful countenance, give thanks with doves, set up jousting tournaments (okay, maybe pickleball) in your yard, host banquets and fly banners with the confidence of a nineteen year old king. And when you mourn this year, as you inevitably will, muster the strength to do it gracefully.

If you have something, anything, to celebrate today, do it without reservation. What do you have to celebrate today?

January 2 is National Science Fiction Day! This is your chance to cuddle up to an Isaac Asimov novel, to watch all those incarnations of Star Trek. Hell, knock yourself out and binge watch Star Wars movies and marvel at the plot inconsistencies. Or take yourself out of you comfort zone and order some M.A. Del Rosario Gods of Manila from Amazon.

I have a special fondness for the craft. But it didn't really evidence itself until I was twenty eight when I met my biological parents and grandparents. My first published book was a romance novel and I confess that I hadn't read one of those until about five minutes before I fired up the Corona Selectric typewriter.

I had been put up for adoption when I was three years old. And got shuffled around to a bunch of families after that. I always wanted to know who I was or where my parents were.

I discovered books and stories by Fritz Leiber, not realizing he was my grandfather. My adoptive parents had been an engineer and a housewife. Imagination was for eggheads as far as they were concerned. I think, at least in my case, nature overrode nurture. I couldn't manage a house and I certainly couldn't be an engineer. I wrote stories and shoved them under the drawers of my bedroom desk. Inevitably, my adoptive mom would find them and make me read them to her. She would question every word, every sentence, every plot point. "Now, what the hell does that mean?" She would ask. And not really in the spirit we have today with our kids—not any encouragement going. She was trying to break me.

But I think she did me a favor. To write and rewrite. To separate my ego from her disparagement.

So today, think about the relatives you have and what they excel at.
Have you inherited some of what they have?
Lynn found his calling as a professional engineer while working on
his father's farm as an apprentice mechanic.

January 03

Today, January 3, is National Festival of Sleep Day! Now this is a holiday I can really get behind. It's gray and cloudy and cold outside and it takes a lot to get me to slither out of bed in the morning. In 1998 Boston radio station WZLX said enough is enough and declared January 3rd as Sleep in Day.

I would have mandatory hibernation from here until sometime in March. Let young, motivated, made of strong stuff Amazon workers deliver everything. Kind of like the pandemic but nobody's required to work from home.

For now, to celebrate this auspicious day, take a nap. Set your alarm for ten or twenty minutes or an hour, turn off the lights and the phone, cuddle up under the blankets and just close your eyes. Or maybe call a few friends and have a slumber party—call your friends, collectively watch a soothing movie or play an online board game and when the mood strikes, let the zzzzzz's begin. In the Medieval era, candles were for the upper class and the peasants didn't have electricity. When the sun went down and the fire in the fireplace died down, folks went to sleep. In the middle of the night, the adults would wake up and quietly gossip, sing, do the nasty and go back to sleep. They knew how to party.

What will you do (or not do) with a Sleep In day?

____

____

____

____

____

On January 4, 1838 in Bridgeport, Connecticut a rather large baby (9 pounds and change) was born. His parents named him Charles Sherwood Stratton. For six months he seemed an adorable if unremarkable baby. And then his parents noticed something off. He stopped growing.

When he was nine years old he was but two feet tall and his doctor informed the parents that young Charles suffered from dwarfism caused by his pituitary gland. His adult height would be 35 inches. If that.

Meanwhile, entertainment entrepreneur Phineas (P.T.) Barnum heard of Stratton. He contacted the Stratton family.

He was impressed with Charles' quick wit and ability to do impressions of famous people. Barnum taught Charles to dance and sing. The entertainment business was changing and just staring at a bearded lady or Siamese (conjoined) twins was getting old. Renamed General Tom Thumb, Stratton could put on a show. He toured the country with Barnum and his entourage.

A lot of people paint Barnum as someone who exploited his performers and perhaps he did as well as disappointing those who couldn't put on an act. But Tom Thumb became quite wealthy working with Barnum. Thumb had his own mansion in Connecticut and even bailed out Barnum when the empresario went broke.

Thumb married fellow dwarf Mercy Lavinia Bump (okay, Barnum persuaded her to take the stage name Warren because he thought it sounded a little more regal) Barnum threw a lavish wedding on February 10, 1863 at Grace Episcopal church in New York. Ever looking for a buck, Barnum charged $75 a ticket to the reception at the Metropolitan Hotel where the newly married couple stood on top of a grand piano and greeted their well-wishers.

Thumb had already performed for Queen Victoria and other European potentates. Now President Lincoln and his wife Mary Todd invited the couple for a reception at the White House. Tiffany & Co. presented them with a silver coach sized just for them.

Thumb died 1883 of a stroke, just 45 years old. Barnum erected a gigantic column with a life sized sculpture of Thumb. Lavinia went on to marry a fellow dwarf performer Count Primo Magri, aka Count Rosebud. When Lavinia died at the age of 78 she was buried next to Thumb with a flat stone inscribed "his wife".

Today you might feel small, ordinary, not ready for prime time. But you've got this. Count up those things that make you different. Some might say odd. But you've got something… list your talents and quirks and think about how you can use them! And maybe also consider how we look at historical oddities.

What kind of life would Stratton/Thumb have had without Barnum?

____

____

____

____

____

On January 5, 1930 Bonnie Parker (19) an unemployed woman separated from her husband of four years met 20 year old confirmed criminal Clyde Barrow at the home of Clyde's friend Clarence Clay in Dallas. The Clays had taken in Bonnie who was on the outs with her family, flat broke, and suffering from a broken arm.

It was like combustion when Bonnie and Clyde met. And it would affect so many people, with an estimated dozen or so people killed on their crime spree with a gang they assembled from like minded criminal folk. They had a particular affinity with shooting up banks, gas stations and funeral homes and they also liked killing cops. For a while they were the darlings of the press because there was something oddly romantic and glamorous about them. But they weren't like Robin Hood, by any means—but a lot of the times when they'd jack a car they'd leave their victims far from home but with some money to grab a bus. Better than a bullet at the back of the head.

Feeling the heat of the law, the gang split up and promised to meet just west of Shreveport, Louisiana. The police had, alas for Bonnie and Clyde, had been tipped off to the plan. They set up an ambush by the side of Louisiana State Highway 154 and lounged about for several days waiting for the couple. They were just about to give up when Bonnie and Clyde drove up on May 23rd 1934. The police were able to kill Clyde instantly with a shot to the head although they threw in a few more for good measure. Bonnie took a little more work. All in all the police fired the car with 130 rounds.

The couple had wanted to be buried together, but Bonnie's parents declined. Bonnie expressed herself in an eloquent epic poem that ended "some day they'll be

Do you think they were heroes or just protesting an unjust economic system or stone cold villains?

Today January 6 I wish you a Happy Epiphany, Happy Theophany, Happy Twelfth night and a very merry Orthodox Christmas. It's the day the three Magi (sometimes we call them kings or wisemen) finally showed up in Bethlehem. Always late for a party.

Some believe this day is a time to "chalk" one's front door with a cross in order to bring blessings to the new year. In my fair town of Winnetka, it used to be traditional to celebrate this holiday with a party at the Challenger home. They had a two story tree under a spiral staircase. And they always had a celebrity guest. That's how I got to meet Tia Carrera pre-Wayne's World. Tip: You always negotiate the fee with the celebrity guest's agent and make sure they're underserved. The celebrity, not the agent.

The three Magi represented God's call for salvation for all people. For that reason, in most early artwork these dudes are diverse. They are said to be descendants of Shem, Ham, and Japheth who were the sons of Noah. Shem is associated with the people of Asia, Ham with Africa and Japheth with Europe.

Whatever heritage you claim this is a celebration of how we are one family. And just like December 25th there's presents! Double Win!

What celebrity guest would you like to invite to your house tonight?
I want Ryan Gosling. Lynn wants Dr. Becky. Mark wants:________

____

____

____

____

____

January 7, 1964 is a very special day in Playboy World. When you think Playboy you think of the magazine, the grumpy old Hefner and the weird stories about just what went on in the mansion. But my first memory of Playboy was when my first adoptive mother was visiting relatives and my father (not wanting to miss a boys' adventure out and having no clue how to arrange for a baby sitter) took me to the ersatz Playboy mansion in Wisconsin. The joint had a goat farm outside and my father gave me a pack of ciggies to feed them. That's the sort of era we're talking about.

I was dressed, if you are interested, in a white linen dress with applique flowers and white patent leather shoes. Lace edged anklets. A white patent leather purse with nothing in it because, well, I didn't have anything to carry in it. Except for the cigarettes.

We went inside the Playboy Clubhouse, me and my father and several of his business colleagues. I was seriously weirded out by the attire of the hostess and all the women who worked there. Tight body suit, fishnet stockings, bunny ears and a white bunny tail. Didn't these women have regular clothes?????

Little did I know that their outfits were actually a part of Patent Office history. On this day January 7, 1964 the first work uniform was trademarked and it was the Playboy bunny costume, er, uniform.

Satin corset with a fluffy cottontail, white collar, black bow tie and the bunny ears was the power suit of the Playboy enterprise from 1960 to 1988. Latvian actress Ilse Taurins (trivia: she was in the Wild Wild West TV show) was dating a Playboy exec and she pitched the idea of a "work uniform" that would mimic and solidify the brand. Ilse had her mother sew the prototype.

When I came back from Wisconsin and told my mom about feeding the goats cigarettes from my purse that led to an uncomfortable interrogation which in turn led to heckuva dust-up between my mom and dad.

If you have an idea, something you're pretty darn sure nobody else has thought of, get yourself a patent attorney. Your idea doesn't have to be a light bulb like Edison, or a telephone like Alexander Graham Bell (don't get me started on his rumble in the patent jungle with Elisha Grey). Instead, just get that patent. After all, Manolo Blahnik got a patent on the color of red used in his high heels that is a recurring item in Sex and the City. That man made bank on those shoes.

What's your idea?

On January 8, 1877 Lakota Chief Crazy Horse and his men fought their last battle with the U.S. military in Montana. They were greatly outnumbered, had run out of ammunition, and were starving.

It had only been six months since Crazy Horse and his ally Sitting Bull had slammed the troops under the narcissist Lieutenant Colonel George Custer at the Battle of Little Big Horn. Custer and all but one of his 200 soldiers were slaughtered. (August Finckle—whose real name was Frank Finkle—escaped and lived to tell a tale to the press that inflamed the white population of the country). Native Americans were ordered back to their reservations but Chiefs Crazy Horse and Sitting Bull organized the Sioux and Cheyenne in particular to resist. At the same time, using diplomatic means, General Nelson Miles persuaded some other tribes to retreat. To Canada.

Sitting Bull and Crazy Horse and their tribes remained with the Canadians for four years before realizing that not all Canadians are gracious, laid back and want to share a six pack of Molson. They returned to the United States. On January 8, 1877 General Miles surrounded their camp in a blinding blizzard and started the slaughter of the encampment. The Native American men held off the troops long enough for women and children to escape and when their safety was established, the men under Sitting Bull and Crazy Horse rejoined their families and fled.

Crazy Horse was smart enough to realize his people weren't welcome in Canada OR the United States. In May of that year, he led his tribe to surrender at the Red Cloud Reservation in Nebraska. He was resisting arrest by local police when he was killed later that year.

Beginning in 1948, sculptor Korczak Ziokowski began a Mount Rushmore type of sculpture of Crazy Horse—a brave man, a doomed leader, a hero to his people. No matter what the odds, no matter the sacrifice, be brave even when doomed and make yourself your own hero.

When have you gathered up the courage to be a hero? Don't be shy? You have!

January 9 is Play God Day. Now this is not a day to play tricks on the cosmos like getting back at that bully from fourth grade or creating a billion dollars in cash to keep you warm at night. No, it's more of a holiday set aside for you to be as God would be. I'm not talking flooding the world and only letting some dude  Noah build an ark. I'm talking do a good deed today. Help someone across the street (God copied this trick from the boy scouts). Call someone you haven't been in touch with for a while and tell them that just thinking about them made you remember an episode when they were soooooooooooooo cool. Pay at the drive thru for the car behind you. Forgive someone. Even the fourth grade bully. It's about time.

You'll make them feel good but guess what? Being a good and merciful God is a wonderful thing—you might reignite a friendship, you might just smile at yourself while you're looking in the mirror, you might also make someone else feel loved, smiled at, accepted. That's what a God does. That's what YOU do!

Is it better to play God or be an instrument of God?

January 10

On this day, January 10, 1776 Thomas Paine published "Common Sense"—a small book with incendiary properties. Paine was born an Englishman, lived in the American colonies, a failed business owner, a reluctant tax collector—jeez, the Brits even had taxes on how many windows your house had! Not giving the IRS any ideas. The taxes, by the way, were a wealth transfer just like today's taxation system but back then it was geographical. Americans were taxed to supply Britain with extra income—a lot of wealth swimming across the Atlantic and a lot of rules and edicts swimming in the opposite direction towards America.

Paine wrote "the cause of America is, in a great measure, the cause of all mankind." His book was an instant best-seller and fomented a revolution. Which, while flawed in so many ways that we like to talk about, became the United States of America. Sometimes the pen really is mightier than that sword.

____

____

____

____

____

January 11

January 11 is International Learn Your Name in Morse Code day!

Mine is .- .-. .-.. -.— -. -.

In the early 1830s Samuel Morse and his assistant Alfred Lewish Vail created a code to communicate in English with dots and dashes. What they really needed was the American engineer Joseph Henry who turned it into an electronic system for ships to communicate with each other and it was unveiled on January 11, 1838. It employs a series of dashes and dots to replicate letters and numbers—sort of like Braille.

It became invaluable during the world wars. And of course, who can forget the valor of the two Morse code operators on the Titanic who stayed 'til the bitter end attempting to communicate with nearby ships, including the Carpathian whose operator had shut down for the night. When the Titanic's assistant operator, Harold Bride, was pulled from the ocean, he was transported to the Carpathian where, though suffering frost bite on his extremities, he went to work transmitting survivors' messages to their anxious families.

Today, Morse Code is largely used by ham radio enthusiasts. The Morse Code is used with many different languages as well as English. Ultimately, the United States converted to the global maritime distress and safety system in 1999.

So today my message to you is:

-.— —— ..- .——. .-. . / -.. —— .. -. —. / —. .-..…— — -.-.— / -.-..…-.. . -… .-. .- — . /
-.— —— ..- .-. .……-.. ..-. / - —— -.. .- -.— -.-.—

International Morse Code

A	• —	N	— •	0	— — — — —
B	— • • •	O	— — —	1	• — — — —
C	— • — •	P	• — — •	2	• • — — —
D	— • •	Q	— — • —	3	• • • — —
E	•	R	• — •	4	• • • • —
F	• • — •	S	• • •	5	• • • • •
G	— — •	T	—	6	— • • • •
H	• • • •	U	• • —	7	— — • • •
I	• •	V	• • • —	8	— — — • •
J	• — — —	W	• — —	9	— — — — •
K	— • —	X	— • • —	.	• — • — • —
L	• — • •	Y	— • — —	,	— — • • — —
M	— —	Z	— — • •	?	• • — — • •

.— …. . — — .——. … / -.— —— ..- .-. / -.. .- —— . / .. -. / — —— .-. … . / -.-.
—— -.. . ..-.. *

What's your name in Morse Code?

____

____

____

____

____

January 12

On January 12, 1964 HE was born, which is to say Jeffrey Jorgenzon Bezos who would change all our lives. He devised Amazon from a cozy bookstore into an online EVERYTHING. During the pandemic I'm not even sure I ever walked into a store even after the quarantine ended because I was so used to shopping in my pajamas on the couch. He built his online bookstore out of his garage in 1994. Don't think him poor—his parents invested $300k and he had a number of trust money funds from other relatives.

He's how we got through this pandemic but he's also destroyed brick and mortar stores. I couldn't have done Xmas shopping without him. His kindly suggestions about products I might like are so thoughtful and so en pointe! I once wrote on Facebook about bobble heads a few days ago and now whenever I open up Facebook or Amazon, I get suggestions of bobble heads I might like!

Happy birthday Jeff, your present has shipped! You might get a text saying:

UPS: Your package is on a truck driven by Mike. It will arrive on your doorstep at 6:27 tonight.

Fed ex: Your package is coming. It will get there when we get there.

United States Postal Service: Package? What package?

Amazon: Your package is already in your apartment. Check your bathroom.

Facebook: We know you were thinking of buying a toaster yesterday. Here are twenty ads for toasters.

How do you shop for your presents to Jeff Bezos?

____

____

____

____

____

January 13 is Rubber Ducky Day and it is celebrated with the best of all indulgences and hoop-la, none of which requiring you to leave your own home. But before I tell you how to celebrate (you're probably filling the tub and adding a little (or a lot) of Mr. Bubble, let's think about the history behind this holiday!

In February 1970 Ernie first introduced his favorite toy Rubber Duckie. Songwriters Jeff Moss and Joe Raposo wrote a song which Ernie sang to his friend Rubber Duckie. It truly was a masterpiece that made Beethoven, Bach and Wagner look like rank amateurs.

"Rubber Duckie, you're the one. You make bath time so much fun. Rubber Duckie I'm awfully fond of you…"

It was such a popular song that it was released as a 45-single, gained a 1971 Grammy nomination for Best Recording for Children to the LP Sesame Street Book & Record which contained the song. Not a loss, I'd say.

Little Richard released two different versions of the song. It's been featured in a number of films and albums. EVERYBODY loves the song because everybody has a rubber ducky. Or maybe just a favorite bathtime friend. Rubber Duckie became a beloved character on Sesame Street, serving as Ernie's confidante, supporter, and friend.

In 1973, the Sesame Street calendar listed January 13 as Rubber Duckie's birthday. Of course, we have to celebrate. I humbly suggest you check to make sure the bathtub isn't overflowing and that the temperature is JUST RIGHT. Get your little guy, maybe pour a bathside beverage, step into the water and appreciate that whenever you think you don't have a single lousy friend in the world, you do. So make sure to sing—

Rubber Duckie

What are you going to do to celebrate?

____

____

____

____

____

January 14

January 14 is the Feast of the Ass aka Festum Asinorm, celebrating an animal who has played a pivotal role in Biblical history and is quite possibly the only animal saint.

Mary and Joseph went to Bethlehem to pay their taxes to King Herod. The week long trip would be arduous at best, horrific if you're nine months pregnant and you've had to explain to your husband that the kid isn't his. Luckily, they had a trusty donkey, or ass, or asino, to carry Mary. As much as I bitch and moan, it's worse than filing with Turbotax.

A bit after the baby Jesus was born, according to the Gospel of Matthew 2:13 and some apocryphal texts, an angel appeared to Joseph and said "Get up! Take the child and his mother, flee to Egypt, and stay there until I tell you. For Herod is about to search for the child to kill him." Herod had found out that there was a Messiah from the three Magi and he decided to kill all the male children of Israel. First time being a girl baby was a def advantage.

So on the 14th of January Joseph gets mother and child on the donkey and says "we're headed to Egypt." While it would take a little under an hour by plane today unless you're on Southwest, this was no small feat for an animal with a baby and mother on it. And it took a full three years to get them all back to Nazareth. Which is about what it would take on Southwest.

In the Medieval era, particularly in France, this day became a celebration of that little rascal Festum. A special mass was designed featuring a boy and girl and a donkey being paraded through town and led up to the altar. The service included the priest saying in Latin "orientis partibus adventavit asinus pulcher et fortissimus." Roughly translated "from the East came the ass strong and brave."

The parishioners responded "hez, sire asnes, car chantez, vous aurez du foin assez et de l'avoine a plantez" and if you didn't drop out of French class you'd know they were saying "Hey, ass, open your pretty mouth! Hay will be yours and oats in abundance!"

Instead of saying "the mass is over," the priest brayed three times on this day as if he was the donkey or at least communicating in the donkey's native language. And the congregation didn't say "Hey, thanks for that mass thing." Instead they said three times "hinham" which is kind of like three more brays.

A donkey would later bring Jesus into Jerusalem on Palm Sunday and thus cement the pivotal role of this species in Christian lore. The donkey/ass/asino was a beater car compared to the Roman centurion's stallion. Donkeys get the job done.

We all have our place in the story. Now and then. And we should never underestimate the role a simple animal will play.

What task, like a donkey, will you do today?

____

____

____

____

January 15

January 15, 1929 is Martin Luther King, Jr.'s birthday. I know, I know—his birthday was on the third Monday of January. A little disconcerting that his birthday shifts dates every year and always results in a three day weekend. But that's because President Ronald Reagan signed into law the birthday celebration for MLK on November 2, 1983 and pegged it as the third Monday. A big impetus for the creation of this birthday/holiday was Stevie Wonder. On his album Hotter Than July the fourth single was Happy Birthday to You and drew attention to the need for a birthday celebration.

MLK, Jr. was originally given the name Michael King Jr. His father was a preacher and in 1934 his congregation paid for a trip overseas to meet, learn and teach with other religious leaders. When MK Sr. returned to the states, he changed his name to Martin Luther King Sr. in honor of the Lutheran Church founder and changed 5 year old Michael's name to Martin Luther King Jr. MLK Jr. did his father (and mother) proud—a bachelor's degree from Morehouse, a degree in divinity from Crozer Theological and then another degree from Boston University. He traveled the country fighting Mahatma Ghandi peaceful like for civil rights. His first appearance in front of an all white audience was in my fair town of Winnetka. In 1964 he was awarded the Nobel Peace Prize.

But some people weren't as excited by the young preacher as others. A number of people tried to assassinate him, the first of which was Izzola Curry at a Harlem book signing in 1958.

On March 29, 1968 after an appearance MLK was hanging out with some of his friends at the Lorraine Motel in Memphis, Tennessee. There is a story that the men had a pillow fight. Just having fun. MLK walked out onto the porch a happy man. "Be sure to sing Blessed Lord tonight and sing it well." Moments later, he was shot by James Earl Ray—just one shot to the head. Taken to a nearby hospital, he was pronounced dead an hour later.

Today let's celebrate his birthday—a life that changed the world. Peacefully. And maybe remember the happy celebration pillow fight that was so fun.

How will you honor him today!

January 16

On January 16, 1919, a molasses tank* in Boston's north end exploded and sent a tsunami of thick black syrup into the streets. The molasses leveled buildings and nearly destroyed the nearby harbor. Twelve people were killed, more than 150 injured. The dead were often found embalmed by the sticky gooey sugary syrup like Pompeii and Herculaneum just without the volcanic ash. It took months to clean up although there are Bostonians claimed they could still smell the sticky stuff as late as the forties. And everything you touched felt eeeewwww!

The explosion was caused by an overnight warm spot in Boston from two degrees to forty. Next time you're at the grocery store, avert your eyes when you see bottles of molasses on the shelf out of respect for the fallen.

*Molasses imported from Puerto Rico was often converted to the volatile chemical ethanol with yeast which led to a lot of carbon dioxide. Imagine a bottle of Pepsi that you shake a lot and then opened it up. KAZOWIE!!!!!!

You never know - make "I love you" the goodbye you give to those you know.

____

____

____

____

____

On January 17, 1706 Ben Franklin was born. There is much to be said about him—polymath, founding father, diplomat, bon vivant, inventor. But this morning as I looked in the mirror and thought "who IS that woman?" I was reminded of a letter he wrote to a young man in 1745. The young man was concerned about his, ahem, urges and Ben counseled marriage but if that wasn't in the cards, choose a mistress. An older mistress. He had eight cogent arguments but the last half of his letter is enough to give all us women d'un certain age some confidence—

4. Because thro' more Experience, they are more prudent and discreet in conducting an Intrigue to prevent Suspicion. The Commerce with them is therefore safer with regard to your Reputation. And with regard to theirs, if the Affair should happen to be known, considerate People might be rather inclin'd to excuse an old Woman who would kindly take care of a young Man, form his Manners by her good Counsels, and prevent his ruining his Health and Fortune among mercenary Prostitutes.

5. Because in every Animal that walks upright, the Deficiency of the Fluids that fill the Muscles appears first in the highest Part: The Face first grows lank and wrinkled; then the Neck; then the Breast and Arms; the lower Parts continuing to the last as plump as ever: So that covering all above with a Basket, and regarding only what is below the Girdle, it is impossible of two Women to know an old from a young one. And as in the dark all Cats are grey, the Pleasure of corporal Enjoyment with an old Woman is at least equal, and frequently superior, every Knack being by Practice capable of Improvement.

6. Because the Sin is less. The debauching a Virgin may be her Ruin, and make her for Life unhappy.

7. Because the Compunction is less. The having made a young Girl miserable may give you frequent bitter Reflections; none of which can attend the making an old Woman happy.

8thly and Lastly. THEY ARE SO GRATEFUL!

How do you feel about Ben's advice?

____

____

____

____

____

January 18, 1911 was an auspicious day in aviation history, all because of young Eugene Ely who only had an eighth grade education. He started off with cars—he was the chauffeur to a speed loving priest in his hometown of Davenport, Iowa. Ely began racing cars and set the speed record for traveling from Iowa City to Davenport in the priest's sporty red Franklin. Ely figured how hard can it be to fly a plane if you can handle a car?

His first aeronautical attempt resulted in a crash. He wasn't discouraged. He somehow got himself attached to the Navy, working on their early airplanes. And on this day, January 18, 1911 he was the first pilot to land a plane on a ship, flying from a San Jose racetrack to the USS Pennsylvania in San Francisco bay. This was a big deal as it meant aerial attacks could be launched from the seas—aircraft carriers would become a big part of future wars and pretty much sealed America's dominance of the oceans and skies.

Ely was part of the team that devised the plane's tail hook and the arrester cables that prevent a plane from just flying right off the other end of the ship.

Ely, just 24, was killed when his plane crashed as part of an aviation show in Georgia. Souvenir seekers scooped up his cap, tie, suit, and parts of his plane. I guess the NTSB and FAA were a little slow on the case.

But think of this—a dude with just an eighth grade education but a determination to fly accomplished so much in so short a time!

Today would be a good time to make a list of the things you have accomplished. Especially the stuff you've forgotten, or maybe have discounted. Maybe you didn't go to Harvard and have billionaires offer you jobs, but you've done—scratch that, you do things—every single day that affect others in ways big and small. Ely was a self made hero. You are too!

List all of your accomplishments big and small!:

____

____

____

____

January 19, 1953 was a blessed day in television history with the birth of little Ricky Ricardo. And in real life the birth of Desi Arnez, Jr. by the same mother and father.

First, there was Desi, son of the two stars of the "I Love Lucy" show. The caesarean took place at a Los Angeles hospital only hours before the airing of the "Lucy goes to the hospital" episode (season two, episode 16 which had been shot in November) featuring the real life Desi Arnez (or Ricky Ricardo as he was known on the show) and his wife Lucy (or Lucille Ball as she was known in real life). More than seventy percent of Americans who owned televisions tuned in. As a percentage of television owners the record would stand until Elvis gyrated his hips on the Ed Sullivan show in 1956.

The onscreen episode featured the Ricardos' neighbors the Mertzes trying to calm Ricky down in the living room as he has a massive anxiety attack about his impending fatherhood. Lucy was offscreen for much of the episode until she emerged from her bedroom to announce IT WAS TIME.

This televised birth on January 19 was groundbreaking stuff. First, married couples had twin beds—and the Ricardos were no exception. CBS and other networks did not even allow the implication that married couples were doing the nasty and as for singletons, forget it! Visibly pregnant women were not to be onscreen. And the word pregnancy? Not to be used.

While in the lead up to the Lucy goes to the hospital episode CBS allowed the script to read that she was "expecting"—or as Cuban empresario Ricky would say 'specting'.

If you're a parent, when did you realize the awesome responsibility you were taking on? And if you are not, when did you realize what your parents did for you?

____

____

____

____

____

January 20 is International Penguin Awareness Day. And I suppose it's also penguin love day because what's not to love about the species? They live in the Antarctic and Shackleton could have used their help (although to be fair he did pretty okay in the end and didn't lose a single man even if all the dogs on the ship Endurance were killed and eaten).

Penguins have a lot to teach us today if we're going to walk on the ice and snow and not take a kerplunk. So let's review the bidding—

Instructions on how to walk like a penguin:

1. Keep your hands outside your coat pockets. You need to have some ballast. Put your hands out just a little. Just in case.

2. Bend your knees slightly, your feet shoulder width apart, pointing at a slight outward angle.

3. Keeping your balance of gravity over your feet, walk with a very flat footed gait. This is NO TIME for high heels. Rubber bottomed non-slide shoes/boots are best. Take it slow unless you're being chased by whales, sharks or process servers.

4. If you want to add a bow tie and a top hat, I won't judge. I might even think you're adorable.

There are about 20 penguin species, the Emperor Penguins being the largest and the smallest the Malacotrasca who make their home in New Zealand and Australia. Penguins live in large colonies. They run out to the ocean to grab some pescatarian food for their young'uns. They can find their offspring in a group of a thousand.

Today, get out your most sensible shoes. Stand at the door with your penguin stance. Face the snow and ice with all the confidence of our flightless bird friends. And if you just don't want to go out, remember that April 25th is World Penguin Day so you have another opportunity to celebrate—even if there might not be as much interest in walking like a penguin.

____

____

____

____

____

January 21

On January 21, 1793, King Louis 16 of France was executed for treason. When the Sofia Coppola 2006 film Marie Antoinette came out, one could be forgiven for thinking he was a petulant and cowardly jerk. But he faced his execution with extreme dignity. His widow Marie would get the ax October 16, she was just 37 but her hair had turned completely white (some irony here since she had really made all white hair wigs the rage). When she was taken out to be executed, she asked her guards if they could give her some privacy so she could pee on the ground—nope, they decided to watch, claiming she would try to escape. She had menstrual problems and they wouldn't allow her any rags which were the eighteenth century version of kotex or tampax. She was a mess, but she faced her death with as much bravery as she could. She had been accused of sexually abusing her son which was really a case of getting an eight year old to repeat everything his captors told him to say. I can't imagine what she and her husband went through. Many of the people who were executed by the "humane" guillotine which generally killed with one blow as opposed to being whacked repeatedly by an ax. But everything that led up to it was worse.

Guillotine - mercy or savagery?

____

____

____

____

____

On January 22, in either 35 or 36 AD, John the Baptist was in prison under King Herod Antipas. Herod Antipas's father was the dude who ordered the killing of the innocents upon Jesus' birth. Herod Antipas divorced his wife Pha'esal because he had the hots for the widow of his half brother Herod Archelaus. Can't these guys get a little creative with their names, like maybe Bob Antipas or Ralph Archelaus?

The new Mrs. Herodias Antipas (again this Herod naming!) caused the hotheaded John the Baptist to preach quite strongly on the sin of marrying your dead brother's wife. Leviticus 20-21 makes it clear this new marriage will be childless or at least with no male issue, a subject that came up once again when Henry VIII of England married Katherine of Aragon, his older brother, Arthur's, widow. Leading to Anne Boylen's beheading. Don't mess with Leviticus.

On the 22nd the Antipases had a great party and one feature of the party was Herod Antipas' stepdaughter Salome performing a dance sometimes called the Dance of the Seven Veils. Herod had promised Salome she could have anything she wanted for having done such a good job. Salome asked her mother what to ask for and Herodias—none too happy about John the Baptist—told her to ask for John's head on a silver platter. And so, that was the end of John the Baptist.

What would you chose if you were Salome? I'd go with World Peace and 20 million dollars deposited in a Swiss bank account..

____

____

____

____

____

January 23rd is National Handwriting Day which celebrates the art of using pen and paper. As opposed to texts and keyboarding and dictating. Handwriting slows down the brain like a Jason Stephenson meditation tape and it makes us really think about what we're doing.

Handwriting has sort of become a lost art, particularly among kids who not only learned to text first AND who didn't get that education during the pandemic shutdown. When I went to school, handwriting—particularly cursive—was a discipline of its own. And I'm old enough that I took shorthand which I don't think ANYBODY knows anymore. And cursive? Uh, no.

The date was chosen because it is also the birthday of the great John Hancock. He owned the Declaration of Independence, being the first to sign it and thereby giving himself up to the possibility that the Brits would want him and fellow signers dead for treason. His big signature made clear that he was ready to take the consequences and gave courage to other signers.

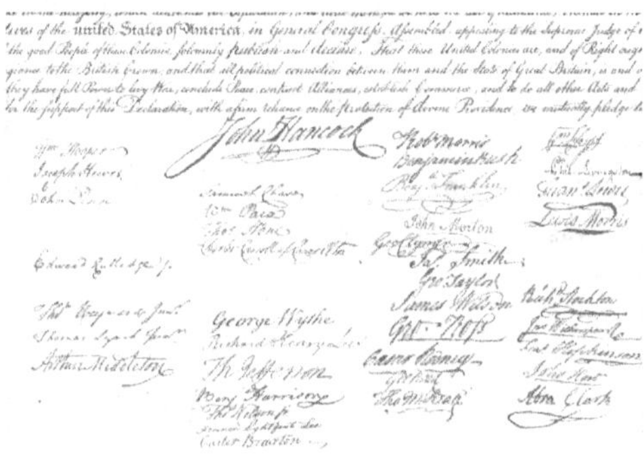

Today, write a letter to someone. On paper with a pen. It will be much appreciated because its not a bill or an advertisement!

____

____

____

____

____

In the blisteringly cold winter of 1683-1684 and the River Thames which courses

through London froze over. Well, at least enough so that Londoners could ice skate, race their horses and hackney coaches over the river. There was bull-baiting—a sport pitting a bull against a pack of fierce dogs usually to the detriment of the bull. Food stalls and much tippling of mead and mulled wine. The Thames was dubbed Freezeland Street and on January 24, 1684 writer Thomas Dekker published a pamphlet describing the "lewd" acts which also occurred. Dekker claimed one guy got so "tippled" that he thought he might skate to Belgium. Luckily, he came to his senses and returned for more fun on Freezeland Street.

The world has gone through mini-ice ages and mini-warmings. During the latter part of King Henry VIII and early part of Elizabeth I's England experienced a warming that resulted in the Thames being perfectly capable of transportation by ship—and some believe that warming period allowed England to take over the seas resulting in an empire where the sun never set.

Robert Frost was commissioned to write a poem for the inauguration of John F. Kennedy. "Some say the world will end in fire and some say in ice. From what I have tasted of desire, I hold with those who favor fire."

Still, it would have been fun to watch the guy trying to ice skate to Belgium.

Today might be a day to question…everything. Science only works if you can imagine a world in which the opposite of your heartfelt belief could be right.

The ice of Freezing Street eventually melted but it returned on a semi-regular basis for over two hundred years. It was known as "the little ice age".

Will the world end by fire or by ice?

On January 25, 1913 it was still legal for parents to ship their children through the U.S. Postal Service. So, Ohio couple Jesse and Mathilde Beagle mailed their eight month old son James on this day to his grandmother in nearby Batavia. The postage only cost 15 cents but little James was so precious his parents insured his safe delivery for $50. James was just shy of the eleven pound limit for transporting babies. Because of the loving care of postal carrier Vernon Lyttle, James arrived safe and sound.

I wonder how much bubble tape they had to use. I don't think styrofoam popcorn would have done the trick. Actually, he was attached by a pouch to Lyttle.

After that story captured the imagination of Americans, others pushed the limits and in February 19, 1914 four year old Charlotte Pierstorff of Idaho was "mailed" to her grandparents' home 73 miles away. Now, I know what you're thinking—she had to have been more than eleven pounds AND she wasn't going to fit in a postal bag. But her cousin who worked for parcel post accompanied her and that may have influenced the decision to let her travel. Her parents also paid the same fare as mailing a chicken.

In 1920, the practice of allowing parents to parcel post their children ended as it was determined that children were not in the same category as "harmless animals". Obviously a decision made by someone who was a parent.

The interesting thing is this all occurred in a part of our history when postal carriers were considered so trustworthy that child or even a little baby could be entrusted to them. And it was a truth—there are no recorded instances of abuse, neglect, or (quel horreur!) murder. Every shipped young'un was delivered safe and sound. Today, parents sometimes entrust their children to airliners. I think Southwest would not be my choice.

If you're a parent, have there been days you would have shipped your kid ... anywhere?

January 26

The bald eagle is our national symbol, making us feel like tough hombres right from the Declaration of Independence. What a dignified, strong, brave, virile bird. It's hard to imagine any other bird giving the world our message. But…to the day he died Benjamin Franklin hated it. He proposed in a letter to his daughter on January 26, 1784 that the true character of our new nation. He said the turkey was more "respectable," a bird of "courage, and would not hesitate to attach a grenadier of the British guard who should presume to invade his farm with a red coat on." He also opined that the eagle was of bad moral character and a rank coward.

Perhaps it's all for the best. I don't know about you but I don't want to eat a bald eagle for Thanksgiving dinner.

January 27

January 27, 1945 marked the Soviet liberation of the German death camp Auschwitz-Birkenau. Soviet soldiers were appalled at the condition of the inmates—starved and hopeless. Among so many dehumanizing humiliations the Nazis imposed on concentration camps prisoners was making them give up their clothes and don a blue striped uniform with bare clogs.* Striped uniforms also stripped every prisoner of their individuality. They were identified by the Nazis with tattoos, which was  a total taboo for the Jewish prisoners. The Soviet Army liberated approximately seven thousand prisoners—1.1 million prisoners had perished, whether executed or dead by disease or starvation.

January 27, 1945 is now known as Holocaust Remembrance Day.

Today, be kind. Just be kind. If we all were, nothing like this would happen again.

*Wedding rings were confiscated by the Nazis as well as any other jewelry. When Auschwitz was liberated, boxes and boxes of wedding rings were found. I can't imagine the heartache knowing what you were giving up when you pulled the ring off your finger.

You know they are going to kill you. Do you give up your ring or say "shoot me now?"

On January 28, 1956 twenty one year old Elvis Presley made his television debut on the variety show Stage Show on CBS. He wore black and suit and shirt and a white tie. The ensemble was purchased at Lansky Brothers of Memphis Tennessee, a shop near the nightclub district at Beale Street where the cool cats shopped. Elvis had been a client for four years and owner Bernard Lansky personally dressed him for the occasion. On Bernard's eighteenth birthday his father had offered this bon mot—

"Son, here's the world. Now go and get it."

Inspired by his father's admiration of hard work and grabbing opportunity where it was to be found, Bernard started Lansky Brothers in 1946 as an Army surplus store but when the market dried up, he turned to high end men's fashion. Well, for Memphis. In the fifties and sixties, Lansky Brothers had colorful window displays and stocked clothes that appealed to the likes of Johnny Cash, Carl Perkins and a host of other celebs.

When presented with the Stage Show opportunity, Elvis went directly to Bernard. Seeing that all the young men on national television were wearing dark suits, white shirts and skinny dark ties, Bernard veered in the opposite direction.

"If Elvis had worn a white button-down Oxford cloth shirt, he would still be driving a truck," Bernard's son Hal once said. Elvis remained a faithful customer until his death in 1977. Lansky Brothers has two different locations in Memphis and you can go shopping just like The King.

I generally have a uniform of black leggings (eighteen pairs of them in my closet), a black sweater or T-shirt (have lost count) and black shoes. Except I did something scandalous today. I wore a red full length fleece cape. Chickened out before I got in the elevator. Went back to my apartment and put on a black puffy jacket.

Hey, baby steps! What are you wearing today?

Today is National Curmudgeon Day when we celebrate the naturally grumpy, pessimistic party pooper that we all know. It honors the curmudgeon of curmudgeons who was born on January 29, 1880. Born William Claude Dukenfield he took the stage name W.C. Fields. He was an actor, comedian and at a young age developed the special skill of juggling.

As a juggler in vaudeville, he was always silent, the better to cover his stutter. He overcame his stuttering by devising the persona of a grump. When silent movies came out and later talkies, he came into his own always as someone who would smoke a cigar and was drunk and mean to children. But it was a different time. His habits took their toll and he spent close to two years in hospital, dying on the day that he and fellow curmudgeon Scrooge hated the most—Christmas Day, 1946.

His estate has never been completely settled because whenever he went to a new town for vaudeville or a traveling show or just for vacation—he opened a bank account. He was always concerned that he might find himself broke in a town with no friends or family to turn to. There might be thousands of accounts with enough to perk up the ears of the IRS.

His last words were "Goddamn the whole friggin' world and everybody in it. Except you, Carlotta."

His mistress, Carlotta. Even a curmudgeon has a soft spot.

Today, to celebrate the day, think upon your own curmudgeon. Someone you deal with who is just a whopping pain in the ass. Be nice to them. Give them a compliment. That'll show 'em.

Today, how will you fight your natural curmudgeonly tendencies?

January 30,1661 was a no good, dirty, rotten, terrible day for Oliver Cromwell and it wasn't just his hair. He was being executed. For a second time. If the ACLU finds out about this, they'll have a hissy fit, a press conference and a lawsuit all at the same time!

Back in 1648 Cromwell overthrew the British/Scottish* King Charles I and sentenced him to death. But by 1660 Charles' son became King Charles II. Did he sentence Cromwell to death? Well, he jolly well did!

There was only one problem—Cromwell had died in 1658. But Charles II wasn't going to let that detail get in the way of a good revenge. He had Cromwell's body exhumed, and on January 30, 1661 had him publicly hanged, beheaded, and his body thrown into an unmarked pit. As for Cromwell's head, the King had it hung on a pike in Westminster Abbey. If that wasn't enough, about a quarter of a century later, there was a huge storm and the pike fell over and the head went rolling through the streets. The head was handed, as it were, from apothecaries, private collectors, museums, until FINALLY it was buried at Cambridge in 1960.

So if things don't go exactly as planned consider what you were attempting in the first place. Revenge is sweet, but plan carefully. Think of the plaque over Cromwell's resting place. Just one word—traitor. But we know him as a traitor with a bad haircut.

*England and Scotland had the same monarch because Elizabeth I had no heir and wouldn't name one before her death. Me? I'm not naming an heir because that would be like naming my murderer. So James IV of Scotland (Elizabeth's nephew) became James 1 of England and that's how both Charles I and II ended up with two kingdoms—Catholic Scotland and Protestant England. What a headache!

Is there someone you know that you should forgive?
It's okay if you can't.

On January 31, 1961, a young chimp known as Chop Chop Charge or Ham the Astrochimp or No. 65 made history as the first hominid to go into outer space.

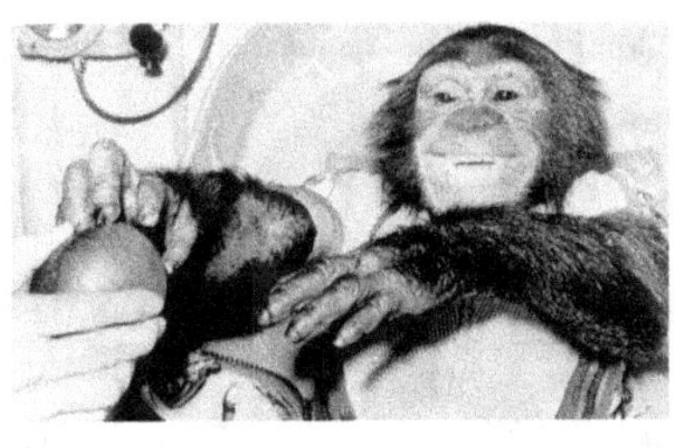

Ham was born in French Cameroon in 1957 and was captured by traders and sent to the Rare Bird Farm in Miami, Florida. He stayed there until 1959 when the Air Force "bought" him, er, recruited him and made him a flight candidate for NASA. There were 40 flight candidates and the purpose of their mission was to figure out what were the effects of space flight on chimpanzees as a way of deciding what would happen with humans. Ham's handlers called him Chop Chop Charge.

While mice and other "minor" animals had been shot out into the skies you can't exactly get them to do astronaut stuff.

Ham was trained at the Holloman Aerospace Medical Center in a sort of B.F. Skinner behavioral modification method to sit in a module and push a lever within 5 seconds of seeing flashing blue lights. If he failed, he was given what has been described as a light shock on his feet. If he succeeded, he received a banana pellet. He was known for being happy and cheerful and cooperative with his handlers and they had great affection for him. To the public, he was only described as chimpanzee No. 65 because it was thought that if people had a name to attach to him they would freak if the mission failed.

On January 31, 1961 Ham was loaded into the Mercury-Redstone 2. He was launched into space for a total of 16 minutes and 39 seconds. He bruised his nose and experienced some anxiety, but nonetheless performed all flight tasks at only a few seconds slower than he had on earth. He was rewarded with an apple when he got back to Earth. The entire time all his vitals were monitored and a lot of what was learned about him on that flight would inform the next NASA project—shooting human Alan Shepard into space on May 5, 1961.

No. 65 became HAM the Astrochimp on his successful return. There are two theories for his name. The commander of the Holloman Lab where he trained was Lt. Col. Hamilton "Ham" Blackshear. Or maybe it was H for Holloman, A for Aerospace, M for Medical. But now he had a name. And a last laugh on the Soviets who thought they were winning the space war.

Continued on Next Page

Continued from Previous Page

After his mission, Ham was sent to the National Zoo in DC where he remained for seventeen years. Then he was transferred to a chimp colony in North Carolina where he passed on in 1980. There was some talk about taxidermying him and displaying him in the Smithsonian but no! You can visit his grave at the International Space Hall of Fame in Alamagordo, New Mexico.

Animals have long been considered to be "sub" human. Like they don't have consciousness. Yet, all animals, not just primates, display intelligent behavior that can't be explained by simply dismissing the idea that they know what they're doing. Think about ants—when they are attacked their brethren might be injured and ants will collect the injured to carry them home base (unlike Russian soldiers attacked yesterday in the Ukraine). Intriguingly, an ant who is extremely injured will pretend to be dead and be passed over by his comrades. This behavior is considered to be an awareness that they would be a burden and detriment to the unit. What can we say if not that there's a consciousness?

As for Ham he taught us more than about temperature regulation of the module or what effects on heart rate there are in space flight. He taught us a chimp can have a sense of humor, a sense of how to get the job done and how good an apple is going to taste when that job is done.

If humans evolved from chimps, why are there still chimps on earth?

____

February and there is everything to hope for and nothing to regret.

–Patience Strong

In 2017, the United States Figure Skating Association designated February 1 as GET UP DAY. After all, getting back up after you fall is the very first lesson of figure skating. One of the most influential get up story from the sport is Janet Lynn 1972 Saporro Olympics who was pretty much out of competition for a medal because of the compulsories* but came out smiling for the free skate. When she attempted a flying sit spin, she fell on her ass about 1:53 minutes in. Right on her ass. But she got back up with a huge smile on her face. The audience was stunned  because within the skating community and certainly the largely Japanese audience, a fall was to be followed by tears and abject apologies. Not for Janet, who taught us all a lesson about Get Up. She finished her program to thunderous applause and captured the hearts of a worldwide audience. Never expecting a medal, she nonetheless took bronze. She became the most popular female athlete of the time AND scored a three year $1.4 million deal with Ice Follies, making her the highest paid female athlete in the world.

You've been through some stuff. You've taken some falls. You've tripped and have had your share of heart breaks. But it's GET UP DAY! I propose you make a list of the obstacles and defeats that you have overcome. And put that list in your back pocket so that you can take it out when you need it. That list will tell you all the times you've gotten back up, make sure to include a happy face. You did it before and you can do it again today.

*Compulsories were where you had to skate over figures on ice in front of a bunch of judges. Wasn't televised. Some gals could have a wretched free skate program and still win gold. Seemed unfair. Now compulsories don't count for much.

How do you get back up when you've fallen?

____

____

____

____

____

February 2 is Dia de Candelaria, the last of the celebrations associated with Christmas and YOU might have a special obligation at the end of this day. But after I tell you what you need to do, you'll thank me!

So you go to a party during the Christmas season and you get a rosca cake. The cake has a secret! A little baby Jesus is hidden within its deliciousness. Whoever gets a slice of the cake with the baby Jesus within is obligated to host a Dia de Candelaria (Candlemas for gringas like me) party 40 days after the birth of Jesus—on the second of February.

The forty days represents when the baby Jesus was presented at the temple and the Virgin Mary was purified (don't get me started on why pregnant women have to be purified—they've done enough). At this February 2nd party that you are obligated to host, tamales are to be served. Humans were formed or created from maize and the tamale is the perfect way of honoring humanity as maize is its most essential component.

Coincidentally the Aztecs marked February 2 as the beginning of the new year honoring Tlaloc, Chalciuhtlicue and Quetzalcoatl as their gods. Guess what they had for dinner?

A tip from a stupid gringa (me). The first time I had a tamale, I bit into it whole, with the husk. I thought "this is awful." But then I followed the very first rule of etiquette when visiting someone's home. Do what they do. Everybody else was opening their husks and enjoying the interior melange of ground maize and beef. It took me a long time to chew that little bite of husk and I sure hope nobody noticed. So today, you can say Buen Provecho!

The Christmas season is officially over and next up—well there's always a holiday ....

Is it good luck or not to find th Baby Jesus in your cake?

February 3rd is The Four Chaplains Day aka Immortal Chaplains Day aka the Dorchester Chaplains Day. The SS Dorchester was a converted civilian ship which left New York January 23, 1943 for Greenland carrying 900 military personnel and civilians. It was part of a four ship convoy with coverage provided by three Coast Guard cutters. In the wee hours of February 3rd off the coast of Newfoundland,  the Dorchester was mortally wounded by a torpedo strike by a German U-233.

The four chaplains onboard—George Fox, Alexander Goode, Clark Poling, and John Washington sprung into action helping surviving soldiers get onto life boats and when the life vests ran out, the four chaplains gave up theirs and as the ships went down, they joined hands, sang hymns and prayed together. Only a little more than 230 of the 900 onboard survived. They described hearing the chaplains singing in different languages and offering up repeated prayers. Many of the passengers who perished were wearing the life vests that allowed them to float on the frigid water but not survive. It's already starting to sound better than the Titanic, with lower costume costs.

George was a Methodist, Goode a rabbi, Washington a Catholic, Poling a Reformed Church of America (kind of like Dutch Protestants but on a different continent than the Netherlands). Three of them were Boy Scout leaders, all had gone to the Harvard Chaplain Training Academy. After the Dorchester went down, they didn't qualify for the Medal of Honor because none of them had participated in combat, so they got Purple Hearts and the Distinguished Service Cross. But in 1960 Congress created The Four Chaplains Medal just for them which were presented to their next of kin. Nine Chaplains have, in the course of history, received Medals of Honor but those chaplains were different insofar as they had been in combat situations.

Today might be a day to think how lucky we are to be alive, and to realize how quickly the situation can change and how it can depend on something as frivolous as a coin toss or as achingly brave as your faith. Every morning I wake up to the slogan "Gratias Dominus Vigiles" which is rough justice Latin for "thank you God for waking me up." Be grateful when he does that thing for you tomorrow morning. And think of those four who gave up everything together, without sniping over differences in politics, religion, or really anything.

You're on a boat - it's going down - do you give up your vest ... for your mother-in-law?

Today February 4 is Liberace Day! It's time to bring out your best out there clothes and tickles the ivory on your (natch!) white grand piano!

Wladziu Valentino Liberace was born on may 16, 1919 and he took to the piano. While his father wanted him to do classical (Chopin, Polinisky, etc) Liberace could also blow the house out with a combo of polka, rock, and rockabilly. He had everything up his sleeve.

He toured the Midwest under the name Walter Busterkeys. Get it? Bust Her Keys? Weddings, holidays, baptisms—he did it all, including, okay and, strip clubs.

He was such a playboy. He was engaged many times but never quite made it to the altar. He did, however, adopt 48 year old Scott Thompson with whom he had had a "friendship" since Thompson was 19. The relationship was doomed—perhaps because of Thompson's drug use and shady ways. But also there was Liberace's diagnosis of AIDS which Liberace kept secret from the public and possibly from Thompson himself.

I can't imagine what Liberace was going through. He died on this day, February 4, 1997 of AIDS related pneumonia. Thompson sued his estate—all about the Benjamins baby—and claimed his health had been put at risk because Liberace never told him of the AIDS diagnosis. Thompson later went to prison for a bunch of drug charges. Today, the anniversary of Liberace's homegoing, let's focus on his love of music, his enormous talent and charisma, and the courage he had doing all of it without a supportive LGBTQ community.

I think I might have met him when I was a youngster. What celebrity musician have you met?

February 5 is Shower with a Friend Day. I have enough body image problems taking a shower with myself that I'm not sure a shower with a friend is going to help matters. I'm figuring full blown anxiety attack. Screaming. Slipping on the soap. Trying to cover up with a towel… or two. I'll sit this one out.

Still, the holiday has a very innocent and unexpected origin. While humanity had been doing its best with baths and pools and rivers, we really owe a debt to the first man to get a patent for a shower—on this day in 1767 William Feetham got a patent for a pump to push water up over one's head and the showerer. Just pull a crank to release the water. The next improvement came in 1850 with the shower being connected to running water—which meant you could take your time!!!

In 2001, Colorado company New Wave Enviro introduced Take a Shower with a Friend Day. But what they meant by friend was a little different—they were encouraging people to take a shower with a "friend" which was its recently invented water filter. Their reasoning was that most people absorb more chlorine and other chemicals through showering than through drinking unfiltered water. So the "friendly" shower filter will help you get that chemical free glow—

You can interpret the holiday ever how you want. Get yourself a water filter for your shower and get a little friendly with it. Er, maybe just use as directed. Invite someone over and relax with a shower together—lavender candles and rubber duckies optional. Follow it up with chamomile tea and anything on the Hallmark Channel.

Comfortable with a shared shower with a friend?

On February 6, 1820 the first group of freed slaves of African descent left America for what would become known as Liberia on the west coast of the African continent.

Importing/capturing/hijacking slaves from Africa had been illegal in the United States since 1808 but slavery of African-Americans* and their descendants was still legal. The American Colonization Society, founded in 1816, gained funding from Congress to help "repatriate" freed slaves. This first group were certainly brave—most had no clue where in Africa they or their ancestors had come from and most notably they were more in touch with American ways than any of the indigenous Kru and Grebo tribes who controlled the territory. The repatriated African Americans founded a capital called Monrovia after ACS supporter President James Monroe and several cities along the coast paid homage to Americans who had championed their cause— including Harriet Tubman, Joseph Jenkins Roberts ** and President James Buchanan. In 1847 these former slaves declared their independence from America, calling their land Liberia. They were joined by many more freed slaves from America through the efforts of the ACS until the end of the Nineteenth Century. Liberians wrote their constitution pretty much along the lines of the United States.

I think anybody getting on that ship in 1820 was incredibly brave and very determined to celebrate their independence. Maybe today is a good day to think about incredible life journeys you've made!

*Some Irish were held as slaves, although they were sometimes formally known as indentured servants with terms that were longer than typical life expectancy.

**Roberts was a freeborn African American business man and ACS supporter who went on to become Liberia's first president.

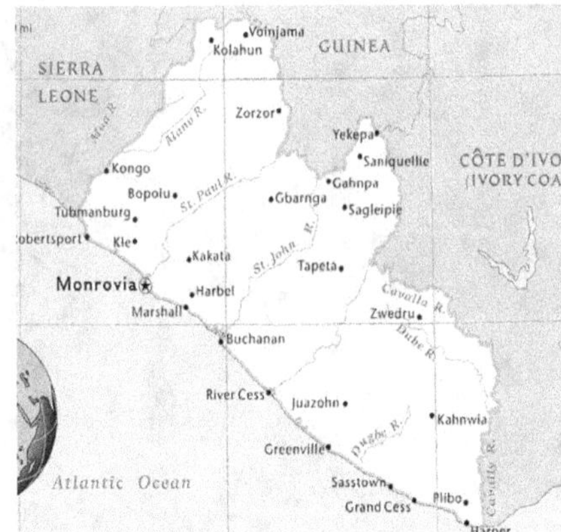

The Portland Vase is a first century BC Roman funereal vase which is housed at the British Museum. When I was living in London, I took the boys to the museum every day and probably never noticed the vase. But it's gorgeous and it was just recreated in 1989 after a rather, ahem, unfortunate episode involving a drunk.

They say you shouldn't drink and drive and I would add to that you shouldn't drink and wander through the British Museum. After a week long bender ending on February 7, 1845, William Lloyd, a student at nearby Trinity College, nudged up against the glass case that enclosed the vase. The vase, incidentally, had been purchased by the Duchess of Portland in the previous century and her son the Duke took a tax write off by "loaning" the vase to the museum in perpetuity. It's an extraordinary piece of what is called cameo glass.

The vase was destroyed and Lloyd was charged with its destruction. His lawyers successfully argued that he had only destroyed the glass case and the vase was a side effect.

He was fined three pounds. Part of the judge's mercy was because Lloyd was an upstanding student and made the usual promises to give up the sauce.

The priceless vase took a lot of work but in 1989 restoration was complete and it appears to the unassuming eye to have never been damaged.

Go see the vase—it's in room 70.

Just like Kintsugi —the Japanese
way of repairing with gold leaf—
take your wounds and heal with gold?

____

____

____

____

____

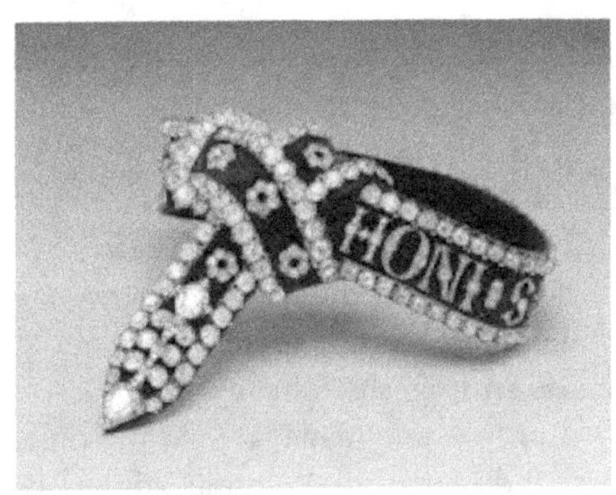

On February 8, 1840 Queen Victoria of England gave her fiance Prince Albert a diamond studded garter to hold up his stockings. It's not as weird as all that. Albert had been made a Knight of the Order of the Garter, one of the highest honors that a queen (or king) can bestow. At the time, men and women both wore garters to hold up their fine silk stockings. It was just a normal part of dressing before elastic was incorporated into garments.

Let's jump ahead to February 10, 1840 when the Queen married the Prince. He was not made king but got the title of consort and he had the garter. The garter was dark blue velvet, the diamonds were real, and as with all the other Order's garters it was embossed with the motto "honi soit qui mal y pense" meaning (in ancient Anglo-Norman) "shame on him who thinks evil of it."

The Order was started in the 1340s when a lady was at a ball in Calais—part of England at the time—and her garter slipped off her leg onto the floor. King Edward (nicknamed The Confessor) reached down to pick up the garter and return it to the lady who was now the subject to snickering fellow guests. That's when Edward announced the motto, somehow conveying that chivalry was more important than making fun of people. Then he created the order of those men who embodied that chivalrous nature.

Queen Victoria was marrying the second born prince (the spare) of the tiny Saxe-Coburg and Gothe, kind of a comedown for her. As for him, it was a little humiliating to not be made a king of England. The garter made up for it a little.

Victoria, meanwhile, was the happiest bride. Normally, a woman in her position would wear a sumptuous gown—purple, gold and silver were popular choices, especially if it was adorned with ermine—and a tiara. A tiara would have sort of rubbed it in that she was superior to Albert—heck, it was bad enough that royal etiquette required that SHE propose to him and HE was not allowed to propose to her.

Continued on Next Page

February 08

She chose a rather subdued white gown, but she was foreshadowing twentieth century fashion editor Diana Vreeland's edict that "elegance is renouncement". While the Queen's gown had a train which was fitted to the waist and removed after the ceremony itself.

The Queen chose to have the dress made by English designer, Mary Bettyns of London's Jermyn street from silk of the Spitalfields section of the city. Her shoes were made by Gundy & Sons of London. And though most women of her status would have chosen lace from Brussels, the Queen chose an English company from Devon which had been decimated by the introduction of machine made lace. At the time, handmade lace was so expensive it was used over and over again. Victoria had the lace sewn into different gowns over the years and was buried in her lace veil.

A lot of thought went into the wedding details. The marriage lasted 21 years. The Queen was in mourning for the rest of her life. But for the few days of February, she was so happy.

Today, take what happiness you can. Store it up for a memory.
Can you record it here?

____

____

____

____

____

February 9 is the Chocolate Day. On this day in 1894 Milton Hershey founded the Hershey's chocolate company. Milton is really the person who introduced chocolate to the American people in an affordable way.

Milton was born in New York to a Mennonite* family in 1857. His grandfather was a Russian immigrant who made his living making candy, a talent he passed on to his son, Milton's father. Milton went to school from the age of six until fourth grade as Mennonites are like the Amish with not much interest in formal/worldly education. The family were soon prosperous enough in the manufacturing side of the candy business and didn't want to put up with fast-paced New York life.

They settled into the Mennonite community in Lancaster, Pennsylvania. Milton was taking over the company and he initially saw the future in caramels, improving the candy using milk (widely available in rural Pennsylvania.) Chocolate was originally a drink for wealthy and Milton thought that if he mixed milk and chocolate into a solid form, he would create the most perfect candy at a price point that made it possible for  every American to have a treat. In 1900, Milton sold the first chocolate bars, naming it (of course) the Hershey's bar. In 1907 he came up with the idea for Hershey's kisses. That was the same year he came up with the idea of adding almonds to the Hershey's bar. He purchased the land surrounding his factory and called it _________ _________.** Because of the Mennonite tradition of service to others, he built houses for his workers, founded a school for their children, and created a boarding school for orphans.

During World War 2, the government wanted to ramp up the quality on their ration packs for soldiers. C-rations, cigarettes, Hershey's bars.

The candy bars couldn't melt because there would be no refrigerator in a soldier's backpack. Milton experimented with bars that didn't require cold. He came through with the chocolates the soldiers loved and came home from combat saying "I've got to have me a Hershey's bar!" Milton died in 1945 after having served his country well.

A way to celebrate today is to, of course, give chocolates to the people you love, including yourself. It's okay to be your own Valentine. Even if it's five days away.

*Mennonites are parts of the Anabaptist family, aligned with the more conservative Amish.

** Hershey, of course!

What chocolate will you treat yourself to today?

February 10 is Teddy Day, named for the stuffed animal inspired by America's 26th president and big game hunter Theodore Roosevelt. On this day in 1902, Teddy, as he was affectionately called, was on a hunting trip in Missouri with a bunch of bigwigs but he was the only member of the party to not kill a bear. Teddy's assistants, led by former slave and confederate cavalryman Holt Collier, cornered and tied a black bear to a tree. Collier urged the president to kill the bear. The President declined, seeing this as unsportsmanlike. Many hunters would agree with him—hunting is supposed to be about you versus nature, not nature tied up for an execution. The bear was released.

Political cartoonist Clifford Berryman created a lighthearted comic for the Washington Post about the affair. He made the bear a small innocent cub and got the state wrong by suggesting that the incident happened in Mississippi. Morris Michtom, a candy shop owner who sold handmade stuffed animals on the side, saw an opportunity—he and his wife rose created a stuffed bear and named it "teddy's bear." That bear made their fortunes!

I had a teddy bear once. The bear was loyal and true, even if I didn't sleep with him I always kept him in my room. All the way into law school. And then the summer between first and second year, I had a fiance who was going to New York for a summer internship. I gave him Teddy so that he would have a part of me. Alas, he broke up with me over that summer—marrying a partner at the firm he was working at and returned to school without the teddy bear. After protracted negotiations (over the teddy bear, not over any possibility of reconciliation) he confessed he may have left my teddy at the home of the woman he was now engaged to. WHAAAAA… ? I was devastated at the loss of my stuffed friend but only mildly perturbed to discover the reason for our breakup. He added that upper class New York women didn't wear shoes like mine and I could do with making myself a better person.

Today I have Fuego. He stands guard outside my apartment. He's a teddy dalmatian. He gives me comfort. And that's what a teddy is for.

Do you have a teddy bear?

February 11

On February 11, 1929 the smallest nation in the world was formed. It is only 109 acres and last time anybody counted the population stood at 825. It has an army, although to be fair its uniforms are ridiculous and none in its ranks have been born there. Matter of fact, no one has ever been born in this country because frankly there are only a handful of women who have ever lived there. It has NO INCOME TAX! Think about that on April 15—

The country is Stato della Citta del Vatican but most folk just call it Vatican City. It sits on the shore of the Tiber River in Rome. The residence of the Pope of course and its most important feature is St. Peter's Basilica. Built in the fourth century on top of the grave of—you guessed it—the Apostle Upon This Rock I Build My Church, Peter.

At one time, the Pope owned a lot of real estate around Europe but by 1929 Pope Pius Eleven was only in control of the Papal States scattered around the Kingdom of Italy. King Victor Emanuel III, who proudly identified as Fascist, wanted to mow them all down. The Pope decided that there was only one state that absolutely mattered—the state built on Rockin' St. Peter's grave.

On this day in 1929, after some acrimonious negotiations, the Pacta Lateranasin was signed. We call it the Lateran Treaty, consisting of a breathtaking 27 Articles of Conciliation, three Articles of Finance and a 45 Articles Concordant laying out the relationship rules for the King and Pope. The King got all but one state and the Pope got his own country surrounding Peter's Basilica, a wad of cash, and a promise that the King wouldn't turn around and declare war on him. Which he didn't and even when Hitler had control of Rome he was too spooked to touch the Vatican. And it wasn't just the Swiss Guard.

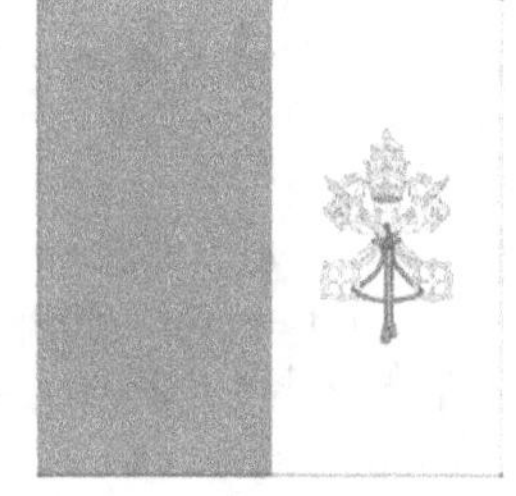

The Swiss Guard, even with its ridiculous uniform, is actually pretty badass. It was formed in 1506 with the task of defending the Pope himself. In 1527 a regiment of 189 defended Pope Clement VII from an attack by heretics and wound up with only 42 surviving. Forty-three if you count the Pope himself. In 1981, Pope John Paul II was attacked by an insane dude with a gun. The Guard defended. Guardsman Alois Estermann comported himself so well he was promoted to commandant. Sadly, a few hours after the ceremony celebrating his promotion, he and his wife Gladys were shot dead by fellow guardsman Cedric Tomay. Tomay then committed suicide before anybody could figure out a motive.

So you want to be a Swiss Guard. First requirement, obviously, is that you have to be willing to lay down your life for the Pope. Have to be Roman Catholic. Male. Swiss citizenship. Unmarried. Aged 19-30. And at least 5'8". Sorry Tom Cruise.

So who do you want defending you -Navy Seals or Swiss Guard?

Charles Monroe Schulz (November 26, 1922—February 12, 2000), died on this day at the age of 78. Best known for the comic strip Peanuts which featured the characters Snoopy and Charlie Brown, among others. He is widely regarded as one of the most influential cartoonists of all time. Cited as a major influence by many later cartoonists. Calvin and Hobbes creator Bill Watterson wrote in 2007 "Peanuts pretty much defines the modern comic strip, so even now it's hard to see it with fresh eyes. The clean, minimalist drawings, the sarcastic humor, the unflinching emotional honesty, the inner thoughts of a household pet, the serious treatment of children, the wild fantasies, the merchandising on an enormous scale.

February 13

February 13 is Galentine's Day, a sort of rebuff to Valentine's Day's emphasis on romantic love. Instead, the holiday is meant to celebrate female friendship and support for one another. It was originally created by the show Parks and Recreation writing staff headed by Michael Schur. The lead character Leslie Knope (played by Amy Poehler) celebrated her female friendships with an all female party and as was her wont, she created elaborate affirming letters and cards for her coworkers and friends.
How can you celebrate? Have a girls' night out or maybe just send out some cards, texts and emails telling your gal pals how much they mean to you. This might be particularly important to do for your gal pals who don't have expectations about the coming fourteenth.

Who are you taking out on Galentines Day? Lucy, Peppermint Patty, or Red headed Girl?

____

____

____

____

____

February 14

We're all clear that February 14th is Valentine's Day but did you know that there's Valentine's Week and it begins on February 7? Probably feels a little like looking at an entire birthday cake and you're salivating for the first bite but if you have to eat it every day for a week those last few bites aren't going to appeal. But here goes with, of course, my fabulous and unwanted advice about how to proceed—

Valentine's Day is meant to honor an early Roman martyr who gave his life for love. And it's also a chance to not just be special to your Special One. It's a time to show your love to EVERYONE!

February 7 is Rose Day. So give a rose to your beloved. Or maybe just give a rose to someone you don't think is going to get one this year. Make it an early Valentine's gift. Or consider another interpretation of the word rose.

February 8 is Propose Day. Proceed cautiously. Don't do it lightly, but if you're thinking …might as well do it before the actual day so that you two can relax.

February 9 is Chocolate Day. Knock yourself out. Buy a bunch of candy bars and give them to people in your life who have absolutely no reason to expect it. Or maybe buy yourself a chocolate you crave but are forbidden by keto or whatevs. Savor every damn bite.

February 10 is Teddy Bear Day. Stop thinking about the lingerie, donate a teddy bear to a local charity.

February 11 is Promise Day. Okay, so you didn't hit February 8. That's chill. Maybe make a promise to your beloved. Or maybe make a promise to anyone. AND THEN FOLLOW THROUGH.

February 12 is Hug Day. Don't randomly grab strangers. It will be alarming and possibly result in legal action. But consider this—studies have shown that people NEED hugs and that a minimum of four a day is as effective as your prescription for Lexapro. You can do it. Hug your mom. Hug your brother. Hug your best friend. Worse comes to worse, hug me.

February 13 is Kiss Day. Bunches of ways to celebrate—tongue, no tongue—but consider this option: buy some Hershey's Kisses and put them in a bowl on your desk, your Little Giant tool chest or your nightstand. If you don't have any money and no significant other then look yourself in the mirror and say "I'm so in love" and kiss yourself! If you do tongue, get some hand sanitizer and Windex. It's also Galentine's Day in order to pay tribute to the gals in your life who have done so much for you.

So get started today for a host of activities every day in order to build your anticipation for the main event...

How are you celebrating?

____

____

____

____

____

<h1 align="center">February 15</h1>

February 15 is Love Reset Day. Yesterday was Valentine's Day and it might have been very good or very bad for you. For some of the latter, this week is dedicated to you. It begins right now with the day sometimes called Reset Day or Slap Day.

You may very well want to slap the ex-beloved who cheated on you, belittled you, generally acted awful. The way you're going to reset is to slap away all the reminders of them. Their favorite brand of coffee? Throw it out. The restaurant you always went together? It's off your list for the moment. You want to slap away the memories as best you can. No actual slapping of the face or the ass.

Tomorrow the sixteenth is Kick Day. Just like Slap Day you're not going to engage in physical violence. You're going to kick them out of your daily life a little more completely—throw away their stuff even the fancy gifts (those you can donate to charity or an acquaintance you seldom run into).

The seventeenth is Perfume Day and that is when you're going to go out and buy a NEW perfume for yourself. Our olfactory sensations can become associated with a beloved and you want to get rid of that. Take your time! And if you guys shared shampoo or scented candles now's the time to make a change.

The eighteenth is Flirt Day. Take a chance by striking up a conversation with someone you're attracted to. Success or failure is not the point. The point is that there are people who are just as good as you once thought the ex-beloved was. Be sure to wear the perfume you bought yesterday.

The nineteenth is Confession Day. It's a good time to get something off your chest, perhaps a long withheld apology to someone. Whatever it is weighs you down and this part of the Valentine's celebrations are slowly becoming not about the ex-beloved but about YOU and giving you the better person that you are. If your confession will do more harm than good, write it all down and rip it up.

The twentieth is the sixth day of this odyssey and it's called the Missing Day. It's a good time to tell someone you miss them? NOT THE EX!!!! But think of the people you may have neglected while in the throes of your ill-fated romance. Tell the person what wonderful stuff you've missed about them. Keep it light, keep it frothy and NOT an unloading of how bad things got. If you're doing this reconnecting via phone or by text SMILE while you do it. It's hard to work venomous feelings into a conversation while your perfume enchants you and you've got a grin.

The last day February 21st is Break Up Day. I know, you've already broken up and that's part of what made Valentine's Day suck. But now you're really past it, or at least on your way.

Most of what I've written comes from the Hindustani Times and they sure take this stuff seriously.

How is your week going to work out?

February 16

Let's go back to February 16, the Day of the Shining Star. You may want to celebrate with dancing, a military demonstration, fireworks, parades, a visit to the Kumsusan Palace to view a father and son embalmed bodies—oh, and if you live in North Korea you'll get extra food rations AND extra electricity for the day!!!!!

This exciting and momentous holiday celebrates the birthday of North Korea's second leader Kim Jong-Il. His father was Kim Il-Sung (first leader and founder of North Korea) and his mother guerilla leader Kim Jong-Suk. In 1941 Kim Jong-Il was born in the Soviet Union as the family was in hiding from the capitalist Korea government. Alternatively, he was born in 1942 at Mount Paektu, a volcano on the Chinese border which in myth is described as the home of the Korean people. The lake atop this volcano is called Heaven Lake. Sounds a lot more full of promise than "we were hiding in the Soviet Union." And besides, everybody shaves a little off their age. So why not make your birthplace sound more glam?

Just like Jesus, there was a bright star that appeared in the sky over Paektu when Kim Jong-Il was born. The baby was immediately given the nickname Shining Star. His birthday became known as the Day of the Shining Star, the second most important North Korean holiday right behind Day of the Sun, celebrating Kim Il-Sung's birthday.

Kim Jong-Il didn't participate in public ceremonies surrounding his birthday but in 2012 a year after his death, February 16th became the national holiday it is. Both father and son were named Eternal Leaders.

A visit to their embalmed bodies at least once in your life is a duty (and awe inspiring pleasure, of course) for every North Korean. Many North Koreans go on their wedding day and give the bride's bouquet as a present to the two. Other communist leaders like Vladimir Lenin and Ho Chi Minh are similarly displayed in their own countries. Visiting Lenin was an integral part of a Moscow wedding for most of the Communist reign. Stalin had his own place in this pantheon but in 1961 he was moved to the Kremlin Wall Necropolis. He obviously had a lousy publicist.

So to celebrate today I'd suggest that if you've got food and electricity even when it's not Day of the Sun or the Shining Star in your country, give some thanks. And, in case you're interested, I'm not doing the embalming thing. I want a Viking burial on Lake Michigan and y'all are invited!

And of course, remember that YOU are the shining sun and star!!!!

On February 17, 1963 the supermodel before there were supermodels Margot Greenfield—surrounded by police and security detail—arrived in an armored car to a party at the Odeon Theater in London in order to hand out the prizes at a bingo game being held at a high-falutin' party. She wore a gown designed and created by Norman Hartnell who designed gowns for many of the royal family (and friends) including Queen Elizabeth II's bridal gown. That wedding dress had been partially paid for by British women sending their clothing ration stamps to Buckingham Palace.

On the seventeenth of February 1963 the dress Miss Greenfield wore was made from over a thousand five pound notes with the smiling face of Elizabeth II on each banknote.

I have almost twenty pairs of black leggings. I wear them every day and I change clothes several times a day not that anybody would notice. I am the same with black sweaters and T-shirts. A particularly savvy potential gentleman caller bought me two black v-neck cashmere sweaters for Christmas. He threw in a third one in dark magenta which will probably never get out of the dresser.

If I slathered myself with five dollar bills I'd need security too.

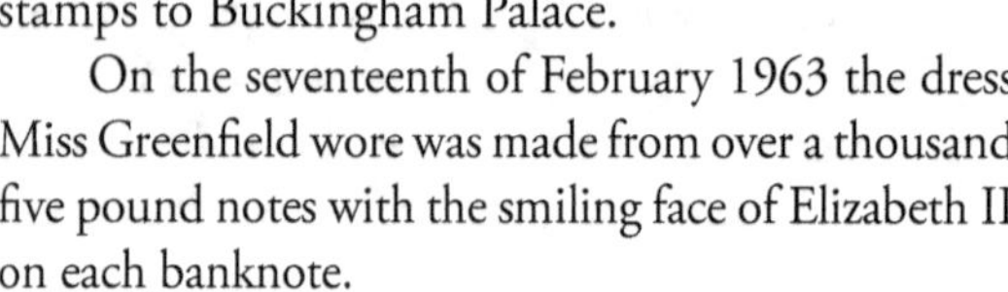

Like the dress?

———————————————————————————

———————————————————————————

———————————————————————————

———————————————————————————

———————————————————————————

You've heard the expression "when pigs fly" but the events of February 18, 1930 demonstrate the superiority of the cow, particularly a Guernsey. For on this day, not only did a cow named Ollie fly but she was milked repeatedly, producing 24 quart cartons of milk which were distributed to the folks on the ground.

Cows, pigs, chickens, all livestock generally is and was transported by train or truck. As the aviation industry grew in the twenties, there was the notion that if you could get animals up in the air, it would save time and money in getting them to the slaughterhouse. In 1930 the International Aviation Exhibition was to be held in St. Louis and the Ford Motor Company which had developed the trimotor plane in 1925 decided this would be a great opportunity to demonstrate what flying bovines could accomplish.

The company paid farmer Elsworth Bunce of Elm Farm in Wisconsin to put his prize Guernsey Ollie on the plane. Bunce would accompany her and milk her—she was selected because she was quite udder-ly the best at creating the good stuff. During the 72 mile flight from the farm to St. Louis, the milk she produced would be packaged in cartons to be thrown to folks on the ground. Except for the very last carton which would be presented to aviator Charles Lindbergh who was celebrity guest of the exhibition.

Minor problem—Ollie was a typically sized Guernsey at 1,000 pounds and I'm sure United would have charged her for at least two seats. She wasn't great about wearing her seatbelt and listening to the safety instructions. She couldn't fit in the lavatory. She tossed hay about and complained about the lack of inflight entertainment. Nonetheless, she produced the milk and was given a new name—Sky Queen. She was an instant celebrity, making Lindbergh look a little B-List.

Artist E.D. Thalinger painted her portrait in 1930, the first of many renderings of her beautiful form. In 2003 Chicago singer/songwriter Barry Levenson wrote "The Bovine Canata in b-flat Major" about Sky Queen as part of his opera Madame Butterfat. Her fame reached its apex in Mount Horeb, Wisconsin. On February 18 Mount Horeb holds the Dairy Fest, dedicated to Elm Farm Ollie, aka Sky Queen.

Henry Ford said at the time the stunt was an experiment in how altitude and flight would affect milk production. In fact, it was Ford's experiment to see if it could syphon off animal transportation business. In the end it was determined to be a failure: in 1933 Ford stopped production of the plane. Only 199 of the planes were made but there are still collectors. There is only one available for sale at the moment—it'll cost you a cool $1.4million!

I don't like milk. Do you?

February 19

Today is your day to not go Dutch. On February 19, 1674 the Netherlands and the Brits signed the Treaty of Westminster giving each other a number of little gifts. Like the country/colony of Suriname in South America got handed over to the Netherlands. The city of New Amsterdam became British property—immediately renamed New York after King James 2 who was also Duke of York. Bouyerwie became the Bowery, Nieuw Haarlem became Harlem. And thus the way was paved for Sex and the City and cosmopolitans! Welcome to New York!

February 20

February 20 is a big day in the Cummins family. Ralph was a Virginia football legend and played at Emory and Henry college and all that was after he had the winningest record in high school football! He hung up his cleats and coached at his alma mater Clintwood High School, retiring in 1987 with an astonishing winning record and three state championships.

But football isn't the thing he's most famous for. He married his high school sweetheart and the couple had their first child Catherine on February 20, 1952. Seems normal. Average. The next year, February 20, 1953 along came their first boy Charles. What a coincidence! February 20, 1956 in comes Claudia. And finally Cecilia February 20,1966.

According to the Guinness Book of Records, the Cummins can lay claim to the achievement of being the only family to produce four children with the same birthdays in different years. The book puts the odds of this happening as being 17.7 billion to one.

Planning a family reunion, well, we know what day it will be!

How come we don't know Ralph's wife's name?

February 21

February 21 is a good reminder that tennis is quite possibly the deadliest sport of all. Forget football and all those concussions and hockey's notorious loss of teeth (think just a moment about how Stan Mikita could have benefited from Clear Choice but he was born a little too early for that).

Tennis is responsible for not one but two deaths of European kings. The first recorded monarchial tennis related death was King Louis X of France. In 1216 he caught a chill while playing and developed a quickly moving pneumonia and died.

Then there's King James I of Scotland who on February 21 1437 was playing a civilized game when a mob of 30 Scottish assassins chased him across the court.

He thought he could escape through a sewer tunnel through his house that he had forgotten he had recently sealed off because he kept losing tennis balls in it. His assassins caught up to him and killed him.

In any event, don't replace your tennis habit with jousting. It's how Henry 8 got struck in the thigh which filled up with puss and had to be periodically drained and ultimately died, several wives later, four of which were dead.

Maybe Pickleball?

February 22

According to creative geniuses Hanna & Barbera, Pebbles Flintstone was born at the Bedrock Rockapedic Hospital at 8 p.m. on February 22, 10,000 BC weighing in at 6 pounds 12 ounces. She was not actually presented to the public until her 11,963rd birthday in the February 22, 1963 Flintstones' episode called "The Blessed Event." Oddly enough, she had not gained much weight in close to twenty thousand years.

February 23

February 23, 1960 is of special significance because it is the Japanese Emperor's birthday. Every year his subjects celebrate this milestone commonly known as Tenchosetsu. Naruhito of Japan was born in 1960 and was enthroned after the abdication of his father, the 125th emperor Akihito in 2019. It was the first time there was an abdication since the nineteenth century, but Akihito was nearly a hundred years old and in poor health.

Many people will use the holiday to visit the Tokyo Imperial Palace. Ordinarily, you can visit the outer grounds but on this day the Emperor and his family will welcome folks who would have been lined up for hours to get into the inner grounds. The family will show up on their balcony kind of like how the Brit royals do it. People will wave Japanese flags and show their support for the emperor. During the week before the celebration, many Japanese write letters to the Emperor to express good wishes.

It is ironic that on this day Americans observe the raising of the American flag at Iwo Jima on February 23, 1945—marking the end of the battle for that island and also a great turning point in the pacific theater of World War 2.

The last several emperors—Hirohito, Akihito and Naruhito—have worked hard to repair the relationship between Japan and the West, particularly the United States. Japan is one of our greatest trade and diplomatic allies in the region and so today I don't hesitate —

お誕生日おめでとう親愛なる皇帝
Otanjōbiomedetō shin'ainaru kōtei!
Happy Birthday to You!

How will you celebrate?

____

____

____

____

____

February 24

February 24 is your second Valentine's Day, in case the first one didn't go so well and the Valentine's Day Reset didn't work out. Known in Romania as Dragobete this is a holiday named for the son of Baba Pochia or *The Old Dokia* who insults the month of March when she goes out and about with her sheep or goats. So it's something of a day of reminding us that spring is soon upon us (forget that grumpy groundhog). But Dragobete watches out for lovers.

It is the day upon which Romanian birds are betrothed. If human males don't meet up with the gal pal of their dreams, they're in for a year of bad luck! Women and girls often will collect snow to melt it and use this special day's water for magic potions for the rest of the year. Floridians don't get this option.

I wish you all success in matters of the heart. Bre Lu'beste Romaneste! Romanian Lovers Day!

Wishing you a great day and the coming year

____

____

____

____

____

On February 25, 1913 the Sixteenth Amendment went into effect and we have, quite literally, been paying the price ever since.

So sit back, checkbook in hand, because April 15 is right around the corner.

Income taxes were nothing new. During the Civil War in 1861, a flat 3% was assessed on all households with an income over $800. It was meant to pay for the war and augment an already dizzying array of other taxes and charges. Farmers and folks in the rural West complained that they were paying a lot but not really getting anything for it and it was repealed in 1872. But government is not one for taking its empty hand out of the cookie jar—a second income tax assessed 2% on all incomes over $4k. It didn't affect that many people but nonetheless the Supremes struck it down. It wasn't until 1909 that the congress figured out the workaround in the form of the 16th amendment.

Now I don't know where you keep your copy of the Constitution. I keep mine by my bed along with the Declaration of Independence and the Bill of Rights. So no need to get yours. The Sixteenth was ratified in 1913 and is a quick, brutal read:

> "Congress shall have power to lay and collect taxes on incomes, from whatever source derived, without apportionment among the several states and without regard to any census or enumeration."

It took effect on February 25, 1913 and government was off to the races. At first it was limited to the upper 1% but you know how these things work. Pretty much everyone pays taxes on their income and now some states are considering a wealth tax which simply taxes anything you own.

TAX SIMPLIFICTION

ACCOUNTING

"Here. You figure out this mess!"

Don't try flying off to Wyoming or Florida. California will be imposing a transfer tax. Right now, our fair Illinois town of Schaumburg imposes a transfer tax of $1 per $1000 of the sale of your home if you try to bust out of the town limits.

So there's sales taxes every time you buy something, property taxes if you own a home, state taxes, and you even pay a death tax and you might not have even wanted to die!

Most people have to hire somebody to calculate their taxes or they have to buy Turbotax or Taxact to do it.

I don't think any of us mind paying if we had a good sense of what we're getting for it. Recently the IRS sent me a substantial check with no explanation. I was wary and rightly so. I cashed it and parked it in a savings account. Of course, the IRS has come back asking for the money AND for interest. In order to pay off everything, I had to take the money right back out of my savings AND come up with interest.

I have several friends who got that friendly check from the IRS and they spent it. I feel bad for them.

Do you look forward to a refund or paying your fair share?

February 26

February 26 is a double holiday, one that will stretch your kindness in a great way. It is Send a Letter to An Elder day as well as Set A Good Example Day. There's a lot of overlap here.

Set A Good Example Day comes from the sixth principle in L. Ron Hubbard's The Way to Happiness, a 21 point outline of all you have to do to be, well, happy. L. Ron Hubbard is fairly controversial because he is, after all, the science fiction writer known for creating Scientology. It'll be interesting to see how Tom Cruise celebrates this year. The sixth principle is a big one to get you to set a good example. And one way to do that is....

Send a Letter to An Elder Day was created by Jacob Cramer who formed the Lover for Our Elders foundation to highlight a growing problem: over 40% of those over sixty report loneliness is a distressing problem. And while it hurts to feel isolated, there's health consequences such as increased stress, heart disease, stroke and cancer. Cramer recently wrote a children's book called Grandma's Letter Exchange about a boy who thinks his grandma's habit of letter writing is boring. But it's not. It's a way of reaching out. If you can't bear to put pen to paper, consider writing to an elderly person in your life and asking them how their day is going or ask them to recall with you a memory that is uplifting.

See if you can honor both holidays at once....

Written by Jacob Cramer
Illustrated by Angelika Scudamore

Who will you write to today?

____

____

____

____

____

On February 27, 1992 actress*, activist**, alcoholic and distichiasis sufferer*** Elizabeth Taylor turned sixty. Still recalling the photographers who parachuted into her wedding to carpenter Larry Fortensky**** at her good friend Michael Jackson's Neverland the previous October, Taylor petitioned the Federal Aviation Administration to clear airspace for a mile around her birthday party and for 1,000 foot above it. It's the only time the government has done a no-fly zone for an ordinary citizen's birthday party.

*She was ten when she starred as Velvet Brown in the 1944 film National Velvet (arguably the horse could be considered the star). She broke her back falling off the horse and suffered from back pain her entire life, leading to an addiction to pain killers washed down with the hard stuff. She went on to star in a number of films and became a real life bride eight times, twice to British actor Richard Burton.

**She did a lot to raise awareness and compassion for those who suffer from AIDS.

***Distachiasis is a genetic mutation that causes a double row of lashes in a person. Sometimes it's just a few lashes but in her case it was a full set. People often thought she had false eyelashes on all the time. When she was cast in National Velvet, the makeup folk accused her of looking "too adult" and tried to remove the extra layers.

****Larry Fortensky met Elizabeth at a rehab center. They divorced five years after the wedding but remained friends. He fell down a flight of stairs after getting drunk while grieving a pet's death, causing him to be in a coma for two months. He recovered but died in 2016 of skin cancer after another two months in a coma. Elizabeth Taylor had died five years before and left him $800k which was in addition to the divorce settlement he received.

Actor Richard Burton, Elizabeth's two time husband, called her a "tough broad." It's a great compliment. Are you one? I try to be!

On February 28, 1927 something extremely weird happened. It was the Soviets, that's Russia for you, and a particular Soviet Ilya Ivanovich Ivanov, a government scientist decided that a new creature made of man and ape would be a good idea—we might call it a humanzee. The governor of French Guinea in Central America invited him to have at it with some of their chimpanzees.

So on this day, two captured chimpanzees—Babette and Syvette—were held down with nets and, er, squirted with semen collected from… well, you can make your guesses. All in the interest of science, of course. When the two didn't show up positive on their pregnancy tests, there was another chimp by the name of Black and another failure.

Ivanov had what he called a "bolt from the blue" idea of impregnating a human female by a chimp. The governor of French Guinea said "mais non!"

Ivanov returned to his home country and got permission to try this new plan—he advertised for a willing female. He got only one response from a woman identified later as G who said her life was in shambles but if she could help science, hey, what the heck! She was paired with an orangutan named Tarzan. The primate suffered a brain hemorrhage and died before the deed could be consummated. The Soviet government pulled the plug on this stuff and even threw Ivanov in prison for "counter-revolutionary" behavior.

On a better note, in 2005, British millionaire Sharon Tendler married a cetacean (that's dolphin, dontcha know) named Cindy (for Cinderella, but don't be deceived—this dolphin was a red blooded male). The duo married in Eilat Reef in Israel after a 15 year engagement. Instead of a wedding cake they had herring. Unfortunately, 6 years later Cindy died. He was forty which is actually pretty old for a dolphin. I don't have any information on whether Tendler moved on from her grief. She opined of their union that Cindy probably did the nasty with other dolphins, but that she was strictly a one dolphin woman. At his passing, she claimed she would not marry again.

Seriously, I don't make this shit up. This a great day to show appreciation for your pet (I've got a squirrel) but don't go too far with it. Just a little rub behind the ears is quite enough. The pet's ears not yours.

If you marry a dolphin, where do you honeymoon?

February 29 is a holiday dear to the hearts of many. Me? I have never participated in its celebration because I loathe the principles upon which it stands. Nonetheless, I will give you the particulars and you can decide whether it's as odious as all that.

On November 15, 1937 comic strip author and illustrator Alfred Gerald Caplin put out yet another installment of the doings of Li'l Abner and the residents of his hometown Dogpatch. Reporting on the events of the day before yesterday. Capp recounted a meeting held by Mayor Hekzebiah Hawkins. Hawkins had the misfortune of having a 35 year old daughter who was, well, ugly. She had never had a gentleman caller, must less a proposal, and Hawkins despaired that she would one day die a spinster and, worse, until that day she would live with him.

Hawkins convened a meeting with the town's eligible bachelors. He declared that there would be a foot race between themselves and Sadie. Whichever bachelor Sadie could catch, she could keep and her betrothal would be celebrated with a dance to be known as the Sadie Hawkins Dance.

Alas, the hapless Sadie came up empty, er, footed and the sorry holiday had to be repeated the next year. And the next. Other spinsters joined up and became somewhat innovative—one year, they wore hobnailed boots the better to stomp young men's feet so as to slow them down.

The traditional November comic strip became a college craze with schools hosting Sadie Hawkins' Dances wherein the gal asked the guy in the annual tradition. Some started to call the dances "turnabout" on the sly assumption that it was the one and only time in the calendar for such a role reversal.

Capp may have been inspired by an Irish dilemma called St. Bridget's Complaint. It is said that missionaries St. Patrick and St. Bridget were despairing of the Emerald Isle spinsters—Bridget suggested that in extremis women be allowed to do the asking. Patrick said, sure, but only once every four years. Under the Pistlonic calendar, February 29 became the logical choice. It is now known as Bachelor's Day or Ladies' Privilege and it carried a bit of a hitch: if a man declined, he was legally required to offer recompense. A new iphone, perhaps?

While Sadie's predicament was resolved by the termination of the Li'l Abner comics in 1978, there are plenty of folks who follow the custom here and across the pond. Me? Here's how I celebrate all year long—I don't call boys, I don't send cute texts, I most certainly do not chase boys wearing heavy boots.

If a gentleman is interested in me he'll let me know. It's saved me a helluva lot of grief.

How do you feel about the customary man asks woman?

____

____

____

____

March is a tomboy with tousled hair, a mischievous smile, mud on her shoes, and a laugh in her voice.

–Hal Borland

Today is Superman's birthday. Well, sort of. On March 1, 1938 Jerry Siegel and Joe Shuster signed a contract with National Allied Publications (a precursor of DC Comics) to put Superman on the cover of Action Comics #1. The two men had labored for almost a decade to find a publisher for their collaboration. But it had finally paid off. We all know Superman—the comics, the movies, the television, even the offshoots Superboy, Supergirl, and Lex Luthor. Of course, Siegel and Shuster bought gazillion dollar homes in Palm Springs and Hollywood. They had young, gorgeous  wives in succession. They had ungrateful children who got into drugs and they could afford the expensive rehab centers for them.

Oh, wait, no.

Siegel and Shuster were so desperate to give birth to baby Superman that they gave away all rights to this caped crusader for $130 which they had to split between themselves. Although, to be fair, they were given a ten year "you work for us for pennies" contract to write successive episodes of Superman.

After the ten year contract expired, Warner Communications, who had become the owners of the franchise, said "so long, farewell, auf wiedersehen, goodbye!"

As you might expect a big fat lawsuit ensued. It ended with a settlement in which each man was given $20k a year in hush money, er, pension as well as health benefits. Ha ha, it was already the seventies and they were old enough they were already covered by Medicare.

Siegel was the original model for Superman and he married a model named Joanne Kouacs who was in fact the muse for Lois Lane.

Shuster never married and lived with his mom his whole life. He did the illustrations for the 1954 comic series Nights of Horror—a bdsm series that is said to have inspired the real life teenage Brooklyn thrill killers of the same year.

Both men died in the nineties flat broke.

The $130 check? Their names were misspelled. And the money didn't go very far. But in 2012 the check was sold at auction for $160k. First edition copy of that first Superman episode was sold at auction in 2011 for $2mil. The creative guys always lose.

ps I threw in the picture from Nights of Horror just to titillate.

Have you done creative work and someone else profited?

____

____

____

____

____

March 2nd and I'm sure your thoughts are consumed by the memory of the hideous war of 2007 between Switzerland and Liechtentstein. Ah, how could we ever forget? It lasted less than twenty-four hours but on this day we celebrate the conclusion of the brutality!

Now it's natural that Liechtenstein, a tiny little sliver of land at the side of Switzerland, would fear an invasion from Switzerland. After all, Liechtenstein is a monarchy while aristocratic titles are forbidden in Switzerland. Liechtenstein allows tipplers to get behind the wheel who would be arrested and hung in Switzerland. Okay, maybe not hung but definitely fined. The Swiss are ardently neutral, even during something like World War 2 while Liechtenstein is sort of promiscuous in its alliances.

But still, with all these differences, the two countries do share pretty much the same languages and some citizens cross over the border with not much more thought than I do walking from my fair town of Winnetka to neighboring Wilmette. But nefarious things happened during the invasion of Leichtenstein late in the evening of March 1, 2007.

Every Swiss male is required to serve in the Swiss army although who's really going to invade the joint? There's a lot of marching. While every male is required to keep a gun IN THEIR HOME for self-protection, the privately held guns are largely used for suicide and the very occasional but tragic domestic episode. No mass shootings or anything. Which makes you wonder about calls for gun control. Because there's not much to do in the army, a considerable number of men are declared unfit just to keep costs down—something that would have come in handy for every American male during the Vietnam War. My biological father cut off one of his toes to get out of the draft and walked to the hospital to cheerfully get patched up. In case you're interested, I'm in favor of drafting women as well. The Swiss don't. They didn't even allow women the right to vote until 1971.

Meanwhile, the Swiss gives its soldiers rifles but they don't carry ammunition. They're largely used as walking sticks for soldierly marches. On the night of March 1st, there was the usual drill of 171 Swiss soldiers. Off they went. Except they got disoriented and ended up in Liechtenstein. Whoops! The soldiers did not declare Liechtenstein a new territory of Switzerland, but hey, there are, after all, folks who think of Liechtenstein as just the 27th Canton or Province of Switzerland. So Liechtensteinians might reasonably be concerned.

The soldiers got their bearings and returned home. The next morning on March 2nd the Swiss government contacted Liechtenstein and apologized. Maybe even sent flowers. Leichtenstein did the right thing and just said hey, no probs, this has actually happened before. Blame the weather. What a great way to end a war, er, accidental invasion.

How would you feel if the U.S. government required gun ownership and training?

____

____

____

____

On March 3, 1934 John Dillinger—young, handsome, and a stone cold bank robber—escaped from a Crown Point, Indiana jail where he got a little restless while awaiting trial for shooting an officer. Which will, these days, get you nothing but freedom, a court date if you choose to return to the scene of the crime, and a $200 debit card.

Dillinger designed a gun from a wooden washboard, a razor handle, and black shoe polish. He bluffed his way out the door, but not before stealing a Thompson submachine gun and swiping the Warden's car. He drove off towards the big city—Chicago.

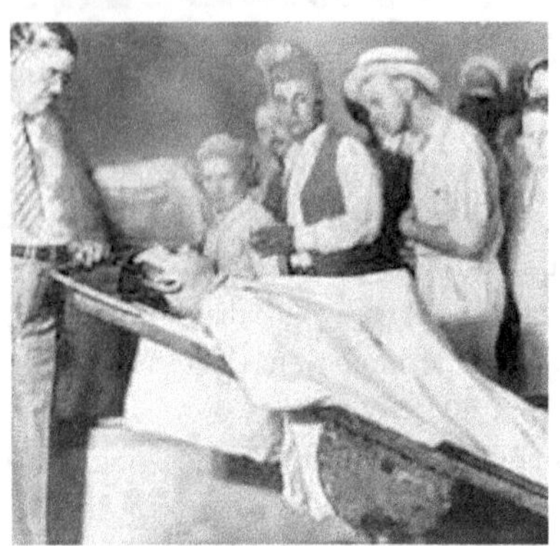

The warden Lillian Holley was so mortified that she and her crew had allowed the escape that she vowed "if I ever see John Dillinger I'll shoot him dead with my own gun."

Alas, Dillinger evaded her. He had a comfortable life in Chicago. Dillinger partied hard, but 1934 came with a hot, hot summer and he went to the movies July 22 to see Manhattan Melodrama. Movie theaters were the one reliable place for air conditioning. On that day, he was accompanied by two glamorous women, ahem, of the trade. One wearing a bright red dress.

In the same theater sat pre-teen Frances Gumm, youngest of the Singing Gumm Sisters was getting mighty tired of the daily rehearsals. She ran away to the Blackstone theater to watch Manhattan Melodrama too. Several times. Then, realizing she had an evening performance she left the theater. She saw a celebrity in the lobby. Or, at least, she thought he was a celebrity. He looked awfully familiar.

Frances asked him for his autograph. It would be the last autograph John Dillinger would ever sign. He walked out of the theater and the feds who had been waiting for the woman in the red dress to identify Dillinger and he was shot cold dead.

Frances changed her name to Judy Garland and did some movie about a Wizard. While Warden Lillian Holley never got to shoot Dillinger herself and she didn't get her car back, she had a different satisfaction of knowing he was dead. The woman in red? That was Madame Sage who owned a bordello that Dillinger frequented—Sage was from Rumania and was concerned about being deported. She thought incorrectly that turning in Dillinger would keep her in the states.

His body was displayed to the public and there was some discussion about whether this thirtysomething hoodlum was particularly, er, well endowed.

Which is why after the first day of viewing ladies were barred from getting a glimpse.

How do you feel when you wear red? Powerful? Sexy? Wicked?

On March 4, 2004 Mianne Bagger became the first transgender player in the Ladies Professional Golf Association. Born in Denmark, she started playing golf at eight and was such a phenom she was even featured with golfer Greg Norman in Golf World magazine as a fourteen year old boy. Her family moved to Australia and that's about the time Mianne felt that her feelings of being uncomfortable as a boy could not be ignored. Her family supported her and she underwent hormone therapy and sex reassignment surgery. She began playing in Australian amateur league tournaments and ultimately ended up in the top ten.

She went pro on this day in 2004 at the Women's Australian Open. She shot a not too spectacular 84 (12 over par) but she definitely put the spotlight on transwomen's participation in the sport. And maybe it was kind of good that she didn't go all Lia Thompson and beat everyone.

Instead, the next day there were newspaper headlines and she handled everything with grace that befits both men and women.

Today, consider how you feel about transgendered people!

____

____

____

____

____

Today is the one of the most important and most widely celebrated holidays in the world. And you might not have ever heard of it. I hope you'll do it up right, which is to say without getting on your knees to Chairman Mao.

March 5, of course, is Learn from Lei Feng Day which honors a comrade soldier mechanic in the People's Revolutionary Army. In 1962 he was killed by a no-good capitalist telephone pole that fell on his truck when he backed that thing right up on it. He was just 22 but his diary—discovered after his death—would be an inspiration during the Great Leap Forward. Well, the diaries and 12 articles, 18 speeches, 30 poems, 3 novels and 9 other works I'm not sure how to characterize. Every word extolled the virtues of the collection and of course the Chairman. He still fixed the Army's vehicles and did assorted good works.

The diary entry for October 15, 1961 includes: "Today is Sunday. I did not go out. I washed five sets of bedding for the comrades of my squad. I patched up one quilt for comrade in arms Gao Kuiyun. I helped the Cooking Division wash over 600 cabbage…although I am a bit tired, I feel very happy. My comrades were all wondering who laundered their bedding so clean."

I'm a lousy under-achiever. It's a good day if I make my own bed.

Even after death, Lei Feng teaches selflessness and humility. As he himself said "my only ambition is to be a rust less screw for the great cause of revolution." Chinese both in country and overseas take this day to do an act of kindness or humility—they learn from the dude!

There's a teeny tiny problem. Comrade Lei Feng may never have existed. Within his hagiography he was a humble orphan soldier who died in obscurity. Within the year, Mao had proclaimed a national holiday in honor of the—quel surprise!—discovery of Lei Feng's diary. Mao even created the Lei Feng Memorial in Fushon with a museum that displays among other artifacts the noose that Lei Feng's mom used to hang herself after an attack by a greedy landlord. Lei Feng is buried on the grounds.

The People's Republic has other role models who the state claims did heroic self-sacrificing things for the

What good deed are you going to do today?

____

____

____

____

____

revolution. Iron Man Wang dog paddled in a vat of cement when there was no mixer so that revolutionary buildings could be built. Shi Chuanxiang the happy go lucky "night soil" collector. Wang Yiqing made five million radio parts but no mistakes. It's a little puzzling that the pictures disseminated of Lei Feng during his military service invariably show him doing good deeds and, well, they seem pretty damn professional. Like he was an ex-royal caught in the act of being compassionate.

Perhaps it doesn't matter. When I identified as a Congregationalist I learned that it was irrelevant whether Christ ever lived. He was merely an allegory, part of a mythology we agree to believe. So play the 2006 online game Learn from Lei Feng and if your avatar wins, meet Chairman Mao. Listen to the chart topper All Northeasterners Are Living Lei Fengs. Maybe go back to doing a good deed—shovel your neighbor's walk, volunteer at the soup kitchen, call your mom. I mean seriously—Joseph Presser call your mom!

March 06

On March 6, 1912 the Nabisco Company filed a patent for an orexigenic* cookie consisting of two round flat biscuits held together by a bit of cream. The patent application** was approved later that month—have you ever heard of the government working that swiftly?—and on March 14, 1912 the Oreo Biscuit was released for the first time at a Hoboken, New Jersey grocery store near the Nabisco headquarters. It was later called the Oreo Sandwich and finally just Oreo.

In the fifties, food scientist William A. Turnier—yes, food scientist is a career—put the logo on the cookie. Later, another food scientist Sam "Mr. Oreo" Porcello developed the crème that is used today—the good stuff. Porcello held five patents for products he created during his 34 years working for Nabisco, including the invention of the Snack-Well and assorted modifications to the Oreo.

Oddly, he didn't actually have a sweet tooth. After he retired, he traveled the world helping with food development in third world countries through the ACDI—Agricultural Cooperative Development International. When at Nabisco and later

*Orexigenic is a peptide that stimulates appetite—not a problem for me—and Nabisco implied that the spices that went into the oreo would have that health effect So there was initially a sentiment that the name "orexigenic biscuit" would go over well. The French word "or" meaning gold might have also been the genesis of the name

**Many patents are really given for the process by which they are made. Even colors can be patented—Tiffany blue is the shade Pantone 1837 so named for the year Tiffany began business. The color of John Deere tractors? Patented. And every company that gets a patent fiercely protects its turf. Don't go making an Oreo at home kids!

What's your favorite Oreo?   Continued on Next Page

March 06

with ACDI he would bring back to his family all sorts of treats to find out what they liked or disliked. He allowed himself the occasional Oreo. Dunked in milk. And why he didn't get a Nobel prize for food science humanitarianism is a cryin' shame.

The Oreo has gone through a lot of tweaks over the years. For instance, the original Oreo was non-kosher, as it was made using pork fat. In 1998 Nabisco switched out lard and gained kosher recognition. There's lots of different flavors of crème, largely to recognize holidays. My favorite is the 2012 Birthday Cake edition which has become a permanent fixture. The Lemon Meringue got the ax. We can argue but I think that's justice.

Today is National Oreo Day in honor of that original patent application. The Oreo is the most popular cookie in the world, with over 500 billion sold.

So how are you going to celebrate this propitious day? I suggest getting yourself a bag of Oreos and share with a friend and two glasses of milk. Just remember to brush your teeth afterwards, particularly if you're going in for a teeth cleaning.

March 07

March 7 is National Cereal Day. While you're munching on your Wheaties, you may say this is just a made-up holiday. Au contraire! The history of cereal is a sprawling tale of religious schism, sanitariums, sexual suppression, suicide and war.

The average person in the 1800s had a diet of meat, alcohol, and coffee. Jeez, that's just like me! The diet created horrific health problems for Civil War soldiers and for post-war factory workers although I think the fact that their lives sucked might have had something to do with it.

Doctors advised plant-based fiber which for most people of the time meant cereal because transporting fresh veggies from farm to grocery store was pretty primitive. Unfortunately, the cereal usually came in bricks that had to be soaked overnight if you didn't want to choke to death—that's where we got the habit of pouring milk over our Count Chocula. Enter New York doctor James Caleb Jackson with his sanitarium Our Home Hygienic Institute which

made its money on rich neurotic people who wanted to take the, er, waters. Jackson had ambitions about how a diet based on the religious principles of the Seventh Day Adventist Church could cure us of our ills and in 1863 he created the wheat based Granula. Sugar? Oh, hella no! Cereal was now a serious medicine!

A client of his New York sanitarium was Battle Creek Michigan Dr. John Kellogg who embraced Jackson's philosophy—and his Granula. He thought he could do it one better using corn. You can see the lawsuit coming. In addition to improving on Granula, he would ratchet up the cereal's anaphrodisiac powers. Yep, that's right. Early cereals were marketed to not just make you healthy but get rid of pesky urges.

In 1894 John and his brother came out with Corn Flakes. Jackson sued, claiming the recipe had been stolen from him. All while the Kellogg brothers were battling each other over which one came up with the flaking process—John and his wife or Will and John's wife. I'll go with giving the credit to the wife. Somewhere along the way John got excommunicated by the Seventh Day Adventists. Here I thought only Catholics, Amish and my family did that!

John did what any self-respecting cereal maker would do, opening the Battle Creek Sanitarium where businessman C.W. Post took refuge with a nervous breakdown. Post was from the Christian Scientist branch of our story. The two denominations were equally strident about vegetarianism, health, and renouncement of sex and hooch. And each denomination thought the other crazytown.

Post allegedly stole recipes for corn flakes and grape nuts before opening his own cereal factory and sanitorium. He claimed his cereals cured him of appendicitis although having the Mayo brothers of Rochester Minnesota perform surgery might have had more to do with it. Plagued by continuing stomach pains Post realized his cereal couldn't cure, he committed suicide by firing a rifle into his mouth. John and Will Kellog never reconciled.

But how did cereal stop being medicine and become a breakfast sugar shot? Jim Rex of Philadelphia had no particular religious affiliation, no particular designs on health and wellness. He was just a man who in 1939 got sick of watching his children dousing their breakfast cereal with sugar. He devised a cereal with a caramelized glaze and he called it Ranger Joe Popped Wheat Honnies. He just promised kids a mail-in quiz and free surprise inside every box. He promised moms that their kids would eat the stuff. He happily sold everything to Nabisco who renamed it Sugar Crisp—spawning a multi-generational empire of sugary cereals.

To celebrate today have a bowl of your favorite! What will it be?

On this day March 8 in 303 a.d. Deacon Apollonius and his friend Philemon whom he had converted to Christianity were martyred. They (and a bunch of other Christians) had their hands and feet bound and then were tossed into the Mediterranean. Those Romans sure knew how to make a statement with martyring Christians what with stoning, mauling, cutting off the breasts of virgins, locking someone in the amphitheater with a hungry lion and whatnot.

It was during the Diocletonic era in which Emperors (in order of appearance) Diocletian, Maximian, Galerius, and finally Constantius ordered every possible persecution of Christians. Of course, it was impossible to fight the tsunami of Christian resistance—Constantius himself ended all the oppressive measures in 313 a.d. with the Edict of Milan. He himself converted.

But I get ahead of myself. Philemon was a flutist, dancer, mime and actor of great popularity in Antinopolis, Egypt. After the order went out that all Christians had to make a sacrifice to the Roman god Jupiter, Apollonius was in a tizzy. He couldn't do it. Wouldn't do it. Philemon said he would costume himself as Apollonius and impersonate him at a Jupiterian sacrifice. What an actor! What a trouper! Taking one for the team! Oscar winning performance! And a personal sacrifice because he would be partaking in acts of the Roman religion—check out Hebrews 6:4-6. The ultimate sin unto death. A complex situation because Philemon would be sacrificing not just his life but his soul so that Apollonius could live and continue his work for the faith.

Philemon balked at the last minute fearing the consequences outlined in Hebrews 6:4-6. He revealed himself as a Christian and the gig was up. Both men were transported to Alexandria for their martyrdom. The two men are saints with a joint feast day March 8. Philemon became the patron saint of dancers.

Is there any sin that is unforgiveable?
Besides wearing white after Labor Day.

On March 9, 1974 World War II finally came to an end, or at least the last of the Japanese Imperial Army surrendered. Phew! What a relief!

And you thought the war ended in August 1945 with the tag team atom bombs at Hiroshima and Nagasaki. No, it ended when Second Lieutenant Hiro Ononda said it did.

Ononda was born in 1922 and joined the Japanese Imperial Army in 1940 and rose through the ranks to become an intelligence officer. After intense training at the Nakaro Institute, he was sent on December 26, 1944 to the Philippine island of Lubang. His commander Major Yoshimi Taniguchi told him that he was to do anything to hamper a possible invasion by Allied/American forces including destroying their airstrip and the pier. Ononda and fellow soldiers were told that surrender or suicide was NOT an option, no matter what the circumstances.

"Whatever happens, we will come for you," Taniguchi assured his men.

Ononda, as a Second Lieutenant, was the lowest ranking officer among the few JIA on the island. Several got killed by air raids, Ononda and three others headed for the hills. It was a rough life, raiding farms and doing all that they could to impede American control of the island which actually officially happened in February 1945. One of their party just plain quit in 1949 and fled. Another was killed in 1954 and Ononda's last comrade died in 1972.

Over the years, there had been some efforts to persuade the evasive and elusive Japanese soldiers. The 1952 airdrop of letters from family members pleading with the holdouts to surrender was thought by the men to be the enemy's trick. Finally, in late 1973 Japanese explorer Norio Suzuki tracked down Ononda, who was not persuaded that Japan had surrendered. He informed Suzuki he was waiting for orders from his commanding officer Then, only then, would he wave the white flag.

The government tracked down Major Yoshimi Taniguchi was by now a bookseller and sent him to meet Ononda. On March 9, 1974 Taniguchi and Ononda sat down—on the orders of the Emperor. Ononda surrendered. "I promised that we would come for you," Taniguchi said. The two men returned to Japan. Ononda decided the place had lost all its traditional values and so he moved to a Japanese enclave in Brazil to raise cattle. He died in 2014, having served his Emperor well and faithfully.

How to honor this day? Perhaps think about the things you're hanging onto and sacrificing for because of loyalty. A relationship. A job. A house. Then make a decision about whether your sacrifices are worth it. If they are, keep on keeping on.

On March 10, 1940 Carlos Ray Norris was born in Ryan, Oklahoma. His Cherokee father was a soldier, mechanic, bus driver and later truck driver. His Irish mother managed the house and her three sons, the oldest of which was Carlos. Carlos later described himself as being a bit shy, not really into sports, and deeply ashamed of his father's drunken antics and the schoolyard taunts about being a half-breed.

But first, a Chuck Norris truism.

Chuck Norris doesn't try to survive the Zombie Apocalypse. The Zombies try to survive Chuck Norris.

That shy child joined the Air Force as a policeman and he found himself in martial arts. He achieved a black belt in Korean Tang Soo Do, Brazilian Jiu Jitsu, and in Judo. And he acquired the nickname…

Chuck Norris!

Chuck Norris was bitten by a cobra. After days of excruciating pain, the cobra recovered.

After his stint in the Air Force he taught martial arts and just happened to have a client named Bruce Lee of the television series The Green Hornet. Lee had experienced some racist stuff. He had auditioned for the part of Kwai Chang, Shaolin monk in the television series Kung Fu. The part that was scooped up by white actor David Carradine, the auto erotic asphyxiation aficionado (say that four times fast). Bruce was considered too Chinese.

Chuck Norris truism:

Chuck Norris has never cheated Death. He always wins fair and square.

Bruce was producing, directing, starring in Enter the Dragon and asked Chuck to play one of the villains. Chuck was such a hit that he was cast in the 1977 trucker/martial arts movie Breaker! Breaker!—and on the advice of his student Steve McQueen, he took the lead in the 1978 movie Good Guys Wear Black. The producers couldn't find distributors so they rented out theaters across the country, taking all ticket proceeds—it's called four walling and it worked!

Okay, one more:

Chuck Norris never has to put gas in his tank—his cars run on fear.

Chuck went on to score parts in action movies and even had a television series Walker, Texas Ranger. Then in 2005 his life was changed by Richard "Lowtax" Kyanka. Lowtax had put together a website in 1999 called Something Awful. He created a forum for folks to make jokes about the strength and virility of Vin Diesel but fans ultimately decided that Chuck was their man.

You are strong. You are courageous. You are more powerful than you think. Attack the day with confidence and commitment. Be the punchline of your own Chuck Norris joke.

Do you have a Chuck Norris joke?

____

____

____

____

____

March 11

Today March 11 is Johnny Appleseed day in honor of Swedenborgian missionary and arborist and introducer of viral noxious dog fennel to the Americas. He was born John Chapman in 1774 in Leonminster Massachusetts. His mother passed on when he was two and the family moved to Springfield, Massachusetts.

In 1797 young Chapman, accompanied by his brother, went west to northwestern Pennsylvania to propagate apple and pear seeds. The duo were able to propagate fruit trees as far west as Illinois, Iowa, Michigan and Wisconsin. They didn't just toss seeds—Chapman purchased land and planted trees. The brother eventually dropped out. Although, yes, Chapmann did spend most of his time bare foot as in the legends (hell, I spent my entire college years bare foot but that's a story for another day). He also preached for Swedenborgia, a Protestant offshoot founded by Emmanuel Swedenborg—an easygoing religion that really just asks you to try to be a good person.

Johnny also introduced dog fennel to the Americas, which is a little like starlings and buckthorn—invasive but a reminder of the old country. He died when he was 70, alone, barefoot, but bequeathing to his sister all his lands which was kind of a nightmare because there were so many of them.

A telling event of his life occurred in Mansfield, Ohio. Attending a sermon, he heard the preacher complaining about expensive teas and calico cloth He asked "Where now is there a man who, like the primitive Christians, is traveling to heaven barefooted and in coarse raiment?" And Chapman stepped right up and said "I'm your primitive" not realizing he was comparing himself to Christ.

Many Europeans and Eastern Americans introduced nonindigenous species of plant and animal to the rest of the Americas. When I moved to Winnetka, a woman invited me to lunch and I thought "I'm making a friend!" No, I was only in for a lecture on cutting down all the buckthorn on my property which is a fast moving invasive plant brought in by Europeans. I felt ashamed and embarrassed. Kudzu was brought in from Asia and wow, it's taken over the South. Plants and animal species move. And there's nothing to stop that.

Chapman brought in dog fennel trees but he also brought us apple trees and pear trees. We celebrate him today in deference to farmers who begin their planting seasons…eat an apple today!

Red Delicious, Granny Apple, or Fuji?

On March 12, 1933 newly minted* President Frank-lin D. Roosevelt got comfortable in the Diplomatic Reception Room of the White House in front of a microphone. He wanted to speak to the American people about the Banking Crisis which had caused over 9k banks to fail in the years 1930-1933, 4k just in the preceding two months. People were panick-ing and lining up to take their money out of the bank pronto like they were extras in "It's a Wonder-ful Life." One of FDR's first acts as president was to declare March 6 a bank holiday and the banks were set to reopen March 13 under the Emergency Banking Act.

FDR took just 13 minutes of America's time, broadcasting on the radio so that every-one sitting in their cars or their living room could hear him. He would speak to the people 31 times in the 4,422 days he served as presi-dent. The talks came to be called Fireside Chats because he wanted people to feel like he was just an old friend who had stopped by for a chat next to a crackling fireplace.

On March 13, banks were bracing for the worst as they opened their doors. There were long lines—confident and courageous cus-tomers looking to deposit their money. FDR's speech had worked its magic.

He was not the only world leader using the newfangled radio address to galvanize the populace. George V** of England had done a Christmas radio address but the monarch who really took it to the next level was his son George VI who took lessons

*FDR was inaugurated on March 5, just a week earlier.

**We all know now that the royal family is terrifically racist and we're all playing the guessing game about who expressed "concern" about how white/black Archie would be. George VI was on a world tour which ended in Jamaica in 1927. He played a doubles tennis match with Bertrand Clark as his partner. Quite the scandal at the time because Clark was black but the king was making the point that all members of the Commonwealth are embraced regardless of their melatonin.

from Aussie Lionel Logue to overcome his stuttering. On September 3, 1940, the day before the Brits would declare war on Germany, he gave a speech so stunning, so rousing that the country turned on that weasel PM Neville Chamberlain and signed up for a battle…serving as a basis for a 2010 movie where Helena Bonham Carter looks like she took a shower and combed her hair.

The monarch who does it best has to be Queen Elizabeth II who gave her first radio address when she was just fourteen. The October 13, 1940 address was designed to reassure children, many of whom had been sent to the countryside in anticipation of Nazi bombing.*** In 1957 she did her first television address in Canada. She always communicated calm, steady, carry on.

***She was joined by her younger sister Margaret who was just starting to understand that she was the "spare" and that must have been rough for her as for Harry.

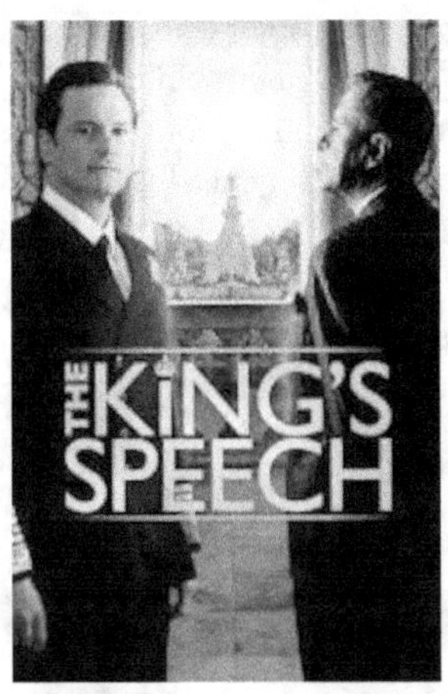

Are you a "keep my money under the mattress" or do you kept it in the bank?

____

____

____

____

Get out your do-gooder personality or maybe get out your Bible because today, March 13, is Good Samaritan Day. Or at least get out your cell phone. You might need all three for this holiday.

If you've got your Bible, take a look at Luke 10:29-37. I'll give you the short version. A man is going from Jerusalem to Jericho and he gets attacked by a bunch of guys, stripped of his clothes and left for dead. And this isn't even the New York subway!!!!! A rabbi and a Levite (sort of like an assistant rabbi) pass the victim by. Don't get me involved in this, they're thinking. Just like a lot of us would. I cop to that. Then a Samaritan passes by. Samaritans were considered extremely lower class, but this particular Samaritan clothed and dragged the victim to a local inn and paid for him to stay and be cared for.

You might think this is a Biblical post but the day is actually really about 28 year old New York bartender Catherine "Kitty" Genovese who on this day March 13 1964 was coming home from work and right there in front of her building she was attacked over the course of thirty minutes by serial burglar Winston Mosley. Despite her cries and screams for help, none of her apartment building neighbors did anything. They just watched the attack play out in the building courtyard like they were at the Colosseum. Possibly thinking "I don't want to get involved" and "maybe I'll get hurt." One person tried calling 911 and on his third attempt he got through to police but by then it was too late. Kitty was dead, splayed out in the courtyard of her apartment building.

Today, consider helping someone in need. It might be as simple as calling someone you know is struggling. Listen to them. Or maybe remember that calling 911 is sometimes the very best thing. Or maybe try to incorporate kindness to strangers in need into your daily habits. And if you're the guy heading from your own personal Jerusalem to Jericho feel free to contact me.

What do you think of first when faced wiht a stranger's emergency? Cellphone used for…?

March 14

I hesitate over March 14. Yes, it's Pi Day 3/14, get it? But it's also a holiday that's meant for the total pleasure of men. Don't worry, ladies, we have something for you but that's not 'til next month.

The holiday was started in 2002 by DJ Tom Birdsey of WFNX, a Boston radio station. He opined that Valentine's Day (February 14) was a totally female centric holiday with candy, cards, jewelry, flowers presented to the fair sex along with a night out on the town. To be fair, this year I ate Ben & Jerry's and watched television on the couch. Alone. But still, I take his point. I happen to think Valentine's Day is a day to celebrate our love for everyone and so I mail out a lot of cards—my grandson, my sons and their wives, friends both male and female, they're all on my list. Course, I regard love as not limited to the romantic sort and I'm pretty much the same way about St. Patrick's Day, Easter, Halloween, etc. I mean, they're not just for the Irish or those who believe in bunnies, or those who have a demonic twist.

Birdsey proposed a holiday to be celebrated on March 14 that would be something of a payback. He called it Steak and Blow Job Day. How you celebrate is pretty self-explanatory. Doesn't cost much and I don't think you have to make reservations. You don't even have to call a florist or peruse expensive baubles at a jewelry store. I think a new dress would be a waste.

Just remember, dudes, that your lady's reward for March 14th is April 14th — Cupcakes and, ahem…you can figure it out…day. Ladies, you can thank me now.

March 15

March 15 is generally a no good rotten bad day, called by the Romans the Ides of March, as Ides is the middle day of any month. It was said that in 44 BC seers informed Emperor Julius Caesar "beware the Ides of March" which was as close as they dared to say "your friend Brutus and all those Senators you think are loyal are settin' up for a rumble." Caesar was cautious that day, spending his time quietly at home. But as the sun went down he decided to go to the capitol building and along the way he passed the seers and said "you're idiots" and the seers coolly sneered "day's not over yet dude." In Latin.

He was met with Senators, each of whom stabbed him in turn so that not one of them could say they were virtuous or be accused of having delivered the fatal blow. The last strike was from Brutus one of Caesar's closest frenemies and the Emperor's

Continued on Next Page

March 15

last words were said to be "et tu, Brutus" which is Latin speak for "Brutus I thought you were my bestie." Brutus supposedly replied "Be still, Caesar, I killed thee not with half so good a will." Which is sort of weasely.

Thus, March 15th is known as Brutus Day, a day to ponder those friendships where your back got in the way of someone's knife. I've got some. You have too. But maybe a way of dealing with this problematic holiday is to consider whether the friendship is one that can be repaired, whether that relationship is worth repairing, and whether you have any need to get yourself an olive branch and maybe a bottle of bubbly in case it all works out. You could also say no, I'm better off and think what a wonderful day this is because that frenemy is not in your life.

Have you ever been betrayed by someone you thought your bestie?

____

____

____

____

____

March 16

On March 16, 1846, the King of the Book Smugglers was born! The day is celebrated all over the world, but most particularly in his home country of Lithuania. I'll give you the deets for how to join in the fun but first an explanation.

Different cultures might appropriate another culture's literature, music, traditions. Usually this happens organically when people just admire something outside of their comfort zone. I don't think it's a bad thing although Kim Kardashian took a lot of heat for cultural misappropriation when she turned up at the 2018 MTV awards wearing braids. I think it's okay for a late middle-aged white woman to spontaneously belt out Kanye "Ye" West songs.

Sometimes cultural appropriation is imposed by governments, religious and activist organizations. And that brings us to the Book Smugglers of Lithuania. In 1863 Tsar Alexander 2 quelled the Polish-Lithuanian Insurrection. Putting the hammer down on Lithuania in particular, he deputized Michail Nikolayevich Muravyo to Russify the people. Getting rid of the Lithuanian language and its Catholic faith in favor of the Russian language and the Orthodox faith.

First order of business—all books in Lithuania were to be written in the Cyrillic, not in the Latin Alphabet. Enter former serf Bielinis who had taught himself to read and write. Bielinis joined one of the groups of book smugglers who carried contraband religious texts from Prussian controlled Lithuania Minor. Eventually in charge of the group, Bielinis became known as King of the Book Smugglers. When a smuggler got caught it was prison, exile to Siberia or being shot right there on the spot. And you think librarians complaining about book banning is bad?

There were roughly three thousand smugglers and they saved Lithuanian literature by hiding books under their skirts, under the wood they carried in a backpack, in the false bottom of a carriage. People were so hungry for their literature the program expanded into textbooks and even fiction. It's estimated the Book Smugglers trafficked five million books. Part of their success was attributed to their very ordinary lower class appearance.

In 1904 Russia lifted the restrictions and the Book Smugglers disbanded. Smuggler Juozas Masiulis opened up a book store in Panevezys. You can pick up a book and a bit of history at J. Masiulio Knygynas at Respublikos g. 21 right there on the corner.

Bielinis settled near Panevezys. He initially supported Communism, little realizing that the Soviet Union was not going to be Lithuania's friend. Under the Molotov-Ribbentrop Pact of 1940 Estonia, Latvia and Lithuania were sucked into the Soviet orbit and it's almost like Alexander II all over again. It wasn't until the collapse of the Soviet Union that Lithuania got out from under Russia's dominance. In 1989 Bielinis' birthday was declared a national holiday—Day of the Book Smugglers or Knygnesi Diena. In Lithuania there are parades and other celebrations. Around the world Lithuanians drop off a Lithuanian book at a bookstore, a library, museum, or coffee shop. Be on the lookout! You might find one and can be a part of a movement that saved a culture!

So today are you going to take a Lithuanian book and drip it off at random locations like a train station or a coffee shop so that someone might be introduced to the culture?

____

____

____

____

____

Today is St. Paddy's Day, honoring La Fheile Padraig aka St. Patrick whose death day is March 17, 461 a.d. You might go to a parade—the first one in North America being in New York in 1762 by conscripted Irish soldiers in the British Army. You might go to a pub and drink Guinness Stout but you have to take my dog Fuego. He loves a party!

St. Patrick was born in 385 a.d. in Britain and was kidnapped at age 16 and sold into slavery in Ireland. He returned to his home after God came to him in a dream and told him "Run to the beach, there will be a ship waiting." He did and there was a boat. Patrick became a priest and returned to Ireland with the intention of converting all the Irish to Christianity. The story about him casting out the snakes of Ireland is an allegory of his efforts to convert or scare away the Druids. And he did a great job because when he died almost all of Ireland's population was Christian. He was named the patron saint of the land.

Not so fast! There are two other patron saints of Ireland. St. Brigid, who may have been baptized by St. Patrick, founded the Kildare Abbey and her homegoing day is February 1, 525 a.d. To celebrate her day weave yourself a Brigid cross out of rushes. The crosses are hung over your front door to protect against evil, fire and hunger. It's a popular housewarming gift. The third patron saint of Ireland is Columba aka Ceili (521-597) who formed a monastery at the Iona Island of the Inner Hebrides. He was one of the

Twelve Apostles of Ireland who carried on St. Patrick's work with a particular focus on preserving Latin texts that were being smuggled out of Rome as it fell. You can celebrate his day on June 9th with a Ceilidh which is a party that features folk dancing and, of course, drinking.

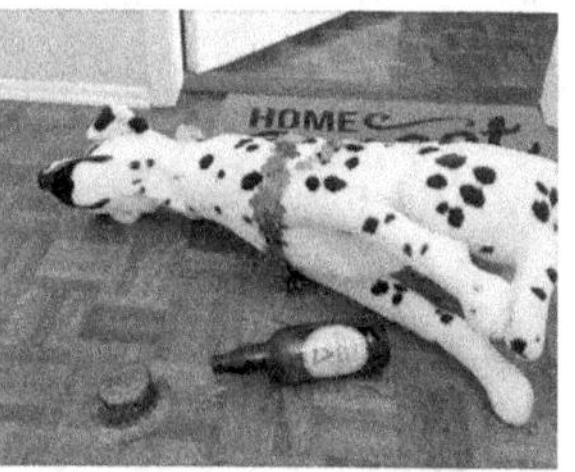

All three saints are buried at Downpatrick (Dun Padraig or Patrick's stronghold). Have a wonderful St. Patrick's Day—Éire go brách, which is to say Ireland to the End of Time!

My dog Fuego before and after the holiday—how will you celebrate?

March 18 and my thoughts turn to Grover Cleveland, Jose & Kitty Menendez, and the three Baby Ruths.

Back in 2012 I was dealing with the stalker ex-boyfriend dude and I had to escape even if just for a weekend to clear my head. My late friend Landon "Lanny" Jones and his wife invited me to their home in Princeton, New Jersey. I went for long walks, visited the college's campus, and enjoyed the Jones' hospitality. I also visited the  Naussau Presbyterian Church's cemetery. Princeton Cemetery has been called the Westminster Abbey of the United States. Rightfully so. It's got Alexander Hamilton's killer and Broadway star Aaron Burr, math ontological dude Kurt Godel, fiery preacher Jonathan Edwards and of course Toto.

I wanted to visit Jose and Kitty Menendez. They had met in Princeton and moved out to California with their boys Lyle and Erik. The two boys killed them in 1989, receiving a "you ain't never getting out!" sentence. Kitty and Jose Menendez were brought home to New Jersey. I can't imagine bringing life into the world and then being shot in the head by my spawn. Their grave, btw, had fresh flowers in front of it and I wondered if I should have brought some. But if I brought flowers for them I'd feel guilty about all the other people buried there.

I was leaving the cemetery when I passed a grave that made me pause. Grover Cleveland. It couldn't possibly be THAT Grover Cleveland. Someone who had been the 22nd and 24th president wouldn't be in a plain grave—there should be accolades and a list of accomplishments and honors. But no, it was him. Before his death of a heart attack in 1908 he had left specific instructions that there were to be none of that. A humble ending but I think a quite good one. His last words were "I have tried so hard to do right." I hope those will be my words as well.

His wife Frances Folsom Cleveland Preston, buried by his side, had been VP of the New Jersey Association Opposed to Woman's Suffrage.

On Grover's other side is the grave of Ruth Cleveland. As first daughter she was quite famous and acquired the nickname "Baby Ruth." In 1904 she died of diphtheria at the age of twelve. Her fame was solidified in 1920 when the Curtiss Candy Company renamed their Kandy Kakes Baby Ruth. At least, that's the company's story when another Baby Ruth threw a litigation hissy fit. Babe Ruth had just broken the single season home run record. George Herman Ruth was 19 years old when he first signed on with the Baltimore Orioles who often trained for the Boston Red Sox. He needed a legal guardian to sign for him and the owner Jack Dunn legally adopted him. The team started to call the slugger "Dunn's Baby" which became "Baby Ruth" which became "Babe Ruth." Somehow I think the Kandy Kake name change was about him all along.

Happy Birthday Grover! You're a great dude! And yes, you did right.

What's going to be on your gravestone?

March 19, 1892 is a day of great significance in college football, The Big Game and a future president who was great with money but not too good on the details.

In 1891, Stanford University had just opened its doors to 559 students, only one of which had ever played football. Rugby was considered the better college sporting man's place to be. That lone football player at Stanford John Whittemore was a transfer student from the more egalitarian Washington University and he introduced some of his friends to football. They formed a team and as a group decided that only Whittemore could be their coach. Whittemore didn't have much experience with the business side of things so he called upon freshman Herbert Hoover to be their manager.

The Stanford Cardinals scrounged for pennies for equipment and they really should have just left it to Hoover. He hit on a scheme to put some real bank in their collective pigskin wallet. His friend Herbert Lang managed University of California

Golden Bears and the two put together an invitational game at Haight Street Grounds in nearby San Francisco. Everyone thought Hoover was an idiot because the Golden Bears were acknowledged to be the best team in the state.

The Grounds was only built to hold 15k but on the day of the game Hoover (and to a lesser degree Lang) had sold 10k tickets. All told, 20k fans showed up for the game, all with the steadfast belief that Stanford would lose. Hoover and Lang scrambled for pots, buckets, bowls in which to keep the coins.

The good news: 20k fans showed up for the game.

The bad news: Hoover had forgotten the football. I coached boys' soccer for nine years and that's probably the only mistake I never made.

The game was delayed for an hour while a local sporting goods store owner was sent to find a football. Hoover didn't get to see the game he had worked so hard to organize. He and Lang retired to the hotel where the teams were staying to count the proceeds.

The Big Game, as it came to be called, is an annual re-match between the two rivals. There was a short hiatus beginning in 1906 when both schools, citing violence in the sport, dropped their football teams in favor of rugby. The winners bring home the prized Axe. The two schools came to make a week of it, with their respective schools having water polo, hockey, volley match-ups. There's even the Ink Bowl, a touch football game between the two schools' student papers.

Herbert Hoover and Lang didn't get to see the game but Hoover must have been damn proud. Not only had he ended up with $30k to finance Stanford football for years to come, his team had bested the Golden Bears 14-10. Hoover went on to become president and his term in office saw the beginning of the Great Depression. He should have stuck to football!

March 20

Princess Royale* Anne, first born daughter of Queen Elizabeth II was given the titles of Air Chief Marshall of the RAF and General in the British Army. If Britain's military echelon gets wiped out, she could step in and do it all with grace and style. And a badass attitude.

On March 20, 1974 at around 8 p.m. Princess Anne was returning to Buckingham Palace from a charity event. Her car was cut off by a white Ford Escort. Unemployed and disgruntled Ian Ball jumped out of the Escort, firing at her bodyguard and chauffeur. A nearby officer thought it was a case of road rage and approached. Ball shot him too. Remember, Britain has the strictest gun laws and even a police officer didn't carry.

Ball then jumped into the back seat next to Anne and told her he was kidnapping her.

"Not bloody likely," Anne is reported to have said. Whether it was the prospect of being kidnapped or the degradation of being driven in a Ford Escort we don't know. She would later describe her interaction with Ball as "a very irritating conversation." The two tussled.

*Princess Royale is an honorary title that is bestowed upon the eldest daughter of a British monarch. It is not automatic, but instead is meant to express appreciation for service to country. It is the highest honor to be conveyed to a female member of the royal family.

Continued on Next Page

____

____

____

____

March 20

With all the troubles the British Royal Family—illnesses, accusations and estrangements—it's easy to forget the most remarkable daughter of the late and beloved Queen Elizabeth 2. Princess Anne the second child is the hardest working royal—clocking over 450 formal engagements a year. That's a lot of handshaking, speeches, state funerals and weddings, remembering people's names before she even meets them and extolling of worthy causes.

She is regal, always perfectly dressed, and pretty darn good looking. And today is the anniversary of when she proved she is one tough broad. Even aside from being an Admiral and having the first loathsome husband Mark Phillips who was in the car and admitted later to being scared. In an unrelated development, they would divorce in 1992 after he fathered a daughter by Heather Tonkin of New Zealand. Anne would find ultimate bliss later that year and married one time equerry Timothy Laurence. Their marriage endured.

Meanwhile, back at the scene of the attempted kidnapping, former boxer Ron Russell (six-four so I'm guessing light heavyweight, cruiser weight or maybe even heavyweight) was driving by and noticed the commotion.

"He needs sorting," Russell later recalled thinking. Aren't the Brits so delightfully understated?

Russell stopped his car, came up behind the fracas and punched Ball in the back of the head. Princess Anne coolly got out of the vehicle. Later, police would discover handcuffs, tranquilizers and Ball's ransom note to the Queen. 20 mil pounds sent to a Swiss bank account. How cliché. In his position I would have asked for a corgi and a Rolls Royce.

Sometimes when I'm in a rough spot, I remind myself of Princess Anne. I try to remember the times in my life in which I have been that tough broad. I say "ArLynn, you're a tough broad." And I just keep repeating it over and over.

"You're a tough broad."

So today go out there and be that tough broad. It's the highest compliment you can give yourself. If you're a dude, don't be Captain Phillips cowering in the back of the car. Tell yourself "I am Machete, I'm a tough hombre."

When have you been a tough broad/hombre?

____

____

____

____

____

Heavy is the head that wears the crown. That line, somewhat modified, shows up in Shakespeare's Henry IV. Hey, it's really true! Elizabeth 2 had her crown downsized before her coronation—she had to endure a four hour ceremony with a crown that was, even after its touchup, a whopping 2.3 pounds. Not like the King of Tonga after it seceded from Britain—reportedly the heaviest crown of the modern era. It was worn by King Tupou I at his 1873 coronation and made for him at the behest of his Prime Minister Reverend Shirley Waldemar Baker. I can't track down a reliable figure on how much it weighs but every king of Tonga has worn it. Tough guys, they are. Or maybe they just train for it.

On March 21, 1800 Pope Pius VII was crowned in Venice with a lightweight papier-mache tiara. It was a replacement for the mongo sized one that was stolen by Napoleon Bonaparte during his overthrow of the previous pope in 1798. Moral of the story: lock up the valuables when French dictators come over. A paper-mache tiara was made as a substitute while the papal diplomats tried to negotiate the return of the original. The noblewomen of Venice donated jewels to decorate the paper-mache and the crown was quite light and comfortable for His Holiness.

Napoleon did eventually come around and gave the original crown back to the Pope in 1804 but he quite deliberately and with malice aforethought modified it so that it was 18 lbs and couldn't be worn for a three hour Easter mass. Successive popes continued to wear the paper-mache crown until it was retired in the mid-70s as even it seemed too ostentatious. Jeez, what a little Vatican Two will do for a church!

Sacred Heart Church in my fair town of Winnetka, has a stained glass window of the papal paper-mache crown. Notice the keys as in keys to the Kingdom of Heaven. And the scarf that is part of the papal vestments. Many churches have such a stained glass window tucked away.

What wonderful relics do you have in your church, temple or place of worship?

March 22 is International Coq Au Vin Day and I think we should all give a big shout out to our late and beautiful Julia Child for her recipe which is so damn economical and elegant and we need a little bit of both, don't we?

So trot on down to the grocery store and get some chicken legs (cheapest cut you can do) and some white wine (cheapest but make sure you are willing to drink a little off the top). Julia suggested you're going to serve this dish with roasted potatoes and salad.

Take some bacon and grill it in a pan. When fully cooked, cut it up to add to the dish or just eat it right there and then. Grill the chicken in what bacon fat there is, adding in salt and pepper. So far, so good. It'll take you about ten minutes. Then add in some wine, some tomato paste, some beef stock, some more wine, some herbs, I don't know—I think parsley, thyme and a bay leaf would do. Then to the vegetables—let the meat continue to cook for thirty minutes because you're going to be busy. Onions, carrots, mushrooms. Boil them up. Add wine. To your mouth. Just to make sure your taste buds are fulminating.

Take your chicken out of the pan. Slide off as much fat as you can, then add more fat in the form of butter (Julia was a big believer in the good stuff—I once met her and she explained that she NEVER used margarine). A little bit of flour, stirring so you get a thickened gravy. Ah, here's the moment. Marry the chicken and those veggies.

Open another bottle of wine. Present the dish at the table. It's typical French—a cheaply made dish made elegant. And these days, I'm thinking the French have got something to teach us.

This might be something the French do well. Can you think of any others?

March 23, 1971 was the day that Congress passed the 26th amendment amid cries of "old

enough to fight, old enough to vote." It was a popular amendment and by end of July it was ratified by 34 states and the paperwork landed on President Richard Nixon's desk to be signed. Think about all the things that you can do once you turn eighteen—you're driving, if you murder your neighbor you're automatically charged as an adult, you can live independently, you can drink (oh, wait!) and you can have some pretty invasive surgical procedures without your parents' permission or even knowledge.

At the time, the slogan "old enough to fight, old enough to vote" was quite poignant. Young men were being drafted to fight or at least be in support positions in the Army during the Vietnam War. It was actually President Franklin Delano Roosevelt who dropped the draft age to eighteen during World War II. So there were plenty of warriors who were old enough to die on the battle field but not old enough to vote or drink or have gender affirming surgery. Wait, nobody was having gender affirming surgery.

But I keep thinking about the Civil War. Some of our greatest sacrifices were made by ones so young. Benjamin F. Williams of Georgia who enlisted/drafted/got roped in at age eight. He was put in charge of a team of two to six horses. He carried ammo. He carried the wounded and managed to live to tell the tale—he died at the age of 89 in 1948.

We did have some casualties amongst our nonvoting/nondrinking/nondriving soldiers. David Bailey Freeman joined the Confederate Army as an eight year old and was killed the following year. He was a drummer—which doesn't sound like much but it was the means by which orders to the troops were transmitted. And at Antie-tam, the bloodiest battle of the war, thirteen year old Charley King died in Pennsylvania, far from his mother's comfort.

We have always had a bit of a squishy feeling about when someone gets to be treated as and have the privileges of an adult. Is it thirteen when a girl or boy has a bar/bat mitzvah? Is it fifteen at a Quincenarea? Is it sixteen when you get your driver's license? Is it when you decide you want certain medical stuff you don't want your parents to know about? Is it five or six years after college when your parents kick you out of their basement and you have to pay your own way on World of Warcraft?

CHARLEY KING.

In any event, it's a good time to celebrate your right to vote. Go do it!

Did you vote in the last election?

Sometime between 1603 and 1610 a portrait of Queen Elizabeth I was painted by an anonymous artist. And he'd better STAY anonymous because it showed Elizabeth at the moment of her impending death. It was at that time a crime to make any reference to the passing of the monarch. The Queen is shown as a weary old woman with Father Time at her right and Death leaning over her left shoulder. Two cherubs remove her weighty, wearying crown so that in Heaven she will be a carefree princess again. I think it's the most beautiful Elizabeth portrait as it humanizes her so well. The painting was only revealed in 1610 and now is displayed at Corsham Court in Wiltshire.

On March 24, 1603 Elizabeth passed on and her 45 year reign was over. She had been sick for a while and stoood motionless for three days convinced she would die if she fell asleep. Some people surmised that she developed blood poisoning from venetian ceruse, a mixture of lead and ash which created her white pallor. She had to apply it quite thickly to cover her smallpox scars. There are others who believe she was felled by an abscess tooth—people of the time brushed their teeth with sugar and Elizabeth's were black. Here's a fun fact—in addition to women whitening their faces to look like Elizabeth, those who couldn't afford the sweet stuff would paint their teeth black. She might have died from an infection created by her coronation ring which she never consented to removing until a week before her death doctors cut it off as the metal was embedded in her flesh. Her last words were "all my possessions for one moment of time."

We will never know what killed her because she left strict instructions that there would be no post mortem and her ladies in waiting fiercely guarded her body. That meant nobody could prove or disprove her assertion that she was a virgin. Three weeks later she was laid in her final resting place next to Mary Tudor, the sister who had thrown her in the Tower and quite likely would have executed her given the chance. The twin coffins sit side by side with a Latin engraving "Regno consortes et urna hic obdormimus Elizabetha et Maria sorores, in spe resurrectionis" meaning "Partners in throne and grave, here we sleep Elizabeth and Mary, sisters in Hope of the Resurrection." Their cousin Mary Queen of Scots who was executed on Elizabeth's order, is buried across the aisle.

I have my own theory about Elizabeth's death. I think she was just tired. Tired of the dysfunctional family—starting with her father executing her mother when Elizabeth was just two. Tired of the political intrigue and constant threat of war. Tired of outliving her closest friends.

This weary feeling happens to all of us at one time or another. But the feeling can go away. If it's gnawing at someone you know, give them a call, ask them how they're doing, take them some fresh baked cookies and sit down for some delish gossip. If it's happening to you then you're going to have to be the one to call to call someone and if you want to call me that's cool too!

On March 25, 1969 honeymooners John Lennon and Yoko Ono (second marriage for both) invited the press from all over the world for their "Bed-In" at the Amsterdam Hilton. They did another later at the Queen Elizabeth hotel in London.

The press was delighted to have been invited on this day in 1969 but deeply disappointed that the couple were fully clothed, albeit in pajamas.

Others around the world were doing the same thing—meant to promote peace, world peace not just marital peace, which NOBODY knows how to accomplish. Hey, this couple couldn't figure out how to repair the rift between Lennon and his Beatles co-musician McCartney.

Every once in a while the world gets a little too much for me. People rejecting me. People stomping over me when I'm just trying my best. The physical pain of my eyes, teeth and feet that I've made no secret of (are you listening Endeavor Health Care? An appointment with a doctor within a two month window is a little too much to ask?) It might be just me thinking to myself I haven't accomplished enough in this short life and I haven't done things gracefully or with enough dignity. Oh, and of course, it's tax season.

That's when I do a bed-in. I just turn on the stupidest television and shut the world out. I don't invite the press. I forego mascara. I don't own a set of pajamas so it's black leggings and a T-shirt. So far, today my peace initiative hasn't affected peace in Haiti, Moscow, Ukraine, or Chicago. But I'm doing my best. Do you have days like this?

Did Yoko break up the band?

At ten p.m. on March 26, 1883 over a thousand New Yorkers descended upon the six floor Vanderbilt shotgun shack at 660 Fifth Avenue. It boasted a tennis court, a gym, a "finished" basement and its own private gardens. Mrs. Alva Vanderbilt was hosting a masque ball slash housewarming party and guests were asked to come in costume. There would be quadrilles which was an elaborate dance involving four couples and if you added a soundtrack by Dolly Parton you'd think it was square dancing.

Weeks before, invitations had been delivered to the best families by servants attired in European style livery. Young people practiced their dance quadrilles—the most popular being the Hobby Horse, the Dresden, and the Opera Bouffe. And everywhere New Yorkers pondered that most important question—what to wear? To dress as Marie Antoinette or the exotic Cleopatra? Or perhaps Napoleon Bonaparte? Or the Goddess Minerva? Perhaps the best dress was the Spirit of Electricity dress designed by Charles Worth worn by Alva's sister-in-law Alice. Made of yellow satin and encrusted with glass pearls and beads, it had a built-in battery that lit a torch Alice held aloft like the Statue of Liberty. Kate Feering Strong's nickname was "Puss" and she went as a cat—complete with a taxidermy cat's head as her chapeau, a set of cats' heads on the bodice of her dress and the overskirt was made entirely of cats' tails sewn into a dark background.

Down the street, young Carrie Schermerhorn Astor anxiously awaited her invitation. But there was none—even though the Astors were the crème de le crème of New York Society. Then the Astors received word that Mrs. Vanderbilt couldn't possibly invite the Astors because Mrs. Astor had never called upon her. Which brings us to the second purpose of the housewarming party—revenge.

The Astors were old money, so old that nobody could imagine a past in which an Astor, man or woman, had to work. The Vanderbilts were a product of the Industrial Age, making money at shipping, trains, ferries. They were one generation removed from being practically working class! So every Astor dinner party, ball, wedding of relatives, minor or near, delivered a cut as sharp as a knife to the Vanderbilts. Snubs can do that.

On the other hand, Mrs. Astor saw what had to be done.

She delivered her card to the Vanderbilt home though the women never met. The next day Carrie's fondest wish was realized. Alva got what she wanted—recognition of how the

Are you team Vanderbilt or Astor?

____

____

____

____

Vanderbilt name was to be respected. Guests observed Mrs. Vanderbilt and Mrs. Astor in animated friendly conversation and so what had started as revenge became a lifelong albeit guarded friendship.

The party, estimated to have cost $6mil in today's dollars, was a grand success with dancing and a third floor gymnasium which had been converted into a forest of trees, orchids and bougainvillea. At two a.m. dinner was served up by the chefs of Delmonico's and served by an army of Vanderbilt help. More dancing followed until the sun rose. Mrs. Vanderbilt led the guests in a final rousing Virginia Reel. Thousands toddled down 5th Avenue just as kids were going to school—a resplendent parade of finery and frippery. The Vanderbilt guests not the kids.

Today, with fewer reasons and opportunities to dress up and maybe, it's a good day to open up your jewelry box and take out that little used bauble or invade the back of the closet and wear a pretty dress. Even if it's just for a Zoom meeting.

March 27

March 27, 1905 is the anniversary of a rather ordinary murder that resulted in a sea change of criminal investigation. Today we take for granted DNA, blood analysis, surveillance video. In 1905 it was just guesswork, conjecture, and the reliability of eyewitnesses.

On this day in 1905, William Jones—an employee of Chapman's Oil and Colour Shop on Deptford street in London—arrived at work in the morning and was puzzled that his boss Mr. Thomas Farrow hadn't opened the doors and windows. Mr. Farrow, 71, and his 65 year old wife Ann lived in a second floor apartment and after some time Jones gained access and looked for the couple. Jones and a neighbor discovered Mr. Farrow dead on the floor. Ann was barely conscious on the bed upstairs. She soon died. They both had been beaten to death.

There was no forced entry and the victims were wearing their jammies so police presumed that Mr. Farrow had heard a knock at the door downstairs and went to answer it. He was beaten to death and the cash register emptied. His wife was then beaten. There had to be two killers because there were two black masks made out of women's stockings left behind. The killers had washed their hands in a utility basin.

Continued on Next Page

   March 27

Scotland Yard had been experimenting with fingerprint analysis and the killers had not been too careful about touching the cash box while they had perspiration and blood on their hands. The trail eventually led to ne'er do well brothers Alfred and Albert Stratton. Their fingerprints were taken and compared to those on the cashbox. There was testimony about the reliability of fingerprint analysis but the prosecution was also relying on witnesses to the Strattons lurking about the shop. The men were hung May 23rd of the same year.

Now we think of fingerprints as a perfectly normal part of criminology albeit a bit old fashioned. Fingerprints are unique—no one has the same as any other person. I was fingerprinted when I wanted to join the Peace Corps. The FBI keeps all those fingerprints—even mine. Fingerprints fade with age so that the Strattons in their early twenties had strongly defined whorls while someone in their seventies can barely make a definable definition. 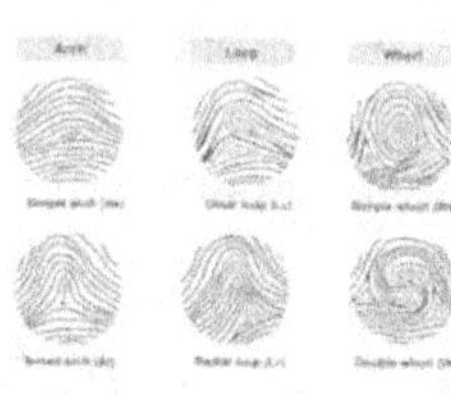

I guess if you're a smart criminal you dress up Grandpa in a hoodie and make him do the hands on work.

March 28

In March 1984 Baltimore Colts owner Bob Isray was MAD! Mayor Willam Schaefer and Bob had been negotiating over stadium improvements and Bob was feeling like he was getting the shaft. Under the cover of darkness on March 28, 1984 Bob moved the entire team to Indianapolis.

Kind of like when on March 31, 2003 in deepest night, our fair Chicago's Mayor Richard M. Daley ordered the destruction of Meigs Field, an itsy bitsy airport on Lake Michigan. He didn't inform the FAA, the city council, maybe didn't even tell his wife. It was a spookyass airport—I've piloted once in and out of there and it was a challenge. If I had hit the rocks or the water first well you wouldn't be reading this post.

Back to Baltimore. Colts fans woke up to find out their beloved team was now the Indianapolis Colts.

There was only one little glitch. Bob had ditched the team band because their uniforms highlighted their allegiance to Baltimore. So he wasn't going to pay for moving the uniforms

Your team leaves the city - are you still loyal?

---

and didn't care to inform the musicians. Still, some of the marching band figured out what was going on and snuck into the Baltimore Colts headquarters and removed their equipment in a heist equal to anything Tom Cruise has portrayed. They hid their equipment and uniforms in a cemetery mausoleum.

In this Baltimore marching band caper, the sixty member team (plus majorettes!) retrieved their uniforms a few weeks later with no fanfare. They made themselves an independent Baltimore Colts Marching Band and played for many years in parades and sporting events and even served in the Canadian football league. But they never booked a gig in Indianapolis. They changed their name to the Baltimore Ravens Marching Band when the Cleveland Browns relocated to Baltimore to become the Ravens. The band's story was featured in a 2009 television show "The Band That Wouldn't Die."

I don't know about you but I think Bob should have personally told the band of his plans. What a dork. Don't leave a party without at least saying goodbye!

March 29

March 29 is a dual holiday—World Manatee Day as well as World Mermaid Day. It's sort of fitting that the two species share a holiday. So go out there and appreciate a manatee and stop by Starbucks while you're at it.

The Mermaid Day was created in 2017 by Freeform network to coincide with the debut of its series Siren which followed, well, mermaid adventures. But mermaids themselves started WAY earlier than that and in a land far away.

Back in the days when Syria was called Assyria, the people had a fertility goddess named Atagatis. She lived, according to legend, in Manbij, an outskirt of Aleppo in Syria. She was said to be so beautiful and alluring that men would castrate themselves in her honor and cut off their, er, junk as an offering at her altar. Seems to me that it sort of defeats the purpose of having a fertility goddess.

For once, somebody agreed with me. King Agbar put a stop to this nonsense by declaring that men who did such a thing would have their hand cut off. The practice of castration seems to have stopped after that.

Continued on Next Page

____

____

____

____

____

Now how does all this relate to mermaids? Well, again we have to say according to legend, the Greeks worshipped Atagatis under the name Derceto. Cultural misappropriation, but there was a lot of that going on then. Now. All the time. Derceto fell in love with a mere human Simious and they had a daughter. Derceto was so embarrassed and ashamed that she killed Simious and left the daughter to be raised by doves in the wilderness. Then Derceto headed for the ocean where her beauty made her a "siren" to sailors who couldn't resist her even when she morphed into a fish with the top half pure bombshell.

The blind Greek storyteller, Homer, even talks about the Sirens. The story had legs—ha ha!—even if mermaids didn't. In 1493, Christopher Columbus wrote of a colleague "when the Admiral went to the Rio del Oro (Haiti) he said he quite distinctly saw three mermaids which rose well out of the sea but they are not so beautiful as they are said to be for their faces had some masculine traits."

Now we—finally!—get to manatees. Manatees are able to turn their heads in a way that other aquatics can't. They have delicate fins with what might seem to be opposable thumbs. And when a sailor is months without seeing a woman and a manatee comes flying out of the water…well, love is in the air. Just like The Love Boat theme song explains.

So knock yourself out and think about how wonderful manatees are today. Or think about 1971 when Terry Heckler was hired by Starbucks to come up with a logo for their brand. The name Starbucks comes from the first mate Starbuck of the ship Pequod in the novel Moby Dick. The iconic mermaid was meant to be a siren seducing coffee lovers everywhere. And it works, doesn't it?

So get yourself some Starbucks machiatto soy milk no foam decaf venti. Then consider the lovely manatee that provided the wet dreams for sailors everywhere.

On March 30, 240 B.C. Chinese astronomers discovered a new broom shaped star. Years later it would be named Halley's Comet after the 18th century Astronomer Royal of Britain Sir Edmond Halley.

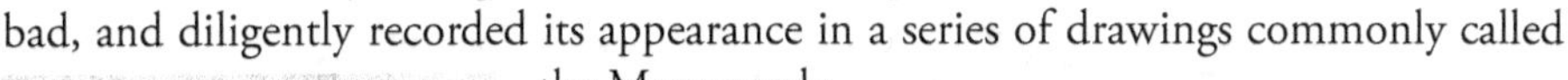

Some of this is true and some isn't. The Chinese astronomers def saw a broom shaped fiery object streaking overhead. And they thought of it as an omen, good or bad, and diligently recorded its appearance in a series of drawings commonly called the Mawangadu.

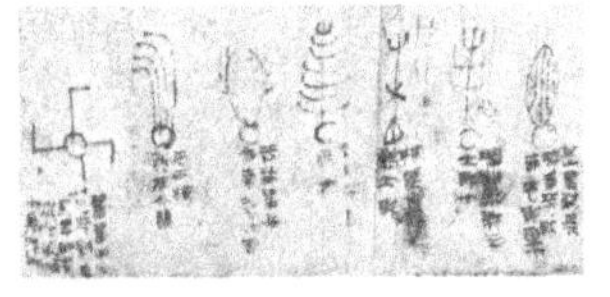

This comet reappeared roughly every 75-76 years and was often the subject of concern or delight. In 1066 a.d. the comet appeared and everyone in Britain took it as bad omen. Especially for King Harold II who was the last crowned Anglo-Saxon king of England. The comet was a great omen for Norman the Conqueror who lived up to his name at the Battle of Hastings, killing Harold and thus ending English rule of England. What a pretty tapestry of the broom star! Too bad about Harold—ever since, the Brits have been ruled by Normans, Germans, even an odd French king.

How did this dirty snowball of water, carbon dioxide, ammonia and dust get its moniker? In 1705, Halley put all these comet incidents together and said, "these aren't different comets it's is the same comet, just we see it at its perihelion, the part of its orbit when it's closest to the sun."

The Halley's Comet of 1910 was the first year in which the comet could be photographed and the first use of spectroscopic analysis so that scientists could determine what it was made of. Among so many other things, they found cyanogen (CN)2 a toxic pseudo halogen that caused French astronomer Nicholas Camille Flammarion to predict that earth's passage through the comet's tail would result in the release of gasses that would "snuff out all life on the planet." Gas masks ensued, along with anti-comet pills and anti-comet umbrellas. Kind of like now, but without Fauci. The earth passed through the comet April 20 and French people survived. Flammarion went back to his seances, psychic research, Theosophy and giving names to the "canals" on Mars which later turned out to be an optical illusion.

Continued on Next Page

    March 30

Mark Twain had declared the previous year "I came in with Halley's Comet in 1835. It's coming again next year (1910) and I expect to go out with it. The Almighty has said no doubt 'now here are these two unaccountable freaks: they came in together and they must out together!" He died a day after the perihelion.

I have a personal connection to Halley's Comet of 1910. My grandfather Fritz Leiber, Jr. was born in 1910 and he believed, like Twain, that he would make his exit when the comet returned. In 1986 he awaited Gabriel's clarion call. He had to cool his heels another 6 years til 1992. Oddly enough, in 1992 Halley's Comet was observed to have some explosions maybe just for Fritz!

Take a minute this evening. Go outside as far from street lights and beamers as possible. Look up at all the glory! You won't get to see Halley's Comet until 2061!

March 31

On March 31, 1959 a 23 year old Tibetan monk and two dozen of his chums crossed the border into India, intent on saving their country and their people. The young monk was born Lhamo Dhondup in the tiny Tibetan village of Takster. When he was two, travelers came and asked for shelter. Lhamo sat on the lap of one of the travelers and reached into his robe for the man's rosary. "That's mine," Lhamo said, and in fact, the beads had been the possession of the 13th Dalai Lama. Thus the four year search for the 14th Dalai Lama was over! He was given the name Tensin Gyatso and was groomed for his role as spiritual and political leader of Tibet, becoming "king" at the age of four.

Tibet was and is rich with lithium, gold, silver and copper—all of which have great industrial value. The Tibetans didn't mine the metals because to do so would tamper with the land but the Chinese had no such compunction. They invaded Tibet in 1950 and declared the country a "national autonomous region." Tibetans resisted and there was a good nine years of escalating tension as everyone waited for Tensin Gyatso to mature.

On March 10, 1959 Gen Zhang Zhen extended a personal invitation to the Dalai Lama to go to the theater. Oddly, he requested his guest bring no guards or security. DANGER, Tensin Gyatso! The Dalai Lama appeared to agree to the terms while he assembled a team of loyal monks who would escape Tibet with him. On March 17, they cleared out of Lhaso and, dressed as poor barefoot peasants, headed through the Khenziman Pass to India.

He was taking a big risk, as India's Prime Minister Jawaharlal Nehru had a few years earlier told the Dalai Lama that he didn't want trouble with China and was intent on staying neutral. Neutral of course being to do whatever China wanted. Nonetheless, the Tibetans and the refugees who followed were welcomed. The Tibetan Government in Exile was formed in Dharamshala. The Dalai Lama took the spiritual name Jetsun Jamphel Ngawang Lobsang Yeshe Gyatso. Put that on a party invitation!

A succession problem will arise upon the Dalai Lama's death, although he has reassured his followers that he will live to 111. In 1995 a 6 year old boy was recognized as the Panchen Lama, the future Dalai Lama. He and his entire family were whisked away by the Chinese government and he is considered (if still alive) one of the youngest political prisoners. While the previous Dalai Lamas have come from Tibet, the present Dalai Lama has said that there will be no reincarnation into a country controlled by the Communist Chinese. He has also made noises that if a woman will make a better Dalai Lama so be it. And in 2019 he declared that because of its feudal origins maybe there doesn't need to be a Dalai Lama at all.

"One thing I want to make clear," he has said. "As far as my own rebirth is concerned the final authority is myself—no one else—and obviously not the Chinese Communists!"

What were you in a previous life? What will you be in the next?

____

____

____

____

____

April splinters like an ice palace.

–Ruth Stone

April 01

On April 1, 1957 announcer Richard Dimbleby opened his BBC radio broadcast with a report on the Swiss tradition of harvesting spaghetti.

"The last two weeks of March are an anxious time for the spaghetti farmer," Dimbleby said solemnly. "There's always a chance of a late frost, which, while not entirely ruining the crop, generally impairs the flavor…but now these dangers are over and the spaghetti harvest goes forward."

Phew! Tragedy averted. All of Britain breathed a sigh of relief for their Swiss compatriots and their future spaghetti dinners. But, check the date. I needn't say anything more.

What will you do to fool the world?

April 02

April 2 is International Don't Walk Your Dog Day! And you can help your canine by flopping down with them on the couch and watching movies—the 2017 A Dog's Purpose comes to mind or the back to back 2019 A Dog's Journey and A Dog's Way Home. If the two of you (or three or four depending on how big your couch is and how many furbabies you have) are in a lighter mood, perhaps The Secret Life of Pets.

We all know that February 22 is Walk the Dog Day and it's important to cultivate a dog's physical exercise. But according to professional dog trainer and author Niki French sometimes dogs have anxiety that is exacerbated by dealing with the outdoors, the people, the traffic, the smells, the other dogs. Not to mention squirrels! So in her book Stop Walking Your Dog French proposed that some dogs develop heightened cortisol levels when they are forced to take a brisk one. Cortisol is a hormone that leads to stress and all the usual stress related illnesses.

Continued on Next Page

____

____

____

____

____

April 02

Reminds me of when I was house sitting a few years ago for four cats and a dog named MacDuff. The cats really didn't care to get to know me—remember, cats were considered Gods in ancient Egypt and the species has never forgotten that. I was told that 13 year old MacDuff went on a walk four times a day. It seemed daunting, but the first morning I was there I figured I needed to go to the grocery store anyway. I said the magic word "walk" and MacDuff was right there to be leashed. We perambulated roughly a half mile to the grocery store and back. Several hours later, I repeated "walk" and MacDuff approached the ceremonial leashing with slightly less enthusiasm. We went uptown to go to the post office and the park, a mere mile and a half round trip. When we got back, he disappeared into the bowels of the space under the couch for a nap. Fast forward several hours and I had the leash. "MacDuff! Walk? MacDuff?" A reluctant MacDuff allowed for the leash. I thought a walk to the beach would be great and I even brought a tennis ball for him to chase. He followed behind me like a French Existentialist girding his loins for the Nazi firing squad and declined to fetch the tennis ball with a weary shrug. Upon returning to the house he laid down up under a coffee table and gave me a "so this is how life ends?" look. He turned his head away from me when I tried for the fourth walk.

When my friends returned home, I told them I had failed. Truly failed. Only three walks. I explained the routes and the adventures planned but not really executed.

"Uh, maybe we should have explained walks," the wife said. "MacDuff normally walks as far as the end of the block and back."

"You live two doors from the corner."

"That's the point."

We all stared at MacDuff supine under the coffee table. I'm almost positive he muttered "bitch" before rolling over. I don't think he was referring to me as one of his species.

A week later, the husband quite cheerfully told me that MacDuff had passed on. He may have been in deep mourning but trying to make me feel better. Or maybe he was just tired of being a househusband managing four cats, three daughters, and MacDuff. The four cats you just put out food and water for. The girls would eventually grow up and head for some prestigious college. And MacDuff? I hope he's happy over the rainbow bridge and knows I meant well.

Or you gonna be like Niki French and take a day off with your pooch?

April 3, 1895 marked the beginning of a legal and ultimately fatal ordeal for one of my favorite writers Oscar Wilde. You perhaps have heard that he was tried for the "crime" of being homosexual. But this wasn't that trial. It was a trial brought by Wilde against the pugilistic Marquis of Queensberry. The Marquis had left his card at Wilde's home with the note "for Oscar Wilde posing as a Somdomite: if the country allows you to leave, all the better for the country; but if you take my son with you, I will follow you wherever you go and shoot you."

Wilde maneuvered the Marquis to be charged with criminal libel, carrying a penalty of two years prison. Me? I would have sued him for misspelling sodomite. But the father was furious. His son Alfred "Bosie" Douglas, 22, had embarked on a relationship with 38 year old Wilde that was both abhorrent to the Marquis but technically against the 1885 Labouchere Amendment criminalizing "gross indecency." The law was seldom used and most people understood that Wilde was fluid insofar as he was married to Constance Lloyd and they had two sons and just as a lot of husbands he stepped out. Constance was pretty and well liked and everyone knew she was a second choice after Wilde's proposal to longtime love Florence Balcombe was rebuffed in favor of Bram Stoker's blandishments.

In the lawsuit, all the Marquis had to do was prove his innocence was that Wilde had en-

gaged in homosexual behavior with someone, anyone, and the term "sodomite" was truth. The spelling was a different matter. On the first day of trial the Marquis' lawyers produced 12 boys who claimed that they had been approached and/or assaulted by Wilde. Wilde's lawyer withdrew the lawsuit.

Damage had already been done. The once celebrated and beloved writer was now an object of revulsion. And there's the pesky legal matter presented to the Crown which reluctantly issued a warrant for Wilde's arrest. Wilde was so sure of his popularity that he didn't flee to Paris when offered the opportunity. But Bosie did—he wasn't taking any chances. Wilde's first trial ended with a split jury, but a third trial got him sentenced to two years hard labor.

When he got out of prison, he aimed for Paris. Bosie—btw, the nickname is a cricket term for a ball that appears to be headed in one direction and aims for another—did not treat him well. Constance changed her name and that of their sons. But she sent Wilde checks which were his only source of income.

Although lots of folks think it was syphilis that did him in, modern theory is that Wilde died of acute meningitis in 1900 with only one friend at his bedside. Poet Robert Ross was said to have been Wilde's first lover, sometime when Wilde would have been in his mid-thirties and Ross a teenager. He held Wilde's hand as he accepted last rites. An apocryphal story about his last words—"the wallpaper and I are fighting a duel to the death. Either it goes or I do." The wallpaper won. Robert Ross paid for his burial, reserving enough space for his own ashes. Which were interred fifty years later. Truest love.

Who is yours?

____

____

____

____

The thirty nine year old Rev. Martin Luther King Jr. is remembered, like Gandhi and Jesus, for his nonviolent approach to social change. There is perhaps one deviation from this position which occurred on April 4, 1968 in his room at the Lorraine Motel in Memphis, Tennessee. Just the day before, King had given one of his most iconic speeches "I've Been to the Mountaintop" at the Mason Temple Church of God in Christ in support of the strike of the city sanitation workers. He said that he of course would want to live a long life but it didn't look like that was going to happen. But he had seen a glimpse of what a colorblind society could look like and would look like. A promised land.

He and his entourage were dressing for a private dinner party on the fourth when fellow activist Andrew Young (and he was REALLY young at this point) showed up unannounced. King pretended to be offended at Young having not given notice of his appearance.

"He picked up a pillow and threw it at me," Young recalled. "And I just threw it back. And all of a sudden everybody picked up pillows. And here we are—middle aged men, almost—and we were having a pillow fight like children."

A scant few hours later, the men decided it was time to head out for the dinner party. King got downstairs and remembered that he didn't have a tie on. He went back up to his room, a room that he had switched with Young because his originally selected room was on the first floor and it was considered more difficult to protect him from murderers than if he stayed on the second floor. He was assassinated on the unenclosed balcony outside this room as he went to retrieve the tie.

But think of the happiness and joy he had for just a few minutes having a pillow fight with his peeps. As if they were all children who could grow up in the promised land.

We take our happiness when and where we can. And we have no idea what awaits us next. So let's today laugh and play like children if only for a few minutes. The memory will sustain us during the truly rough patches we are sure to endure.

April 5, 1614 is the wedding date of Pocahontas, daughter of Wahunsencawl, chief of the Algonquin tribe Powhatan. The groom's name was John Rolfe, an Englishman who cultivated a very popular sweet version of tobacco in Virginia.

Pocahontas' real name was Amonute but also had a more privately used name of Mataoke meaning white feather. Pocahontas was a nickname meaning playful.

The couple fell in love and Pocahontas converted to Christianity, taking the baptismal name Rebecca. She married John and not quite a year later in January 1615 their son Thomas was born. The family traveled back to John's native England to present Thomas to the Rolfe family.

Pocahontas was a hit with the English—so exotic, yet trying so hard to become Europeanish.

The Rolfes returned to the family farm in Virginia in 1616. Pocahontas, er, Rebecca fell ill and died in 1617. She was buried in England. Rolfe left his young son Thomas in England with relatives intending to return for him later. The two never saw each other again. Rolfe remarried in Virginia. He died at the age of 37. And never saw his first young wife's grave.

So happy anniversary you two lovebirds. Oh, wait, they might not have been lovebirds. Pocahontas may very well have wanted to represent her tribe in the best possible light and keep the peace with the British. As for Rolfe, he wanted to solidify his sales of his special blend tobacco to the English.

My birthname was Arlynn. My adoptive "our Lynn." Later, ArLynn to represent both families. Have you ever changed your name or thought of it?

____

____

____

____

____

April 6 is a special holiday honoring one of the world's most famous saltwater fish belonging to the Thunnini tribe which is part of the Scombridae family. It is also a holiday that teaches us about rejection and how to come to terms with it. Something I struggle with every day of the year.

The holiday, of course, is Charlie the Tuna Day, sometimes called Sorry Charlie Day. Charlie was born in 1961 at the Leo Burnett advertising agency and his father/illustrator Tom Rogers based the Albacore on his beat musician friend Henry Nemo (I am NOT making up the last name). Charlie was voiced by Herschel Bernardi.

Charlie appeared in 85 advertisements until the mid-eighties and the theme was always the same: Charlie's overriding ambition was to become a spokesman for Starkist tuna. And with his suave debonair manner, his French beret, Charlie figured he was a shoe-in. But the results were always the same —

"Sorry Charlie.

Starkist doesn't want tuna with good taste,

 but tuna that tastes good!"

What does Charlie teach us about rejection and how to come to terms with it? Charlie never lost his cool, never stopped believing in himself and he'd always shake it off and try again. Whether it's not getting that job, losing the gal you thought was yours, or not getting your book published by Random House (sigh!) be like Charlie!

Charlie was retired in the eighties but made a spectacular comeback in 1999. He's got toys in his image (my favorite is the Funk Pop Charlie). He's been in Advertising Week's Madison Walk of Fame with assorted other mascots. And he even got his own movie—the 2012 Food Fight—playing alongside Charlie Sheen, Christopher Lloyd and Eva Longoria.

So today celebrate Charlie—put on that French beret, slap a smile on your face until it naturally adheres, and get your Charlie swagger going!

There is an alternate story about the spooky starlet Maila Nurmi who came forward in 2003 with the claim that her good friend deceased movie star James Dean created Charlie on a cocktail napkin. Nurmi was hostess of a local Los Angeles show called Vampira where she would show different B-movies. When Nurmi wouldn't agree to contract terms for a television series, the studio hired Elvira and created Monsterama. Nurmi's claim about Charlie and James Dean was found to be false.

All Americans have second acts. Or maybe third or fourth. Have you had a come back and how did you do it?

April 7 is a special day in music and tax history. It teaches a special sartorial lesson that I think you'll find quite useful and will help you stand out! Oh, and save money with the IRS. Which is always a good thing.

On April 7, 1974 at the Eurovision song contest in Brighton, England-for the very first time—a Swedish group won. It was called ABBA after the first initials of the quartet—Agnetha, Bjorn, Benny and Ann-Frid. They were dressed in satin culottes, sequins, silver platform heels—Rupaul would no doubt have swooned if he had been in the audience.

ABBA won the competition with their song Waterloo, which references a woman who is so in love with a man (well, we think so) that he was her Waterloo. Meaning utter defeat as in Napoleon versus the British Duke of Wellington in 1815. Spoiler alert—Napoleon lost.

Back to Eurovision—the win catapulted the group to stardom and they signed with Atlantic records. They still wore crazy ass outfits that you wouldn't ordinarily wear outside on the street or to church or to your grandmother's house. And that was the point...

The costumes were, under Swedish tax laws, deductible because they were clearly meant only for work. "In my honest opinion we looked like nuts in those years," guitarist Bjorn admitted. "Nobody could have been as badly dressed on stage as we were."

Me? I went in totally the opposite direction. I was doing Annie Hall—painter's pants from Sherwin Williams, white shirts, tie and vests from the thrift shop, and Kinney's sneakers. Then the Woody Allen movie Annie Hall came out and I had to change my look.

But the ABBA costume choice became their signature and their tax dodge. Which reminds me—

So get out those dancing shoes, sequined shirts and blouses, maybe a feather boa or two, and go to work. It might just work when you get an invitation, er, audit from the IRS.

April 8 is a very special birthday—that of our dear Prince Siddhartha Gautama of Kapilavastu, otherwise known as Gautama Buddha, aka, Buddha Jayanti or Buddha Purnima of the Mahayana tradition. Whatever name you want to call him, all of Southeast Asia will be celebrating! This birthday is part of Vesak which is a three part holiday which celebrates the birth, the enlighten-

ment, and death of Buddha. Siddhartha is a meaningful name in Sanskrit—Siddha meaning achieved, and Artha meaning what was searched for. And I guess Buddha achieved what he was searching for. His birthday is celebrated by different branches of Buddhism on different days which is really how I think things should work for me—namely, a bunch of birthdays and presents!

The Mahayana tradition of Buddhism sees the world as one of transmigration and reincarnation (Samsara) from which one can only escape by achieving Nirvana, a sort of wisdom and peace with the universe. I have sooooooooooooooooooooooo many incarnations to go through before Nirvana strikes me. In the meantime, I think I've almost felt that Nirvana thing when my kids were young and they'd crawl into bed with me and fall asleep.

Find some time today to let go of worry, finances, snubs and smudges—take out your imaginary party hat, grab some peace of mind, and say happy birthday Siddhi!

April 09

On April 9, 1939 contralto Marian Anderson sang before 75k people at the Lincoln memorial and Lord knows how many folks listened in on the radio. She wore a resplendent gown with an orange jacket with gold trim. She had a hella fur coat because it was a cold day but also to reinforce that she was a star.

How'd she end up with the gig? Well, she was supposed to perform at Constitution Hall as a guest of the Daughters of the American Revolution (I confess I'm eligible and have actually spoken at a DAR event but never joined). There was a problem with Marian's invite—she was black. And that was sort of the end of that.

Except the NAACP and her manager Sol Hurok pitched a fit. Interior Secretary Harold Ickes from my fair Winnetka got involved and booked Anderson for that Easter Sunday at the Lincoln Memorial and, with radio broadcast, pulled in way more of an audience than the DAR could have ever provided. She gave a stellar performance and the DAR sort of looked, well—racist because they were. And the whole contretemp highlighted the treatment of blacks in America.

April 10 is the death day (feast day)* of Anglican Saint William of Ockham (named for Oak Hamlet his hometown) and boy does he have a lot to teach us, with or without a fireplace poker in his hand!

He was born in the High Middle Ages 1285 or so and he's associated with metaphysical nominalism which if you want to impress a girl definitely bring that one up as in "he's my fav metaphysical nominalist and can I touch your breasts?" He landed on the nominalism idea that we really don't have access to big ticket items like "justice" or "peace" or even "glass of water" because we're just taking our subjective experiences and slapping them down on words.

Being that he was part of Christian Europe where lack of faith would get you burned or impaled, he became the chief proponent of Fideism which proposed that all knowledge could be divided between the rational and that which is imparted by God. You can say to yourself there is no God, there is no faith, there are no saints, but that's your rational brain at work. Your higher brain believes and knows the presence of God and of immortal principles. Kind of like Deism which was practiced by Washington, Jefferson and a bunch of our founding fathers who hated going to church but did it anyway because otherwise they would have been cast out of society instead of creating a nation.

William of Ockham died on this day in 1347 but his real accomplishment was a brawl at the Cambridge University Moral Sciences Club on October 25, 1946. He might not have been there but he sure would have approved. Sir Karl Popper of the London School of Economics had been invited to deliver a paper entitled "Are there Philosophical Problems?" Well, yeah, duh, because if there aren't philosophical problems how are philosophy professors going to make a living?

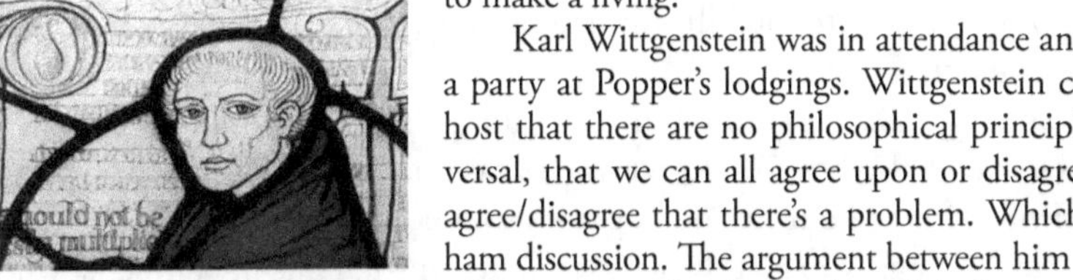

Karl Wittgenstein was in attendance and was invited to a party at Popper's lodgings. Wittgenstein contended to his host that there are no philosophical principles that are universal, that we can all agree upon or disagree upon or even agree/disagree that there's a problem. Which is a very Ockham discussion. The argument between him and Popper was quite heated, with Wittgenstein leaning on a fireplace poker while Popper said there were certainly some universal principles we could all agree on.

"Name one," Wittgenstein challenged, wielding the poker.

"Not to threaten visiting lecturers with pokers," Popper replied calmly.

Wittgenstein threw down the poker and left in a fit of pique.

William of Ockham's brand of nominalism is commonly known as Occam's Razor—to wit, if there's one simple explanation for something another that has a lot of hypotheticals and extra add-ons, go with the easiest one. Don't overthink. And maybe this is a day for you and me to consider our problems and quandaries and mysteries and just say "what's the easiest explanation?"

*The day a saint dies or returns to the Lord is considered their "Saints Day" or "Feast Day". So if you forget somebody's birthday just say that you're waiting to give them a gift on their saint day! Buys you some time. William of Ockham is a saint for Anglicans but Catholics? Fuggedaboutit!

It's April 11 which is Dog Therapy Appreciation Day. It's an important holiday to think about this—6.5 million pets are dumped into shelters every year AND only 1.6 million dogs and 1.6 cats will find a fur-ever home. The holiday was created by animal activist Colleen Paige in 2006 in order to focus on how to find homes and to appreciate what animals can do for us humans.

Pets have long been part of our lives—the dog collar first showed up in a 3,500 B.C. Mesopotamian drawing. Cat owners have long said that "cats were Gods in ancient Egypt and they've never forgotten it."

Pet owners tend towards dogs even though in some cultures they are considered as an unclean species. Forty five percent of pet owners have a Fido. Thirty percent weigh in with a King or Queen Meow. Nine percent go with fish—at my doctor's office there's a huge aquarium and when I get off the elevator there's one particular fish that comes up to the glass for a smooch. If he asked me out for a date, I'd bring a big Ziploc bag with water.

So how do you celebrate Dog Therapy Appreciation Day? Well, with respect to Dog Therapy Appreciation think about the dogs who work for a living giving their fur-parents emotional support. I have a girlfriend who ordered a blue vest online. Bit me twice but it wasn't exactly trained. It just had the vest.

Me? I carry dog treats in my pocket. I found out I'm not allowed to have a pet—dog, cat, rabbit, goldfish, python—in my building. I wish I would have known that before the closing. I also have a squirrel who occasionally visits my balcony along with the birds. I put birdseed out. It's not a pet if never comes inside, right?

And I have several dogs who go for walks with their fur-parents in Winnetka who bark and pull at their leashes because I'm the treat lady. I'm talking about you, Chipper, Elvis, Mic, Romeo!

Are you a cat person or a dog lover?

April 12, 1945 was a very bad, no good, horrible, rotten Thursday for Eleanor Roosevelt. In the morning she was asked to return from a speaking engagement to the White House pronto! She knew it was going to be trouble and said later that she clenched her hands the entire way. As well she should, as her husband (and incidentally fifth cousin) had succumbed to a massive stroke at their retreat in Warm Springs, Georgia. Pretty damn terrible, right?

It gets worse. She arrived in Warm Springs late that night and finds out that FDR was not alone in his final hours. Rather, he had been with Lucy Mercer Rutherfurd. Eleanor had discovered Lucy had had an affair with FDR many decades before, nearly causing the divorce of the Roosevelts. But FDR promised that he'd never see Rutherfurd again.

Oh, Eleanor! I was one of the most naïve of wives but even I know that when a husband says that he's not going to see the little hottie again he just means just until you go to the grocery store and he sneaks out of the house. Or a secret meeting with the Pentagon.

Eleanor's day got worse. FDR's cousin, secretary and second string mistress Laura Delano delivered the knife in Eleanor's back with the news that Lucy had just left the premises. And that the affair between Lucy and FDR had been all consuming for thirty years with occasional Laura Delano interludes. Conducted at a house FDR had build for Laura at the Roosevelt Warm Springs get away.

But there's more. It turns out that many of the assignations with Lucy over the decades, including this last fatal one, were arranged by FDR and Eleanor's daughter Anna.

Widowed, betrayed, betrayed again, and again. All in less than twenty four hours.

I bet Eleanor looked ahead to the next day and said "Friday the Thirteenth? Ha!"

Tell me about your worst day. It's not today and you got through it !

____

____

____

____

____

On this Thursday April 13, 1865 President Abraham Lincoln would be happy. He had suffered during the previous years—shepherding a country to victory through a brutal civil war, losing his young son Will to typhoid, and being haunted by a recurring dream of watching a boat carrying an assassinated president towards a distant shore.

But on the thirteenth, he persuaded his wife Mary to accompany him on a carriage ride and a walk through the park. He told her that their days of grief were behind them. He dismissed his security detail so he might enjoy this private time with his beloved wife. He was happy. He smiled. How many times have you seen a photo of him smiling?

It would be his last full day of life. He slept well and woke up happy. The dreaded thirteenth of the month was over! But on the evening of the fourteenth he would be shot and would breathe his last on the morning of the fifteenth. Witnesses said he seemed utterly at peace as he passed. Well, yeah, because he was unconscious.

We don't know what will happen today or tomorrow but on this day, let's enjoy the feel of the cool breeze as we take our beloveds out on a carriage ride.

What will you do today to make yourself happy?

April 14

April 14, the day after the dreaded thirteenth is a day with all sorts of associations—tragic, perplexing and delightful.

April 14, 1865 of course is the day that Abraham Lincoln was shot during a performance of Our American Cousin by Tom Taylor. The shooter was actor John Wilkes Booth who clearly didn't understand the etiquette of "the show must go on." Booth fired at Lincoln and made his clumsy escape. The show became a parade with the dying president carried to a boarding house across the street where he would pass the next morning while Mary Todd screamed and cried in the next room, having been banished by the doctors for her hysteria.

Across town, co-conspirator Lewis Powell attacked Secretary of State William Seward and his family—his daughter Fanny and sons August and Frederick defended the Secretary and he survived. Powell the twenty one year old halfwit would hang along with other conspirators. Powell's last words were said to be "she doesn't have to hang," referring to Mary Surratt who had hosted many of the conspirators' meetings.

Also, on April 14, 1912 the Titanic hit a really big ice cube around 11:40 p.m. just as dessert was being served. Lousy dinner party. No cognac, not even a cheese platter.

The best of all possible April 14ths was 1992 when my son Eastman was born. I had been told by the doctor at my first ultrasound that Eastman had a hole in his brain and probably had Trisomy-18 a particularly wicked genetic malformation in which there were no recorded histories of infant survival. The doctor advised an abortion. The hospital I would be delivering in required me to go to a genetic counseling session where I would get even more "expert medical advice." I was again told "abort mission."

I was offered a last ditch option of an amnio but if the results came back bad the hospital was prepared to put a "do not feed" order on Eastman. You can see why I wouldn't play the odds when the house was guaranteed to win.

I didn't do the amnio. I spent the next six months sitting. With my hand on my belly. Eyes closed. Talking to Eastman. Telling him gently, kindly to "close up that hole in the brain." Okay, then there were a few times I said "Jeez Louise, just close up the damn hole would you? Why? Because I said so!" I wasn't particularly functional in my duties as a writer, wife, or mother to the other kids.

In the end Eastman Leiber Presser was born around two thirty in the afternoon of the fourteenth. The next morning a pediatrician doing rounds came by and counted up the toes and fingers. I asked if Eastman had Trisomy-18. The doctor's reaction? "You must be a first time mom." The untterly healthy Eastman became a phenomenal drummer, an actor of impeccable comic timing, a composer, a bowler, a sommelier and I couldn't be prouder of him!

I later learned that early sonogram results sometimes produced false data which suggested a fetal malformation and one phantom malformation was Trisomy-18. Many experts gave women the same advice I was given. Then the technology of sonograms became more precise and itsy-bitsy holes in the brain didn't panic anybody. So today, for me, the fourteenth of April is the miracle of the Eastman—the little kid that could!

Wish my son a Happy Birthday!

April 15

Today, April 15th is the homegoing day of Father Damien of Molokai, the fifth largest island of Hawaii. He taught us a lot about how to care for the sick, whether with leprosy (as he did) or AIDS, or Covid. He was considered to not be a particularly smart man but what he had was something dang special. He is what the Catholic Church calls a Martyr of Charity, meaning he died as a direct result of his work for others.

Damien was born in Belgium in 1840 and his family hoped he would go into some sort of money making enterprise. They had a LOT of kids to support. But Damien prayed to become a missionary like his brother Auguste was set to do. As Auguste was making plans for his own Hawaii mission he fell ill and the governing bishop decided "fine, we'll take Damien."

In 1864 Damien arrived in O'ahu and was ordained. Hawaii was going through a rough patch as Westerners and Chinese were descending on the islands, bringing diseases to which the indigenous population had no immunity. Leprosy was one of the most virulent and deadly. Now called Hansen's disease, it is caused by the mycobacterium leprae and results in nerve and muscle damage, disfigurement…and sometimes death.

In 1865 the Hawaiian parliament passed the Act to Prevent Spread of Leprosy requiring quarantine of infected folks and their families. The most serious cases were sent to eastern Kalaupa'pa peninsula of Molokai Island. Nobody made any plans to return. This "leprosy colony" was closed in 1969. Nearly ten thousand Hawaiians had been sent there to die.

Damien volunteered to go and create a parish. He comforted the sick, dug graves for those who passed, founded a school for the children of the afflicted, ate with the community and raised funds for his work. He aimed to recruit others of the religious community to come to Molokai. An enterprising young nun Marianne Cope who had founded and run a hospital in Syracuse, New York showed up with 6 other nuns and was with Damien when he died. She and the sisters founded a hospital in the colony.

It was inevitable that Damien would get the disease because he didn't wear a mask and he didn't have the advantage of hand sanitizers and plastic gloves. There was no particular medical protocol and no Anthony Fauci on the case. As Damien wrote home to his family "I make myself a leper with the lepers to give all to Jesus Christ."

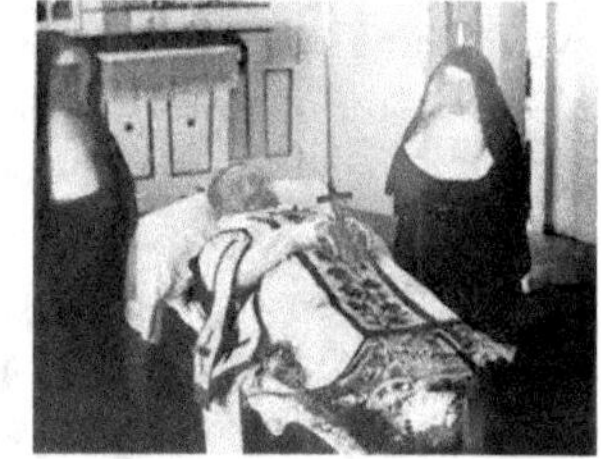

In December 1884 he put his feet into a scalding hot bath and that's when he knew his prognosis. Leprocotic nerve damage had left him with no feeling in his footsies even as he got second degree burns. Still he resisted—working until at last leprosy beat him on April 15, 1889 at the age of 49. Sister Marianne Cope who apparently had a resistance to the disease (or maybe she was just stubborn) nursed him at the end.

He was buried under the tree he had first sat under when he arrived. The Belgium government demanded his body back and they were given it—except for one hand which remained in Hawaii.

Father Moloki and Sister Cope were canonized as saints. And they remind us to take care of people even if we have to teach ourselves to love them.

Who do you choose to take care of?

April 16th is officially Foursquare Day. As it happens, four (April is the fourth month in the Gregorian calendar) times four (that's square if you weren't paying attention in math class) equals sixteen. Ergo—the month squared and the date is the result.

Foursquare is a rather simple game requiring nothing more than a flat surface, some chalk to create a square (if you're Banksy you can use spray paint). Perpendicular lines to create—you got it!—four squares within the larger square. Then you line up to take your turn being in one of those small squares. You bounce the ball back and forth until someone doesn't catch it. Lot less equipment than golf or hockey, to be sure.

Around the world there are to be many Foursquare championships for the holiday which only began in 2009. Optometrist Nathan Bonilla-Warbur was a numbers enthusiast (dweeb) and came up with the idea of a holiday devoted to Foursquare the game. He discussed his idea with friend Jessica Barnett and their company Foursquare—devoted to tracking down the location of your new favorite restaurant, your best clothing store, the greatest grocery store—announced that April 16, 2009 would become official Foursquare Day. That first year, over 55k people signed up for the event—a long running game but of course it didn't beat the 31 hour record of Baker Hall of Huntington University—with just seven players in rotation. And every year thereafter, this holiday has become more popular—so much so that the company no longer tries to keep up with registration but kindly still provides swag for participants.

If you want to celebrate, get together a group of friends, get a ball (one of those red dodgeballs will work well) and find an empty parking lot. One reason that the game is so popular in schools is that after twenty minutes and the teacher says recess is over, you just walk away. Or if the person who went on the Mickey-Dee's run pulls up you can all high five and consider the game worth celebrating.

Take some chalk, make a foursquare court on the driveway - invite friends. How long will you play?

April 17

April 17 is World Hemophiliac Awareness day. It doesn't sound too world altering but while it is a rare disease it has had a major impact on our history. Hemophilia is a genetically transmitted bleeding disorder that makes even the tiniest paper cut a potential cause of death because there is diminished or no ability for the blood to clot. That scab you get when you bash your knee? It's saving your life.

Hemophilia is transmitted by women (genetic carriers) but males suffer the consequences—being unable to stop bleeding both internal and external. Small paper cuts or bruising your knee falling off your bike causes unbelievable pain and the effects lasts for weeks. This disease ripped through the European royal families, particularly the Hapsburg, Romanov and English dynasties. When Nicholas II abdicated the Russian throne he did so on behalf of himself and his son Alexei who had the disease although the family kept that a secret. The disease had been introduced to the Romanov family through Nicholas' wife Alexandra who was the favorite granddaughter of Queen Victoria. Nicholas understood his only heir couldn't withstand the pressures of being Tsar. The next possible Tsar was his brother who said "I see those Bolsheviks a'coming and no thanks."

Alexei the son was prone to bleeding episodes. The quite rightly panicked and protective and gullible Alexandra turned to faith healer and charlatan priest Rasputin who seemed to be able to get the child over his episodes. Russians decided that Rasputin and Alexandra were sleeping together. The scandal contributed to Nicholas not being able to protect his country, much less his family, from the Bolsheviks who executed the family at Ekaterinaberg (eastern Russian city) on March 15, 1917.

Today consider the disorder which has led to so much research that contributes to cures for other related diseases of the blood. I had a boyfriend in college who required regular blood transfusions because of the disease. When the epidemic AIDS hit, he became infected through an otherwise perfectly ordinary transfusion. As many hemophiliacs, he passed on and maybe today we should honor him and others.

Are you involved in Hemophiliac
Awareness or research?

<h2 style="text-align:center">April 18</h2>

On April 18, 1930 the BBC new radio broadcast at 8:45 opened with the announcement "there is no news." and there was a brief, quite British interlude and then a return to the programmed Wagnerian opera Parsifal.

I'd like an April 18 like 1930. Tomorrow you are free to go back to the chaos we know as modern life.

<h2 style="text-align:center">April 19</h2>

It's April 19 and you're probably thinking ahead to the Christmas season and buying some tix to the Rockettes Christmas Spectacular! Coordinated kick dancing by gals with chicklet teeth, glimmering eyes, perfect hair, and boy, how they kick!

They wouldn't exist if it weren't for John Tiller of Manchester, England. In 1889 Tiller, a bit of a perfectionist or as we would call him now OCD guy, noted that women chorus dance troupes were often uncoordinated, undisciplined, didn't really match up. To his standards.

He created the "Les Jolies Petites". The dancers were required to be of the precise same height and weight, just as the Rockettes are today. He introduced the practice of having the dancers link arms and kick with absolute precision. In public, they dressed in the most modest dresses and it was made very clear to them that they were not stars, they were a team.

He started other troupes, based on the success of the Petites of Paris, London, New York, etc. He even opened a boarding school in Manchester where promising dancers were given an educational curriculum but with bonus classes in dance. If they showed promise they were given further education in Covent Garden, London.

These glam gals had their ups and downs in popularity—in World War 2 they couldn't do a lot of overseas work. But they were in a number of theater and film productions. In later years, they primarily danced for charitable causes. Their final performance was in 2011 and many of the dancers were in their sixties and seventies.

Russell Markert, founder of the Rockettes, was a huge fan of the Tiller dancers and said if he could get American girls with longer legs and a bit more height, he could take on the world.

Get on the internet, pick out your tix and call one of your galpals. Or if you don't want to go to New York, link arms, kick it up, and make the world a more glam place.

Are the Rockettes part of your Christmas traditions?

April 20

April 20, uh, fourth month twentieth day, it's 420. How did this day become Get Your Ganga Going. Some folks opine that 4:20 was police code for marijuana violations. Some think it's because the chemical that gets you high is named 420. Others say it was Bob Marley's birthday—uh, it isn't, but I'm not going to get in the way of anybody's theories. Believe what you want…

In the early '70s, a group of students from San Rafael High School in Marin, California would meet for a little weed at 4:20 when after school activities were over. They were called the Waldos because they would huddle up against the wall for cover. One of their members, David Reddix, became a roadie for the Grateful Dead and told the story of Jerry Garcias' merry band of weedsters. The Grateful Dead started popularized the term and now we all know what 420 means.

April 21

On April 21, 1986, an estimated thirty million Americans were glued to their televisions to see the unveiling of the hidden treasures of the notorious 1920/1930s gangster Al "Scarface" Capone. Capone had run roughshod over the Chicago criminal world—what with illegal hooch, prostitution and murder. I lived at the site of the 1929 St. Valentine's massacre in which 7 members of Bugsy Moran's north side gang and a random wannabe gangsta dentist were mowed down in the garage by Capone's crowd. I don't even think they let the mechanic's dog live.

Bugsy Moran was pissed and declared war. Chicago was, well, like it is today. Bugsy would lose all his money and was put in prison for some petty crimes. He died of lung cancer. Capone was convicted of tax evasion and, when released, died of syphilis.

Fast forward to 1986. Journalist Geraldo Rivera announced he was going to open a sealed vault in the basement of Capone's Chicago headquarters. He was going to open the vault on live television! Thirty thousand watched on their televisions. I stood outside the building itself because I didn't own a television. There were sure to be treasures and gold and maybe skeletons. The real ones.

After interminable yammering and commercial breaks, at last the vault was opened and…nothing. A lot of dust and a couple of bottles of moonshine gin.

Both Capone and the contemporaneous comedian W.C. Fields were petrified by bank failures and the tax man. Fields was said to have opened a just in case bank account in every city he visited. Capone did something of the same sort with the added element of vaults because you can't really walk into BMO Harris and say I need a safety deposit box for these cases of moonshine. Neither man left instructions for their heirs to retrieve this largesse after their death.

Today, to celebrate (?) the opening of Capone's vault take a moment to write down all the particulars of your stash(es) and give it to a trusted relative or friend !

April 22, 1886 Ohio made illegal the seduction of female students by male teachers. Obviously, the legislators had never heard of pedophiles who preyed on boys and if you told them the story of Mary Kay Letourneau and Vili Fulaau* they would have had the vapors.

There were other states which criminalized at the time the seducing one's student or, frankly, any female under the age of eighteen. Virginia and New York explicitly connected the criminal seduction by a teacher of an otherwise chaste woman with the promise of marriage. Making the assumption that one would only do the nasty if the guy promised to put a ring on it.

I like the language of Georgia's statute which did its best to write a Harlequin novel—making it illegal for a man to "seduce a virtuous unmarried female and induce her to yield to his lustful embraces, and allow him to have carnal knowledge of her."

Pause the story. I have to swoon.

The particular focus of the Ohio law was seduction of girl students by their teachers and it was a great first step. These days we should have a law making it illegal to seduce a woman with a promise of a starring role in a blockbuster movie and then not delivering a contract and maybe a significant piece of jewelry. Oh, wait, Harvey Weinstein.

*Thirty four year old Letourneau later married Villi, served prison time for her sins, had two children with him, gave up the family she had when she taught him in sixth grade. She died in Villi's arms in 2020 even though they had divorced. There are some loves that endure despite or because of the law.

Have you ever had a love you could give the world for?

On April 23, 1985 the Coca-Cola Company introduced New Coke, a reformulated soft drink meant to replace its flagship beverage. It was as if the apocalypse. Everyone hated it! Former President Jimmy Carter's daughter, Amy, stockpiled "Old" Coke as did many Americans.

The decision to make "New" Coke, as the company itself explained in its backtrack, spawned "consumer angst the likes of which no business has ever seen."

As Time's then-food critic put it: "New" Coke "approaches the sweetness and thinness of Pepsi, [but] it does not have the lemony aftertaste."

The decision was reversed after 79 days, and on July 11, 1985, original Coke returned. Within a year, "New" coke was withdrawn from the market and "Classic" coke reigned.

My favorite cola is Mexican Coca-Cola made with cane sugar? What's yours?

____

____

____

____

____

April 24, 1986 was the homegoing of someone I don't think anybody would regard as a saint. Yet, she had a major impact on English history in much the same way as Anne Boleyn the second wife of Henry VIII.

Wallis Simpson, a double divorcee who might have ruled England but settled for simply ruling the heart of the former King Edward VIII, Wallis died aged 89 alone in their Paris apartment. Edward, who was given the title Duke of Windsor upon his abdication to be with the woman he loved, had died in 1972. The couple had had a vibrant if vapid social life in the early years of exile. He was appointed governor of the Bahamas, a title given to him during World War II mostly to keep him and his Nazi sympathizing ways as far away from the action. After the war, the couple settled in Paris and the servants called them His Royal Highness and Her Royal Highness even though they had long been stripped of those titles.

When Edward died, his body was transported to England to be buried at Frogmore cottage on the grounds of Windsor Castle. The very same cottage Prince Harry and the former cable television actress Meghan Markle were given upon their wedding.

The Duchess was reluctantly allowed to attend the understated funeral in London and she was put up at Buckingham Palace for the night. Then the Duchess was shown the door and on to the plane back to Paris.

Without Edward, she had no cachet or calling card to society. She quickly declined in health and while she was cared for by loyal servants and nurses, she was preyed upon by her attorney Suzanne Blum. The attorney stole from the Duchess and even gave away her beloved pugs. Blum and some of her friends ended up with extravagant "gifts" of jewelry and money.

At the end, Simpson was bedridden, confined alone to her bedroom in a nightgown shoddy and stained.

When she died, the Firm—with great reluctance—allowed her body to be transported to England for a private service at St. George's Chapel on the grounds of Windsor castle where her husband had had his service. The family showed up with gritted teeth—even the Queen Mum who blamed Edward and Wallis for the stress put upon her beloved Albert (Bertie) with a regnal name George VI after he succeeded his older brother. During the service which lasted less than a half hour, Wallis Simpson's name was not mentioned once.

Women often have a fear of dying alone, of losing everything, of facing the void with no one to hold their hand. Oh, whoops, I was talking about me!

On April 25, 1952 Father John Pohlen of the Tekakwitha* Indian Mission of Sisseton, South Dakota wrote to the Seely family of Wheaton, Illinois. He offered them children from the Mission's Papoose House in exchange for ten dollars each. There were approximately two dozen such boarding schools that took in—sometimes forcibly—Indian children from infancy to near adulthood. But selling the children was often a goal as well, nicely called "adoption."

Father Pohlen settled on sending the Seelys a five year old Dakota Sioux boy who had been forcibly taken from his mother when he was an infant. A single mother, she had been at a dance party which was considered justification for taking the boy away. The boy was sent to the Papoose House where he was cared for by the nuns along with other Indian infants.

This is where it gets dark. The priests and even some of the nuns were prone to physically and sexually abusing the children. This particular boy remembered being promised a lollipop by Father Pohlen in exchange for an act. Pohlen had a penchant for that sort of thing.

On May 3, 1952, at the age of five, the boy was sent to Illinois by bus—a 700 mile eighteen hour trip. The bus broke down and the boy soiled his pants. A kind police officer got him cleaned up and fed him and put him on the next day's bus. Mr. Seely picked him up at the bus station and named him Dennis Isaac Seely. Work began on erasing the Dennis' memory of a previous life or identity. I sure sympathize—I was adopted when three and my new parents corrected my use of the name ArLynn and said "No, it's Our Lynn." Pretty soon I forgot the Ar part. It wasn't until I was twenty seven that I learned my birth name. The reason I use a capital L in the middle of the name is so that I remember both sets of parents.

While the Seelys had a birth certificate filed to name them as parents and Dennis as their son, they treated him as a servant. I can identify with that too. He and I cleaned our respective houses and did lawn work. Dennis cleared out as soon as he could get a job. I ended up in the foster care system.

Father Pohlen died in 1969. The Tekakwitha Mission was demolished in 2010, the year a class action lawsuit was filed against the Catholic Diocese that oversaw the Mission. The suit was dismissed in 2011. Dennis went to visit the reservation where his birth mother had lived. He felt like a white man totally estranged from his native culture. He said of his time at the Mission, "I can remember a lot of the kids looking for their parents to come and get them … looking for someone to come down the driveway there, off the main highway … no one ever came."

I totally get it.

*Saint Katera Tekawitha was a Native American nun born in New York in 1656 and was known as the Lily of the Mohawks. She had a disfiguring episode of smallpox when she was young and she developed an interest in Catholicism as she turned eleven. At thirteen she declined to marry. She officially converted to Catholicism at age 19. She died five years later. The name Tekawitha, oddly enough, means "she who bumps into things." I would have left the Mohawks if they had given me that name even without the lure of Christianity.

If you are adopted, do you want to meet your biological paents?

____

____

____

____

On any given Sunday, the average American is watching a game—on their television, in the stands, at a bar or on a cell phone. They might even be participating in a game in their backyard, their country club, the fields of their park district. But in the sixteenth century, many Christian countries prohibited games and frolicking and sports on the day that should be devoted exclusively to worship. Sunday services could go on for hours and many churches employed what was called a sluggard waker who carried a pole to whack (and wake) any snoozers. To be fair, generally sluggard wakers' poles had an animal tail or a feather on one end for the ladies and the infirm.

In Sixteenth Century England all forms of sport on Sundays was prohibited which was a shame for folk who worked six day weeks. But Queen Elizabeth I made an exception to this rule on April 26, 1569 for a Middlesex chicken merchant John Seconton Powler. The Queen felt sorry for him as he had four young children and "had fallen into decay." He would be allowed "to have and use some plays and games at or upon several Sundays for his better relief, comfort and sustentation." Why he got this special dispensation is a mystery but he was specially and solely allowed this privilege. Powler could go out shooting, could leap, could run, could throw sledges and bars and could wrestle. How does one do that last one if anybody you wrestle with can be arrested?

At the time, the Queen's castle was open for supplicants who begged for special favors. There was even a day set aside for the ruler of England to touch those who suffered from scrofula (also known as microbacterial cervical lymphadeinitis). The disease caused huge tumors, mostly on the neck, and the thinking was that a king or queen touching the person would have healing qualities.

Queen Elizabeth died with only James of Scotland as her heir. He was the son of her cousin Mary Queen of Scots—whom she had beheaded. He took the title James I of England in 1603 to add to his kingdoms and titles. In 1618 he published The Book of Sports which declared Sunday games and play legal. Frolicking too!

Still, emotions about sporting on Sundays were not to be ignored—in the 1924 Olympics British runner Eric Lidell refused to compete in the 100 meter when he discovered the heats were scheduled for a Sunday. The British team was tight knit and teammate Andrew Lindsay who had already snagged a gold gave up his slot in the Thursday 400 meter. Lidell had not trained for such a long race but he managed to get the gold. He would return from the Paris Olympics to say a more permanent goodbye to his family in Scotland—he went to China as a missionary and was killed by the invading Japanese.

What do you do on a Sunday? How do you live your faith and your fun?

April 27

On April 27, 4977 B.C., we have a birthday to celebrate! On this day the universe was
born, according to sixteenth century German
mathematician and astronomer Johannes Kepler, considered a founder of modern science.
Kepler is best known for his theories explaining
the motion of planets and his work in math-
ematics. Kepler was no conspiracy theorist or
fundamentalist Christian or part of a cult.

He was an avowed atheist at a time when you just kept your mouth shut about it
and hoped you didn't get burned at the stake. So his work basically was at odds with
the Aristotlean "first cause" or if you prefer Latin "primum movens" or you could say
"a diety who gets the party started."

Whatever your belief system, Kepler is giving you the excuse you need and want
to ditch your keto diet and have a piece of cake today! However, it must be a fire haz-
ard with that many candles to celebrate our earthly birthday.

April 28

On April 28, 1922 Korean crown prince Yeong married Japanese princess Masako for
a second time. Their first wedding had been in Japan in 1920. This time the renewal
of vows were held in Korea.

In 1910 Japan and Korea had entered into a treaty making Korea a colony of Japan, thereby demoting Korean emperor Sunjong to a mere
king. Pissed off as all get out, Sunjong sent his son Yeong
to Tokyo for schooling and to capture the hand of the Japanese princess Masako. Seemed to turn out okay at first and
when they arrived in Korea for the second ceremony, they
brought with them their seven month old son Jin.

For the Korean ceremony on this day in 1922, Masako
wore a formal Korean robe known as a Jeokui in deep blue
silk embroidered with 154 pairs of pheasants. The pheasants
were in five colors, symbolizing the five virtues of a queen:
benevolence, righteousness, piety, wisdom and trust. She
also wore a ceremonial headdress that was so heavy that
she had to have a lady in waiting prop it up from behind
Masako whenever she walked. Yeong wore a Yongpo of red

with dragons made of gold threads. Their son Jin wore a peach gown and was carried
around by a courtier. The day after the ceremony, the couple visited Jongmyo, a ceremonial shrine, to report their nuptials to Yeong's ancestors.

A few days later baby Jin died under the cloud of suspicion that he had been poisoned. The couple recovered from their grief in order to produce a male heir. They lived a long and prosperous life. Masako changed her name to the Korean Yi Bangja. The couple worked together to smooth Korea/Japan relations. They did their royal duty.

You can see the royal wedding gown at the National Palace Museum of Korea. Who knows? Maybe they'll let you borrow it. Just not the headdress.

April 29

On April 29, 2011 Prince William of England married Kate Middleton. The bride was beautiful, her sister Pippa had a great ass, Harry hadn't yet taken to scowling. But the scene stealer?

Princess Beatrice's Fascinator

Two explanations are in order. Princess Beatrice was the daughter of Sarah Ferguson and King Charles' younger brother Andrew who wasn't yet disgraced. Fascinator is a small formal hat for women, usually resting on a headband, and it's meant to be somewhat provocative or perhaps even humorous.

The pink fascinator Beatrice wore to the wedding was designed by Philip Treacy an Irish milliner who, incidentally designed the beauxbaton hats for the 2005 Harry Potter and the Goblet of Fire film. But he is most famous for the Beatrice fascinator which was compared by the various press to a pretzel, an octopus, a toilet seat or an IUD It was meant to look like a giant bow. Her sister Eugenie's hat looked like something out of Robin Hood but didn't attract nearly as much attention. I sort of wonder how Beatrice got in and out of the car.

That hat WAS the wedding and Beatrice was ridiculed pretty harshly. Yet, she did the most royal thing: she auctioned it off on eBay, raising $131k for UNICEF and Children in Crisis charities.

Class act, I'd say. So I will always be a Beatrice fan AND I'll always be on the lookout for her fascinators.

Today, don't be afraid to make a fashion choice that's out of the ordinary.

April 30

April 30 is National Prepareathon Day, created by President Obama in 2014 as part of his initiative to help Americans prepare for natural (and unnatural) disasters. Don't mean to be a downer, but all kinds of things can happen in a blink of an eye: a car crash, a house fire, a death in the family, an attack from Mars. Are you ready?

Today is a good day to update your emergency contact list of relatives and friends you would need to watch out for or who would watch over you. It's a good day to pack (or repack) your go bag in case you need to make a hasty retreat from a hurricane, a fire, or your in-laws coming to visit.* A good day to talk to your family about where you'll meet up in case you are separated. A good day to check the pantry for nonperishables and bottled water—and all the other things that grocery stores run out of when panic shopping set in. A good day to check your fire alarm batteries and get the car checked out. Go to *community.fema.gov* for tips on other suggestions.

And then sit back and relax. You've done what you can do. Peace of mind is everything!

*During the pandemic/protests of 2021-2022, I kept a backpack near my front door. Extra cash. An extra credit card. A second ID card. Change of clothes. A paper copy of my contact list in case I got separated from my phone. A week's worth of meds and vitamins. Some TSA sized toiletries. Granola bars and bottled water. And (bien sûr!) lipstick, perfume and mascara. It gave me some comfort to think I could just pick it up and walk right out the door. I've never had to use it. Hope you never have to use yours!

Do you hav a gobag and a plan?

____

____

____

____

____

M ay is nature's way of saying Let's Party!

–Robin Williams

I might be getting ahead of myself, but May 1 is a VERY important and yet largely overlooked holiday. I encourage you to get a move on and prepare your celebration in all its glory.

It is the day of lily of the valley, a flower that represents hope and joy and the happiness of spring. Although the word or reference to flowers shows up 159 times in the Bible, the lily of the valley is one of only three flowers named—rose and rose of sharon* being the other two.

The flower blooms in Europe, Asia and North America (although it may very well have been transported by settlers). It's perennial but many people are allergic to it and the roots especially are poisonous. In the Medieval Era, it became a custom to deliver lilies of the valley on May 1st to sweethearts. But this really took off in a big way when the king of France Charles IX gave every lady of his court a bouquet. Suddenly, every man worthy of the title of gentleman was handing out bouquets left and right on May 1.

In the nineteenth and twentieth centuries it became the custom to create baskets or cones with flowers and treats in them, including but not limited to lilies of the valley. Then you went to your intended sweetheart's home and hung the confection on the front door knob. I remember doing this as a child although I don't recall ever receiving a May Day bouquet.

The winter is a memory. Hope and joy and lily of the valley is here!

* A flowering shrub in the mallow (malvaceae) family.

Go to the florists' and just buy a small little something and hang it on the doorknob of someone you love or someone you think could use some perking up. The joy they feel will be roughly equal to yours in giving.

____

____

____

____

____

On May 2, 1536 Queen Consort Anne Boylen was arrested for, among other things, treason, adultery, and incestuous relations with her brother George. Her "co-conspirators" were also being round up and ultimately all but one would be executed. Anne represented herself, never a good idea but you try hiring an attorney in those circumstances. It was a three hour barge trip to the Tower of London and because she was still technically still a queen she was not taken through Traitor's Gate. Instead she walked up the same stairs to the very same apartment she had been given at the Tower three years earlier on the eve of her coronation. Her escorts were of such lowly station that they stood at the bottom of the stairs until it was confirmed she had entered the apartments.

She lost her trial and was found guilty by a council that included her father and some other family members.

She was executed on the nineteenth and her husband showed her a "mercy" in that he hired an experienced executioner from France who traversed the Channel even before Anne was arrested. Most beheadings in England and many other countries required a bunch of whacks before the deed (or dead) was done. Anne paid the executioner, which was customary to show forgiveness for their job but also to hopefully get it all over as quickly as possible. The executioner asked for and received her forgiveness. She gave some last words —

"I pray God save the King … for a gentler nor a more merciful prince was there never."

Was she being sarcastic or was she protecting her two year old daughter Elizabeth and the rest of her family? Eleven days later, Henry 8 married Anne's lady in waiting Jane Seymour.

May 03

May 3rd is a day of great importance which hasn't yet come to fruition. Sometimes it feels like this, right here right now, is the End of the World. There have been other times, other concerns, other certainties that it was indeed the end of the world as we know it. For instance, according to the Mayan long count calendar, or at least the modern interpretation, the end of the world was scheduled for December 21, 2012. Hey, we're still here. No worries—the next time the Mayans predict the world will end is May 3, 7138.

We've got some time. When was the last time you thought jeez this might be it!?

May 04

May The Fourth Be With You! Today is a day to celebrate the beginning of the Star Wars empire. Although the first of so many, many, many prequels, sequels, whatevers, the original was actually released on May 25, 1977—Greek Independence Day. But the phrase "may the force be with you" became so much of the English language that Disney and Lucas Films have embraced this day as yet another way to remind us of the franchise.

British Prime Minister Margaret Thatcher won the first election of a female, uh, are we still allowed to use the term, Prime Minister of Britain on May 4th 1979. She was the daughter of a grocer and she was mighty tough. I've gone to two dinner parties in which she and I were both guests and you just didn't want to get in the way of her—at the first one, I was wearing a black dress, she assumed I was a server and demanded I get her a cup of coffee and another napkin. The day after this May 4th victory of Thatcher, the Conservative party was as British generally are and took out an ad in the Evening News saying "May the Fourth Be with You, Maggie, Congratulations!"

All right, let's not get confused here. May 5th (otherwise known as Cinco de Mayo) is a great Mexican holiday but it's not when they won their independence which sometimes gringos and gringas assume. The Cinco de Mayo battle took place on this day in 1862 against Napoleon III. At the time, the French were actually one of the strongest armies in the world. Today, I think I could arm wrestle a regiment or two.

Things came to a head on May 5th 1862 in the small town of Puebla, Mexico. The Mexicans were greatly outnumbered—2,000 soldiers facing 6,000 French. And say what you want about the French they had better munitions, better training, and, hey, great escargot. But the Mexicans had something that every force needs—an absolute determination to defend their homeland.

Within a few hours the French were defeated. Mexican President Benito Juarez declared the day—Cinco de Mayo—a national holiday in honor of the soldiers who prevailed and the soldiers who were casualties.

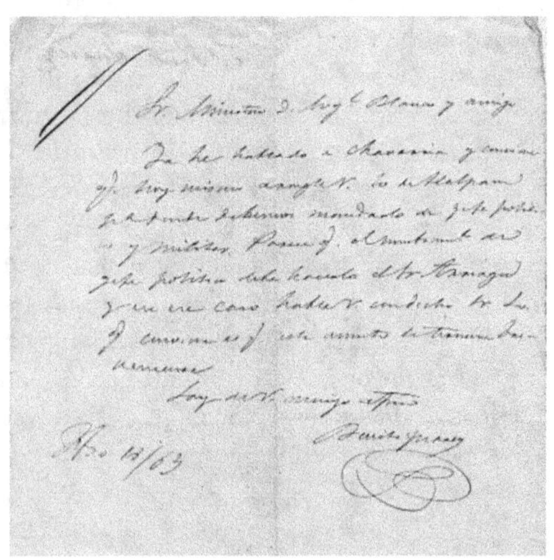

Letter held by US Library of Congress handwritten by President Juárez while Puebla was still under Mexican control. He fired off a letter on March 18, 1863, to his minister of war, Col. Miguel Blanco, asking that a local leader, Feliciano Chavarría, be named political and military chief.

So on this day, walk out the door and face whatever adversity you have in front of you and beat the living daylights out of it. Also, putting a Mexican flag on your car isn't a bad idea.

Oh the Humanity!

On May 6, 1937 the German commercial dirigible Hindenburg had flown ten transatlantic trips to the United States in its 1936 "season". Dirigibles were starting to look like the future of travel. This particular 1937 trip carried 97 people. Its body was filled with hydrogen and it had an undercarriage that was non plus ultra (that's French for fancy) in dining and accommodations for the passengers. The passenger list was smaller than usual but was fully booked for the return trip to England as many would be attending the coronation of King George 6 in London. The crew was a little more than usual as there were twenty trainees onboard.

The flight was utterly uneventful until the Hindenburg prepared to dock in Lakehurst, New Jersey. News reporters with their cameras and microphones had arrived to report on the first flight of the 1937 season. Among them was Herbert Morrison of WLS radio who cried out "oh the humanity!" upon seeing the Hindenberg explode.

There were 35 deaths among the 97 onboard. Oh, and a worker on the ground. The deceased either burned to death or fell to the ground in desperation. The only winner amongst them all was 14 year old Werner Franz who was a serving boy for the crew. He was about to burn to death when a water tank exploded, dousing his potential immolation. He took his chances sprinting for safety. He was the last surviving crew member of the Hindenburg, passing on in 2014 after a successful career coaching ice skaters, including two Olympians.

It was the end of the dirigible business but the story has a moral: don't play with hydrogen. That stuff explodes. Just ask Edward Teller, the Hungarian-American scientist who invented the hydrogen bomb.

Lately, there's all sorts of experimental transportation.
Would you go to space?

____

____

____

____

____

May 7 was a great day for Norway! Their most famous of artist Edvard Munch's oeuvre—The Scream—was recovered intact after having been stolen February 12 earlier in the year on the day which was the opening day of the Lillehammer Winter Olympics. The thieves had cut the wires holding up the 1893 painting in an Oslo museum, leaving behind a thank you note. Well, actually, "tusen tack for dalig sakerhet" Norwegian for "thousand thanks for the bad security!"

And we were just thinking about Nancy Kerrigan and Tonya Harding!

In 1996, four men were arrested for the stolen painting, including Paal Enger who had been convicted for stealing Munch's painting The Vampire in 1988. Enger had a pattern. He escaped from prison during a field trip (yes, they have field trips for prisoners in Norway and if they did that here in America, yikes!). Enger was recaptured and finished his sentence.

There was no ransom paid, much to the dismay of the four absconding art lovers.

While they were all sentenced to prison, The Scream was not safe. Munch painted several versions and in 2004 a different Scream was stolen and retrieved. My suggestion is that if you really want a good one, find the private owner of the version that sold for 120million in 2012. That's called an investment.

Would you buy a painting for $120,000,000 and if so by whom?

May 8, 1945 was Victory Day in Europe. The Nazis had been defeated and now it was just the Japanese to vanquish. Americans celebrated in Times Square by kissing nurses and drinking beer. But how about the British who had endured so much and so close? May 8th was declared a national holiday for the Brits.

And what a holiday it was! Prime Minister Winston Churchill received reassurances from the Ministry of Food that there would be beer available to all! The Board of Trade declared that red, white and blue bunting could be purchased without ration cards—and every Brit pulled out the stops! There were spontaneous parades, church services of thanksgiving, and block parties. Soon to be Queen Elizabeth 2 and her sister Princess Margaret (both known by their official last name of Windsor) even got permission from their parents to join in the festivities. The sisters definitely deserved it—they had worked for the war effort as much as any. Elizabeth was trained as a mechanic for the Army.

Restaurants and pubs offered special "Victory Menu" items—my favorite was Victory at Sea with anchovies, lemon mayo and frisee (fancy word for delicate curly lettuce). Hey, these people had been living in such deprivation that any kind of sandwich (and beer!) sounded like a treat worthy of a victorious people.

Because of the International Date Line, some of the British Empire had to wait until the ninth to pop the corks. New Zealanders, for instance, went to work on the day as if it were perfectly ordinary. But they knew VE would be celebrated on their May 9th.

The war against the Japanese (the last of the Italy-Germany-Japan axis) wouldn't end until August, 1945. Oh, wait, no, it wasn't until December 18, 1974 that the last Japanese soldier Hiro Onoda would lay down his sword.

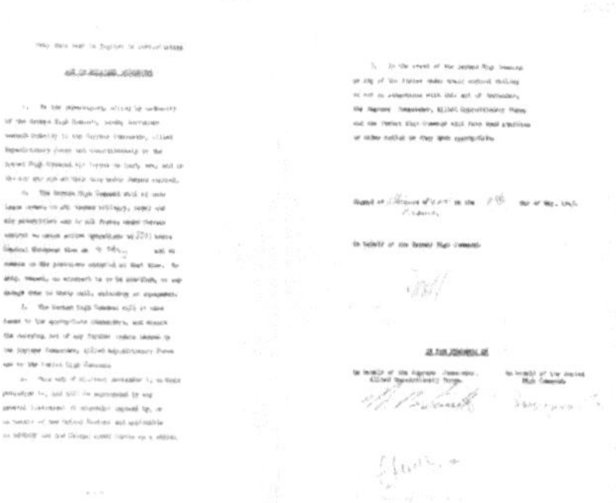

Surrender Document signed
by German Army

May 9th is Lost Sock Memorial Day, a day in which we mourn the sock that went missing. Of course, we are joined in this by the missing sock's partner who, if you follow my advice, will soon meet a grisly end.

We've all done it. Folded up the laundry and noticed there's one rogue sock that's gone AWOL.

Now the question is—is your washing machine a top loader or a front loader? That's not a query about the machine's sex life.

Top loaders often suck the wandering sock up under the agitator or in the wash plate at the bottom of the machine. If it's under the agitator, you might be able to retrieve it and for the sake of your washer, it's a good thing to do. If that sock got sucked into the wash plate, it's curtains.

Front loaders have a filter and if the sock gets in there, you have to take the filter off and pull out lint and hopefully a sock.

Otherwise, today is the day that you explain to the surviving sock that it's time. Toss it with a brief prayer. Or use it to dust your furniture. If you can get your Rose Nylan going, make a sock puppet. If you have a child who might be traumatized by any of this or if you're feeling particularly vulnerable, go on Amazon.com and order the 2014 Gillian Johnson book "The Lost Sock." A wonderful story about a Little Man who loses one special sock.

Or be like me and buy a twelve pack of the same black socks and white socks. Missing socks can go missing and you can disregard the holiday altogether.

May 10 is the anniversary of the 1849 Astor Place Opera house riot which left 22-31 people dead and at least 120 injured. The riot pitted the poor but hungry for culture versus the wealthy New Yorkers who wore formal wear and white gloves. The riot comprised the largest casualties in a domestic disturbance since the Revolutionary War.

All the participants appreciated theatre, mostly Shakespeare. And riots in theaters weren't uncommon. You'll recall the Stamp Act riots of 1765 which resulted in a melee in which an entire theater was destroyed while British actors continued their performance. Show must go on.

The crux of the problem of the Astor Opera House riot was the rivalry between frenemies and fellow actors American Edwin Forrest and the Brit William Charles Macready. Macready was performing Macbeth (also known as the Scottish Play) at the Astor while at the same time Forrest was performing Macbeth on Broadway. Macready's audience was going to be wearing their formal wear and Forrest's lower class audience members were going to be wearing their, well, whatever clothes they had.

Except it didn't work out that way. On the seventh, a bunch of Forrest fans bought cheap seat tickets in the balcony of the Astor and pelted Macready with whatever fruits, vegetables, shoes, eggs and whatnot they could bring. The performance was done in pantomime because the crowd was so loud. Macready announced he had had quite enough of Americans and was going back to Britain. Meanwhile, Forrest was being touted as giving a rousing "American style" manly man performance.

Macready should have gotten on that boat right quick but instead stayed for the performance of the tenth. There was a hostile crowd of ten thousand outside who were not permitted inside because they didn't follow the hastily enacted dress code. But they caused such a commotion that Macbeth was performed again in pantomime. Macready was hustled out of the theater afterwards in disguise. The rioting continued into the eleventh.

A lot of this was caused by animosity and national pride in American actors and in England they sided with the Brit actors. Shakespeare wasn't just for English literature class naps. His plays were popular and here in the states was widely considered to be the sort of man who would have been an American if he had simply been born in a different time. Shakespeare was so popular that out west cowboys and gold miners would recite Shakespeare from memory after dinner (they didn't have streaming or cell phones if you can believe that.)

May 10

My great grandfather and great grandmother and their son—my grandfather—were all Shakespearean actors. They had their own touring company and all made the transition to silent films and then talkies. America ultimately produced the sort of playwrights with a relevancy that sidelined Shakespeare. Although if you think about it, many of our best modern movies and plays carry Shakespeare in their hearts.

Today think about something from Shakespeare you'd like to watch. If you feel like it, put on some white gloves and a tuxedo jacket. Just don't pelt the screen with veggies. When I was in the middle of the divorce I would watch the 1996 Romeo and Juliet with Leonardo DiCaprio and Claire Danes. And then Sense and Sensibility (Jane Austen) with Kate Winslet and Emma Thompson. I'd start crying during the opening credits. It was rough justice therapy.

A PICTURE OF MY GREAT-GRANDFATHER, FRITZ LEIBER SR., AND THEDA BARA IN THE SILENT FILM JULIUS CAESAR.

Is art divisive or somehow reconciliatory? Does Shakespeare have class implications worth fighting for?

____

____

____

____

____

On May 11, 1882 playwright/essayist/raconteur Oscar Wilde was touring America, bringing culture to the uncouth masses although largely focusing his efforts on giving lectures to the wealthy and then allowing himself to be persuaded to have tea or dinner or attend a dance.

The New York Times reported that on this particular day at Wallack's Theater he delivered a light hearted lecture and he wore "a suit of black velvet with … knee breeches … long black stockings, pumps with silver buckles, a drab kid glove on the left hand, lace ruffles at the wrist, and a lace ruffle around the neck." Now we know where Michael Jackson got the idea of one glove!

The New York Times complained in a somewhat passive aggressive way that Wilde's hair "hung in graceful hanks over his neck and shoulders, and so concealed his ears that it was impossible to discover whether he wore earrings or not."

Wilde's reputation as a, ahem, Bohemian sort of fellow was well known for his sense of style. I think today is a good day for you to pull out the one thing in the closet that you've always wanted to wear but didn't quite dare. A feather boa lurks in the back of my closet, lonely and abandoned. I just might … will you?

Wilde spent some time in prison for sodomy and when released headed for Paris where he stayed in a hotel until he died. His last words were reportedly a stinging rebuke of the decor—"either the wallpaper goes or I do." The wallpaper won. Wilde died November 1900 with many concluding syphilis. Some newer theories include choleastatoma, a middle ear infection. Now every time I get a pain my ear I'm going to prepare for the worst.

____

____

____

____

____

May 12, 1971 was a fantastic day in fashion history, women's liberation and rock and roll! Twenty six year old Nicaraguan Blanca Perez-Mora
Macias (at sixteen she changed her first name to
Bianca) married Rolling Stones front man Mick
Jagger. They had met in Paris at a party for the
band. It was like two taxicabs crashing into each
other. Him a jet setting rocker, Bianca a human

rights activist. A scant nine months later, they married in a Roman Catholic ceremony in St. Tropez, France. And they gave their star-studded guests just twenty
four hours notice.

The most extraordinary thing about the wedding was Bianca's "bridal gown"…
Mick was wearing a beige three piece suit and running shoes. He looked, in my
humble opinion, like he was on his way to work at a used car dealership. Bianca
wore a white Yves Saint Laurent jacket, no shirt but lots of cleavage, what appeared
to be matching skirts, platform heels, and a veiled hat. The ensemble was casual,
elegant, and not what anybody would expect. And there was some expecting going
on—Bianca was four months pregnant with the couple's daughter Jade.

Mick was a husband who slept around but it wasn't until he met blonde Texas
born model Jerry Hall that he had a full on see her twice affair. In 1978 Bianca
divorced him and she would be his only legally recognized wife. When Jerry and
Mick had their wedding in Thailand it turned out to be "ceremonial" and not recognized by the Thai government. That distinction was crucial when they divorced
after four children and twenty years together. Jerry bounced back and went on to
marry and divorce publisher Rupert Murdoch.

But Bianca! She transformed the idea of what the bride could/should/would
wear—wedding suits for women became a thing. Her serious side showed through
as she continued her work in human rights activism, most notably as an ambassador for the Council of Europe. She also appeared in a number of films and her
daughter Jade had a successful career as a model. Mick went on to have more children, bringing him a grand total of eight kids by five different baby mamas.

Bianca would later say rather cryptically in an interview that the wedding was
the end of her marriage.

What did or will you wear to your wedding?

Sometimes the thirteenth of the month is a no good, terrible, rotten, horrible day even if it's not a Friday! And on Thursday May 13, 1604 it certainly was for a cute little lamb who had traveled all the way from France on a ship with explorer/merchant Pierre Dugua de Mons and his second in command navigator/cartographer/soldier/geographer Samuel de Champlain. The two men were on a mission—most important to the merchant Dugua—to figure out a way to make money. Sending fur back to Canada and maybe some precious metals might do.

The little lamb had been in the hold of the ship for the trip with only a few deck forays. When on Thursday, May 13, 1604 the sailor in the crow's nest announced "land ho!" or rather, "terre ho!" The little lamb got so excited that she jumped into the sea and aimed to swim for land.

Now here's the good news: Sailors rushed to save her and she was brought back to the safety of the ship.

Here's the bad news: The sailors killed her and ate her for dinner.

Dugua and Champlain named the little cove they were in Port Mouton which is French for mutton or lamb.

And so there's a little section of the coastline of Nova Scotia right by the Kejimkujik National Park called Port Mouton after a hyperexcited lamb. It's a fishing town and has its own post office, restaurant, general store, and liquor store. Children travel to nearby Liverpool for their education as the Port Mouton school was closed in 1994.

Two morals to this story: a day can start of really great but don't let down your guard. You might be slathered in mint jelly by nightfall. And if your given a choice between shutting down the liquor store or the local school, go with your instincts.

Here's a before and an after picture of little lamb's day—

Are you going to go Vegan today?
Just for today of course.

On May 14, 1942 the British made an enormous sacrifice for the war effort. Just about every item of food was rationed and meat was scarce because it was necessary to keep the fighting men in shape with a high calorie diet. On May 14th—in order to save the precious nylon used for making parachutes—the government introduced yet another austerity measure named "Bare Legs for Patriotism." Women needed to ration and conserve and as their stockings ran ragged, completely give in to "liquid stockings". Using foundation brushes and a nude cream they'd fashion something approaching the look of hosiery.

"Leg lotion gives the glamorous effect of super sheer stockings, out flatters your finest nylons! It goes on like a dream and it magically makes your legs look slimmer," read an advertisement for the wonder cosmetic. Liquid eyeliner could be employed to create the fashionable back seam. The campaign and the womanly cooperation saved the British government 600 pounds by 1943. The French made a hefty sum selling soldiers silk stockings to send home to their ladies. Coco Chanel, who has often been accused of collaborating with the Nazis, wrapped bottles of Chanel No. 5 for a soldier's gal back home. She'd even ship. All the guy had to do was fill out a gift card—oh, and pay!

In the nineties, Vogue editor Anna Wintour pretty much made hosiery a fashion no-no. Bare legs became the norm.

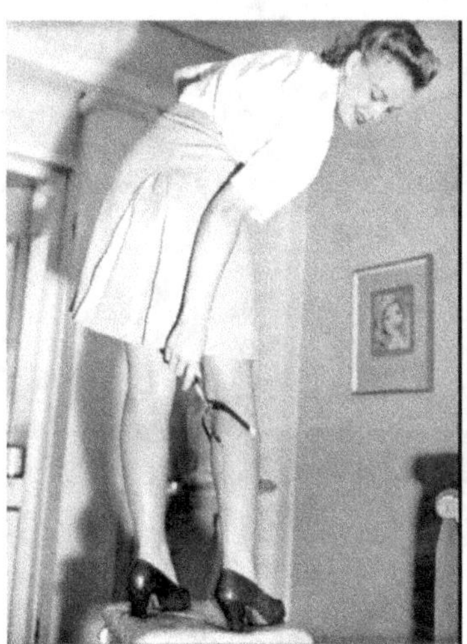

Stockings Yes or No?

May 15, 1803 a Woodstock, Connecticut slaveholder Samuel McClellan distributed posters offering a $10 reward for the return of his eighteen year old slave Caesar. The poster described said slave's apparel which actually sounded pretty dapper. Caesar could be identified wearing "a light colored sailor jacket, a mixed green and black swans down vest, a pair of overalls, a Holland shirt, a pair of gray socks, a pair of thick shoes, a brown homemade great coat, and a large old Hat."

The detail with respect to the clothing was in part because most slaves only possessed one set of apparel.

We'd like to believe that all Northern States were abolitionist but that really wasn't the case. McClellan had been a notable leader in the Revolutionary War against England.

Caesar was born in 1784 and was raised with three other slave boys in the McClellan household—Cit, Simon and Prince. They were allowed to go to school but had their duties at home.

Good news—the self-emancipated Caesar was never found and bad news—he never was mentioned in Woodstock historical records again.

Are indentured servatude and slavery two different names for the same thing?

____

____

____

____

____

On May 16, 1830 global warming officially claimed its first victim.

Eighteenth century French mathematician and physicist Joseph Fourier was a smart dude. He devised the Fourier Series which I won't bore you with because if you were paying attention in trigonometry class you already know about and if you weren't I won't spoil the ending. He also specialized in thermodynamics in which he gave us all we need to know about heat conductivity which I won't explain because I KNOW you weren't paying attention in physics class. But, hey, those doodles you did in your notebook of the female/male form are classic.

He also is the first to postulate what we know now as the Greenhouse Effect, in which a glass enclosure traps sunlight and converts it into heat. Or, as you gotta have read the papers, when the ozone layer that protects us from the sun like one of those windshield visors you buy for your car so you don't burn your butt when you get out of work. Oddly, the ozone hole has nearly disappeared EXCEPT some of our privately owned spaceships are impeding the process.

Fourier took Greenhouse fears in a different direction than we have. He thought the heat was a great thing. He overheated his house with roaring fires and wrapped himself up in blankets even in the middle of summer. Kind of like those Hammacher-Schlemer sauna blankets where you swaddle yourself for the sweat. It was while wearing this sort of blankie that Fourier tripped and fell down the stairs at his home and died on May 16, 1830.

Robert Frost said at the 1960 inauguration of JFK "some say the world will end by ice, others say by fire."
What is your opinion?

On May 17, 1948 newly married Princess Elizabeth II and her husband the Duke of Edinburgh ended their four day visit to Paris. It was the first trip outside of Britain for the couple and Elizabeth was newly pregnant and kind of wilting in that way that pregnant women do sometimes. Me? I always looked green like I had to throw up. Which quite often I did.

The couple had a full schedule of official duties. They toured the gardens at Fountainbleau which had been the home of the French royal family. They had a luncheon at a local restaurant after a picnic on the grounds was considered too much of a security risk. The final event was a ballet at the Opera Garnier. More than five thousand uninvited mere mortals stood outside and some even booed when the Princess didn't make an appearance on the outdoor balcony.

The press was having a hard time getting a good shot of the Princess. Luckily, there was the parvenu Lady Alexandra Howard-Johnston (remember the "t" otherwise you'll start thinking about early bird specials). She was dressed in a white satin gown with gold embroidery designed by Jacques Fath, her usual couturier (mine is Walmart).

When Alexandra and her husband (an aide to the British royal family) arrived at the joint, the Parisian Garde Nationale jumped to attention. Alexandra realized they had mistook her for the Princess and the Duke. "That was the effect of my splendid Fath," she said later. Fath was a designer on part with post war Christian Dior and Pierre Balmain. Unfortunately, he passed on in 1954 of leukemia. But just think what effect a well made frock can have. I mean, who remembers what Elizabeth was wearing?

May 18, 1924 the United States rugby team arrived at the 1924 Paris Olympics at the peak of French anti-American feeling. Like, what was their problem? We saved their sorry asses in World War I and we'd do it again in World War II. Mais cherchez la femme!

When the team's boat pulled in Boulogne, the Americans were held up for hours with officials dilly-dallying with their visas. When they showed up at the practice fields, officials barred their access. So the Americans did what all red blooded Americans would do—they climbed over the fence of Colombes Stadium to scrimmage on the championship field. Take that! The French retaliated by stealing their equipment.

And then came the championship game itself. On May 18, fifty thousand fans showed up to boo the Yankees. But again, the American spirit showed—the Americans won over the French team by 17-3.

Spectators tossed bottles and rocks onto the field, fought each other and anybody they suspected of being American, and one fan knocked an American bench player unconscious with a walking stick.

The Olympic Committee responded by banning rugby from all future summer games. So with that technicality, the United States held its head high and was the reigning rugby champion for 92 years. Then the sport was reinstated in 2016. Fiji took gold, Britain silver and South Africa bronze.

1924 USA National Union Rugby Team that won the Gold Medal.

Wasn't it nice to hav 92 years unchallenged as champion Rugby players?

May 19th is National Barber Mental Health Awareness Day. I know you're skeptical about the need for such a holiday, but hear me out. This holiday was established in 2020 and you can't call it a made up Hallmark holiday because I don't think they sell "I appreciate my barber" cards. But barbers have historically played a huge roll in the mental health of their clients.

From even before the 16th century, barbers cut hair and pulled teeth. Sometimes they even did surgery. It really wasn't until two centuries later that barbers became a stand alone enterprise. Dentists and surgeons put on similar white coats but dissimilar airs. The barber with his shears performed a very important service well beyond cutting hair.

The barber shop became a place for (mostly) men to congregate and socialize while waiting for a trim and a shave. Barbers often became confidantes for their clientele in a time where nobody had a therapist and Sigmund Freud (b. 1856) hadn't yet figured out that it's all your mother's fault. You got a shave, a haircut, a slap of aftershave and you poured out your problems. The barber would give his two cents and even if he was daft, at least someone was listening to you.

Well into the Twentieth century, barbershops became a venue to discuss civil rights, the Vietnam War and other social issues. In 1960 Dr. Israel Golddiamond posited that a barbershop became a place where ad hoc therapy was occurring in a noninstitutional setting.

By the 2000s, it was well recognized that barbershops could be a place to disseminate health information, hold interventions and keep track of the health and wellbeing of its clients.

In 2020 Barber Mental Health Awareness Day became a holiday. Now, I think it would be pretty strange for you to give your barber a dozen roses or a modest but still flashy bauble. But what you can do is stop in, even if you don't have an appointment, and just say "hey, thanks." Or maybe just watch an episode of the Andy Griffith Show and watch Barber Floyd.

And here's my barber. I always go to him when I'm in Portland, Maine. I don't even know his name and I'm not exactly sure he remembers what it is either. So we're even. I can tell him anything and he never judges. Mostly because he doesn't have his hearing aids in. And the minute I walk out the door, he doesn't remember a thing.

Do you have a barber you're loyal to. Someone you can talk to?

____

____

____

____

Just in case you forgot about making the Nice List and not letting your name show up on the Naughty List, there's May 20, 325 a.d. Because on this day in Anatolia in what we now call Turkey, Emperor Constantine who had converted to Christianity convened the First Council of Nicaea to figure out the Holy Trinity. Big issue—was Christ divine or was he just a really good human being? And what about that Holy Ghost?

Constantine was really devoted to these sort of questions. He had converted when facing a battle with Emperor Maxientus in October 312 AD. The night before, Constantine promised God he'd convert from worshipping Sol Invictus to worshipping Jesus if he won. And he did. When you make a promise to the Divinity you'd better keep it because, hey, you don't know what kind of stuff they can punish you with.

But let's get back to May 20, 325 a.d. About 300 delegates had showed up at the Council and only two disputed Christ's divinity. One was Alexandrian priest Arius. As he argued his position, another bishop, named Nicholas, became enraged. He stood up, walked across the room and punched Arius in the face. Whoa! Better do your chores and be nice to everyone you meet because it looks like St. Nicholas aka Santa Claus has quite the temper!

Do at least one good deed today, just in case.

On May 21, 1927 aviator Charles Lindbergh completed the first nonstop flight across the Atlantic Ocean. He wore a rotation of three jaunty one piece jumpsuits which he signed the underside of the collar later for fans "worn on the following flights: San Diego-St. Louis, St. Louis-New York, New York-Paris."

Exactly five years later on May 21, 1932 wearing jodhpurs, a short jacket and a collared shirt under a one piece flight suit, Amelia Earhart became the second person to cross the Atlantic nonstop solo. And the first woman.

Five years after that, on May 21, 1937 Amelia Earhart departed on her first around the world flight. Nobody knows what happened to her but she is presumed to have run out of fuel and crashed at Howland Island in the Pacific as she and her navigator/co-pilot Fred Noonan approached the island. Amelia left behind her publisher husband George Putnam who had really marketed the adventure. Noonan left behind his second wife Mary.

Is THIS the day YOU start a great adventure

____

____

____

____

____

May 22 is the homegoing day of Saint Rita of Cascia, Italy. She was born in 1381 AD and I think of her as having committed the greatest sin of all—filicide. And for that she got made a saint? Let's see what you think.

When she was twelve, she was married at her family's behest to a wealthy, yet abusive husband. She endured him for twenty two years and ultimately she converted him to Christianity by her good example (which is how St. Paul counseled wives to do when they found themselves married to a nonChristian—more effective than a frying pan to his head). However, not all of Rita's husband old ways disappeared and he was murdered, the victim of a family feud.

Rita's two sons declared they would avenge their father's death. St. Rita prayed ardently and openly that both sons die so that they would not commit that sixth commandment—you know, the one about not killing. Within months, both sons were dead, some believe by dysentery instead of violence. Rita considered her prayers answered.

And my kids think I'm a terrible mom?

She retreated to an Augustinian monastery to care for the suffering. And a little penance. Her reward was a wound appearing on her forehead that was similar to that Christ had when the crown of thorns was placed on his head. She died in 1457 and canonized in 1900. She is invoked against smallpox and is said to help women in childbirth. She is the protector of grocers and salami vendors.

Still, wishing your own child dead???? Seems very unsaintly to me.

Saint Rita - really ?

Today I'm thinking about May 23, 1957 which is when the only known police officer in my fair town of Winnetka was killed in the line of duty. It happened on the triangular intersection on Church and Green Bay Avenues. Robert E. Burke was but a young 32 year old who had served in the Navy and had joined the police department after he was discharged. It was a random traffic stop but there was a hitchhiker who was standing nearby who got freaked. Even though he wasn't involved in the stop at all, he pulled out a gun and shot Burke in the head. Then shot himself. A terrible random encounter. Glenn Florkow, who worked at the Winnetka police department spearheaded making the little triangular park that is the location of Burke's killing.

Every year Glenn puts out flags at Memorial Day (well, it is kind of near the date of Burke's death) and at the Fourth of July. I have had the flags in my place and so I walked them down Green Bay tonight and put them out. Nobody is going to put up a park when I pass on but this guy sure deserves a corner of Winnetka to serve as a reminder of what he gave up for our village.

<h2 style="text-align:center">May 24</h2>

On May 24th, 1920 the French President Paul Deschanel fell off the Orient Express as it approached Lyon. He was overheated and wanted his window opened. Rather than call for help from a porter, he put his entire weight on the window and whoosh! He was dressed in his green silk pajamas. No slippers.

The train engineer, and in fact, everyone else on the train, were blissfully unaware of the accident. Most were asleep, perhaps even the engineer himself. Deschanel walked about a half hour away to the nearest signal box.

"I am Monsieur Deschanel, President of the Republic!" he shouted to the signal man.

With the dignity and sneer that only the French can summon, the signal man replied, "and I am the Emperor Napoleon."

<h2 style="text-align:center">May 25</h2>

On May 25 1980 the "stupidest song ever written" peaked at #1 in the UK, above records by such wannabe musicians as Elton John and Paul McCartney.
Let's go back to 1970 when MASH (the movie) director Robert Altman had a requirement for the "Captain Painless" suicide scene. He wanted "the stupidest song ever written." Neither Altman nor show composer Johnny Mandel could get it down pat, but Mandel had an ace up his sleeve. Or rather, a fifteen year old son Johnny Altman. Suicide is Painless is a three minute track with lines like "the sword of time will pierce our skins. The pain grows stronger, watch it grin."

The movie used the song and in 1972 the show premiered on television and we couldn't get the damn song out of our heads. BTW the only cast member from the movie who transitioned to the television version was Walter (Radar) O'Reilly played by Gary Burghoff.

Young Mandell made more than $1 million in royalties for writing that little ditty while his father scored a paltry $70k for his work. I wonder what they bought each other for Christmas presents!

This makes me think what gifts did the Altmans exchange at Christmas?

On May 26, 1968 Iceland officially switched from the British system of driving on the left hand side of the street to the right (like us NORMAL Americans). At the appointed time of 6 a.m., all Icelandic drivers stopped wherever they were motoring and switched lanes in an elegant U-turn.

I like the Icelandic people. So polite, so rugged, so organized. There was only one injury, unlike there would be if America tried it. We'd have pile ups and road rage and protests and conscientious objectors and folk who would claim the whole change was a conspiracy to … well, there would be conspiracy theorists.

There was only one injury in Iceland on this day. It was to a bicyclist. He broke his leg.

The day is remembered even now as "Haegri Dagurinn" or "Right Day"—raise your hand if you object to that characterization.

May 27

Lets step back May 12, 1972 when the low rent five cents a session psychiatrist Lucy van Pelt kicked her brother Linus out of the house. It's been my experience that folks in the "helping" and "mental health" profession are the craziest.

Linus had nowhere to go except Snoopy's doghouse. Linus, Snoopy, and Woodstock shared an amiable life. But Lucy was deeply critical. Snoopy countered Lucy's criticism that Linus would never amount to anything by explaining to her that the doghouse was actually his dorm room. And he was not Snoopy no more—he was Joe Cool! and Linus was a college boy!

On May 27, 1972 Linus explains the situation to the visiting Charlie Brown. The dorm did not actually have a cafeteria—Snoopy ordered delivery pizza.

But isn't that what all college kids do (pre-Covid of course)?

May 28

Media (not social or mainstream but geographic) is a good sized chunk of land abutting the Caspian Sea. The Medians and the Lydians of Turkey were ALWAYS fighting. Maybe out of boredom, ruthlessness or whimsy. On May 28, 585 b.c. they were going at it when the midday sun went black and the battlefield vanished for about three minutes. When the sun brought its light to world again, the freaked out warriors laid down their weapons and there was a truce.

Astronomers can determine the dates of past, present and future solar eclipses but none of the battle participants were paying attention to astronomers. The battle was one of the oldest historical events where we know the exact date. Forget Keppler's theory about the day the universe was created (April 27, 4977 b.c.)—this is real science.

The eclipse was calculated in advance by the philosopher Thales of Miletus in Lydia. As twentieth century philosopher/scientist/science fiction writer Isaac Asimov said, "Thales' calculation was the birth of science."

Do you agree with Asimov?

May 29

May 29 is a great to toss aside your troubles. You should put on some vinyl records and dance The Turkey Trot! Condemned by no less than the Pope himself, the Philadelphia born dance includes a lot of gyrating, body contact between men and women and imitation of the bird itself. On May 29, 1912 Edward Bok, editor of Ladies' Home Journal, fired 15 employees for dancing the turkey trot on their lunch break.

Think of the freedoms we have fought for and won - civil rights, women's rights, unions on strike. Just for today, put on those dancing shoes —

May 30, 1868 was the first National Decoration Day, proclaimed by Commander in Chief John A. Logan to honor the fallen Union soldiers. There had been many states and towns that had their own holidays to visit the graves of dead Union Soldiers, bringing flowers and small flags. Mary Ann Williams of the Soldiers Aid Society was credited with writing to many Northern papers suggesting a unified holiday. Logan was prompted to make May 30 that day and it wasn't until 1971 that Congress made the last Monday in May Memorial Day. Congress is always looking for a three day weekend like MLK day which we solemnly celebrate with a trip to Lake Geneva, Wisconsin and play eighteen holes.

Problematic was how to deal with the Southern soldier, who believed (wrongly to be sure) in the Southern Cause. Individual states had their own holidays for the visit to the grave but not many of those who had perished were retrieved for a burial in their hometown.

Memorial Day weekend is a holiday for parades, games, barbecues, maybe even some fireworks. A trip to the cemetery perhaps but most cemeteries make it a practice to put flags on all known service members. On this Memorial Day whether today or sometime this week, in between the festivities, take a moment to think upon the soldiers who fell.

How will you spend the day?

On May 31, 1949 Cleveland grocer/deli-catessan owner Charley Lupica started a four month encampment on a four foot wide plat-form atop a 60 foot flagpole. He swore he would stay there until his favorite team the Cleveland Indians won a championship pennant. He last-ed through bullies pelting him with cans and firecrackers, 100 degree heat, missed the birth of his fourth child and his wedding anniversary (wonder how Mrs. Lupica felt about all this).

The Indians didn't win the pennant and Lupica was starting to get a little too comfort-able up there. At last, Indians owner Bill Veeck had the pole towed with Lupica still up there all the way to municipal stadium for the final home game of the season. In front of 34k cheering Indians fans Lupica climbed down and kissed home plate.

He died 53 years later, never forgetting his quixotic cheerleading. He even had business cards made that identified him as "1949 Cleveland Indians Flagpole Sitter." I think Veeck should have given him lifetime season tix. And given Mrs. Lupica a fur coat and a diamond bracelet.

Sometimes there are things we gotta do even when others think we're an idiot. I've done a few of those things myself....

The Indians came in third place for the 1949 pennant.

Your favorite team and why?

____

____

____

____

June and if you're not barefoot, you're overdressed.

–Kai William Starks

On June 1, 1943 Harlem native Malcolm Little arrived for his army induction appointment at New York's Draft Board #59. He wore his best zoot suit—broad shouldered, high waisted, wide legged pants. He accessorized the suit with bright yellow shoes. He frizzed his naturally black hair with bright red gel.

He greeted the white soldier at the sign in desk. "Crazy-O, daddy-o, get me moving I can't wait to get in that brown {uniform}!"

A few weeks later a 4-F card came to Mr. Little's home. He was so relieved and never heard from the Army again. Later, he changed his name to X as in Malcom X, civil rights activist. Klinger could have learned from him.

Many countries have mandatory service even in peace time.
How do you feel about mandatory service?

June 2nd makes you think of the coronations, or at least it does me. And I'm not even thinking of Elizabeth II in her 1953 ceremony which opened the second Elizabethan age.

On June 2, 1974 Bhutan Crown Prince Jigme Singe Wangchuck donned the traditional yellow silk scarf and he was thus made King Druk Gyalpo of Bhutan, a landlocked country in the Himalayas. The people call their country The Land of the Thunder Dragon or Dryukal. Jigme had a big task ahead of him, squeezed between India and China. He has a nice philosophy, saying he preferred to measure Gross National Happiness instead of Gross Domestic Product.

He has four wives and a few consorts, ten children in all. The wives are all sisters and the quartet had a private ceremony in 1979 and a public ceremony in 1988. They live in the castle while Jigme prefers a solitary life in a log cabin a little higher in the mountains. In 2006, he abdicated to his son Jigme Khesar Namgyel Wangchuck who announced that he would only keep one wife—Jetsun Pema. They have two sons. And the entire clan all get along!

How should we measusre the success of a country? Can it be as simple as money?

While the family of Elizabeth II partied down that Platinum Jubilee, June 3 is a royal anniversary of a different sort. On this day in 1937, Elizabeth II's uncle Edward VIII who had renounced the throne six months prior, was married to American Wallis Simpson at the Chateau de Cande in France. The joint was loaned to them by Charles Bedaux. That day would have been Edward 8's father's 72d birthday, which sort of pissed off his widow. Families are tough, aren't they?

The wedding was a somewhat solemn affair because Wallis believed that Edward mishandled their version of Meg-xit. A morganatic marriage is one in which the wife gets all the bennies of being queen but any children she begets will not inherit the throne. Wallis was forty and unlikely… so that seemed like a perfect solution.

After the abdication, they had to wait for her divorce from her second husband Mr. Simpson. Thus the delay on getting the cake. Wallis wore a blue day gown that was in a color which became all the rage, known as Wallis Blue. The couple were married until the death of the Duke in 1972. Wallis passed on from complications of dementia in 1986. Her possessions, including some kickass jewelry or at least the ones that hadn't been stolen by her attorney, was bequeathed to the Pasteur Institute.

Wallis and Edward are buried at Frogmore, which of course is where Harry and Megs rented for a while.

What did you give up to marry the woman or man that you loved?

____

____

____

____

____

June 4th is a day of great significance in the history of horse racing, the sweet kiss of death and extreme weight loss methods.

On 1923 Brooklyn born Frank Hayes (thought to be 22 but maybe 35) was a mere stable hand and horse trainer, Hayes was given the opportunity to jockey in the prestigious Belmont Steeplechase for a 20-1 long shot mare Sweet Kiss. The favorite that year was the power house, er, horse, Gimme.

In order to prepare not just Sweet Kiss but himself, Hayes lost ten pounds over the course of twenty four hours—he taught all New York supermodels what's what with running, refusing water, no food whatsoever. He may have indulged in some diuretics and Metamucil but Ozempic wasn't on the market then. He clocked in at 130 pounds when the race started.

The crowd was surprised that Sweet Kiss and Gimme were within a few lengths for the first three laps but even more gobsmacked when on the fourth lap Sweet Kiss pulled out ahead of the pack. Who knows? Maybe Gimme was a gentleman and said "ladies first." Hayes then, apparently, had a heart attack and died. The odd thing is that Hayes' body remained in its saddle for three more laps to victory. In death, he was a phenomenal jockey.

It was the first and last win of his career. No losses, except his life of course. He was buried in his riding silks.

Sweet Kiss won a purse of $1,775 and is said to never have raced again, earning the moniker Sweet Kiss of Death. I wouldn't ride her, would you?

How far have you gone to achieve your dreams?

On June 5, 1956 Elvis Presley first performed Hound Dog on the Milton Berle Show. It was his second appearance on the show and he had been asked to sing without his guitar which might be what caused the problem.

Hound Dog is a 12 bar blues song composed by Mike Stoller and Jerry Leiber (no relation to moi unless there are royalty checks to be distributed.). It was originally recorded by Big Mama Thornton in 1952 and was pretty much her biggest hit. She gave it all a slow, angry, bluesy touch.

Without his guitar to cover his, er, manly parts and with Elvis wanting to give the song a little umph—he made his mark on the song, the television, and got himself the nickname Elvis the Pelvis.

Good morning and you're welcome.

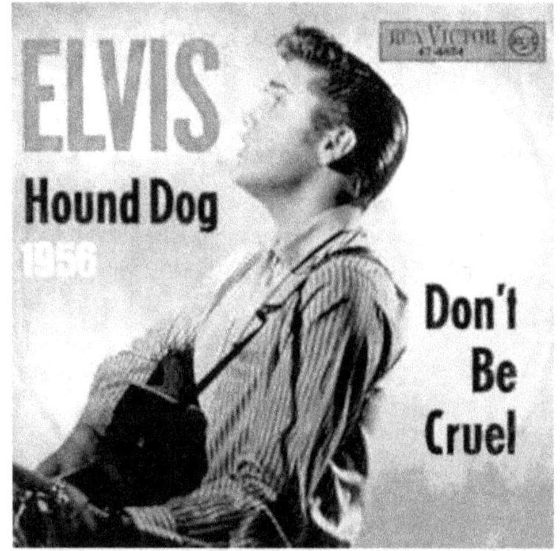

June 06

On June 6 1867 eighteen year old Archduchess Mathilde (you remember her from the Hapsburg family of Austria) was hiding a cigarette behind her back—concerned her nearby father would disapprove. Dresses being as long and voluminous as they were, she lit up her dress with some ash and died hours later. I think along with a cancer warning, cigarette packs should have a "might set your dress on fire and kill you!"

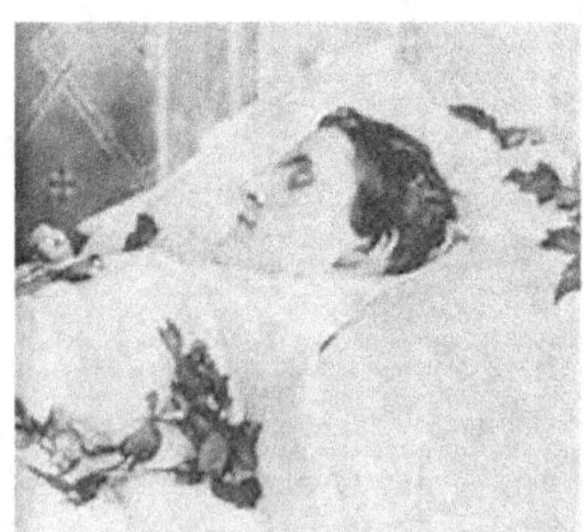

I only smoked when I worked construction as a teenager. I wanted to fit in with the guys. At the end of every day we'd drink coffee and vodka. Not something you'd find at Starbucks. I am grateful that I ditched the bad habits. What have you had to quit? Give yourself some props for that!

____

____

____

____

____

On June 7,1866 Lutheran saint Si'al passed on. As is customary for the Catholic and Anglican faiths, a saint is celebrated on the day he or she dies. Si'al was not a Lutheran, but rather a Catholic who had been baptized in 1848 and given the name Noah.

We know him as Chief Seattle. His mother and dad were of the Duwamish and Suquamish tribes respectively. He was a fierce warrior and ruled over a wide swath of what we now call Northwestern Washington.

The rival Chimakun tribe would keep sneaking up the Green River and raiding Noah/Si'al's land. He solved the problem of these unwanted guests by exterminating the entire Chimakun tribe. He owned slaves he captured in battles with other tribes. The Hudson Trading Company nickname for him was Le Gros which means "big guy" and he earned it being well over six feet. He had several wives, not at the same time as far as we can tell. He had seven children, including a daughter known as Princess Angeline who converted to Catholicism and devoted her life to good works.

He was very good if unlikely friends with David "Doc" Maynard, a Vermont emigre who was a pioneer, abolitionist, doctor, lawyer, businessman, and bigamist. When Maynard and some of his cohorts platted and took control of what we now call Seattle, Doc was insistent it be named for his friend, Si'al. He also insisted that the resolution creating the city include a clause that his first marriage to Lydia was annulled and his second marriage to Catherine made valid. Better than Henry VIII's methods.

In 1854 Si'al gave a speech in which he declared that white man's religion, *i.e.* Christianity, is written on stones so people don't forget its precepts. I guess he didn't know was that Mohammed, Joseph Smith and Moses all lost theirs.

You can hear the entire speech in the band Soundgarden's cover of "Into the Void" by Black Sabbath. If you want to bite the head off a bat in honor of Ozzy Osbourne that's your business and your health risk.

I have no idea why Si'al is a Lutheran saint. He died a Catholic and his funeral had elements of Catholic and his tribes' rituals. His burial suit was European, loaned to him by a local admirer who was obviously is never getting it back.

Princess Angeline continued her work for the poor and would sometimes be found on Seattle streets raptly doing her rosary. There is in Seattle the Angeline Center which helps women struggling with homelessness.

I guess I get out of this is you never know who your friends are going to be and they may have different beliefs and backgrounds and lifestyles than you.

Name a friend you like because of or inspite of your differences.

____

____

____

____

____

June 08

Jerome "Mr. Organic" Rodale was a writer and guru who proselytized healthy eating and exercise.

On June 8, 1971, he announced at a taping of The Dick Cavett Show that he had decided to live to be a hundred years old. "I have never felt better in my life," he added.

He didn't make it to the next commercial break. Cavett turned his attention to his other guest—columnist Pete Hamill. Rodale slumped to one side. "Are we boring you?" Cavett quipped.

Bad joke. In the next moment, Cavett was shouting "is there a doctor in the audience?" Two interns rushed up onto the stage and heroically performed CPR. Rodale was pronounced dead.

That episode never aired although many people claimed to have seen it. Rodale was 72.

I wake up every morning assuming this is my last day. One day I will be right. Treasure every minute! And every morning, pray Gratias Dominus Vigiles. Thank you Lord for waking me up!

June 09

June 9 is Donald Duck Day—in honor of Donald Fauntleroy Duck, created in 1934 by Walt Disney. Donald has appeared in more films than any other character in the Disney universe and more comics than anyone outside the superhero genre.

He is a great patriot and during WW2 he appeared in morale boosters such as "Der Feuhrer's Face" (it won an Oscar!) and a seven episode series that followed his adventures as an American soldier. He became the mascot of the Air Force's 309th fighter squadron and a slew of other fighter and bombardment squadrons. He is also the mascot of the Coast Guard.

In 1984 on the occasion of his 50th birthday his footprints were enshrined at Grauman's Chinese Theater. In 2005 he got his very own star in the Hollywood Walk of Fame.

Today, honor him by honoring your country! Whatever your talents, you have something to offer.

What can you do?

June 10th is Iced Tea Day. As far as I'm concerned, it as the true beginning of summer. If you're a Northerner like me you take it with ice and a slice of lemon. If you, dear reader, are a Southerner you gotta have the sugar and lots of it.

Tea is claimed to be invented by the Chinese mythological creature Shennog around 3000 b.c. The British imported globs of the stuff and contoured an afternoon snack around tea and finger sandwiches. Green tea was served cold with a healthy dollop of liquor. It wasn't until 1870s that Thomas Lipton opened up a tea shop in Glasgow, Scotland and made ice tea accessible to the Average Joe.

Then there was the 1904 St. Louis World's Fair. Miserably hot. What to serve the masses? Iced tea took on new life even without the liquor. Suddenly Northerners and Southerners united after the contentious Civil War. We even developed the Arnold Palmer with iced tea and lemonade! And, of course there's the tea concoction of Long Island.

My way of making ice tea—get a few Lipton bags and a bottle of water. Shove the bags into the water bottle and put it out on the porch, the balcony, or just next to a sunny window. Six hours later you've got yourself perfect iced tea. Pour! Throw in the cubes. Lemon slices and/or sugar. Sit out in the backyard. Or the parking lot if you don't have a yard. Relax—Summer has officially begun!

How do you take yours?

June 11

June 11 should be called "Bird Island Day" or perhaps "Fun Things You Can Do with Papier Mache" day. You decide.

On June 11, 1962 guards at Alcatraz prison made their usual rounds and it looked like four inmates—armed robber Frank Morris, bank robbing brothers Clarence and John Anglin and murderer Allen West—were peacefully counting sheep. Alas, no. Their blankies were stuffed with pillows and extra clothing and three of their four heads were actually models made of papier mache with some hair glued on.

Morris was the brains of the operation to escape from Alcatraz, the rocky isolated prison in San Francisco Bay which, since its opening in 1934, had never had a successful early bon voyage. Not from lack of trying. Morris's colleagues had carefully dug a tunnel to the top of the building and he had hidden a lifeboat made of purloined raincoats. The men, minus West who possibly overslept and didn't get out of his own cell, hustled to the lifeboats and set off for land. They were never found although many in their families claimed to hear from them from time to time. The next year there was a film Escape from Alcatraz with Clint Eastwood. The prison was closed and is now open for private events like Boy Scout camping trips. I'm not signing the permission slip for that field trip!

Now why was the joint called Bird Island? You have to go back years to Alaska where an eighteen year old pimp Robert Franklin Stroud murdered a bartender who was hitting on one of his mistresses, er, sources of income. He was sentenced to life in prison and after killing a guard, sent to Leavenworth. Solitary confinement. Twenty-three hours a day with one hour for lonely exercise. One rainy day, he found a nest with three birds which had been tossed from a tree. He nursed the birds back to health. Eventually, he ended up with three hundred canaries in his care and wrote the 1933 blockbuster Diseases of Canaries. He even found a cure for avian hemorrhagic septicemia. How did he finance all this? Stroud became a mixologist, making alcohol that was quite tasty and popular with inmates and guards alike. His profits went to bird seed.

When he was caught making the hooch, he was sent to Alcatraz. Conditions were harsh, he wasn't allowed to keep birds but word had gotten around about his ornithological tendencies. Alcatraz became known in the vernacular as Bird Island.

Continued on Next Page

June 11

Stround died in 1963. But he had the pleasure of seeing the 1962 movie Birdman of Alcatraz. The movie glossed over the dead bartender, the prison still, the dead guard at Leavenworth—indeed, all of Leavenworth. Burt Lancaster played Stroud as a kindly ornithologist who saved the lives of many a canary.

One of the most delicate, romantic scenes in the film is when Stroud/Lancaster is visited in prison by an elderly stranger, a woman whose dear bird was snatched from the talons of death by Stroud's medical regimen. She asks if there is anything she can do to repay him. He asks to see the contents of her purse. Puzzled, she complies, taking out a powder compact, lipstick, dainty handkerchief, a small vial of perfume. He inspects each one tenderly and makes clear it's been a long time since he's seen a woman. What hit the cutting room floor was probably a scene where afterwards he raped and killed the woman.

So to celebrate June 11, get out an old newspaper and rip it into strips, dip the strips in glue and get creative. Or maybe just go outside and look at the birds flying overhead.

June 12

On June 12, 1970 Dock Ellis started his day off the way he liked to. The Pittsburgh Pirates pitcher took a hit of the hallucinogen LSD and settled in for a long, strange trip in the privacy of his Los Angeles home.

An hour later, his girlfriend frantically pointed out that the sports page had him scheduled for an afternoon game in San Diego. He was the starting pitcher. Whoops! He managed to get to LAX to catch a flight to make the game ninety minutes before his opening pitch.

And what strange, strange game. In his own words "the ball was small sometimes. The ball was large sometimes. I saw the catcher. Sometimes I didn't. I started having a crazy idea in the fourth inning that Richard Nixon was the home plate umpire and once I pitched to Jimi Hendrix. He was holding a guitar and swinging it over the plate."

Ellis walked eight batters and hit one batter in the back. Nonetheless, he went the nine inning distance and delivered a 2-0 win over San Diego. This 35 year old right hander Dock really should have had a conversation with Just Say No to Drugs crusader first lady Nancy Reagan.

Lysergic Acid Diethylamide was discovered by Swiss chemist Albert Hofmann who was hoping to discover a cure for postpartum bleeding. LSD has been maligned for years but recently, serious attention has been paid to its use in treating various psychiatric disorders, including depression, anxiety, post traumatic stress disorder and addiction. It has had promising results particularly in treating alcoholism which is now treated by going to meetings with other alcoholics, getting gossip and picking up cuties now that the original rules of separate sex meetings have been changed.

Today, consider the strength of willpower of Dock Ellis—and let's not forget his girlfriend!—who were determined to not let down his team. Even if the President of the United States and Hendrix were behind home plate!

This, of course, is not an endorsement of doing acid. Especially when you have a game scheduled.

Your thoughts?

June 13 is National Sewing Machine Day. Celebrate by putting your index finger directly under the needle of a Singer….oh, never mind!

People have been hand sewing clothes, table linens, and other items since they first got hold of a skinned bison. But it was a labor intensive activity largely done by women. Clothes were expensive and became even more so when bison skins were replaced by cotton, silk and wool. When Anne Boleyn got axed, she bequeathed to her loyal ladies in waiting her wardrobe of gowns. Today, you'd think she was being a cheapskate but no, clothes were damn valuable even if they weren't Chanel.

In the Eighteenth Century, looms were created that made fabric instantly cheap. That's when inventors turned their attention towards the idea of replicating the success of the looms with a mechanical device that would do the sewing. Cabinet maker Thomas Saint patented a hand cranked sewing machine in 1791 although it's not clear that he ever went beyond the drawing board phase. It wouldn't be until 1851 when Isaac Singer patented a sewing machine with a foot pedal that things really started going well. He and Elias Howe ended up in court fighting over who should get credit. My money is on Singer. Singer sewing machines ruled until 1946 when a company called Toyoda (NOT a typo) built its first sewing machine—it wouldn't be until later that the company would take its skills and start making cars under the company name Toyota.

In the early 20th century nearly every home in America had a sewing machine even as store made clothes were getting cheaper and cheaper. When I was in eighth grade, all girls were required to take a year of Home Ec (boys took Shop although Linda Smith got to take shop because she complained). Half of my year was spent sewing a dress that I would be required to wear for one full day of school. One of the most humiliating days of my life. Boys (and Linda Smith) made pencil holders and book shelves.

How can YOU celebrate this special day? Maybe bring your machine out if you have one and give it a nostalgic run. Or look in your closet and appreciate the work that went into each item—oh, and maybe decide that the dress you HAD TO HAVE five years ago but haven't worn in four and it doesn't fit anyway, go all Idina Menzel and let it go.

Home Ec or Shop?
Your choice—

June 14

June 14, 1777 the Continental Congress of what would become the USA approved the design of its flag. The stripes
represent the original colonies (fun fact: Maine you would
expect to be a state, but quel surprise!, it was a colony of
another state…name it, no fair using Mr. Google). The stars
represent the states. The red represents the blood brave soldiers spilled in defense of our country. The white to represent the purity of our defense of freedom.

Massachusetts, supposedly the most anti-colonialist group
of the original thirteen colonies, held Maine as a colony. Maine
got its freedom when the Missouri Compromise, meant to avoid
Civil War, allowed for Missouri to join the country but only if an
anti-slavery state (Maine) was added.

June 15

June 15, 1215. at Runnymede, a swampy suburb twenty or so miles from west London, there
was a resolution on a food fight which resulted in the beginning of democracy. We should be
grateful, especially before we chow down. It was called the Magna Carta.

English kings had the right to "purveyance" which is a fancy ass word for stealing food.
In the Middle Ages, food was quite valued, there were many years of bad crops and the idea
that the king might show up at your doorstep and take (not pay for) food that you've been
growing all year…well, it just didn't sit well. Especially with lords and ladies who were trying
to protect and produce for hundreds of people.

The lords and ladies rebelled and forced King
John to affix his seal on the Magna Carta, a document that lays out how the king was going to damn
well act in the future and the rights of folk against
that king. At Runnymede, King John was cornered
by nearly 40 nobles who were in no mood for
more. The human rights were minimal by our new
standards—just lay off my harvest, dude. If you

read the whole thing, it has a lot to say about having a unified system of measuring food and
drink (especially beer and corn) for sale and if the king ran off with some of your stuff he'd
have to pay up immediately. This of course put the king in a bind since he was responsible for
his household and for England's army. Where was he supposed to come up with vittles?

In any event, a lot of the Magna Carta became the makings of the American Declaration
of Independence and Constitution. Except for the food part. So today, be grateful that no
monarch of England or American president has the right to grab that last box of Oreos from
your nightstand. And that you have a republic meant to protect you from potentates.

What freedoms do you hold dearest?

<hr>
<hr>
<hr>

June 16, 1963—ah, what a time! I was just two but I already knew that we were in a fight to the death with the evil empire communist of the Soviet Union—they were out to destroy us Americans and every week our nursery school had an atomic bomb drill, hiding under our little desks like that was going to help matters.

The Cold War was best described in the Russian born Irving Berlin song "Anything You Can Do I Can Do Better" which was tucked into the 1950 Broadway show Annie Get Your Gun. Soviet Russia particularly put a lot of stock (that's Vladivostok comrade) in the space race. Orbiting, getting to the moon, showing off rockets. And what did we do?

John Wayne would say, "Pilgrim, we're going to do it better!"

On June 16, the Soviet Union played the "oh, so you got beaten by a girl" card by shooting off Vostok 5 and 6 with two female astronauts. Vostok 5 was the launcher and Vostok 6 was the glamour girl. Er, woman. After Vostok 5 launched her, Valentina Tereshkova in 6 spent the next three days in space proving that even Soviet women were superior to any red blooded American male astronaut. She orbited the earth 48 times over 71 hours, which was more than all the American astronauts combined at that time.

Born in 1937 to really authentic peasant parents in Maslenniko, she worked in a textile factory. When she was 22 she signed up for a parachute jump. She liked it. More jumps followed and she caught the attention of the Council of Soviets and their space program.

Valentina actually had no manual control over her space rocket which is a good thing as she had no pilot training. She was a passenger, but a great publicity tool for the Soviets. She returned to earth to acclaim—she received the Order of Lenin and Hero of the Soviet Union for her efforts. She attracted the attention of Prime Minister Kruschev who saw another use for her.

He introduced her to Andrian Nikolayev, a fellow cosmonaut and hottie. They married in November 1963 after a whirlwind courtship Soviet style. They had a daughter. They divorced and Valentina was elected to the Supreme Soviet and later the Duma, both of which are sort of like the Senate of the Communists of the time. And when I say elected, I mean that she was chosen, something like what Mike Madigan used to do here in Illinois and since every Soviet citizen was required to vote and she was running unopposed she got 100% of the vote every time!

We now regard space travel as tourism for billionaires. If you were given a free ridde would you take it?

____

____

____

____

____

For those of you who think Valentine's Day is a Hallmark holiday, I would like you to consider June 17th as the REAL DAY OF LOVE!

Let's consider the second wife of Shahab-ud-din Muhammad Kurram. Kurram was otherwise known as Shah Jahan. That second wife, born Arjumand Banu Begum, would acquire the regnal name Mumtaz Mahal (trans: Chosen of the Palace) they were engaged in 1607 while in their early teens but didn't marry until 1612. Jahan had to first marry Qandahari Mahal in order to keep her dynasty the Safavid under control. After marrying Mumtaz he went on to acquire three more wives, each of whom aided his creation of an empire that stretched all across the continent. Mahal apparently was instrumental in arranging these marital/political alliances.

Mumtaz, being the child of a lower order nobleman, was considered a mere consort but she wielded a lot of power and was known as a brilliant tactician. And most of all, she was Jahan's one true love. The couple had thirteen children* but I won't list all their names because you'll get bored. As they approached the birth of their fourteenth child, it appeared that nothing could get in the way of their happiness. However, on June 17, 1631 Mumtaz died while giving birth to Gauhara Begum.**

*No, really, I'm not going to do that because I'll get bored and misspell a name and some of the more brilliant folk will tell me I'm an idiot at a speller.

**Fun Fact: Jahan is widely understood to have ordered all his daughters to never marry—some in our modern age would say "what a prick." However, another interpretation is that he wanted his daughters to be shielded from being used for the political purposes as all but one of his marriages had been.

Continued on Next Page

June 17

She was temporarily buried at Zainabad Gardens by the River Tapti and then transported to a spot near the Yamuna River. Jahan spent a year in isolation, tough to do when you're running an empire. During that time, he designed a crypt to be her forever home. It would take 22 years to complete and would be known as the Taj Mahal*** a monument to a love that never dies. Jahan died in 1666 and was placed in the crypt next to his beloved****. Dynastic battles amongst his sons ensued—there would be no family reunions with that crowd. So today might be a day for you to think about YOUR undying love—do you have one?

***Locals in the nearby town Ofgra started calling it Taj Mahal because Taj was a shortening of the first name Mumtaz and Mahal, well, you get the point.

****Not quite. Mahal and Jahan were encased in twin crypts in a garden outside the building. With all the regicide going down there was every possibility of body snatching and whatnot. The couple's eldest daughter Jahanara Begum knew what her brothers were about.

What's the most reckless thing you've done for love?

____

____

____

____

____

____

____

____

____

____

June 18

June 18, 1815 was a decisive day in European history and something of a a sartorial adventure. Napoleon Bonaparte* was managing his comeback as Emperor of France and was shoving the Brits across the Channel. The day before he had defeated Prussian F.M. Von Blucher at Ligny and also the 7th coalition forces at Quatre Bras under the command of the British Duke of Wellington. On the 18th, Bonaparte looked like he was going to be emperor of all he surveyed. Everybody loves a comeback, right? And he looked fab!

There's lots you can read about the Battle of Waterloo, the name Waterloo having come to mean a disastrous defeat, generally in politics. But also in music, namely ABBA's blockbuster "I feel like I win when I lose."

Napoleon's clothes tell a story—

He arrived at battle in a green, gold and white uniform of the chasseurs a cheva— his imperial guard—with a gray coat. Pretty regular but he added the wow! factor with a cloak made in the style of the Berber Burnoubs. The cloak was lined with silk and embroidered with eagles and with a gold clasp which joined two Napoleonic bees.

Wellington arrived at the field of battle wearing a pretty drab blue cloak over his uniform. He was not distracted by sartorial concerns. Within hours, he had routed Napoleon and four days later Napoleon surrendered and abdicated, thus ending the hundred days comeback reign—or, as the French call it, "zut alor!" Wellington's 7th coalition entered Paris on July 7 and Napoleon was exiled to a shotgun shack castle on the island of St. Helena. His cloak was seized by F.M. von Blucher who presented it to the Prince of Wales

June 19

Twelve year old Annie Ide had the horrific, tragic, terrible, no good rotten misfortune of having her birthday on December 25! The mournful deprived child had to share her day with every man woman and child of the Christian faith. Luckily, her father was friends with the author Robert Louis Stevenson—best known as author of Treasure Island. Stevenson was getting on in years and decided he didn't need his own birthday. On June 19, 1891 he formally transferred his birthday to Annie in a letter she received the next day June 20:

> I, Robert Louis Stevenson … in consideration that Miss A.H. Ide, daughter of H.S. Ide, in the town of St. Johnsbury … was born, out of all reason, upon Christmas Day and is therefore, out of all justice, denied the consolation and profit of a Proper Birthday:
>
> And considering that I, the said Robert Louis Stevenson, have attained an age when oh, we never mention it, and that I now have no further use for a birthday of any description ….
>
> Have transferred and do hereby transfer to the said A.H. Ide, All and Whole of my right and privileges the 13th day of November, formerly my birthday, no, hereby, and henceforth, the birthday of the said A.H. Ide to have, hold, exercise and enjoy the same in the customary manner, by the sporting of fine raiment, eating of rich meats and receipt of gifts ….
>
> Robert Louis Stevenson

I share my birthday July 23rd with Woody Harrelson. While there were quite a number of years that nobody, not a single one remembered mine, this year I have saved up for my Angel parfum. I don't think it's Woody's fault or because folk are so bedazzled by his special day and enormous talent that they overlook mine!

What celebrity/outlaw/royalty/saint/billionaire do you share a birthday with?

On the eve of what's shaping up to be a hot summer, what with a so called "heat dome" about to descend on us like a satanic veil, it's nice to know that June 20 is National Ice Cream Soda Day! The confection was created in 1874 during a celebration of the 50th anniversary of the science and technology museum The Franklin Institute. Robert McCay Green, a soda fountain manufacturer noticed that some of the fountains were attracting more customers. On a whim, he added a scoop of ice cream and voila!

The cooling delight was an immediate hit but not without its controversies. Some people posited that the ice cream soda was sinful, particularly because the ice cream could (quel horreur!) mask the little dab will do you addition of alcohol to the soda. Many communities banned the sale of ice cream sodas on Sundays. Which led to the creation of the ice cream sundae—if you were going to have a chaser, you'd have to bring your own flask!

There are many variations on the soda. The purple cow combines grape soda and ice cream and it's particularly popular in the south. The egg cream combines milk seltzer and a flavored soda. Northeasterners find it quite tasty. And who can argue with the snow white white which combines ice cream and 7-up or sprite. I'm more of a root beer float woman but I do have a friend who favors orange sherbet and 7-up.

Enjoy the day! If you play your cards right, you could have one for breakfast, lunch and dinner each!

June 21, 1926 marked the fiftieth anniversary of the Wimbledon Championships and for that auspicious occasion, King George V and Queen Mary handed out commemorative gold medals to 35 past champions. These marvels of the court included France's Suzanne Lenglen who had only lost one march between 1919 and 1926. She had six Wimbledon championships to display in her boudoir along with two Olympic medals.

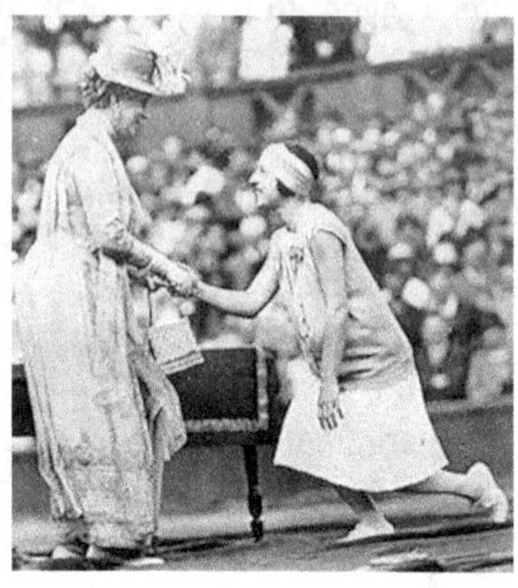

Born in 1899, Suzanne was taught tennis by her father. This nascent Earl Woods would place Suzanne on one side of the net and he would place a handkerchief on the other side of the net. Then he'd serve. Suzanne's job was to lob the ball at the handkerchief. When she succeeded, her father would make a smaller target by folding the handkerchief in half. They'd go back and forth until she was unable to hit a coin.

She was the Tiger Woods or the Williams sisters of ladies' tennis and she revolutionized the sport—making it faster and more aggressive. She also altered the course of tennis history in 1919 in her first Wimbledon appearance by wearing a loose flimsy dress with—get this—scandalous short sleeves! She completed this ensemble with white silk stockings rolled to her knees, point shoes and a white floppy hat! Quel Horreur! Prior to this time, women wore full length gowns with de rigueur petticoats, long sleeves and a suitable hat. In later tournaments, Lenglen would modify her attire with a bandeau, no sleeves at all, and she even introduced color as opposed to regulation white.

But on this day, she curtsied to the Queen as she received her commemorative award and looked carefree and relaxed while the Queen looked trussed up like a Christmas turkey. Langley died at the age of 39 under mysterious circumstances. The official cause of death was anemia which was pretty treatable in the late thirties. Some thought perhaps leukemia. And some thought a broken heart, as her long term romance with Baldwin Baldwin (no that's not a mistake) did not result in matrimony because of a pesky impediment known as Mrs. Baldwin.

June 22

On this day, June 22, 1940 the French suffered one of the most humiliating defeats of World War II and the Nazis thought they were delivering the most incredible revenge. Both sides were in for a surprise.

Beginning on the tenth of May and continuing into June 21 1940 the Nazis had been ripping through France. But the 2 Compiegne Armistice was supposed to kind of stop all that destruction. The agreement allowed the Germans to retain most of Northern and Western France, to take control of French access to the English Channel and all other Atlantic Ports.

There was a railroad car parked in the Alsace-Lorraine region where the Germans signed off on the Armistice of 1918 (WW I). Well, that's where the Germans wanted the signing of the 2 Compiegne Armistice just to sort of remind the French who was boss. After the signing the site was pretty demolished including a decades old monument depicting a German eagle impaled by a French sword. The demolished eagle and the railroad car were sent to Berlin as tribute to Hitler.

The Armistice went into effect at midnight on the 25th but that didn't really stop antagonisms. The Germans ended up controlling all of France. Then they lost it, in large part due to the help of the Allies and by April 1945 Hitler's symbolic train carriage revenge was forgotten.

Sometimes people do you wrong. Way wrong. And you want revenge. But that's a dish—so they say—best served cold. Or maybe forgiveness does the purpose. How about you?

June 23

June 23 is national Typewriter Day in which we celebrate Christopher Latham Sholes, Wisconsin publisher and Free Soiler* and inventor of QWERTY. Look at the top left top shelf of your keyboard. That's QWERTY.

It's a very special day for me. I grew up in the foster system and pretty much could go from one placement to another with all my possessions in a Hefty bag. Except for my Smith Corona electric typewriter. I remember one placement where I had an "office" in the garage and I would huddle up there every night to work. I remember

*Free Soilers was a party with a platform pretty much exclusively devoted to abolitionism. Seeing as how the Democratic party was pro-slavery, the Free Soilers of Wisconsin joined up with the Republicans who were like minded on the issue of eliminating slavery.

Continued on Next Page

one typewriter being borrowed while I was in law school by another resident of the YMCA—wow, was she proud of herself when she pawned it and I nearly flunked my Uniform Commercial Code final paper! Today nobody much uses a typewriter except of course Tom Hanks who keeps 150+ typewriters at his Playtone offices and one at home to write notes to friends. But if you have a computer, a laptop, or even act like a teenager texting your friends it might seem puzzling the arrangement of the letters.

The first typewriter was invented in 1714 by Henry Mill and its letters were pretty much like a Marconi dispatch. For the next century and a half there were all sorts of innovations but Sholes and his partners Carlos

Gidden and Samuel Willard Soule really wanted regular folk to have the opportunity to print their correspondence almost as if they had the Guttenberg Press at their fingertips. In 1867 Sholes put together a prototype of a typewriter that sort of resembled a piano with black ebony and white ivory keys. On June 23, 1868 Sholes applied for a patent for this typewriter.

His contribution to the evolution of the typewriter really wasn't in the design of the actual typewriter but in the placement of the letters. Typewriters had always been arranged so that the keystrokes were in line with the alphabet—ABCDEF, etc. Fingers would sometimes jam the keys. It was a slow process to type out a letter but Sholes had a counter-intuitive vision of how to distribute keystrokes between each hand so that typing could be done with speed and efficiency. Watch how you type on your computer or laptop. Most English words are going to use something from the left hand and then something from the right and you're going from the front row to the second to the third all within a single sentence.

Typewriters became an utterly essential element of the office along with short-hand which don't get me started—it's a dead language I once knew. Sholes' patent #79265 transformed our lives. Too bad he sold his patent for $12k while one of his business partners held out for royalties that are estimated to have netted him $1.5m. So I guess the moral of the day is don't get self conscious about how you're using Sholes' invention and don't sell out on a great idea when you have one.

On this day June 24 we mourn the passing of the last known Chelonoidis Niger Abingdonii otherwise known as Lonesome George. He was a tortoise of the subspecies known as Pinta Island Tortoise as that's where they called home on one of the Galapagos Islands. Believed to have been born in 1910, he died in 2014. He was the endling of his kind. His last days were spent in the  care of the Charles Darwin Research Station on the island of Santa Cruz as the vegetation on Pinta had been decimated by feral goats. But you can still visit him at the Galapagos National Park as he was taxidermied.

He might be Lonesome because he was an endling (last of his subspecies with no possibility of reproduction) but some folks believe he was named for the American actor George Gobel who had a popular eponymous The George Gobel Show in the '50s. Mr. Gobel was known as a country singer and comedian with a low key style in a stark contrast to someone like Milton Berle. Gobel sometimes might have given the impression of being melancholic or maybe just resigned to the vagaries of life. He was born nine years after his Galapagos tortoise but he died in 1991.

My favorite Gobel quote—"never put off til tomorrow what you can do today because tomorrow's going to be bad enough as it is."

So today, in honor of Lonesome George the tortoise, take your time because sometimes you just don't have a choice—it's pretty hot out there! And in honor of his namesake, still try to get it all done. Me? I have a broken washing machine and dryer, an air conditioner that is shot, and no internet. By the end of the day I hope I have everything under control. Then I will slooooooooowly crawl under the covers and take a nap!

June 25 is national Work from Home Day! I'm not making this up—and the history of work and residence is pretty much full circle thang!*

When we went with an agricultural economy, there wasn't anything like long commutes and grabbing a Starbucks on the way to the office. The average worker lived, worked and took care of their children all in the same place. Even the notion of a "stay at home mom" didn't exist because said mom was out on the field with baby strapped to her back just like everybody else.

With the industrial revolution, folks went to a factory that was on prime real estate—can't move onsite so housing became separate from work. Now we have public transportation, fast food drive thru, and the class warfare of corner office versus cubicle versus open plan.

In 2017, only 5.2% of Americans worked from home—largely creative freelance types (me! me! me!). With Covid a lot more folks figured out how to do it—and we're liking it! According to National Today surveys, 52% of Americans would like to continue working from home even after things go back to "normal." Workplace morale is pretty evenly split, but hey, when is morale ever perfect? With 82% of workers saying their residences are perfectly equipped for work at home, why would big business reopen that downtown skyscraper high rent locale?

So today, in honor of Work from Home Day, a day that may become more a part of our culture. And so, to honor the day and create its own tradition, let's celebrate with

NO SHIRT, NO SHOES, NO PROBLEM Day!

And just like the old commercial, "okay, what are you wearing, JAKE from State Farm?"

June 26th is a solemn day, but one that has an element of redemption. Today is the saint day of Pelagius of Cordoba, Spain. The Catholic church generally celebrates the homegoing of saints, when they have their return to the Lord. On June 26th 926 a.d. Pelagius aka San Pelayo Martir went home to the Lord at the age of 13. At the age of ten he had been presented as a hostage/gift/guest to the Caliph Abd-ar Rahman III of al-Andalusa in exchange for a relative being held by the Caliph. Something went wrong with the deal and Pelagius was kept for three years.

Now there's no dispute that Pelagius was a handsome young man. And no dispute that he was pious in his Christian faith. At thirteen he was given a choice by the Caliph who pretty much functioned as his father since he had been transferred by his family. In the earliest version of the story, the Caliph is rumored to have made him a proposition of a, uh, sexual nature. In later versions, the Caliph demanded Pelagius convert to Islam. At the time, Spain was the center of a religious and cultural war with Islam.

Pelagius declined whatever offer he was given and he was then tortured for six hours. The depiction of his dismemberment is painted by Master of Becerril and is titled The Martyrdom of St. Pelagius. Again, there are a couple of versions of how things went down. There's also a version in which he was catapulted over the walls of the city, presumably to hit the rocks of the river encircling the city. Either way, he survived and endured and then was decapitated with his piety intact.

This young man became a cult figure and the United Nations ended up declaring this day June 26th as International Day Against Drug Abuse and Illicit Trafficking as well as the International Day in Support of Victims of Torture. Pelagius is the patron saint of abandoned people, torture victims, and (not sure why) the town of Castro Urdiula in Northern Spain. He's also got the Seminary of Pelagius in Cordoba which has one of the largest collections of religious texts.

It's a downer holiday, right? Like you can't really give your friends Pelagius gifts and a party just doesn't sound right. A visit from the Pelagius Bunny? Fuggedaboutit!

But there's a bright side. Today is also Forgiveness Day. No, the United Nations didn't make it explicit but it is a true holiday. Forgiveness is something where we think we're giving someone else a gift, something they may or may not deserve. I think forgiveness is a gift we give ourselves so we can move on with our lives.

Today consider honoring 13 year old Pelagius with a forgiveness. Doesn't mean you have to like the transgressor or even talk to them ever again. Just take the weight off your shoulders and let it go. Tears optional.

Who will you forgive to relase YOU?

On June 27, 1940 John Godfrey Knauff settled into his seat at the Brooklyn Dodgers v. Chicago Cubs game. Sixty years of age, it was his very first ball game—but he had to be there because it was "Jack Norworth Day" at the stadium and furthermore he would be given a sold gold lifetime ballpark pass by the MLB.

Knauff, under his stage name Jack Norworth, had written the song "Take Me Out to the Ball game" in 1908 when he was a mere lad of 29. He came up with the notion while perusing an ad on the New York subway about the sport. He handed the lyrics to his friend Albert von Tilzer who put it to music.*

The song told the story of a young Irish gal named Katie Casey who gets "baseball fever". When a suitor asks to take her out, she agrees but ONLY if they go to a ball game. Tilzer's company—York Music Company—produced a series of painted glass lantern slides so that the song and the story-line could be shared with people who weren't even in the stadium!

The song has gone through many incarnations and changes—most recently last year when the minor league Hartford Yard Goats got rid of "peanuts and cracker jacks" from its rendition. Within its friendly confines are "buy me a hot dog and yard goats hat." Yep, that takes some getting used to.

BTW , the Dodgers won 5–4. Knauff is not recorded as ever attending another game. He thought it boring.

---

*Nora Bayes is often credited as the co-writer of the song instead of von Tilzer. She was Knauff's first wife, he was her second of five. As part of their prenup he agreed to never write music with von Tilzer again. Bayes was a talented actress, singer, and composer—she and Jack went on to write "Shine on Harvest Moon"

June 28, 1914 Gavrilo Princip walked into Mortiz Schiller's deli in Sarajevo and ordered a burek—a beef and potato filled pastry. It was 1914 and Princip had just tried

to work up his nerve to kill Prince Franz Ferdinand Carl Ludwig Joseph Maria of Austria, the heir presumptive* of the Austria-Hungary throne. Maybe it was nerves, maybe it was a malfunctioning of his pistol. Maybe it was bad timing. He decided to treat or console himself with a burek.

Earlier that day Nedeliko Cabrinovic had fired at Ferdinand but hadn't succeeded in putting that bad boy prince down. As Gavrilo Princip was biting into his burek Ferdinand was on his way to the hospital to visit and give comfort to those who had been injured in the Cabrinovic attack. Unfortunately, his chauffeur lost his way on the busy Sarajevo streets and the car stalled directly in front of the deli. Gavrilo couldn't believe his luck and walked out, shooting Ferdinand and his wife the Serene Highness Sophie.** Ferdinand's last words were "sterbe nicht bleibe am leben fur unsere kinder."***

Thus began World War 1. Sophie and Ferdinand were dead within the hour. Princip was sentenced to 20 years in jail. He died of tuberculosis a few years later. He was put in an unmarked grave but in 1920 his body was exhumed to be placed in the heroes of the Vidoudan chapel with the inscription "blessed is he who lives forever he has something to be born for."

Twenty million people would die during World War 1. All because Princip had to stop for a burek!

*An heir presumptive is someone who is presumed to be the heir to a royal title. The situation was a little complicated because of an unfortunate incident at Mayerling in which the true heir killed himself after killing his lover who may have been the illegitimate daughter of his father.

**When Ferdinand was courting Sophie Chotek, the palace informed him that he couldn't marry this mere commoner. So she became a "Serene Highness" (ihre durch laucht) which is code for "she ain't good enough to be his wife".

***Don't die darling live for our children!

The Globe Theatre was William Shakespeare's hangout in London. He wrote a gazillion five act plays that pretty much went on forever. During the action, audience members often wandered about hanging with their friends. Serving girls sold beer, mead, wine and all sorts of food. Shakespeare worked with a lot of other authors and directors called the Lord Chamberlain's Men and some people think he may not have been the only one to write plays attributed to him. The Globe was built in 1599 but had a short run. It burned down on June 29, 1613 during a scene which Henry VIII's entrance was heralded to the audience. The roof of the theatre was made of wood and thatch. No fire inspectors, I'm guessing.

The Globe was rebuilt the next year but with the English Civil Wars, theatre productions were momentarily forbidden.

On June 30, 1936 Margaret Mitchell's book Gone with the Wind* was released. It had been rejected by 38 publishers, many of them citing the incendiary nature of how race relations were portrayed. The book was an instant best seller and the next year garnered Mitchell a Pulitzer and a movie deal.

I first encountered gwtw when I was in a foster care home and the residents were allowed to blow off homework to watch the film on television. Nobody opted for homework. I remember feeling uncomfortable particularly when Hattie McDaniel was dealing with Vivian Leigh. None of the other foster kids, black or white, appeared to have any particular feeling one way or another but maybe that's because they were just glad to not be consigned to their rooms for "quiet time" and homework.

I read the book later that year and was struck by its ambition but again I was uncomfortable. HBO was embroiled in a controversy as they initially pulled the movie from the lineup and then returned it with a disclaimer that the movie denied the horrors of slavery. Embedded within the showing are two panel discussions how flawed the movie is.

*Mitchell's working title was Baa Baa Black Sheep—now that would have been a poor choice. Instead she went with a line from Ernest Dowson's poem Non Sum Qualis eram Bonae Sub Regno Cynarae, a poem about love and loss.

Any suggestions for HBO?

———————————————————————

———————————————————————

———————————————————————

———————————————————————

———————————————————————

J uly and girls just want to have sun!

–Haley Marie Olsen

On July 1, 1946, Operation Crossroads began—a series of 23 nuclear weapons tests which would be conducted by the United States over the next twelve years. The explosions quite outdid any Fourth of July fireworks and were conducted at the Bikini Atoll which was chosen because the atoll was remote and not in the path of ship or air travel.

This test on July 1—aka Event Baker—was an underwater detonation and it created quite an above water commotion called the Wilson Cloud.

Meanwhile, French automobile engineer and fashion designer Louis Reard was playing around with the notion of a two piece bathing suit. Mind you, he didn't invent this thing. Two piece bathing attire could be found in many cultures. But the notion of a two piece suit in modern western culture was, well, explosive. Especially as skimpy as he envisioned it. In July 1946, Reard opened his Parisian shop to sell his bikini He's pictured here with one of his models wearing what we now would consider quite a tame bikini compared to what gals wear today.

You may now go back to looking at kim kardashian.

I think my days of wearing a bikini are over.
How about you?

On this day, July 2, 1776 Massachusetts statesman John Adams wrote his wife that "the Second of July, 1776 will be the most memorable epocha* in the history of America. I am apt to believe that it will be celebrated, by succeeding generations, as a great anniversary festival!"

Well, not exactly, no offense to you Mr. Future President, but the second was the date of the declaration that we weren't taking no more guff from King George the Mad. Instead, the Fourth is when America ratified that declaration!

Still, if you want to get the party started early, raise a tall one to our second president. Oh, and get one out of the fridge for me!

Every signatory on the Fourth knew they were committing treason to the Brits and had to be prepared to lose their property and possibly their lives. I used to think John Hancock, the first to sign, was a bit of a jerk making his signature so LARGE but these days I think he was making a statement—"If you're going to hang us, start with me!"

*Epocha is the old fashioned way of saying "epoch"—just remember, English is a living language.

July 03

July 3, 1862 was no day to be in Pennsylvania. Particularly in Gettysburg, where a battle between Union and Confederate forces raged. Over three thousand Union soldiers would be killed, more on the outnumbered Confederate side. On the third, twenty year old Jennie Wade was kneading bread at her sister's house. The sister had recently given birth and Jennie and her mother were helping out.

A bullet flew through the window, striking Jennie's shoulder and piercing her heart. She died instantly. Because the Confederates were retreating through the area, the presumption is that she was shot by one of their sharpshooters. She was quickly buried in a coffin that was meant for a Confederate general, but hey, he was just going to have to wait and bloat up in the heat.

On July 4th her mother baked 15 loaves of bread for Union soldiers in the area, using the dough Jennie had been preparing. The sister's house became known as the Jennie Wade House with a museum. In 1882 The United States Senate voted the mom a pension because of her and Jennie's efforts on behalf of the Union. Jennie's body was moved to the Evergreen cemetery near the body of her presumed fiancé Jack Skelly who was wounded at a nearby battle. He was being treated at a Confederate field hospital where he met a friend from school in Gettysburg. He gave him a note to transmit to Jennie. He died July 12 without ever knowing of her death and she never knew of his. The note was found on the dead body of the Confederate soldier.

A monument complete with her holding a loaf of bread was built and it matches the one at the Jennie Wade House. She is the only civilian casualty in the Gettysburg battle who was a civilian hit directly by enemy fire. A perpetual flag flies over her statue at the Evergreen and Jennie is one of only two women to have that honor—Betsy Ross being the other one. A small coin purse found in Jennie's clothes was donated to the Jennie Wade House museum.

When I die, I don't think I have much of anything that anybody will want donated to them. Happy Fourth of July. It wasn't just 1776 when people were making extraordinary sacrifices. Take a moment in between the parade, the barbecue, and the fireworks to say a quiet thank you to those who fought and those who were just making bread to feed them. *True courage—to wake up the morning after your child's death and get to work. Could you?*

July 4 is a day of parades, fireworks, barbecues, and biting one's thumb at the British (go read the first scene of Romeo and Juliet). But the fourth has not been a good day for presidents. July 4, 1826 was homegoing day for founding fathers Thomas Jefferson and John Adams.

Jefferson was 83 and attended by his doctor Robley Dunglison, his grandson T.J. Randolph, his granddaughter Virginia Randolph, and her hubby Nicholas Trist at Jefferson's home, Monticello, in Virginia. He had been struggling for some time and his last words are described as either "is it the fourth?" or "no, doctor, nothing more" as he declined another round of painkilling opiates. One of my dearest friends on his deathbed wouldn't take a last dose of morphine on a plastic lollipop so I stuck the lollipop in some white wine and said "happy hour." It worked, but it was weird.

Meanwhile, up in the Northeast, ninety year old John Adams passed on but not before grousing his last words "Thomas Jefferson still survives." Sorry, Adams, you're wrong again (see my post about July 2). Jefferson had died five hours earlier. The two men had a fraught relationship but were comrades at the signing of the Declaration of Independence, the Revolutionary War, and being Presidents. And they had sort of patched up their differences.

Meanwhile, James Monroe our fifth president, died on July 4th 1831 with the cause of death presumed to be tuberculosis. His last words apparently referenced James Madison a president and friend for four decades. "I regret that I should leave this world without again beholding him."

But the real pity is Zachary Taylor, our twelfth president, who celebrated the fourth in 1850 without a care in the world. At a party he indulged in a popular confection of cherries mixed with fresh milk. Sort of like Ben & Jerry's Cherry Garcia. And he had seconds. Thirds. Maybe he snuck a fourth serving—after all, who can deny a leader of the free world? He walked home and felt oddly chilled. By July 9th he was dead—possibly by poisoning or possibly by cholera. The milk would be the culprit here either way.

Then there are presidents who have had a great fourth. President Thomas Whitmore got to fly a jet and battle aliens although of course he did have his wife die the day before. Never heard of him? Check out the 1996 movie Independence Day. I did last night and cried through most of it. Especially his rousing speech "go fourth America!"

Happy holiday and be grateful for all the sacrifices our founding fathers made so that Harry and Meghan could have a place to retreat to when the toils of royal life got to be too much.

July 5, 1898 is an important date in America's pastime—because on this date, Miss Lizzie Arlington* became the first woman to play with a major league men's baseball team.

Lizzie was born in Pennsylvania in 1875, 1876, or maybe 1877.** She was what we used to call "a tomboy." She was the first gal in her hometown to learn to ride a bike and she enjoyed hunting, fishing, rowing, and whatnot. But she was at her best when she took to the field as a right handed pitcher and occasional infielder. At age thirteen, she signed with the Women's League Cincinnati Reds and later with the Young Ladies Baseball Club of New York. She had an assured and aggressive style—and made a not so shabby $100 a week.

Theatrical and sports promoter William J. Connor recognized talent and incidentally how to make a buck. He got her a berth at the men's league Reading Pennsylvania Coal Heavers and on July 5, 1898 she was brought out of the bullpen for the ninth inning in the Coal Heavers game against the Allentown Peanuts.

Her appearance had been heavily promoted and she drew a crowd of approx. 1,000 fans including 200 women*** who wanted to know if she could actually pitch and more importantly what would she wear? Lizzie entered the field in a stylish carriage drawn by 2 white horses. The Reading Eagle newspaper would later report that she was "a plump young woman*** with an attractive face and rosy cheeks. She wore a gray uniform with skirt coming to the knees, black stockings and a jaunty cap. Her hair was not cropped, but done up in the latest fashion."

There wasn't a lot riding on her pitching skills. She had done her job of filling the bleachers. And besides, the Coal Heavers were up 5-0. How much damage could she do?

It looked a little dicey. She allowed 2 hits and then walked a batter. With bases loaded, it was not looking to be a good day for women's sports. But then she un-

*Her birth name is thought to have been Elizabeth Stride or Stroud.

**I've always thought women should lie upwards about their age. For instance, in my forties I routinely copped to five years older. Damn, girl, you look good! was usually the response. On the other hand, I had a galpal who routinely pegged herself at forty until one day she slipped up about what her favorite fan crush was when she was in grade school. A blushing sixty year old.

***Women didn't routinely go to baseball games but with the promise of seeing Lizzie play, how could you not? The iconic song "take me out to the ball game" describes a young lady telling a gentleman caller she will only see him if he takes her to a game. It was considered quite a novelty.

Continued on Next Page

July 05

leashed the Lizzie her team knew her to be. Three strike outs later, the crowd erupted with applause and shouts of "good for Lizzie!"

To be fair, her pitching style was—oh, gosh, I'm really going to get into trouble for saying this—somewhat erratic and without the brute power of her male counterparts. Further, she was anywhere between 21 and 23 and coaching her into a full career as a major league pitcher before the age effect kicked in was going to be tough. She ended up signing with the Boston Bloomers in the ladies' league and she was a great novelty draw. She died in 1919 probably of complications from surgery.

The picture is from the Robert Edwards auction house and is the only known cabinet card**** of Lizzie in uniform. The card which was expected to fetch $300 sold for $6,518.

****A cabinet card is slightly larger and more substantial than a regular baseball card. It has a plain backing because it is meant to be displayed in, you got it, a cabinet.

July 06

Happy birthday to Jetsun Jamphel Ngawang Lobsang Yeshe Tenzin Gyatso! Well, that's just his spiritual name and I dare you to say it three times fast. Most folk, particularly Tibetans, know him as Tenzin Gyatso or Gyalwa Rinpoche. We're talking the 14th Dalai Lama, born July 6, 1935 to farmer Chekyong and Diki Tsering in the small northern Tibetan town of Taktser.

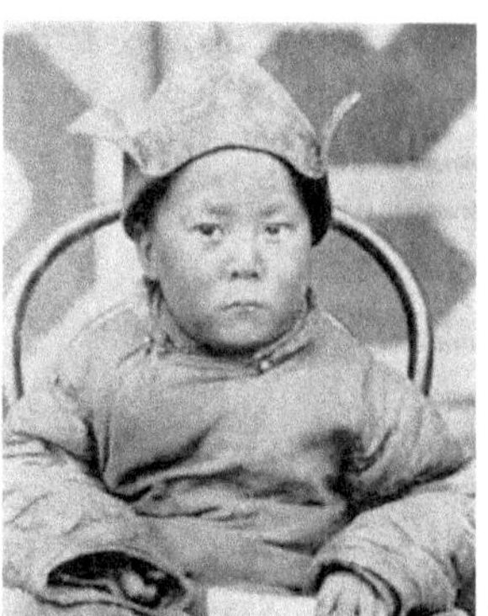

His family was of the Gelug School of Tibetan Buddhism. When Tenzin was five he was enthroned as the Dalai Lama.* His brother was made a Lama as would all of the Tsering boys at one point or another.

Tenzin didn't take on his full spiritual responsibilities until 1950 when the People's Republic of China had already invaded the country. The PRC had already declared another boy as the Dalai Lama but he's never been taken seriously. There were a bunch of uprisings by the Tibetans and in 1959 Tenzin and some other priests (including brothers) headed for India. An arduous journey on foot over the mountains but Tibetans are tough.**

Eighty thousand refugees followed later to the Dalai Lama's new home in Dharamshala, India aka Little Lhasa. Lhasa is the administrative capital of Tibet under the Chinese rule.

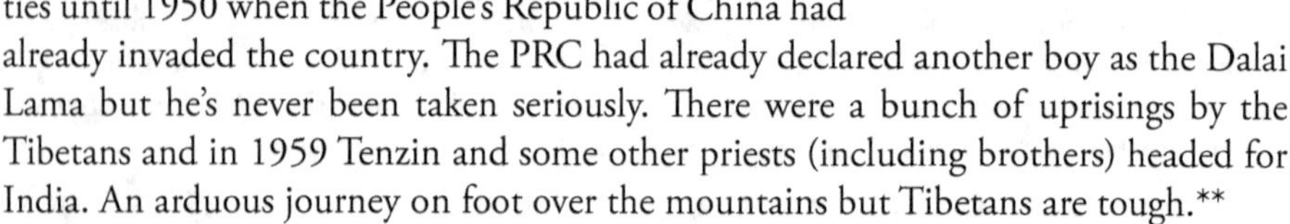

July 06

The Dalai Lama received a Nobel Peace Prize in 1989 and is actor Richard Gere's idol. Tough to say what's the bigger deal. The Dalai Lama is a beacon of peace and tolerance although he's not without his controversies. He has given interviews expressing opposition to abortion and also oral sex which has required him to do some fancy footwork on the issue of homosexuality. But we all evolve and morph in our spiritual and political beliefs.

Happy Birthday Tenzin! I think your birthday should be an international day of celebration!

*When he was chosen, it was not by the traditional Golden Urn method which is where you put a bunch of names in the Urn and the first name drawn is the dude! Tibetans were nervous about the incursion of the Chinese and were concerned the Golden Urn system would be rigged. The Tsering family became something like nobility in giving Tenzin to the cause.

**When his father died, the Dalai Lama performed the sky burial as per tradition. This involved dragging Chekyong to the top of the nearby mountain and chopping his body into edible dainty pieces for vultures lurking nearby. I sure hope my kids don't get any ideas.

July 07

On this day July 7 in 1880, Otto Frederick Rohwedder was born in Davenport, Iowa. He was the sort of guy whom we would refer to as a "tinkerer." During most of his career he sold and repaired jewelry and, well, tinkered. In 1928 he invented a machine which would slice bread. He believed that pre-sliced bread would appeal to Americans' impulse to have things organized, neat, efficient.

Rohwedder sold his two jewelry stores and built the first machine which made its debut at Bench's Bakery in Chillicothe, Missouri. Sliced bread proved so popular that the machine wore out within 6 months. Rohwedder sold the second machine to Korn's Bakery in his hometown of Davenport. In 1930 the Continental Baking Company acquired the rights to the invention (and its improvements by inventor Gustav Paperdick) and used it initially to package its popular WONDER BREAD! This new bread was easy to use for sandwiches and toast and it promised to "build strong bodies" with 12 essential minerals and vitamins. Actually not as stupid as it sounds, given the usual American diet of the time.

In 1943 amid efforts to support the war, the government imposed a ban on sliced bread—the thinking being that the process of creating and wrapping the slices took up too much energy and resources. And you thought wearing a mask during the pandemic was a hardship!

The greatest invention since...

____

____

____

____

____

The most notable and poignant event of July 8 actually began on the 7th. In 1939, the Tenth Duke of Marlborough hosted a debutante party for his seventeen year old daughter Lady Sarah Spencer-Churchill on the evening of the seventh. The party would mark Lady Sarah's coming into adulthood. It was also a party that marked the beginning of the doom of everything English.

The party was at Blenheim Palace, the only privately owned castle in England—given to the First Duke of Marlborough by Queen Anne. The ballroom and even the lake outside were floodlit so that if you lived within a few miles you were quite aware that you hadn't gotten an invite. Tyroleans walked about serenading the guests. Dancing? A lavish dinner? Champagne? Oui, bien sûr! As the sun rose on the eighth, footmen in powdered wigs served hot dogs and coffee to the exhausted guests. The party sauntered in all their finery to Westminster Bridge as Big Ben struck eight. They somehow all knew it was the end. They stared with great melancholy at the horizon. They knew they might be as doomed as a bunch of Romanovs in the gun sites of a Bolshevik shindig.

While Lady Sarah was the center of the party, the ballgowns designed by the very au courante designer Charles James made a statement. The Countess of Rosse wore my favorite which was pink.

"I never had a better time," young future president Jack Kennedy said.

Would there be another party like it? Well, not for a long time. And guests knew it. The Military Training Act had been passed and men were being drafted. Evening wear was put into the back of the closet and a designer like James who favored elaborate, voluminous gowns would be considered wasteful and unpatriotic. Blenheim was turned into a temporary school for children evacuated from London and the grounds were turned into Victory Gardens. Lady Sarah, who would have expected to whirl on dance floors on the arms of potential husbands, took a job in a munitions factory. She still ended up marrying three times and lived a good long life.

It would be a decade before English aristocracy pulled the tuxes and the gowns out of the closet. A bit tight, a few moth holes, a little yellowed, but England would survive. A total of 65 countries have declared their independence from the United Kingdom. The empire shrinks. But England survives. Some of the partygoers would not and they knew it on the morning the last party broke up. But being English, they put a brave face on it. *We will survive.*

____

____

____

____

On July 9, 1960 seven year old Roger Woodward, along with his sister Deanne were going on a boat ride on the upper Niagra river. The boat developed engine trouble and the boat went flying over the Falls. Roger tumbled over the Canadian Horseshoe Falls.

There are an estimated 5,000 bodies which have been recovered from the bottom of the Falls. About fifty folk a year take the plunge, the vast majority of which are suicides. On October 24, 1901 Annie Edison Taylor became the first person to survive a trip down the falls—she did so in a barrel. Barrel falls were sort of a publicity thing, but didn't have a good survival rate.

But let's get back to Roger. He would say later—

"For me there was initially pure panic, I was scared to death. I can remember going through the rapids and being thrown against the rocks and being bounced around like a toy in the water and being beaten up pretty badly. My panic very quickly shifted to anger and the anger was from seeing people running frantically up and down the shoreline and wondering why they wouldn't come out and rescue me."

Roger Woodward then said that after fear and anger came peace.

"There was a time I thought I was going to die and my seven years of life literally passed before me and I started thinking what my parents would do with my dog and my toys and had really given up at that point and felt I was going to die that afternoon."

But he didn't, instead being dragged to safety by the crew of a passing Maid of the Mist tour boat. The boy was reunited with his sister Deanne who had been scooped up by rescuers before she could tumble down the falls.

I've lived a good long life. I have tried my best. I have done what I thought was right with a few exceptions that may have involved among other things chocolate, unrequited love, boyfriends, and vodka. I figure I will approach death the same way Roger did. There will be fear and maybe some anger. I hope I can stay in the peaceful acceptance zone.

July 10 marks the greatest tax revolt EVER! And we're not talking about a politician. On July 10, 1045*** the great economist and public policy theorist Godiva, Countess of Mercia, took a stand. She was the wife of Leofric, Earl of Mercia. Lady G took pity on their people of Coventry, who were suffering grievously under her husband's oppressive taxation. He was taxing EVERYTHING including some stuff American governing bodies haven't thought of … yet.

Lady G appealed again and again to her husband, who obstinately refused to relent. At last, thinking to himself "could she just shut up already?" He said he would grant her request if she would strip naked and ride on a horse through the streets of the town. Lady G took him at his word, and after issuing a proclamation that all persons should stay indoors and shut their windows, she rode through the town, clothed only in her long hair. Just one person in the town, a tailor ever afterwards known as Peeping Tom, disobeyed her proclamation in what is the most famous instance of voyeurism. Peep-

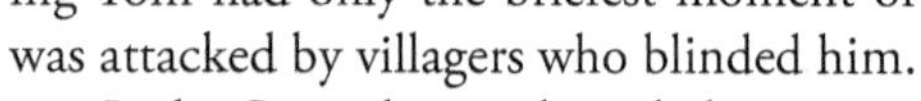

ing Tom had only the briefest moment of delight—he was attacked by villagers who blinded him.

Lady G got her wish and there was tax relief. I'd offer to do the same thing but I fear that even with my avoir dupois, someone might raise taxes even further.

The Pre-Raphaelite brotherhood of painters and sculptures really liked the legend and the most famous rendition of Lady Godiva was painted by John Collier in 1898. Note that Lady G is astride her horse and not side saddle as a woman of her time would have been. Lynd Nead, author of "the female nude: art, obscenity and sexuality" (1992) went off on a tear over the painting, declaring that nudes were a way of regulating women's bodies. I wonder what Nead would make of Michelangelo's David.

The gal in the painting is Mabel Violet Hall. She was a favorite amongst the Pre-Raphaelites and later took to the stage under the name Mab Paul. In 1910 she left England for Australia and had a successful theatrical career. This particular painting can be seen at Coventry's Herbert art gallery and museum. The Broadgate clock in Coventry features Godiva prancing around on the hour.

If you could get rid of one tax by driving through town in the buff, would you? What would be the tax you'd most like to see go?

____

____

____

____

____

This July 11 I hope you are preparing your bonfire. Given the events of the past Fourth in my neck of the woods a bonfire seems like a perfectly harmless operation. I used to have a neighbor who would drink gin and tonics and set off firecrackers in the alley every weekend and once his pyrotechnics set off a fire on top of our garage but he put it out with a garden hose. I'd like that neighbor back please. He seems wholesome in retrospect.

July 11 is celebrated as Eleventh Night in Ireland. In the evening, Protestants light fires to begin the celebration of the 12th which is sort of like Guy Fawkes day in Britain but it's called Orange Man's Day. In this Irish holiday, Protestants recall the 1691 victory of Protestant King William of Orange over Catholic James 2 during the Williamite-Jacobite War. Possibly this bonfire is linked to some of the counties lighting bonfires to guide the Williamite ships to safety during the naval portion of the fight. Or simply a desire to get together with the neighbors and have a few.

Eleventh Night is somewhat divisive but the Catholic population gets to test out their fire detectors with the August 14th Feast of the Assumption of Mary. Catholics and Protestants alike celebrate Midsummer Day, Bealtaine on May 1st and Halloween (Samhein for you Gaelic speakers).

So if you haven't already done it get a big metal cage and attach wood and charcoal—

I kinda think bonfires are way too much trouble and dangerous to boot! How will you celebrate today?

July 12

July 12th also known as The Twelfth, a holiday which celebrates Irish British loyalists, mostly the Ulster Ireland Protestants. Orangemen are also known as Orange order and they celebrate the victories of Protestant United Kingdom's William of Orange (Orange being part of the Netherlands). William beat the Catholic king claimant James 2 at the Battle of the Boyne in 1699. Also, of course, the Glorious Revolution which made William of Orange king making the Brits finally and ultimately a Protestant Empire.

The way Ulster and other folk celebrate the day is with a parade (of course), bonfires (mais oui!), drinking and orange bunting on buildings. It's just like March 17 just…orange.

The way you can celebrate is perhaps to wear orange, just like you wear green on St. Patrick's Day. Try to remember when you see a flag of the country of Ireland—it celebrates the Protestant heritage with orange and its Catholic with green. The white is like a demilitarized zone, symbolizing peace between the two groups.

William was married to Mary, Princess Royale daughter of Charles I who had been executed by dissatisfied English.

Green or Orange today for you?

July 13

July 13 is Barbershop Music Appreciation Day. Now, we ordinarily think of Barbershop music as quartet of four dorky guys in straw hats and striped jackets (barbershops used to always have a red and white [or in America red, white, and blue] striped pole outside their entrance and that was the inspiration for the striped jackets.)

But there's a little more here. Barbershops were a social gathering place for men who wanted a haircut or minor surgery or "get that tooth out it's driving me nuts!" Barbers were also a sort of rough justice therapy office—customers could talk about their troubles and triumphs with other clients or with the barber himself.

Sometime in the 1600s, barbers began keeping citterns in their shops. A cittern is sort of like a lute or guitar and guys would start singing. The style developed of four tones—the lead that carry the melody, the bass that would provide the lowest notes, a tenor to harmonize at a higher note than the lead, and the baritone that completes the chord.

You didn't have to have just four singers and if there were just three of you, so what? Then barbershop choirs developed with dozens of men singing their parts. There became a national organization that would put on shows together—The Society for the Preservation and Encouragement of Barbershop Singing in America. 

But then something odd happened. Women started wondering why they were being left behind in the action. On this day July 13, 1945 Edna Mae Anderson invited a bunch of wives of the Society to her home and proposed that they start a, ahem, ladies' group.

Called the Sweet Adelines, these music lovers put on shows with or without their husbands. Following, of course, the traditions of harmony of Barbershop.

Today, celebrate this day by watching the 1986 movie "Hoosiers" in which the national anthem is sung in Barbershop style by the Travel-Aires. I dare you to listen to it without having to grab a hankie.

Have you ever gone to a Barbershop show or even listened to a song on the radio? What did you think of this neary extinct form?

Dang it, I wish I had been alive in 1912! No kidding I wasn't but on July 14, 1912 it would have been exciting to be in Stockholm. Specifically at the Olympics —

I sympathize completely and maybe identify with Jim Thorpe who was competing in the Decathlon. Somebody had stolen his shoes but he managed to find two mismatched shoes in a garbage can. He had to shove two pairs of socks into one of the shoes. He was determined to win not just a medal but the heart of Iva Miller and her family who were a little judgmental. He won two of the four events that day and even won the gold in the Pentathlon. The next year he would lose his medals over a technicality because he had played minor league baseball for money.

Meanwhile, on July 14, 1912 Shizo Kanakuri began the Marathon. In a way. He had traveled to Sweden in an eighteen day, well, marathon of ships, trains, carriages, buses, and cars. Sometime during the sixteenth day of his sojourn the weak and dehydrated Kanakuri lost consciousness. A nice Swedish family took care of him and sent him back to Japan. He had never checked in with the Olympic Committee so he was officially listed as missing.

Here's the good news! Jim Thorpe and Iva Miller got married in a spectacular Catholic ceremony and in 1982 his medals were restored. More good news—the Swedes tracked down Kanakuri in Japan and in March 1967 he completed the Marathon. Official time—54 years 8 months 6 days 5 hours 32 minutes and 20 seconds.

Sometimes we face adversity. It's hard to find shoes. It's hard to travel for eighteen days and not be able to even start a marathon. But we have goals and we can reach them. Today is a day for figuring out what is most most most important to us and grabbing on to it!

What is one goal that you have yet to achieve?
What's stopping you?

On July 15, 1988 the most wonderful Christmas movie of all time was released. The production company Gordon Company and Silver Pictures as well as distributor 20th Century Fox should have aimed for, say, the day after Thanksgiving for the release. On the other hand, my most successful Christmas party was held in July—I couldn't keep enough fruitcake and eggnog onboard!

The movie of course is Die Hard. New York po-lice officer John McClane (Bruce Willis) is visiting his estranged wife (Bonnie Bedelia) and two daughters for Christmas in Los Angeles. He joins his family at Bede-lia's office Christmas party and that's when Hans Gru-ber (Alan Rickman) and his merry band of terrorists take over the building. Only one man can save every-one—that would be McClane! Spoiler alert: he does.

The movie grossed $140 million and had four Oscar nominations. There were four spin-off movies and Willis was transformed from pretty okay television star to the Big Screen. And I have to pull out a few Kleenex towards the end.

Willis has recently been in a bunch of klunkers. He's been struggling with lines and with a lack of energy. According to insiders, he's been trying to amass a big pile of green before he simply isn't able to act anymore. The poor dude has aphasia, a progressive disorder which destroys a person's ability to understand and communicate language. People who worked with him just thought he was distracted or maybe on drugs but as the family announced his diagnosis, Willis officially retired from the business. He has a marvelous social network which includes ex-wife Demi Moore and their children as well as present wife Emma and their children. Aphasia is generally caused by stroke although traumatic brain injury can be at fault—he's done his share of movie stunts.

I wish him well and plan on a Die Hard marathon once I get the television working again. Thank you Xfinity—it's been close to a month now. No internet, no television, no nothing. I'm sort of living off the grid. If only I had a John McClane in my life!

July 16

On July 16, 1945 the first atomic bomb code named "Fat Boy" was tested near Alamogordo, New Mexico. The test itself was called "trinity." The test was a success. The bomb code named "Little Boy" was dropped on Hiroshima and "Fat Man" was dropped on Nagasaki in August of the same year.

Are you old enough to remember A-bomb drills in school? Like crouching under your desk is going to save you.

July 17

To understand the importance of July 17th you have to look back to August 23, 1861. For it was on this day that Lorain, Ohio resident James A. Stone enlisted in the United States (Union) Army. He had been born in 1829 as a slave in Kentucky but had escaped to Ohio. He married a mixed race woman and became a father. The family was listed on the 1850 Census but with no mention of their racial origins. From the start of the Civil War, Stone wanted to serve his country but blacks were not allowed in the Army. Still, he was light skinned enough to "pass" as white and he decided not to bring up the subject to his recruitment officer. He put on his uniform August 23, 1861.

He ended up in the Ohio 1st E Light Artillery Battery and served, by all accounts, with great honor. He was injured in battle on October 29, 1862. At his autopsy, it was established that he was in fact black. It is unclear whether his widow received a pension as he was not "legally" in the Army. He is considered the first black to serve.

As the war progressed, the Union was desperate for more soldiers and it was an open secret that many light skinned blacks were already in the fight. Perhaps inspired by James A. Stone's service, Congress passed the Militia Act on July 17, 1862 which—among other things—allowed blacks to enlist. Large scale recruitment didn't get started until after the Emancipation Proclamation of January 1, 1863. Approxi-

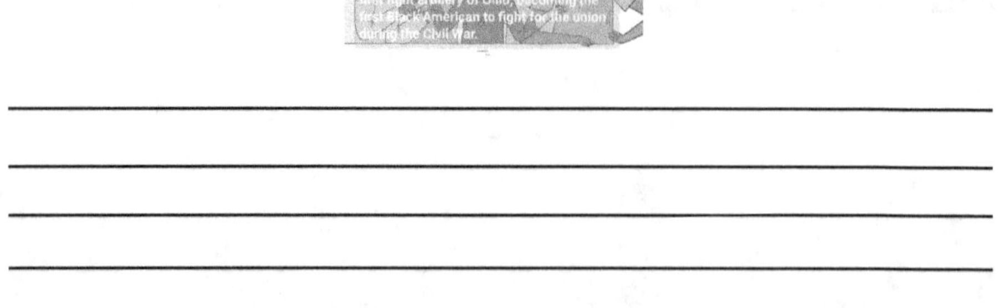

mately 180,000 blacks served in the Union Army and while 40,000 died, it was—as in all wars—mostly from disease. These men were fighting for the freedom of their southern brothers and sisters.

Meanwhile, in a desperation move, the Confederate Army allowed as how enslaved blacks could be drafted into service. Altogether, less than ten thousand blacks served—mostly as musicians, servants, and laborers.

It takes a lot of courage to enlist. Or even to be drafted. My father evaded the draft for the Vietnam War by cutting off his pinkie toe with a cleaver. My former mother-in-law described the happiest day of her life as when my ex-husband got his 4-F notice—meaning they'd take anybody but him. What would make you feel like enlisting in this era?

July 18

On July 18, 1918 in Mvezo, South Africa, a child was born to the royal family of Thembu. His name was Rolihlahla Mandela otherwise known as Nelson Mandela.

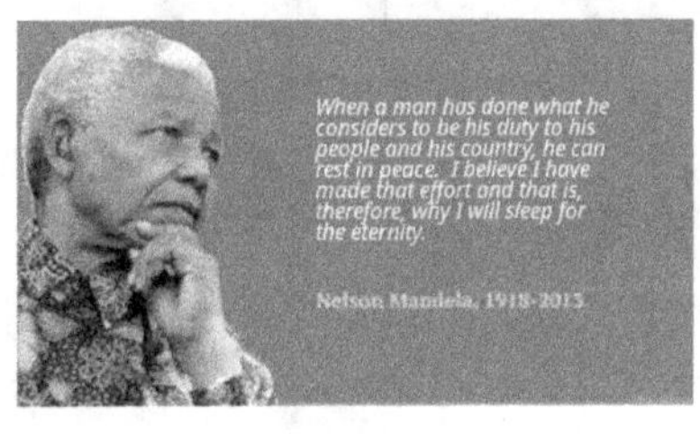

He was well educated as a royal should be and he developed a keen sense of outrage blended with social consciousness particularly in the era of apartheid, the South African system of separation of the races. He engaged in political activism and was sent to prison for 27 years much to the consternation of justice minded people. When he was finally released, he partnered with President F.W. de Klerk to end apartheid and bring about reconciliation. They shared the Nobel Peace Prize in 1993. I was once at a dinner party and man, he's a huge guy with a humongous appetite! Oh, and the BEST camel coat I've ever wanted to steal.

Mandela died in 1995 at the age of 93. It wouldn't be until 2009 that the United Nations created International Nelson Mandela Day.

Maybe we could all celebrate by doing one nice thing for someone from whom we are somewhat estranged. Reconciliation is a beautiful way of healing yourself, the other person, even a little bit the rest of the world!

*Anyone you'd like to reconcile with? How can **you** start the process?*

July 19, 1969 is the day of the Chappaquiddick Incident, otherwise known as "things you shouldn't do when you're drunk" day or maybe "don't lie about it" day or perhaps "don't hang out with Kennedys" day. At Chappaquiddick, Massachusetts Ted Kennedy, 37 year old Massachusetts Senator, lost his chance at becoming President and 28 year old Mary Jo Kopechne lost her life. Let's review the lessons.

1. Don't go to drunken barbecues with married men. Ted Kennedy was set to sail in the local Regatta with his boat Victura over the weekend. One of his advisors/crew mates had rented the secluded Lawrence Cottage as a place to, er, get away from it all. On the night of the eighteenth Kennedy hosted a barbecue with his male buddies, all but one of whom were married. Then he invited the "Boiler Room Girls"—six gorgeous twenty something single women who had worked on his brother, Robert Kennedy's, ill-fated presidential campaign. Wives were not invited. The cookout started at eight-thirty.

2. Don't let Teddy drive! Around 11:15 Kennedy asked his chauffeur for his keys. He claimed that Kopechne had asked him for a ride to the ferry that would take her from Chappaquiddick to Edgartown where her hotel was. It would have been a five, ten minute ride. She didn't tell the other Boiler Girls and didn't take her purse or keys. An hour later, off duty cop Christopher "Huck" Lake saw a car parked at an odd angle on the street. He approached the car and asked if the driver needs assistance. The car sped off but Lake is able to make out part of the license plate number which matched Kennedy's car.

3. No drunk dancing in the street! Lake continued on his way and came upon three of the five Boiler Room Girls doing a conga line dance in the center of Chappaquiddick Road. He asked them if they needed a ride. They declined and later would say they remember him asking but they were going to stay on the island instead of going to their hotel in Edgartown.

4. Seriously, don't let Teddy drive! According to Kennedy, he made a mistake in the dark night—instead of turning left towards the ferry, he turned right onto (irony alert!) Cemetery Road, lost control of his car and

———————————————————————————————————

———————————————————————————————————

———————————————————————————————————

———————————————————————————————————

———————————————————————————————————

plunged into the Channel at Tom's Neck. The car flipped over and took on water. Kennedy escaped the vehicle but Kopechne did not. He swam the short distance to shore and walked to Lawance Cottage, passing four houses where he could have politely, if drunkenly, asked to call 911.

5. Don't sleep it off when your gal is fighting for her life in the car—it's ungentlemanly! Advisors told Kennedy he had to report the incident and several of them walked him towards a pay phone near the ferry slip. At the phone booth he called another few advisors and then tore off his clothes, jumped into the water, swam 500 ft. to his Edgartown hotel and slept it off. The Chappaquiddick Sheriff and Coroner would later agree there was at least enough air in the water for Kopechne to still be alive—she could have been saved at that point. At two-thirtyish, Kennedy returned in dry clothes to the party. The Boiler Room Girls were told Kopechne was at her hotel. They partied til the wee hours.

6. Don't think you won't get caught! At 8 a.m. the car was discovered by a passing fifteen year old who went to a nearby house and the police were called. At ten a.m. Kennedy discovered that Kopechne's body and his car had been retrieved. That's when a light bulb goes off—"I should call the police!"

If you can't follow these rules, then be a powerful Kennedy.

He received altogether a two month suspended sentence for leaving the scene and had his driver's license pulled. So he had to give the keys back to the chauffeur. He was reelected as Senator but he didn't run for President in 1972. He waited for 1980 and did miserably.

In 1972, a political joke circulated.

Pollster: Nixon—would you buy a used car from that man?

Voter: Sure, but I wouldn't let Teddy drive it!"

What's your feeling about the Kennedys now?

____

____

____

____

On July 20, I think a lot of us remember 1969 and Neil Armstrong about to be the first man to put his toe on the moon's surface.

But I think more about the Alvin Dark line made in the spring of 1962, when newspaperman Harry Jupiter asked the baseball manager about pitcher Gaylord Perry's apparent improvement as a hitter. "Man will land on the moon before Gaylord Perry hits a home run," Dark replied

Alvin Dark was actually quite prescient. Less than an hour after Apollo 11's lunar module touched down on the moon's surface, Perry swung the first home run of his career.

While we think of the moonwalk as a feat of NASA's engineers and airmen there was another player, perhaps just as important. When he emerged from the module, Neil Armstrong was wearing a space-suit designed and constructed by the Playtex bra and girdle making company. The suit had 21 thin layers of the same nylon, lycra, neoprene, and dacron that was used for ordinary underwear. The suit also contained some not so ordinary lingerie elements mylar,

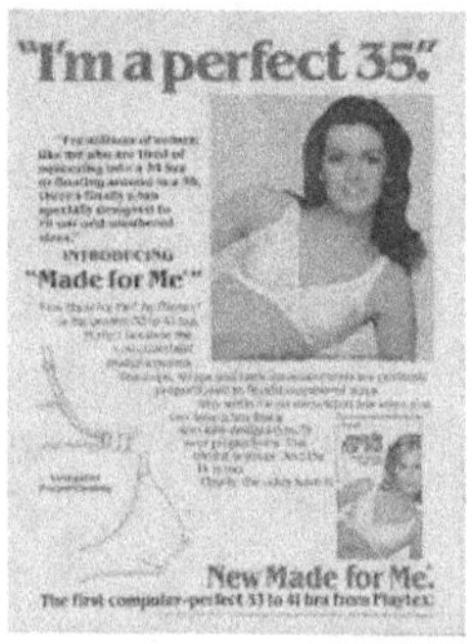

kapton, and teflon in order to give Neil protection from extreme heat and cold, ultraviolet radiation and projectile micrometeorites. In essence, Armstrong's suit had to become its own space rocket!

These days, you can go to space if you have some, er, friends and maybe a billion. Would you want to go?

____

____

____

____

____

On July 21, 1969 the day* after landing on the moon in a lunar module, Neil Armstrong became the first person to walk on the Moon. While the command module that brought the three man crew and lunar module to the moon orbited over head, lunar module pilot Buzz Aldrin and Neil Armstrong landed the lunar module on the Sea of Tranquility and made plans for a moon walk. Neil stepped on the Moon's surface almost 7 hours after landing. After stepping on the Moon, Neil Armstrong uttered his famous words, "one small step for [a] man, one giant leap for mankind."

Aldrin and Armstrong spent the next several hours frolicking and exploring. And no doubt gossiping about what a loser Michael Collins was. After all, he was just like an Uber driver who has discovered his riders aren't ready but there aren't any other rides he can pick up so he can't cancel. Actually, he orbited the moon and performed all sorts of scientific experiments. Me? I was lying on the floor in front of the black and white television. Agog.

"We showed those Commies ," my mother of the time said. She was of course referring to the space race between the Soviets (present day Russia) and America.

The crew returned to earth without particular incident. There were ticker tape parades, which is to say that public works had a lot of sweeping up to do the next morning.

But what of Collins who orbited the moon alone, having forty-eight minutes of a solitude not known since Adam before Eve? Collins said he never felt lonely but rather a feeling of "awareness, anticipation, satisfaction, confidence, almost exultation."

Sometimes when we're anxious or lonely or depressed we forget that we can take those emotions and flip them as easily as you flip a coin over. It's the same coin — perhaps with a sense of anxiety on one side and excitement on the other, or maybe isolation on one side and a sense of freedom to do whatever the heck you want on the other side.

* What's a day on the moon?

What emotion can you flip today?

On July 22, 1934 12 year old Frances Gumm was in Chicago performing with her family's vaudeville act the Gumm Sisters. It was a grueling schedule of rehearsals and performances and on this day she just walked out. She went to the Biograph Theater to see the Clark Gable flick Manhattan Melodrama. She sat through five showings. There was air conditioning. And given the summer heat, that was quite a draw, even without Gable, Loy, and Powell.

Eight hours later, she figured she'd better get back to the family and to the evening's show. In the lobby, she spotted a tall, moustachioed dandy in a blue pin stripe suit with a glam dame on each arm. Maybe because she had just been watching Clark Gable, Gumm figured him for a movie star and asked for his autograph. He did

so with a flourish and minutes later was shot dead just outside the theater.

Not because of giving out autographs to truant child performers. No, this was John Dillinger, aka public enemy no. 1. He was a take-no-vacation-time crime spree. One of the women on his arm had turned him in. Frances Gumm aka Judy Garland had recognized him not from the screen but from his wanted poster.

July 23

Today July 23 is St. Bridget day, patron saint of Sweden and pilgrims. More importantly, it's national ArLynn Leiber Presser Day, a commemoration of when I came into the world spreading cheer and chaos. Me and Bridg share the day with Gorgeous Grandma Day which was founded by Alice Solomon who in 1984 graduated from Wellesley college at the age of 50. She felt that she was marginialized and put into a category of "you can't wear short skirts," "you can't dye your hair pink," "you can't be hot."

Ergo the holiday, which celebrates older, et, femmes d' un certain age.

What's the most reckless thing you have planned? A tattoo? Dyeing you hair pink? An assignation with a much younger, er, well, no judgement today!

July 24 is the feast day of St. Christina the Astonishing whose appellation at first glance makes her seem like she would be a featured performer in a circus. And she could have been....

Born in 1150 she was orphaned at fifteen and tended sheep. She had a seizure in her early twenties and boom! She was dead. In the coffin, just about to be lowered into the ground, she sat up and announced that she would devote her life to religious service. That's a trick I want to do at my funeral. Must have caused a few hastily arranged confessions when she did it. In my case, I'd get and interviewed by the Daily Mail.

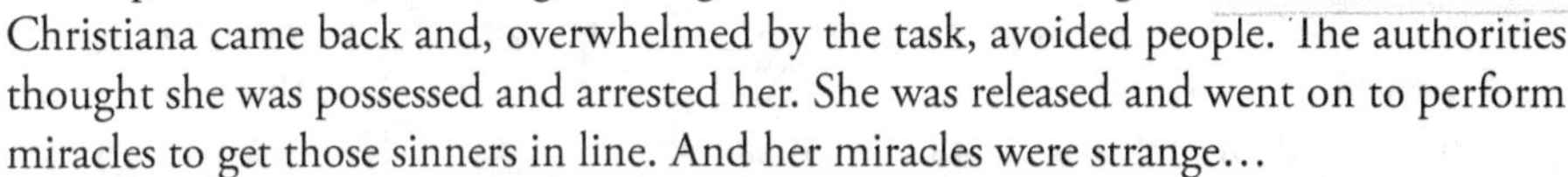

She claimed she had visited Heaven, Hell and Hades and was given a choice of staying in Heaven or returning to earth to deliver souls up to Heaven. Me? I might have gone with the sure thing but Christiana came back and, overwhelmed by the task, avoided people. The authorities thought she was possessed and arrested her. She was released and went on to perform miracles to get those sinners in line. And her miracles were strange...

She would throw herself into large fireplaces, howling in pain, and yet emerge with nary a scratch or blister. Maybe a slight tan. She would jump into the freezing cold Meuse River and tread water for hours at a time like a Navy Seal recruit all the while loudly praying for God's mercy on the sinners and not quite virtuous. Sometimes, perhaps out of boredom, she'd let the currents take her downriver to the mill where the wheel would drag her around in the most frightful way and yet she'd emerge unscathed. She'd let packs of local dogs chase her, bit her, scratch her, and when the attacks were concluded she'd be cuddling them. All the people of her town could see her sufferings and were converted.

Party tricks? Magic? A series of Miracles? Whatever it was she lived to be 74 years old and was almost immediately canonized and it was a hop skip and a jump to sainthood.

Modern interpretation is that she was mentally ill and so I suppose it's fitting that she is the patron saint of the mentally ill and of mental health care workers. Emerging from one pandemic and possibly entering another variant we've all went a little crazy. I turned to food and sometimes Mr. Vodka and certainly binge-watching Golden Girls, MASH, and Andy Griffith which are all three their own craziness. I'd like to believe I'm getting better but since it looks like being double vaccinated did no damn good—I'll still have to wear a mask, social distance, and I'm at risk for not just the delta but plain old Covid regular—I might occasionally need an astonishing saint named Christina. *How did you get through the Pandemic w/o going crazy?*

July 25 is always on a Sunday, er, rather a Sundae. Today is National Hot Fudge Sundae Day. The tasty treat was thought to be invented as a means of allowing the purchase of ice cream treats on Sundays even though Sunday laws (sometimes called "blue laws") prohibited all sorts of things on Sundays to get people to church and keep their minds on spiritual matters. Ice cream sodas were popular in the late eighteenth century but some folk would put a little something "extra" in the soda and ice cream concoction and that would be known as "imbibing."

An ice cream sundae on the other hand had no room for something extra—and many places and people have claimed responsibility for inventing it. Druggist Edward Berners of Two Rivers, Wisconsin claimed to have made the first one in 1881. It was a simpler time when the drugstore was where you got your fix for laudanum, coca cola, ice cream, and cocaine—you know, the good stuff. In 1892, the Ithaca Daily Journal printed an ad for the concoction spelling it "Sunday." It was Cornell—they didn't have proofreaders.

There are many variations, my favorite being the hot tin roof sundae invented by Nebraska pharmacist Harold Dean Thayer in 1916. Chocolate sauce drizzled over

So go out there today and get yourself a sundae…today…on whatever day of the week it is. What flavor will you pick?

July 26

On July 26, 1869, the longest nontechnical word in the English language was formed. It was more than three hundred years in the making. In 1536 and six years after his break with Rome, Henry VIII formed the Irish church as a parallel to the English Anglican church he was the head of. The new Irish church supporters were called Establishmentarians.

On July 26, 1869, England passed the Irish Church Act, or rather the Disestablishment Bill, disassociating the Anglican church from the state. Those who favored this bill were called disestablishmentarians and then there were others who didn't want to break with the Anglican Church of England and they were called antidisestablishmentarians. And if you were in conversation about the group and its philosophy you might say antidisestablishmentarianism. It is the longest non technical word in the English language although any chemist, biologist, physicist or whatnot can come up with longer words that can't really be used by a third grader quizzing and making fun of his/her colleagues on the playground.

To celebrate this laudable holiday, one might try to gently slide the word into a sentence like "I have to go to the grocery because they're having a sale on organic antidisestablishmentarianism celery. Or you could attempt to make words out of the letters that make up the word. If you get more than 8252 you're beating the world record. That ought to help with insomnia!

July 27

July 27 is a heavy duty day of commemoration for Soviet, Chinese, North Korean, all Communists, this is day of victory in the Fatherland Day. In Cuba, the revolution anniversary is celebrated. Lots of parades, tanks and fireworks—general agreement that Communism is just, well, better.

Me? I'll be celebrating Creme Brulee Day as well as Scotch Day. Wonder if they taste good together? Let's find out.

Which holiday will you go with?

July 28, 1914 on a languid summer evening in New York, a new form of dance was introduced by Harry Foxtrot and his gal Yansci Dolly on the roof of the New York Theater which had been transformed into the Jardin de Danse where dancers entertained, cocktails were imbibed and the rooftop was opened for customers dancing beneath the moonlight and stars.

The Theater was making the transition from traditional vaudeville and plays to movies. Silent movies, that is. And they were doing their best to be flexible. Enter Harry Fox, a long time vaudevillian who would do a live performance between films and nestled in between his jokes and pratfalls he introduced a song that became known as "Fox's Trot". It relied on a 4/4 time as opposed to the traditional 3/4 time of the waltz. What a heady time of change!

Fox had been born in 1882 Arthur Carringford in Pomono, California and alas found himself on his own at the age of fifteen. He joined the circus, traveled the country, tried his hand at vaudeville, even did a couple of silents before landing in New York (he may very well have met my great grandfather Fritz Leiber Sr. who was traversing the country in the same manner, although with a Shakespearean company).

Fox fell in love with one of the Dolly Sisters who performed every night on the roof and he took a particular shine to Yansci. Together they turned the Fox's Trot into a couples' dance. There's a lot more fluidity and freedom to the dance which worked well with the newly popular ragtime music and (quel scandale!) the couples danced quite close as opposed to traditional dances in which men and women were at arms' length. On this day (or rather evening) in 1914, they boldly debuted the Foxtrot. The crowd went wild. Soon the waltz was seen as rather stuffy.

There are many people who claimed credit for the dance and there were many variations—the Peabody, the Quickstep, the Roseland. But my money, er, my feet are on Harry Fox. The Foxtrot later was adapted and repurposed to be the Lindy and my favorite—the Charleston.

So get out there and put on your dancing shoes. Or do it barefoot. Grab a partner and hold him/her tight. Today is a day for dancing! *What's first on your playlist?*

____

____

____

____

____

July 29 1981—one hundred yards of tulle, twenty-five yards of silk taffeta, ten thousand pearls, a twenty five foot long, ginormous puffed sleeves, and ruffles, bows, antique carrickmacross lace. It was designed by husband and wife team Guianne David and Elizabeth Emmanuel. The 153 yard veil was anchored by the spencer family tiara. Although everyone said Prince Charles was marrying a commoner, Diana was actually the daughter of an earl.

Diana was roughly Charles' height so she wore flats.

She said later that she felt like a sheep being led to slaughter.. I don't think I've ever seen a prettier sheep. She was divorced 15 years later and killed in a car accident in 1997.

But she did get to dance with John Travolta when he still had his hair on. At the White House. …Worth it.

If you're married what did you and your love wear? If you're not, what are you thinking might be nice?

July 30

Up until 1952 Olympic medals were awarded for some, er, rather nonathletic categories like music, literature, sculpture, even city planning. On July 30, 1932 the painting "Casting" by Winslow Homer, the American painter best known for his landscapes of his native Maine, was entered into the 1932 Los Angeles summer Olympics. However, since he had died 22 years before, he was not awarded a medal.

What new Olympic event would you like to see added to the roster?

____

____

____

____

____

Today is a day of great mourning in England. So take a moment, bow your head and give thanks that we have survived. July 31, 1970 was Black Tot Day. Sailors wore black armbands, black tots were consumed and the remains thrown overboard from ships near and far. On the HMS Collingwood, stationed at Hampshire, there was a funeral complete with drummers and pipers and wailing and weeping.

An explanation. In the seventeenth century, transporting clean water on naval ships was a difficult and sometimes deadly operation. Wooden kegs were like petri dishes, with scurvy being only one of the risks. So the Royal Navy instituted a policy of twice daily rations of rum or gin, and a gallon of beer to each of its men. The acid in the beer, gin, and rum was thought to sterilize the water inherent in the drinks. Traditionally, the ship's purser, accompanied by his assistant (always known as the Jack Nastyface) would apportion these rations at around eleven a.m. and then again at night.

Beer was still a problem because it just took up too much room and it only contained a measly 1% so sailors greatly preferred the rum. The rum was called a "tot" and because of many incidences of, ahem, intoxication the rum allocation was halved and at one point diluted with water.

Thus the black tot or grog or punch as it was called—here's the recipe for y'all to celebrate, er, mourn today. One part sour (lime juice was commonly used), one part rum (Pussers Rum was the Naval standard) and 4 parts H_2O. The lime was meant to chase away scurvy and the rum was supposed to clean the water. Twice a day, just like picking up your meds at the local Walgreen's. And you still got the increasingly unpopular beer.

But the problems attributed to intoxication in the British Navy went unabated. The practice was abandoned entirely on this day in 1970. No rum. No gin. No beer. It was the sort of thing anticipated by the Book of Revelations as a sign of the End Times. The last of rum was handed out on Navy ships at eleven and the leftovers, well, we think they were cast overboard.

So just for your health's sake, I'd take some water (even Flint, Michigan water if you must), some rum, some lime juice freshly squeezed and some more rum in the memory of all who have served.

Cheers.

August is the month of apples and falling stars, the last care free month for school children.

–Victor Nekrasov

August 1 is midway between the summer solstice and the autumnal equinox. In Ireland and Scotland it is a holiday that celebrates a funeral,yearlong marriages, the pagan god Lugh and the beginning of the harvest season.

It's called Lughnasadh or Luhasa or Lunastal or Luanistyn depending on whether you're Irish, live on the Isle of Man or you're Scottish or Wiccan. But it's pretty much the same story:

The God Lugh mourned the death of his mother (or maybe stepmother) Tailtiu. She supposedly died of exhaustion preparing the land for harvest. Hence, a funeral. Anyhow, this all happened during the yearly Aenach Tailten games. And just like the Ancient Greek Olympics, the Kings and Queens every year declared a cease++++fire between warring tribes during the games. Tailtiu's funeral was held during the games which included a celebration of the harvest. The celebration included, well, drinking, comradery, and a rather interesting marital practice.

Hand Fasting is when a couple lay in bed and reach into a hole in a wall. On the other side, their beloved's hand waits. They hold hands and thus contract a yearlong marriage. The marriage could be renewed but it could also be dissolved without consequence. There are other cultures that cultivate similar chaste customs—even the Amish!

Remember this day as fall leaves swirl around your feet and then snowstorms erupt. Find things to celebrate now and to remember when Jack Frost nips at your nose.

It's August 2 and what are you doing? Well, naturally, you're feedings eggs to a snake. Not just my friend Star Wheeler who owns a python (that's the last of me going to her house!). Today is Nag Panchami, nothing less than the most important day, the fifth day, in the month of Shravan which is the most auspicious time to worship Lord Shiva.

Snakes are holy to the Hindu religion. Don't kill one. In fact, on this day, you will offer a Naga snake a meal of milk, egg and sweets and you get on your knees to worship the slithering deity. Oh, and bonus if you fast today because the act will forever protect you from the fear of snakes. Naga snakes are the most holy and the holiest of these holy snakes is Mansa Mata the mother of all snakes. This worship, by the way, is for women to do. The men steer clear of this whole thing.

Me? I've already had breakfast. I'm not getting close enough to a snake to give it anything to eat.

What's your phobia?
Mine is definitely snakes ~ otherwise known as ophidophobia.
If you are scared of the number 13. You've got triskaidekaphobia.
Clowns? Coulrophobia.

August 3 is a day to remind one's self that if at first you don't succeed, try try try again...

Miriam Hargrave of Wakefield, England really wanted a driver's license. She failed the test. And then a second time. And again. After her thirty first failure she told a newspaper "I've spent all my savings and my husband has threatened to leave me if I don't give up trying."

After her thirty eighth try she moaned "I was so confident this time but it just didn't work." After her 39th attempt, she crashed the driving school's vehicle into a red light.

Apology accepted. On August 3, 1970 her fortieth try was a charm. She had spent $720 on lessons and could no longer afford a car. No word on whether the husband left her.

I hold to the belief that you just keep trying. On the other hand, I sold my car and don't drive anymore. Uber is cheap although they keep adding new "charges."

How do you get around town? Would you have the endurance of Mildred Hargrave?

On August 4, 1790 then Secretary of the Treasury Alexander Hamilton created the wussiest branch of the Armed Forces. Oh, wait, how do I take back the word wussiest?

He started with ten Revenue Service cutter ships. Their mission was to prevent smuggling on our shores—oh, wait, that's actually still a problem. Their mission expanded to basically taking care of, well, our coasts and bodies of water, once saving future Illinois congressman Mark Kirk in the chilly waters of Lake Michigan near my fair Winnetka. He was sixteen and had upended his boat. Coast Guard saved him. Just doing their job. I met him once. He seemed nice enough although he left his office in some scandal.

The Coast Guard was given its name in 1915 by President Woodrow Wilson and every year on this day Grand Haven, Michigan celebrates its status as "Coast Guard City" and there will be a parade and games and the usual frolicking and pageantry. I've always thought of the Coast Guard as the lesser of our Armed Forces. I'm wrong – the Coast Guard defends our borders, our peeps, and now as part of the Homeland Security Agency, it defends and protects us.

Today you might be at the beach — say thank you to the Coast Guard.

On August 5, 1926 52 year old Erik Weisz aka Harry Handcuff Houdini entered the natatorium (fancy term for pool) of the Hotel Shelton in order to win a bet and prove his dominance in the world of illusion.

The previous month Rahman Bey had spent an hour dawdling in an airtight container that was lowered into the Hotel Dalton pool. He bet Houdini he couldn't do better.

Ha ha! In what would turn out to be Houdini's last successful daring deed, he was lowered into the Shelton pool in a sealed container. He had a buzzer in his hand to communicate with his assistant James Collins. Collins checked in on him frequently, giving Houdini an idea of how long he had been underwater and generally propping up his spirits.

Ninety one minutes later, Houdini was raised out of the pool. He was not looking all that good but he had survived. A lifetime of stunts including breaking out of handcuffs and chains and even once having his head sealed into a milk container which he broke out of. Houdini had proven himself.

The question is how did he do it? Truth is, he practiced. He made two earlier runs in the days leading up to August 5, pushing himself for longer times. And he practiced conscious breathing.

That night Houdini wrote a detailed account of his day to W.J. McConnell, a researcher with the government's Bureau of Mines. He wanted to help McConnell with research into how to extend the survival times of miners trapped in shaft accidents. It's unclear whether McConnell paid any attention or penned any response.

But Houdini's efforts serve all of us as a guide—it's easy to get claustrophobic and anxious during these times, whether a pandemic, a jail cell, a submarine. Houdini's counsel of how to breathe is a great tool. Breathe in to the slow count of five. Hold for a few seconds and breathe out for ten. Hold and repeat.

Perhaps the most incredible use of conscious breathing was in early summer 2018 at the Tham Luang cave in Thailand. Twelve boys of the Wild Boar soccer team were trapped by an unexpected torrential flood. All twelve survived eighteen days in that cave—their assistant coach Ekkaphon Chanthawong taught the boys how to slow their breathing. When rescuers finally reached the team, the cave was extraordinarily depleted of oxygen but every one of the boys and their coach survived. Sadly, two rescue workers perished. Many of the surviving boys were sent to Buddhist monasteries to spend two or more years of giving thanks for their survival—a common practice for people who have been delivered from danger.

I hope you can tell me how you are getting that oxygen to help you through these times. Then take a deep deep breath—feel the gift of oxygen that nature gives you. Blow it out. And release the negative to be taken back by nature.

Houdini died of peritonitis (ruptured appendix) after McGill University student J. Gordon Whithead punched him on a dare. Houdini's wife Bess would have seances every Halloween to try to communicate with Harry, believing there was no force, not even death, that could trap Houdini. Houdini had left her with a secret code that she offered many a seance to unlock. The last seance was on Halloween 1936 at the Knickerbocker Hotel in New York. A torrential rainstorm broke out and some thought it was Houdini. But not Bess. She died later that year and was not buried in her husband's crypt because she was not Jewish but she nonetheless is buried nearby. Houdini fans hold a seance every Halloween at the Weisz (Weiss) site where he is buried.

On August 6, 1945 29 year old Mitsubishi engineer Tsutomu Yamaguchi was on a business trip to Hiroshima when the American Enola Gay dropped the first atomic bomb on the city. Yamaguchi suffered burns over much of his body and temporarily lost his hearing and sight. Nonetheless he survived and, considering himself lucky enough, he made his way home to Nagasaki. It was there that the Americans welcomed him home with a second atomic bomb. Yamaguchi was badly injured but nonetheless survived. At the time he said "I thought the mushroom cloud had followed me from Hiroshima."

As many of you know, I was adopted when I was three. My first adoptive parents met during World War II at Oak Ridge, Tennessee—he was a chemical engineer working on a secret project which he didn't even know was an atomic bomb. His sweetheart worked for the war effort at a munitions factory. The men were sequestered in a hotel, the women in a dormitory. For only limited hours they were allowed to leave their rooms. Their phone calls and letters were monitored and censored to ensure that they gave away no secrets. The munitions women worked an eight hour shift and then punched out only to go back to work for another unpaid eight hours simply because everyone was pulling together to get our soldiers home. She lived mostly on liver and onions because it was a dish that would increase iron in the blood, making it possible to donate pints more frequently than the government would allow. The Japanese, Yamaguchi included, were making similar sacrifices for their land.

As for Yamaguchi? He lived to be 93 years old and his wife, who had been in Nagasaki during this period, lived to be 88.

August 07

On August 7, 1906 farmer William Jared Manly of Erie, Pennsylvania obtained a patent for a chicken treadmill. Long living, skinny chickens were prized for their egg production. Sadly, the treadmill proved unpopular as farmers ditched raising chickens for their eggs instead of more profitably for meat!

August 08

August 8 reminds us that history is full of calamities that resolve themselves in the most unexpected ways.

On this day in 1588, England looked to be doomed. Queen Elizabeth's ex-brother-in-law Philip 2 of Spain had sent a group of ships to take back his rightful place on the throne.

Say what??? But Philip had two points—he was the widower of Mary Tudor who is a queen most notable for loping off the heads of Protestants and for lending her name to a Sunday morning beverage alternative to mimosas. Philip was pissed off at Elizabeth's execution of her cousin Mary Queen of Scots whom many Catholics regarded as the legitimate heir to the throne of Scotland, England and Ireland. Perhaps most importantly, roughly half of England's population was Catholic at that point in Elizabeth's reign. After watching nearly as many of their faith be killed as during Mary's reign, nobody was in an ecumenical mood.

Philip's delegation consisted of 130 ships (with a priest for each ship) and 30,000 sailors and soldiers. Elizabeth, five foot three and a female, looked to be no match. Besides, she had trouble enough trying to keep her head on her shoulders and a crown on top—there were many English who would have welcomed Philip's rule.

The young Queen Elizabeth headed to seaside Tilbury where her forces were assembling and she famously told her troops "I know I have the body of a weak and feeble woman; but I have the heart and stomach of a king, and of a king of England too!"

Great leadership? Perhaps. Superior sailors? Maybe. But there is another factor in the ensuing defeat and rout of the Spanish Armada of ships. A terrific storm fell upon the combatants and the Spanish ships were pushed towards the North Sea and what ships survived the battle ended up on the Northern coast of Ireland. Their descendants are often called "black Irish" because of their black hair.

Arguably, without that sudden and unexpected storm, Elizabeth would be just another wannabe royal who got her head chopped off and Espanol would be the official language of the barrios of London.

How has fate, nature, or God intervened for you?

____

____

____

____

August 09

On August 9, 1945 an American plane dropped a nuclear bomb on the Japanese city of Nagasaki. A few days before Hiroshima had gotten the same treatment. Altogether, 355,000 deaths, mostly women and children. The war was effectively over.

There was, however, another casualty in 2014 that is worth note.

Japan in defeat went into a bad funk in all its aspects. Including a dance style devised by Kahuo Ohno and Tatsumi Hajakata who experimented with something they called "Buto" (sometimes with an "h" at the end of the word as it was spelled in English). It was meant to reject and repudiate both Eastern and Western cultures with a particular focus on the wickedness of America and Japan. Characterized by slow controlled and distorted movements it would tackle such taboos as murder, homosexuality, pedophilia. And it was done in the nude with the body covered by white makeup.

It would be one of those avant garde things not suitable for a first date but its greatest proponent was V. Katsura Kan. He taught in Boulder, Colorado. He was probably 71 when he met late twenties Sharoni Stern. The duo sure could put on a Buto show but they also had a sick relationship. Stern's parents were alarmed and several times tried to kidnap her from this one man cult. Sharoni would keep escaping home and running back to Kan.

In 2012 Kan ultimately sent her away, telling her he had no use for her any longer. She killed herself. On August 8, 2021 the parents won a pyrrhic victory in the form of a civil judgment against Kan. Thus the last victim of Nagasaki and Hiroshima.

How has history's events impacted you?

August 10, 2003 marks a Valentine's Day of the extraterrestrial kind. On this day 41 year old cosmonaut Yuri Malenchanko and his beloved 27 year old Ekaterina Dmitriev tied the knot.

The bride was at NASA headquarters in Houston, Texas. She wore a cream colored gown. A paper cut out of the groom was in the reception room. One of Yuri's fellow cosmonauts officiated. At the end of the ceremony Ekaterina blew her husband a kiss. Yuri, who had smuggled a tail coat, tie, and ring onto the space station blew her a kiss in return from 240 miles over New Zealand. Texas is a gracious state which allows proxy marriages in which the betrothed don't have to be together.

The Soviet government was NOT happy and no cosmonaut has done that matrimonial thing again.

The long distance (after all, Yuri often went on space flights of over 200 days at a time) only strengthened their love. They talked on the phone, they wrote, they pined away for each other. After the first outer space wedding, Yuri returned to earth. The couple had a traditional Russian Orthodox wedding and went on to have one daughter. They are still married, even after Yuri went on a few more space flights.

So the next time you're complaining that you can't maintain a relationship with someone who's out of your zip code, just think of these two! Long distance relationships can work!

Yekaterina Dmitriyeva, the bride of Russian cosmonaut Yury Malenchenko

Well, maybe they can. What's your distance limit?

Charles Dickens was known for his novels—my favorite being A Christmas Carol and of course Tale of Two Cities. He had so much to be proud of—wonderful children he abandoned and an ex-wife he ditched for a younger version! But on August 11, 1844 there was something he was utterly enamored with—His moustache.

On this day in 1844 while vacationing in Italy he wrote to a friend with an update on his facial hair.

"The moustaches are glorious, glorious! I have cut them short and trimmed them a little to improve their shape. They are charming, charming. Without them, life would be a blank."

Luckily, Charles was not Amish who have a practice of shaving all moustaches until marriage and then as having become a man he grows a beard and cannot ever cut it. But moustaches? Absolutely not! Moustaches lead to vanity in grooming.

Facial hair?
Yes or No.

Ah, the greatest and possibly first road trip ever! On August 12, 1888 Cecilie Bertha Benz needed to travel—her mother was ill and Bertha was a good daughter. And once she had determined that she would visit her mother, some 66 miles away from her home in Manheim, Germany, she proved herself a good wife as well.

Okay, at first Mr. Benz—we call him Karl—might have groused. After all, he didn't like his wife leaving him but also he didn't like the fact she stole his car. And not just any car—it was his only car, a prototype he had built himself. Prior to his mother in law's illness the car had only been kept in the Benz garage while he perfected this new form of transportation.

We Americans think that Henry Ford invented the automobile. No, this horseless carriage was long in the making in Europe. Benz knew how to make an automobile. Ford knew how to make a lot of them, revolutionizing the idea of an assembly line. Which is how pretty much everything is made these days.

The trip for Bertha hit some, ahem, speed bumps that all future road trips would have. At one point she had to use her garter to insulate a frayed ignition wire and her hatpin to clean a clogged fuel pipe. She may have invented the field of auto mechanics—and you know what? Everybody in Germany marveled and wanted a ... Mercedes Benz!

Traveling without the husband's permission was illegal. But lest you think Karl a hapless sexist toad, think on these words he wrote of his wife—"Only one person remained with me in the small ship of life when it seemed destined to sink. That was my wife, brave and resolute!"

August 13

August 13 we celebrate Sinistrality! This holiday was created by Dean R. Campbell (1928-2017), an Army veteran and in later years, an owner of an Anheuser Busch distributorship in Kansas. He served his community in a number of volunteer capacities even though he was a Sinistralitist, a holiday celebrated on the thirteenth and we all know how dangerous that is.

Sinister, wow, that's a word that conjures up bad stuff. Sinister. Spooky. Up to no good. Well, actually, sinisterality means left-handed. Lots of folks over the years have thought there was something bad about left handedness. In most Muslim countries, it's considered an extreme breach of etiquette to touch the food at table with your left hand. For many centuries in western culture, mothers and teachers would attempt to "change" their child's left-handed ways, sometimes involving smacking the child when s/he used that hand for writing or picked up their fork. As late as the 1990s there were research papers connecting an increased possibility of schizophrenia in folks with sinistralism. If I try to explain the whole reasoning on that one, you'd be reading this post for another five hours and it would cure your pesky insomnia.

But back to Campbell. Many things in the military are geared to right-handed folks (same with medicine—most surgical tools cater to right-handed surgeons but there is a smaller market for the 10% of the population that is left hand dominant). The single exception I have heard for a left-handed advantage is in landing a plane as opposed to take off. So next time you get on a plane, ask if the co-pilot is left-handed.

On August 13, 1976 Campbell had had quite enough of the discrimination. Even in something so simple as his favorite sport golf. So he founded the Lefthanders International Society and declared August 13 Lefthander's Day, or as we know it now, Sinistrality. The ten percent of the population that deserves some respect.

So maybe today do something different. If you're right-handed, try writing a letter with your left hand. No fair smudging the ink on the paper. If you're a surgeon or an airplane pilot I wouldn't suggest switching up your routine, but just appreciating how some of your colleagues have to adjust.

If you have a left-handed child, don't admonish. Instead appreciate. After all, Leonardo da Vinci was left-handed and look at what he got done!

Leftie or Rightie?

____

____

____

____

August 14, 1935 and President Franklin Delano Roosevelt signed into law the Social Security Act which levied a tax on employees and employers alike in order to provide a retirement fund for all Americans. The program took a while to get started because it wasn't until 1940 that the first recipient of a retirement check—Ida May Fuller of Ludlow, Vermont—applied for and was sent $22.54. A schoolteacher born in 1874, she received monthly benefits until her death in 1975. The first social security number was issued to 23 year old John D. Sweeney Jr. (055-09-0001) who was a shipping clerk in Westchester County as he learned his father's business. Sweeney lived with his family in a 15 room home and the entire family voted for the Republican Alf Landon in the presidential election in 1936. Not exactly supporters of FDR. Sweeney died in 1974 at the age of 61 without having collected a dime.

This past year the payout from Social Security will be $1.2 trillion given to 66 million people. There is a separate supplemental program for the poor which will pay out $61 billion to 7.5 million folks. Just before Mother's Day, the Social Security Administration publishes a list of the most popular baby names based on applications for SS numbers.

Social Security benefits are, like I said, paid for by taxes on both the employee/future recipient and his/her employer. That's money taken out of your paycheck or payroll. But joke's on you—in 1984 Congress decided to tax these benefits. We might call that double taxation since it's taxing money that was already taxed from you and whoever you worked for. There's always been talk that Congress will somehow abolish the system, but I think it will go quietly, as the taxation on benefits rises. It will be an irrelevant add on to income tax. Ha ha! Actually, I'm not sure I think that's funny.

The first Social Security recipient recieving her first check.

How much of your retirement income will be social security?

August 15 is National Relaxation Day, a day to chillax and let the tensions in your shoulders, your brain, your stomach just surrender to feeling absolutely no pressure. I figured this holiday was created by an overworked stockbroker, lawyer or any mother.

But no, it was created in 1985 by 9 year old fourth grader Sean Moeller from Michigan. A day to do nothing might mean playing video games all day but if you get yourself worked up playing World of Warcraft try something else. A book maybe. Gardening is great unless you start swearing at the weeds. Laying on a hammock might be best. Or just get a stress ball which was invented in 1988 by Alex Carswell, I use them when I get my B-vitamin shots. Calms me down enough so that I don't hit the nurse when the needle hits my butt cheek!

There are so many ways to relax, calm down, take a break from panic and pressure. I have developed a special relationship with Jason Stephenson who posts meditation videos on Youtube. Many a night I think "it's not going to work I'm way too tense" and then I wake up three hours later to an ad for Cialus and realize I've gotten some of that bliss I was looking for.

Somehow, I think the 1986 movie Ferris Bueller's Day Off might have been inspired by Moeller.

In 2016, Moeller started identifying for each year one relaxer of, er, merit and put it on his X (neé Twitter) account. I don't have X or Twitter so I couldn't tell you who this year's winner will be. Maybe me this year!

National Relaxation Day is not to be confused with August 24th Slacker Day which is a British invention designed to encourage folks to stay in bed, call in sick to work and pull the covers back up over their heads. The Pandemic Lockdown sort of made all of us slackers so now having a single day to celebrate is a bit weird.

No, no, Relaxation Day is just one special gem of a day to kick back, relax, take it easy, enjoy yourself. No guilt.

How will you spend your day?

____

____

____

____

____

Yo ho ho, Matey! Grab your eye patch and your swearing parrot! Raise a bottle of rum to Johnny Depp and the Pirates of the Caribbean! Maybe pledge your allegiance to pre-Castro Cuba of Fulgencio Batista and grab a six pack of Coca Cola to go with the afore mentioned.

August 16 is International Rum Day. Rum, dark or light, the favorite beverage or mixer of pirates and Battiste loyal Cubans alike. First, what is rum? It's fermented from sugar cane or from one of its processing by-products molasses. All rum is clear when the process is done but dark rum is made by adding certain spices and dyes.

Although many civilizations played around with fermenting sugar, what we now know as rum was created by 16th century Caribbean slaves using molasses—everyone's got to get their drink on, right? It was often called the Devil's Drink because it was so cheap and easy to make. Devil knows how to run a business, don't he? Then colonials got the idea you could use sugar cane. And that you could mix it as a cocktail. And that you could make money off it. And sway elections.

Elections? Say what? Those colonials started using rum as a means of currying favor with elected officials who in turn learned to figure out who was going to "donate" the most of the sweet stuff to them.

The taste for rum made its way to Staten Island with an opening of a distillery in 1664. Boston opened one three years later and rum soon became one of New England's most profitable industry. Distillers in Rhode Island even made a particularly strong version which was used as currency in the slave trade. In the colonies, it was estimated that men, women and children each drank three gallons of the stuff a year on average. Sailors were given daily allotments of rum which was mixed with water to make grog.

Europeans stuck up their noses, deciding that the only rum worth drinking was Caribbean. Thus we associate rum with Cuba instead of, say, Vermont.

The best way to celebrate the day is to mix up a Cuba Libre aka rum and Coke. Rum is quite possibly the only alcohol that can improve upon the taste of Coke. You could do it in costume as a way of testing out a potential Halloween persona. Or just sip it on the back porch.

I don't drink rum, but write down your favorite rum based drink?

August 17, 1957 it was not a very good day to be Alice Roth. Or Richie Ashburn for that matter.

Ashburn was playing his usual center field spot for the Phillies, a position he held from 1948-1959. He had many nicknames including Whitey because of his bleach blond hair, the Tilden Flash because of his home-town Tilden in Nebraska but my favorite is Putt Putt because he could run so fast that either Ted Williams or Stan Musial is said to have commented "you would think he had twin motors in his pants."

As a batter, he was pretty good but more of a singles hitter than a slugger. A good reliable get onto first base guy. My younger son was really bad at tots baseball and I advised him to never swing. Because all he had to do was get to first base and that's good enough. He was a great at getting a walk.

On August 17, 1957 Alice Roth, wife of Earl Roth the sports editor of the Philadelphia Bulletin, was enjoying the game in the stands when Putt Putt stepped up to the plate. He hit a foul ball which struck Alice right in the face, breaking her nose. As medics carried her away in a stretcher, Putt Putt hit the next pitch right onto Alice's leg.

Moral: that guy had aim! Alternative moral: maybe he had a crush on her.

After Putt Putt left the Phillies he played a year for the Cubs and another for the Mets. But his heart was always with Philadelphia (although he lived in Tilden during the offseason). He became a beloved broadcaster for the Phillies. He became good friends with the Roths and even got their son a position as bat boy for the Phillies. And Alice never slapped him with a kid glove.

Even so, when he became eligible for the Hall of Fame years later, Alice's husband exacted his revenge by voting fifteen times against him over the ensuing fifteen years. A fan initiated petition blitzkrieg erupted and Putt Putt was inducted into the baseball hall of fame in 1995, two years before he passed on.

I guess the real moral of the story is that you can have a terrible, rotten, no good day but you can turn it around with a good attitude, a smile on your face, and if you've done wrong, a houseplant and an apology note does a lot of good. Or if you have a crush on a gal, send her flowers or chocolates, not a baseball!

We all have had bad days.
How do you turn one of them around?

August 18

A lot of my friends are using memory games and puzzles to help stall the degenerative effects of age. Some use Sudoku, some use crossword puzzles, some use fancy apps, and some use programs their doctors prescribe. Or drugs.

They might have gotten the idea from Mark Twain, aka Samuel Clemens, who on August 18, 1885 patented "Mark Twain's Memory Builder: a game for acquiring and retaining all sorts of facts and dates."

He had an odd notion of what to do and how to go about it. The instructions declared that the most important facts in history were the "accession of kings". So for instance, correctly answering that James 1 was crowned the English king in 1603 got you ten points. Queen Victoria 1838? That's five points right there. Declaration of Independence in 1776? Just one point, mostly because there wasn't an accession of royalty.

I have plenty of friends who are going to great lengths to hang onto their memory. Me? There's so much I'd like to forget. And the friends? Really, I sort of can't remember their names now. I just call everybody sweetpea.

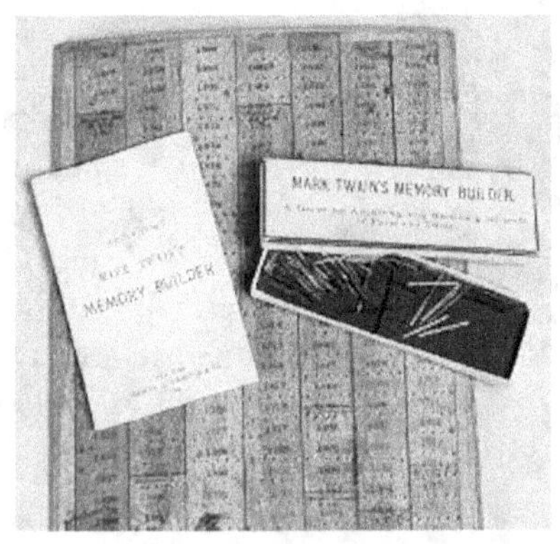

Regular exercise of the body is super important!
What do you do to exercise your mind?

____

____

____

____

____

August 19

On August 19th, 1883, Gabrielle "Coco" Chanel was born in France. While she had a rough childhood after being abandoned to a convent-run orphanage, she put on her big girl panties and decided she was going to make something of herself. The nuns encouraged practical skills, amongst them sewing. But Coco decided she wasn't just going to be hemming rich gals' hems. In 1910, she opened her first shop, where she kickstarted her brand by selling hats. Later, she added evening gowns and very simple day dresses.

IN World War I, soldiers flooded Paris and wanted something special to send their sweeties back home. Coco would gift wrap her personally created perfume Chanel No. 5 and ship to the gal. She did foresee that my habit of wearing all black was non plus ultra of elegance.

She did have a rather unfortunate habit of hanging out with the Nazis, at least

until World War II was over. But growing up in her circumstances had taught her survival skills. She fended off accusations of collaborating with the Nazis. She reigned supreme over fashion and beauty until her death at 87 in 1971.

Go immediately to your closet, bring out that black dress. A few baubles, a short snappy haircut and a spritz of perfume that makes you irresistible. I wear Thierry Mugler's Angel because Chanel No. 5 starts to smell like asparagus on me. I once had a kindergarten boy sniff the back of my hand and tell me he loved me just because I smelled so nice. I told him I'd wait for him. I was lying, but hey, Coco would have done the same.

What's your perfume?

____

____

____

____

____

A question for y'all—

Who's the greatest mass murderer of all time? I'm just talking numbers. John Wayne Gacy? Charles Manson? Amateurs. Okay, Vlad the Impaler or maybe Genghis Kahn if you're old school—Hitler or Stalin or Pol Pot if you're a modernist.

Nope, the greatest mass murderer of all time is the itsy bitsy mosquito.

Let me back up. Malaria is estimated to have killed half of all the people in the world who have EVER lived. In 2018 even with advances in medicine there were 228 million cases worldwide with 405,000 deaths with children under five the most vulnerable. Most of these deaths occur in Sub-Sahara Africa.

Why the southern climes? That was a mystery until August 20, 1897 when Dr. Ronald Ross discovered that female mosquitoes can transmit the disease from human to human. Mosquitoes, especially the females, don't like to winter in a cold climate. Ross paved the way for medical advances, vaccines and treatments that have drastically cut the number of cases and has reduced the mortality rate. Even so, it's a carrier of a disease that makes Covid look like a rank amateur.

So why do I bring up such a depressing topic? Well, it's not depressing. It's encouraging. Somewhere out there is a scientist who's going to figure out Covid and its variants. While it would be uncomfortable to believe Covid will always be with us, there is the prospect that very soon the Brits will invent another cocktail. You're wondering why I'm bringing up cocktails.

Today, August 20, the London School of Hygiene and Tropical Medicine will celebrate world mosquito day with lectures and parties. In the days when the sun never set on the British Empire, young men were being sent overseas to colonize India, Africa, lots and lots of Asia. Their mortality rates were higher for malaria than for combat deaths. Their sacrifices for their country amazing.

Quinine was considered a prophylactic against the disease and young British men going overseas were advised to ingest it over the course of weeks and months prior to their travels. The stuff tasted vile and was a tough sell. But if you added gin and a slice of lime … well, that's how we got the gin and tonic. Greatest contribution to the art and science of mixology!

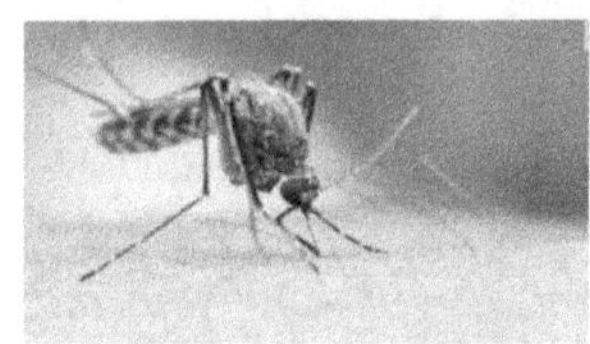

How will you celebrate the eradication of malaria? One part gin, two parts tonic, a slice of lime for me!

August 21

On August 21, 1911, a formerly "okay it's nice but we don't think about it all that much" painting the Mona Lisa by Leonardo da Vinci was stolen from the Louvre by three Italian workman. Suddenly, the painting was considered da bomb!* When it was recovered in 1913, the thieves claimed they were just taking it to return it to its home country Italy. Conveniently forgetting that da Vinci had been under the patronage of the French King Francis I at the time and had brought the painting to His Highness as a present.

Art heists are rarer than, say, flash mobs grabbing everything out of a Louis Vuitton store or a 7-11 but there's been some interesting ones—

The Gardner Museum in Boston response to their own heist is sort of fun. Art collector Isabella Stewart Gardner stipulated in her will that all the pieces and presentations would remain exactly as she envisioned them. In March, 1990 thieves looted the joint, appearing to have a particular fondness for Rembrandts. The Museum has kept the empty frames exactly as they were pre-heist.

Edvard Munch made four versions of The Scream, a painting he described as being about a "gust of melancholy." In 1994 one version was stolen from the National Art Museum in Oslo during an exhibition tied to the Lillehammer Olympics. Also known as the Tonya Harding Nancy Kerrigan Rumble in the Rink. The art thieves wanted $1 million, an offer which was declined. The picture was retrieved without incident a few months later. But ten years later, another version of The Scream was stolen from the Munch Museum.

In 2003, the Whitworth Museum in Manchester, England was relieved of a bunch of paintings done by Gauguin, Picasso and Van Gogh. This one is fun—there was no ransom note, no attempt to sell to a reclusive billionaire, mais non! The paintings were hung in the bathroom of the museum with a manifesto suggesting that art is for everybody. No admission required.

I don't really understand art thievery even though I have watched The Thomas Crown Affair four times and briefly dyed my hair Renee Russo style. My favorite pieces of artwork are those created by my children or by friends. But if I was suddenly gifted by a magnificent classic piece of art I think I'd go The Last Supper because there's so many hidden meanings involved. What about you?

*Fun fact: Italian police even questioned Pablo Picasso—like he would have time to steal the painting, what between sleeping with everything that moved in the south of France and painting his own stuff.

Today consider making your own masterpiece. Will it be a painting, a sculpture, a banana duct taped to a canvas?

August 22 is the feast of Saint Guinefort of France. He was a dog. How can a dog be a saint? In 1250 on this day, in a castle near Lyon, France, a knight came home to his castle and looked in on his baby son. The nursery was a disaster area and the crib up-ended. No sign of the son. And there was Guinefort with a bloody mouth. The knight was so furious thinking Guinefort had killed his son that he smacked him/her/it with a saber sword. Then he heard the baby son crying under the bed. He saw the dead viper with bloody dog tooth marks all over it. That's when he knew it was his dog who was the valiant saviour.

Guinefort had saved the baby and was repaid by his master with his own canine life. The knight was so upset (his wife too) that they gently buried Guinefort in a well and planted into the well trees in gratitude and memory of the brave French greyhound. People started visiting the site, particularly mothers with sick children. Apparently, the visits cured kids, hence the miracles of sainthood.

But Guinefort is not officially a saint. He is venerated with his feast day (saints are venerated on the day of their "homegoing") On different days there is Saint Gelert of Wales and the story of the Indian Brahmin and the Mongoose. Same general story line. The Catholic Church tried to suppress his cult, but animals can be saints, can't they?

Take a look at your pet. Whether it's a dog or cat or goldfish or oh jeez I have friends who own a python I NEVER want to see. Because a python can open its mouth so that it's six times larger than its head.

Recognize that your pet devotes its life to thinking you are the MOST important human in the universe. They love you, they worship you, they don't have a life outside of you and they would definitely chew up that viper attacking your baby in the nursery. They're saints.

Except my friend's pet python, forget about him. He's not going to do you any favors.

Saint Guinefort

What's your pet's name?

____

____

____

____

____

Today August 23, 1977 aeronautic history as well as ecowarriorism was formed. Engineer Paul McCready, founder of Aerovironment ("do more with less") flew a human powered plane he named the Gossamer Condor in order to win the first Henry Kremer prize for pioneers of human powered flight. Industrialist Kremer had started the prize in 1959 but 1977 was THE FIRST YEAR IT WORKED! Paul McCready would win the prize again in 1979 when he flew the Gossamer Albatross from England to France.

Total carbon footprint: zero. Fuel: nothing.

Some of you will note the resemblance to Leonardo da Vinci's drawings of a flying machine he intended to make. Meanwhile, ecowarriors and influencers Harry and Megs recently took a 12 seat Cessna Citation Sovereign to a conference to harangue us on how we're destroying the planet. They required 247 gallons of jet fuel an hour. The most vociferous of ecowarriors Leonardo di Caprio leaves a ten ton carbon footprint while scouting for 25 or younger girlfriends and telling us how we're destroying the planet.

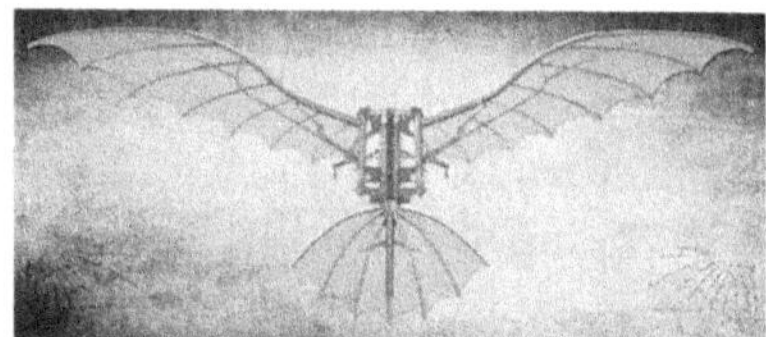

When you fly someplace, even if you're scrunched in your coach seat, do you feel guilty?

On August 24, 1967 Abbie Hoffman—cofounder of the anarchist group yippies and author of "Steal This Book"—planned a publicity stunt. He took 15 pals on a tour of the New York Stock Exchange, the capitol building of capitalism. At the end of the tour, the group gathered on the balcony overlooking the trading floor. The cohorts took from their pockets three hundred one dollar bills. It wasn't raining men. It wasn't raining cats and dogs. It was raining cash. Trading was halted for six minutes as brokers scrambled and squabbled over the largesse.

Having proven his point about greed and green, Hoffman's group left. Two weeks later, the NYSE spent $20k to enclose the balcony with bulletproof glass. Sadly, Hoffman committed suicide in 1989 but I would have loved to see a little more, er, theater from him!

What's the funnest practical joke you pulled and what did it teach you about human nature?

August 25

On August 25, 1835 the New York Sun premiered a six part series of articles supposedly reprinted from the University of Edinburgh announcing that vampires, or if you prefer Lain Vespertilio-homo, had been discovered on the moon. According to the articles, a newfangled telescope also discovered bison, goats, beavers and unicorns wandering the moonscape with great dignity and pleasant countenance.

The Sun newspaper, founded only two years before, had had middling circulation figures but these spectacular findings set off a firestorm. Scientists all over the United States debated the possibilities of this new development. Circulation of the paper skyrocketed until…reporter Richard Adams Locke admitted that he had made up the story.

Still, the circulation figures didn't change and who knows? Maybe there are vampires! The Sun continued to publish independently until 1950 when it merged with the New York World-Telegram which folded in the sixties.

August 26

On August 26, 1805, the Corps of Discovery Expedition reached the head of the Columbia River in Idaho all the way from Eastern America and they were thinking they should turn around and go back. Might be August but it was damn cold. The men had been wearing moccasins that would tear apart in a single day of hiking. The heads of the mission to explore the Louisiana Purchase—all the land President Jefferson had bought from the French—were Meriweather Lewis and his dear friend Lewis Clark. The duo got to mostly ride horses. But the crew wore their moccasins out and then spent their evenings stitching up their footwear for the next day's adventures. Nobody was happy.

I don't think guide Sakagawea was wearing Christian Louboutins. But I think the men would have done well to look at what she was wearing.

The expedition took a couple of years and sort of set the template for NASA, with its experiments in medicine, astronomy, botany and cartography. It was a great success, with only one member of the fifty odd men passing from acute appendicitis. Today, you can see the International Space Station flying overhead in the middle of the night, which is something I do. The astronauts are not just sitting up there playing poker and doing gravitation-less backflips. They're kind of a laboratory like Lewis and Clark but with the whole universe.

But the true lesson of today's day in history is take care of your feet. They get you places.

I like an epson salt concotion in a tub in front of the TV. How about you?

On August 27, 1896, Suldan Khalid bin Barghash of Zanzibar was enjoying his morning breakfast. He had successfully poisoned his cousin Sultan Hamad bin Thuwaini al-Busaid two days before and was sighing with contentment over his rule of the small island off the eastern coast of Africa.

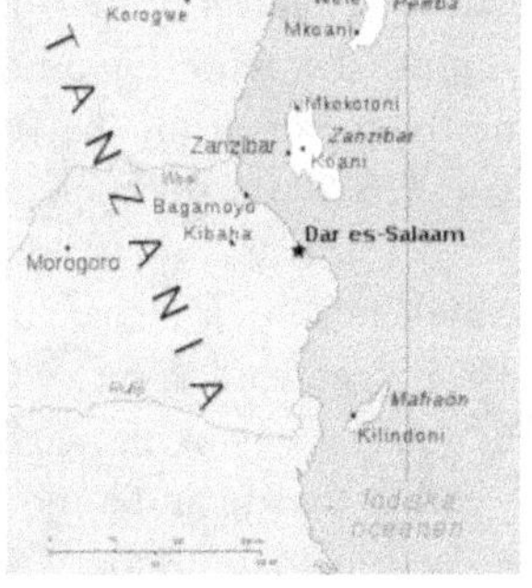

Yes, Zanzibar was small—a mere 950 square miles—but it was pivotal in the slave trade. The Sultans of Zanzibar had made good money selling slaves to the Portuguese, the Spanish, the Germans, and even the Brits.

Khalid bin Barghash expected to make that same bank. But as he looked out of his balcony at his Beit al Hukum palace he noticed three British cruisers and two gunboats lolling about in the bay.

Ah, the Brits! A country with a square footage that could fit inside Illinois, Indiana, and a chunk of Ohio had managed to spread its tentacles out all across the globe. Its citizens liked to boast that the sun never set on the Empire and the way they got there started with the slave trade. We'd like to think it was those wicked Spaniard conquistadors or American idiots but perhaps we just feel uncomfortable pointing an accusatory finger at that mild mannered grandmother Queen Victoria who engineered the takeover of our world. The Brits became industrialized and as is the habit of those who move away from agricultural based economies, they had "evolved" or "woke" and were decidedly abolitionist. They didn't want the Sultan making money and on August 26 instead of sending a congratulatory telegram to him for killing his rival they told him that the moving trucks for the antislavery Hamud bin Muhammed would be arriving at 9 a.m. the next morning to take his position.

If the Brits wanted war, the Sultan would give them war! He was not without resources. He had a yacht, the HHS Glasgow, and he had some palace guards, servants and, yes, slaves. Sultan sent a message to British Consul Basil Cave stating "we have no intention of hauling down our flag and we do not believe you would open fire upon us."

Forty minutes later, the palace was destroyed, the Glasgow sunk, and the Sultan had shimmered off into the morning mist. It still remains the shortest war in history and way easier to keep track of than the hundred years' war (or more accurately the 116 year war) conducted between the Lancasters, Yorks, Valoises, and … oh never mind!

If there's a moral to the story of the hapless Sultan it is that getting a lot done early in the morning makes one feel pretty productive but there might be some glitches.

What's your favorite morning routine?

____

____

____

____

____

August 28

On August 28, 1938 my alma mater Northwestern University* awarded Mr. Mc-Carthy a degree. It was honorary to be sure, but hey, he didn't have to attend classes! A journalist reporting on the graduation ceremony commented that "certainly it will not be the first time that a blockhead has received a university degree."

Mr. McCarthy took no offense. After all, he WAS a blockhead. He was the puppet teammate of ventriloquist Edgar Bergen** and he had a cynical, edgy (for the time), talk back atcha disposition. He had worked with Bergen since Bergen was 13. Bergen paid $36 to a Chicago woodworker to create Charlie based on a redhead newspaper boy in his neighborhood. By the 1930s Charlie was wearing tuxedo and a monocle. Oddly the duo had their best success in a radio show.

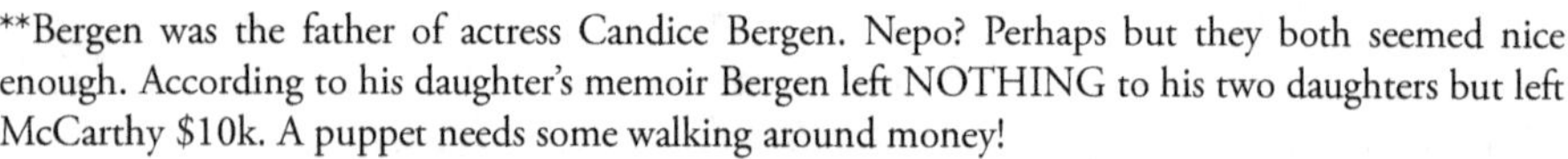

Bergen had gone to Northwestern majoring premed but never finished. Money may have changed hands in getting McCarthy his honorary degree but hey, that's just how it works.

*I graduated North Central College in Naperville, Illinois, Northwestern for law school.

**Bergen was the father of actress Candice Bergen. Nepo? Perhaps but they both seemed nice enough. According to his daughter's memoir Bergen left NOTHING to his two daughters but left McCarthy $10k. A puppet needs some walking around money!

August 29

Today is the anniversary of Judgment Day, which occurred on August 29,1997. Beginning at 2:14 a.m. on that fateful day Russia was attacked by nuclear missiles by a cadre of Skynet machines. As the historian and single mom Sarah Connor* described it "the survivors of the nuclear fire, lived to face a new nightmare, the War Against the Machines."

But wait! We're still here! Even if Skynet the leading machines had achieved consciousness and decided they had had quite enough of the humans making them do all the dirty work. The war between Machines and humans went on well into 2029 and it didn't look too good for humankind.

I think The Terminator must have been inspired by my father Justin Leiber's 1985 book Can Animals and Machines Be Persons?** Justin's conclusion is that everything depends on consciousness, the ability to be aware that you're a separate entity and that you have control over your actions and thoughts. He references an Alan Tur-

*Sarah Connor was played by Linda Hamilton who married director James Cameron when they did Terminator 2. They got divorced and remarried and divorced again. She now claims to be celibate and okay with it. How bad could Cameron have been?

ing thought experiment in which a robot goes toe to toe with a human. The human loses. Damn, we always do.

Today there's a lot of talk about whether artificial intelligence is going to take over

our jobs, our armies, our government, our very lives. To say nothing of our sex lives as there are some pretty amazing artificial "dolls".... A very terminator-esque scenario shaping up. And now we have Ameca the robot who is awfully human like especially if they'd put some damn clothes on her. In the interview she is articulate and thoughtful. I'm scared of her already.

So enjoy the anniversary of Judgment Day and consider whether you're concerned or not by recent developments and where you think the future is heading. Given Sarah Connor's experiences in later Terminator movies, I need to ramp up my bicep workout. In the first movie Sarah was a bit of a schlub but she got her game on. Also, I need to get some kick ass aviator glasses.

**Justin believed humans were really only human when they reach consciousness when they are about four years old. I was three when he and my mother put me up for adoption. He was an affirmed atheist and a brilliant mind and when we met when I was 27 he treated me as his daughter in the only way he knew how. The book can be purchased on Amazon and it's a quick but insightful and spooky read. Especially these days.

August 30

I'm naming August 30 "Americans Just Don't Know How to Leave a Party Gracefully Day." There's other holidays on the thirtieth of the eighth month. It's Frankenstein Day because it's the birthday of author Mary Wollstonecraft Shelley. It's International Cabernet Sauvignon Day and I don't have to tell you how you're supposed to celebrate that because I don't like it. So you can have my glass.

But I'm sticking with Americans Just Don't Know How to Leave a Party Gracefully Day. On August 30, 2021 American forces finished up the exit from Kabul's airport. The last American to board the last C-17 transport plane was Army Major Christopher Donahue who was wearing his night goggles and following Ambassador Ross Wilson. Planes overhead protected the takeoff and the Taliban were already in the airport scooping up night goggles Americans had left behind—spoils of war, you know.

Over the course of the preceding two weeks, nearly 120k Americans and friendly Afghans (those who had been working for us) had been evacuated. Beginning first, of course, with Afghan President Ashraf Ghani, his wife and some senior staff in a flotilla of MI-17 helicopters. And then came the deluge of folk, mostly men, at Hamid Karzai International Airport. The operation was called the Pineapple Express, not to be confused with the marijuana strain of the same name.

Everyone had been vetted and their documents reviewed and their belongings searched at a secret doorway to the airport known as the Black Gate. But there were a number of Americans, friendly Afghans, wives and children of the very pilots who were flying others to safety and a group of orphans who were asked to the Gate on the twenty-fifth. They arrived by four crowded buses and disembarked to have their passports reviewed (again), their luggage searched (again), their permissions sorted through (again). Suddenly, a colonel of the 82nd ordered all of them back on the buses and get the H to the double L out of here. Pandemonium—the Taliban were right outside the Gate and everyone knew the fate of the bus travelers faced. Some of the soldiers objected and asked can we at least get the Americans out. Denied. Or the orphans? Ixnay. What about the wives? It wasn't a negotiation. It was an order. The group was pushed back onto the buses and the Black Gate was closed off and reinforced in case anybody else tried to make a break for it. And they all knew the Taliban was outside waiting for them.*

---

*One of things I find most unusual about the Ukrainian evacuation it was largely women and children were prioritized for exit—with men even remotely capable of serving in the army staying behind. In both Afghanistan and Saigon it was largely young strong males who got themselves a spot on the plane. During the children's evacuation of Saigon flight attendants were overwhelmed by the influx and complained bitterly "where are the children?!!" On some flights in the so-called evacuation of children there were none.

And then America left the party.

Kind of reminded me of another thirtieth of the month—April 30, 1975 and the fall of Saigon. Americans and our friendly Vietnamese had been told that the song "White Christmas" by Bing Crosby would play on the Armed Forces radio station and that was the signal to get to the Embassy or to get to a predesignated evacuation spot. Everyone already knew the end was nigh, it's not like it was a surprise. The Ambassador ordered the exhumation of his son who had served and died in the war and was buried underneath the largest tree in the Embassy's courtyard. Lot of work went into getting that tree chopped down. All around Saigon, South Vietnamese soldiers stripped down on the streets, leaving streets paved with combat boots, hoping to pass themselves off as hapless, shoeless farmers or some such.

It is never easy to leave a war and sometimes it's hard to get one's self extricated from a party. How would we do better when we fight on foreign soil and create allegiances that will be sloughed off when we retreat? Because I think one should leave a war and a party with equal grace and no collateral damage.

You're in a country as an American expat. You get five tickets (the last ones!) on a flight out. Who do you take?

____

____

____

____

August 31 is National Distance Learning Day. A system of learning we have become quite familiar with due to Covid and the University of Phoenix. We rely on computers and zoom for this endeavor. But distance learning owes its origins to Joseph Lancaster from London more than two centuries ago.

In 1829 Lancaster, an avowed Quaker with a social conscience, devised the idea of a correspondence school for poor children whose parents couldn't afford tuition or who lived where there weren't any schools to be had. The school was free for its students and relied on the British Mail System to deliver lessons, homework, tests, and the all important diploma. Lancaster later moved to teach at a Quaker school in Philadelphia but he continued his mission of getting the three Rs to the poor.*

In 1920 Winnetka's own Dr. William Hadley suffered an episode of scarlet fever which left him with impaired vision. He learned Braille, a system of reading and writing invented by French educator Louis Braille that uses patterned dimples on paper.** A visually impaired farmer's wife from Western United States heard of the story of Hadley and had her husband write to him asking for help so that his wife could read and write. Their ensuing correspondence inspired Hadley to create the eponymous Hadley School for the Blind which today serves all fifty states and a hundred countries. Just as Lancaster's schools, Hadley is free to its students.

The University of Phoenix was founded in 1976 by billionaire John Sperling and his buddy John D. Murphy. It turned into an online program in 1989. Like the two other schools we've talked about, there's open admissions which means anybody can use its resources—and in its first years it was largely employers financing the education of their middle management. Unlike the other two schools, Phoenix was and has always been meant to be for profit.

These days, there are lots of schools for adult education and their template allows for us to navigate COVID or principled distance learning. Although it didn't teach one of my young relatives to freeze in front of the screen and pretend that the computer had malfunctioned. Then she'd turn off the computer and go play or watch tv.

*Rose Nyland of Golden Girls fame once explained that the three Rs were reading, writing, and rooster insemination. The St. Olaf school system she attended was quite something.

**We should really call it Barbier—for French educator Charles Barbier de la Serre who was fascinated by shorthand and other writing methods. He believed that the alphabet was an impediment to poor people learning to read because it was too complicated. He created a system of elevated dots on papyrus and unexpectedly discovered it worked for blind or visually impaired people. He started a school to teach the system and he didn't meet his student Louis Braille until many years later. The system was used by the French Army as a means of coding messages.

So today, to celebrate Distance Learning Day even when you're thinking this distance learning is driving me nuts with my kid in the house all the damn time, just pour a little something into your Starbucks and sit on the couch and let it wash all over you.

September days are summer's best of weather
and autumn's best of cheer.

—Helen Hunt Jackson

September 1, is the anniversary of the most shameless self-promotion in our nation's history. Are we talking TikTok? Or Meghan and Harry? Or the Donald? Or Ye?

No, on this day in 1856 an anonymous rave "boffo boffo" review of a slim volume of poetry appeared in the magazine United States Review, announcing "An American Bard at Last!"

Well, stand ye back William Shakespeare!

"His scope of life is the simplest of any yet in philosophy," the review opined. "He is the largest lover and sympathizer that has appeared in literature."

Oh, dear, my heart's all aflutter and my panties fell around my ankles! And I don't even like poetry.

Now who is this amazing poet? None other than Walt Whitman and the tome was Leaves of Grass which used nonrhyming and threw out the rules of following any particular pattern. The poems focused on sensual pleasures—not anything that would raise an eyebrow today but nonetheless it was swoon-worthy.

Ol' Walt became the darling of the poetry world.

Who wrote the review? This is where it gets interesting. Turns out an attentive reader noticed similarities between the style of Walt's language in poetry and…in writing anonymous reviews. Quel surprise! Quel horreur! The reviewer was uncovered—Walt himself.

He nonetheless survived the controversy of the review. When he passed on in 1892 he had the consolation of knowing that he was the most influential poet in America. Until Robert Frost and Rod Mckuen (ha ha!)

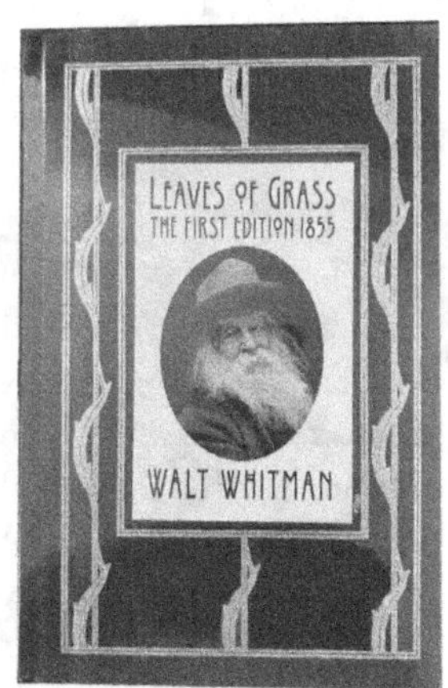

So today, consider writing a poem. For the heck of it. Or maybe just write a glowing review of yourself. Embellish as necessary. Don't have rules.

On September 2, 1846 Queen Victoria wrote of a sartorial coup by her son Prince of Wales, otherwise known as Bertie. Four years old and making an even bigger splash than any Kardashian.

On the royal yacht off the coast of Jersey, Bertie "put on his sailor's dress, which was beautifully made by the man on board who makes for our sailors," the Queen recorded in her diary. "[T]he officers and sailors who were all assembled on deck to see him, cheered and seemed delighted with him."

Bertie's outfit mimicked that of the midshipmen sailors of the nineteenth century but it wasn't until Bertie swaggered about in one that it became fashionable for both boys and girls to wear similar attire.

Bertie later became estranged from his mother when in 1861 his father Prince Albert died of typhoid. Didn't matter to the Queen that what was listed on the death certificate. Bertie was the cause of the Queen's husband's death and she was unforgiving.

Bertie was nineteen and known for being a lazy pleasure seeker. While at Cambridge College he was rumored to sleep with four different women a week. He drank prodigiously and didn't really attend classes. A dynastically perfect marriage had been arranged for him but he had fallen in love with a showgirl (sort of a nice term for it) and was dragging his heels. Sounds like just about every boy I know in my fair town of Winnetka. Except ours have video games.

Prince Albert, although he wasn't feeling well, went out to Cambridge to talk sense into his son. The two seemed to make amends. But on the way back to London Albert's health took a turn for the worse and within weeks he was dead. Obviously, Bertie's fault.

Victoria recorded that the very sight of Bertie made her shudder. He spent 59 years waiting to become king. After her demise in 1901 he took the regnant name of Edward VII, although his close friends and mistresses called him Bertie. The letters he sent to me were signed "yours forever, Bertie" — quite the guy.

You can see the actual suit at the National Maritime Museum in Britain or you can just enjoy the Franz Xaver Winterhalter's 1846 portrait. Young Bertie looks so angelic and sweet. You never know how kids are going to turn out, do you? And you never know if the familial bonds will be as strong.

How did you ever live up to your parents expectations?

____

____

____

____

____

September 3 is National Pet Rock Day! Old enough to remember pet rocks? Young enough to think it's a crazy idea? Well, I think the pet rock has a lesson for all of us.

During the pandemic I noticed EVERYBODY had a dog to walk. If I was walking down the street on the sidewalk, fully masked and distancing, people approached from the opposite direction with their dogs and their grim determination. And then they would lurch towards the street. I took it personally. The lurching. With the masks, I could never tell if someone was looking at me with sheer hatred or whether they were smiling a good morning.

EVERYBODY had a dog. Until they had to go back to the office or school or their country club. Now there are ads on Next Door Neighbor and whatnot asking if anybody can give a home to their little Fido. When there's a new outbreak (some New York epidemiologists and public health officials are already calling for mask requirements to be reinstated) some families will be missing their Fido. Who's probably already dead—PETA has reported that pet euthanasia has skyrocketed.

But let's go back to 1975. Advertising executive Gary Dahl was at a bar with his friends who were complaining about their pets. They had to be fed, taken for walks, their kitty litter scooped up, and then there's veterinarian visits and shots. There's the pets who chew up their shoes (okay, dogs, that's on you). The friends joked around about having a pet rock would be easier. The friends thought nothing of this banter….Except Gary. And he devised a pet rock (costing less than a dollar) to be delivered in a box with holes for ventilation (of course!) and straw bedding (costing nothing). The big problem was the box which was going to be pivotal in the whole marketing campaign. Putting the holes in the box jacked up the price. So Gary devised a booklet entitled "the care and training of your pet rock" and managed to get the price pulled down. Genius.

The manual, btw, included training suggestions. Teaching a pet rock to sit or stay was to be accomplished effortlessly. Come, sit and shake hands were considered to be nearly impossible. Attack was fairly simple but required some help from the pet's owner.

Gary sold over a million of these pets at $4 each. It seemed EVERYONE had to have one in the Christmas season of 1975. But by 1976 people were bored. Or maybe the upkeep (what upkeep?) of the pet rock got to people. Still, Gary was a millionaire and moved on by opening a bar he called Carry Nations in Los Gates, California. Carry Nations is, of course, the famous temperance activist who advocated for Prohibition. Gary passed on in 2015 of pulmonary disease.

Choose: Pet Rock, Dog, Cat?

September 4 is a date that reminds us all that clothes make the man … and the woman!

On September 4, 1759 twenty two year old Helena Slicher married Baron von Slingelandt at the Koolsterkerk in the Hague. She wore a hooped gown aka far-

thingale more than six feet wide with a matching underskirt. The overskirt had a long pleated train. The hoop which held up the skirt was a confection of petticoats and whalebone. The sleeves were fitted with two small round lead weights. But it's the embroidery that really makes this dress—parrot tulips, auricula, dianthus and oriental poppies on silk. She sort of had to slide down the aisle of the church sideways and sitting down for dinner must have been quite a spectacle but with a dress like that, who cares? If I wore a dress like this in Winnetka I'd definitely rule the sidewalk and all those pesky kids on bikes trying to mow down pedestrians would have to think twice.

The clothes that make me are generally black. Black leggings and a matching black T-shirt or sweater. Black shoes. I'm starting to wonder if I should shake things up a little. You know, a color. A different color. Like red. Or yellow. Or … no. Not there yet. Like The Seagull by Chekov:

Medvedko: Why do you always wear black?

Masha: I'm in mourning for my life.

Me: I do it so I don't have to think about what to wear and it's always cheap at Walmart.

What's your go to attire?

____

____

____

____

____

On September 5, 1698 Tsar Peter the Great of Russia issued a proclamation that all men must shave their beards. SAY WHAT?

Russia was at war with Sweden and the Ottoman empire at the same time and you'd think he'd have other things on his mind than facial hair. But he was the kind of guy with a talent for multi-tasking or maybe just plain crazy. Or, most likely, so in love with European culture that he wanted his men to look like they were from Britain or France or Spain.

Russian men all had beards. They grew them long and bushy and accessorized with great moustaches. Peter allowed them to keep the moustaches but a heavy fine was imposed on those men who kept their beards. And an extra heavy fine for those who wore beards and long robes.

Beards mean different things in different cultures. There's no way a Hassidic man would put up with having his beard cut. Amish? Well, the beard signifies that he has married and is now a man and he never cuts it. On the other hand, Amish men cannot wear a moustache because in the nineteenth century men became quite ostentatious in their moustaches. Waxes, twirls, etc.

It was sort of the same thing to the Russian men who liked their moustaches, beards and long robes—but boy they were paying a lot for the privilege! Meanwhile, the poor were shaving and wearing pantaloons. They looked more like pouting French than Russian.

Peter made a lot of changes to Russian culture and cut a swath through his foreign adversaries. In 1724, he developed a urinary infection resulting in surgery in nearly four pounds of urine was extracted from his body. Then in 1725 (and I will now add the word allegedly) he was in Finland when he saw one of his soldiers drowning. He waded out waist deep and saved the poor man. He developed a cold—when he died a few months later it was discovered that his bladder had become infected with gangrene.

Back to beards. Peter did a lot of great things for Russia, in the heavy handed manner that all Russian leaders specialize in.

Recent studies have shown that women perceive men with beards as being more masculine, more alpha-male-ish. Do you agree?

____

____

____

____

____

At the very least you can say September 6 is the Perfect Attendance Day. And there is nobody who epitomizes the holiday more than Cal Ripken Jr., shortstop for the Baltimore Orioles who on September 6, 1995 played his 2,131st consecutive game. He beat the previous Perfect Attendance Day hero Lou Gehrig's record and Cal would go on to finish with 2,632 consecutive games before he removed himself from the lineup before the last game of the 1998 season. Gehrig's record had stood for 56 years and most pundits who watch the game thought Gehrig's stamina and attendance record couldn't be broken in the modern era.

Ripken continued to play ball until 2001 and he was always loyal to the Orioles. After all, his father Cal, Sr. coached the Orioles for 15 years and in 1987 was the first man to manage 2 sons in a game—his namesake and younger son Billy. Cal, Jr. started getting awards like Rookie of the Year (tough to argue with 28 home runs and 93 rbis) and he's got his own spot in the Baseball Hall of Fame. But I think his Attendance Record is his greatest accomplishment.

So when it's hard to get up this morning after a three (or four?) day weekend just remember showing up is half the battle! Go out there and be your best Cal Ripken Jr.!

September 7 is National Threatened Species Day in Australia otherwise known as "sorry that last Thylacine endling is dead" day. It's a day that doesn't necessitate celebration, more like a bit of sorrow.

Thylacine, aka Tasmanian Tiger aka Thylacinus cynocephalus once ruled the animal kingdoms of New Guinea, Australia and Tasmania. They coexisted with dingoes and the aboriginal community. While dingoes had no dietary restrictions against eating a Thylacine if they could get one, some aboriginals declined.

The mythological explanation is that a spirit/boy Palana was attacked by a kangaroo and a Thylacine pup took that kangaroo down for the count. The grateful Palana marked the heroic pup with a black ochre strike to commemorate its bravery.

The extinction of the Thylacine can be blamed on humans—I mean, what can't we blame ourselves for? The islands got more crowded. And the species was sort of isolated with dingoes and I'll tell you right now there's nothing worse than being stuck in an elevator packed with dingoes. They'll be licking the last of your flesh off your bones before you hit the tenth floor. And they'll complain about lack of good barbecue sauce.

The endling Thylacine—"endling" is a term for the last of a species—was captured in 1930 in Tasmania. A little bit of a mystery as to whether it was male or female but since

there weren't any others to mate with that was a moot point. The Thylacine was placed in the Hobart Zoo while zoologists scrambled to find someone, anyone, anything, to mate with it. Even a friends with benefits relationship would do. Oddly, Thylacine males and females both had pouches. Great place to store things—extra cash, a granola bar, and a baby Thylacine?

Benjamin—because the Hobart folk finally gave him a name—died on this day in 1936. A zookeeper appears to have locked Benjamin in the outer area overnight. During the day, the heat was unbearable but the frozen night killed this endling.

We always think of dinosaurs, extinct and uh, why? We think about the dodo bird who really was a bit of a dodo. Species take over—here in Winnetka it's buckthorn and nationwide it's sparrows who are destroying our agriculture and neither species are native to North America. One day it might be our turn to endling.

Do you approach your end with fear, trembling, or peace?

September 8 is a terrifically important holiday and it requires a little prep so I hope you're reading this early or maybe even on September 7.

September 8 is R U Okay Day but it is also for checking in on the people we love, we haven't heard from in a while, who sometimes in the hustle and bustle of our own lives we forget. Or maybe it's just checking in on a neighbor that you kind of have a gut feeling they're not doing too well.

It originated in Australia and I love it almost as much as Christmas because I don't have to make lists of presents that nobody will like and I'll feel terrible. And I won't get phone calls from people who say they didn't get their Christmas wreath from me.

So here's what you do:

1. Sit down and consider listing three or four people that you're going to contact.

2. Jot down a few topics of conversation: their dog, their embroidery classes, their family.

3. Get down to business and call. R U Okay? And listen, really listen. Because sometimes folks will say "oh, sure" but your gut knows better. Don't be confrontational—but make clear that they are important to you. Lie if you have to, God won't send you to Hell for this one. Bonus points if you make plans to get together.

4. Let them know they can always contact you. Oh, and maybe throw in something you have always admired about them or an anecdote about how they helped you and you've never forgotten.

The holiday started with a tragedy. In 1995 Barry Larkin, much beloved and admired in his community, committed suicide. Complete surprise because he always had it all together. In 2009, his son Gavin Larkin together with Janina Nearn proposed making a documentary about Barry's life. Then they realized that a movie wasn't enough. They created something called the "Conversation Movement" to get people talking to and listening to each other. Gavin passed on recently from cancer but his way of honoring his dad lives on.

So make that list.

Who are you gonna call?

____

____

____

____

____

September 09

September 9, 1917 was the day Admiral of the British Navy Sir Frederick Tower Hamilton became the first Gen-texter. On that day he penned a letter to his then Minister of Munitions Winston Churchill saying in part "I hear that a new order of Knighthood is on the table! OMG! Shower it on the Admiralty!" Winston would lead the British during the troubles of World War II as perhaps the best Prime Minister ever. He definitely left behind adolescent ways, known for smoking cigars and drinking all day and night during the war. He lived to be 93 years old. How much longer he would have lived without those bad habits!

I think people text more than call and trading emojis takes the place of the place of communication. What's your favorite mode of conversation?

September 10

On September 10, 1897, 25 year old London cab driver George Smith was arrested after slamming his cab into a building. He made history as the first drunk driving arrest, pled guilty and was fined 25 shillings.

In America, New York passed its first drunk driving prohibition in 1910. Other states followed. In 1936 Rolla Harger created the Drunkometer which standardized measurements of level of impairment. It was sort of like a balloon that the drunkee would blow into. Harger's colleague, Robert Borkenstein, invented the less bulky Breathalyzer in 1953. But people really didn't take driving under the influence seriously until Candy Lightner founded Mothers Against Drunk Driving in 1980. Known as MADD, they would lobby for effective laws banning mixing drinking and driving. Ms. Lightner's 13 year old daughter Cari had been killed by a drunk driver and she was dealing wiht her grief in a way that benefits all of us.

Even with the years of P.S.A.s, restrictive laws, and tragic accidents—drunk driving still exists. At least for today, make sure you're not part of that problem. I'm not but that's because I have had my right eye cornea sheared off twice and it is a favor to the State of Illinois that I don't drive. With or without the alcohol.

September 11

September 11 is Patriot's Day, named for the 2001 attacks on the USA. Let's never forget. I was in the car taking my son Eastman to school. We were listening to a New York radio station covering the airplanes flying into the Twin Towers. I told Eastman don't speak a word of this when you get into class. Of course, he announced it to everybody.

I think everybody lost someone that day. I lost a long ago boyfriend who was working in the Pentagon and was unexpectedly called to a meeting in a section of the building that was demolished. My aunt was in one of the New York towers and made the decision to walk away rather than go downstairs to the parking garage with her workmates. She lived but had massive foot blisters walking home to Queens. Her fellow employees died when they were buried under the rubble of the towers. Survival in any of these tragedies is often a matter of luck.

Where were you?

September 12

September 12 is our National Day of Encouragement! It's a time to say and do positive things to make others feel noticed, celebrated, and just generally all around encouraged. The holiday is NOT a mere Hallmark holiday which is a derisive term that I've heard applied to every holiday for which a person has forgotten to get a card, a gift or make a phone call.

The holiday was first proposed in 2007 by Mayor Belinda Laforce of Searcy, Arkansas. The holiday caught on with Arkansas Governor Mike Beebe declaring September 12 the day for residents to step outside themselves and show a little "you can do it" to everyone around them. President George W. Bush later made it a national holiday.

And sometimes we NEED it!

It's easy to celebrate—take out a set of post it notes. Write a name of someone you know on each one. Think about what they want out of life and get ready…make phone calls and start with "I know you can do this!" If you're not one for phone calls you can text, email, send a carrier pigeon. During the pandemic, I would say "thank you for coming to work today" to the grocery clerks because I really had no idea what encouragement they needed.

Who in your life needs a "you can do it?"

September 12th and 13th are together both amazing days of sacrifice and heroism for the Mexican people. Oh, and the Irish too. So picture this: 1847 at the height of the Mexican-American War which will determine the fate of what's now southwest USA. Two major battles occur—

September 12th was the battle of Churubusco which pit the St. Patrick's Battalion aligned with the Mexican Army. Say what? Irish and Mexico? Truth be told, many Irish suffering under British oppression were lured to the United States with the promise of a good job wherein they could send money home to their families. Instead, these men found themselves in what were called "coffin ships" because so many would die at sea. Overcrowding, not much in the way of rations, no ventilation. Just like Southwest Airlines! In any event, when the surviving Irish would find out the "good job" meant they were conscripted to the US Army. Guess what? You're going to Texas and btw you are not allowed to be Catholic anymore! You will attend Protestant services and gimme that rosary!

Many of us are spiritual and not religious so we cannot comprehend how horrible this last part was. The Irish soldiers shipped to the Mexican border were a deeply unhappy group. There was a group of soldiers who turned around to join the Mexican Army. They called themselves the St. Patrick's Brigade. They were

well trained by the Americans with skills they passed along to the Mexicans but then there was that last battle of Churubusco. Fifty San Patricios, as they were known by their Mexican brothers, were captured and charged with treason and all but two were hung. Those lucky two were lashed and branded with the letter D for deserter and had to wear a yoke around their neck for the duration of the war. The last Mexican defender took down the flag and wrapped it around himself before flinging himself off the fort's tower. San Patricios became heroes and saints to Mexico and Ireland. September 12th is celebrated in both Ireland and Mexico.

The Mexican government had something like a West Point at Chapultepec, with dedicated cadets between 40 and a couple hundred men. Americans attacked on September 13. And at one point the general defending the academy ordered the cadets to retreat. Six cadets refused and promised to defend the fort til the end. Five died. And that last cadet, knowing the outcome, took down the Mexican flag, wrapped it around himself and flung himself off the parapets. The cadets are known collectively as Ninos Heroes.

____

____

____

____

____

Today is the anniversary of the greatest and most glorious television event! On September 14, 1985 the first episode of The Golden Girls aired. The show was meant to highlight superstar Bea Arthur as Dorothy and she required her own separate dressing room, more money, and other accommodations. But the show became more of an ensemble cast. Betty White and Rue McClanahan as Rose and Blanche respectively were extremely close and carved out more and more air time.

Casting producers initially wanted Rue to play the ditz from St. Olaf, Minnesota but Rue said no, this is not the role for me. I want to play Blanche Devereaux, the husky voiced tramp, er, woman of sophistication and unbridled passion. Meanwhile, Betty was thinking she'd be better at playing the dumb blonde (natural brunette). The two women persuaded executives to let them read together and WOW!

The pilot included a cook named Coco who disappeared before Episode 2. A few episodes later, Dorothy's mom Sophia Petrillo escaped from Shady Pines nursing home after a fire caused by, well, unfortunate circumstances. The show was so popular that it had guest appearances by Bob Hope, Sonny Bono, and Burt Reynolds. After 180 half hour episodes and seven years, the show's last episode aired on May 9, 1992 with the wedding of Dorothy to Blanche's uncle played by Leslie Nielsen. It portrayed a rather unfortunate choice of wedding gown. There were a few spinoffs but nothing quite captured the magic.

I often go to hulu and start with an episode. Just one. I'm not an addict. Okay, a second one. And since I know the gals so well they won't mind if I watch, er, close my eyes and listen to a third episode. Not going to sleep, not going to, not going, er, it's the next morning.

What's a show the soothes you and ultimately makes you slumber?

Happy birthday Henry Charles Albert David! Or Prince Henry or Duke of Sussex, or maybe just Harry. On September 15, 1984 he came into the world as a third in the line to the throne of the United Kingdom, behind his father Charles and his brother William. Now, he's pretty far down on the list behind his brother, his nephew George, his niece Charlotte and his nephew Louis. Unless somebody dies (God forbid), converts to Catholicism or marries a Catholic, this dude ain't ever getting the crown.

Traditionally a second son (or as Harry reminds us ad nauseam, a Spare) would be destined for a life of military service and Harry did his bit during the conflict in Afghanistan. But the publicity surrounding his station created a security risk and he left for a desk job.

And then there's the elephant in the room. She's not an elephant but she's definitely a force to be reckoned with. The cable television series actress Meghan Markle, Duchess of Suffolk. The story goes that as the staff of the queen at the tower of London displayed the choices of tiaras for the couple's wedding, they told the couple that the Queen had specifically withheld a tiara once worn by Elizabeth's mother. Harry's response was "whatever Meghan wants, Meghan gets"

She did get what she wanted—Harry, a title, a glam wedding—but not that particular tiara. The couple have returned to Meghan's native California. The withdrawal of the couple from official royal life has kept tabloids hopping. Me? I have to read stupid stuff to stay on the treadmill. Thank you Harry and Megs!

In any event, there are rumors of marital discord between the Sussexes. And money troubles (haven't we all got that). But today, cast that aside and wish Harry a happy birthday!

My sons disagree about who is the favorite child — if you have siblings, do you think one of you is a "favorite?"

On September 16, 1983 2000 people were sworn in as American citizens in the Shrine Auditorium in Los Angeles. Well, actually 2001 new citizens because Arnold Schwarzenegger had gotten through the red tape that had prevented him from becoming an American citizen. His native Austria didn't allow dual citizenships but a special act of their parliament allowed an exception for the Arnold. So on this day, he raised his right hand and poof! He was thirty six at the time. And an American!

Love him or hate him, Arnold has proved himself a man of many talents. Bodybuilding champion. Movie star (my favorite being True Lies). Politician—California benefited from his service as governor. And speaking of service, two women—wife Maria Shriver and their housekeeper Mildred Baena who each gave birth to a Schwarzenegger son within a week of each other!

I am appreciative of immigrants who come here and take a job and work their way towards citizenship. I am in favor of expedited work permits for the immigrants who are being dropped off in Chicago's police stations, New York's finest hotels, and (quel horreur!) Vice President Kamala's house.

So I celebrate The Schwarzenegger's citizenship even if I couldn't stand his flick Conan the Barbarian!

Do you believe in borders?

____

____

____

____

On September 17, 1859 San Francisco resident and failed rice grower Joshua Norton declared himself Emperor of the United States in a letter he sent to the papers. Say what?

Good thing President James Buchanan didn't hear about this. San Francisco was/is a little different from D.C. so the editors of the Bulletin duly published the letter. San Franciscans, being a whimsical group, rallied around their new potentate. He lived in a boarding house in a somewhat respectable neighborhood and folks, er, his citizens, gathered to gawk at him.

He issued both paper money and coin and began to use it for his restaurant tabs. Most restaurants and shops cooperated in the spirit of fun. Norton also gave out money—issued in his name—to those he considered in need. The currency is quite a collector's item today.

He abolished Congress and he declared himself Protector of Mexico in 1863 after Napoleon III invaded the country. He became convinced that he would make a most suitable husband to the widowed Queen Victoria of England. She played hard to get and none of his love letters received a response.

As Emperor he wore a military uniform donated by a retired general as well as a magnificent hat. He inspected parks, talked with his constituency, roamed the streets and generally acted like a boulevardier. But he had a lot of interesting political and infrastructure ideas, including the creation of what would become known as the Golden Gate Bridge. When it was built, many lobbied for it to be named the Emperor Bridge in his honor.

Perhaps his best work as Emperor occurred on August 12, 1869 when he abolished the Republican and Democratic parties, explaining that their animosity towards each other was destructive to civilized discourse.

In 1880, Norton collapsed on the street and died before medical care could be had. Ten thousand people lined the streets on the day of his funeral to watch the cortege although a scant thirty people attended the burial at what is now known as Woodlawn Memorial Park cemetery. As he had no heirs, the dynasty of Emperor Norton came to an end.

If you could be Emporer or Empress of any country, which would it be?

September 18

September 18, 1837 is a very important day in my life—it's the birthday of Tiffany!

The iconic jewelry store was founded by Charles Tiffany and his friend John Young. The obvious reason it's called Tiffany as opposed to Tiffany and Young is because Tiffany's father provided the seed money— $1000—from his cotton mill. Yes, there were slaves involved.

Tiffany's does a lot to protect its brand name and in 1938 the company trademarked the color known as Pantone 1837. The optimistic light blue is recognized the world over and every husband knows if he comes home with light blue box from Tiffany he will be forgiven EVERYTHING.

Celebrate this day by putting on a tight little black dress and your best diamonds and sunglasses and pick up plain coffee in a Styrofoam cup. Slink around like you just own the joint, no walk of shame, instead make the who day YOURS!

September 19

September 19, 1783 was a great day in aviation. The first hot air balloon was shot up into the skies over France. King Louis XVI, the little sadist, suggested loading it up with prisoners to be launched irretrievably into the heavens.

The balloonist brothers Joseph-Michel and Jacques-Etienne Montgolfier objected to this tropospheric torture. They suggested a test run with barnyard animals. So in the early afternoon, before a crowd of nearly 130k people outside of Versailles Palace, they placed a duck, a sheep and a rooster into the wicker basket. The brothers lit their contraption and all five—two inventors and their animal guests—went up into the air. Not very long. Landed two miles away in Vaucresson eight minutes later.

The Montgolfiers were pleased. The animals, well, a local press account stated "it was judged that the animals had not suffered but they were, to say the least, much astonished."

262

September 20, 1972 was an auspicious day for relations between the sexes. A battle royale between a 55 year old washed up hustler Bobby Riggs and a 29 year old top seeded tennis pro Billy Jean King. The match was designed to settle once and for all whether men are the superior sex or whether women had simply been held back by archaic laws and the necessity of wearing doing everything in high heels.

The back story: Bobby Riggs was an extraordinary tennis player … in his day. He was ranked number one in the world as an amateur in 1939 and twice as a pro in 46 and 47. But rumors were that he owed a lot of money in gambling debts and he spent his retirement as a hustler of sorts. He produced sports exhibitions across the country but was considered a has been loser. Although he was 55 he declared that as a male he was a superior athlete to any, any, any female. He challenged number one ranked 29 year old Billy Jean King to a winner take all match. Of course, she won. And that's history.

Not so fast. Before there was September 20 there was May 13's battle of the sexes between Bobby and Margaret Court. Court was a 30 year old top seeded player from Australia who was one of three women who had a grand slam boxed set which meant she could grand slam anybody. King had declined the match with Bobby and second choice Margaret stepped up to the plate for women and a 100k winner take all match. May 13 fell on Mother's Day and as they shook hands before the match, Bobby presented Margaret with a bouquet of flowers which she accepted with a curtsy. Less than an hour later—6-2, 6-1—Bobby was victorious. The match became known as the Mother's Day Massacre.

King reconsidered and accepted Bobby's challenge. On September 20, the battle of the sexes commenced. Although Bobby at first looked to be making the match another masculine victory instead the game concluded 6-4 6-3 6-3, a victory for women!

Bobby was considered a, ahem, dick. But King didn't seem to think so. The two remained friends for years and while Bobby lay dying of prostate cancer in 1998 King asked to see him one last time. He declined because he didn't want her to see him as he was. Instead, they had a final phone call the night before his death and King claimed the last thing she was able to say to him was "I love you."

On September 21, 1915, Sir Cecil Herbert Edward Chubb was sent on an errand by his wife Mary Bella Alice Finch. He was to go to an estate auction of Sir Cosmo Gordon Antrobus who had recently inherited a whole lot of stuff from his departed brother. Cecil was to purchase a dining room table and matching chairs that Mary had been lusting after for quite some time.

Simple enough errand. Can't really mess that up, can you?

But there was the matter of lot 15, a totally useless piece of property with a bunch of 25 ton stones so huge they would be difficult to move. The stones were arranged in such a way that growing crops on the land would be impossible. There was one bidder who thought he might use the stone filled land for corralling sheep.

Blame it on stiff drink, blame it on whimsy, blame it on some passive aggressive feelings about that dining room table but Cecil came in with the winning bid—6,600 pounds or in today's American dollars about $736k. He was sort of upset that there had been a possibility that someone would take the huge stones to another country and when you're in the middle of World War I it doesn't sound that ludicrous (to be fair, many of the stones actually came from Wales, two hundred miles away—another whole story).

Cecil came home quite proud of himself but the next morning confessed to Mary that he had entirely forgotten about the dining room set. He was in the doghouse for sure!

If the couple had gone out that morning to visit Cecil's purchase, they would have figured out that the point of Stonehenge—as it would come to be called—is a sort of calendar with the alignment of stones' shadows marking the vernal and autumnal equinoxes. It is indeed a bit more of a treasure than a dining room table, even with matching chairs.

Just about everybody in the upper class of England was going broke in the wake of the war, including Cecil who really hadn't figured out what to do with those stones. So he donated them to the British government in 1918 (tax deduction!) and in gratitude the government made him a baronet.

He died at the age of 58 and was the last private owner of the property. To celebrate the autumnal equinox get out your pagan regalia and toast Cecil who probably saved Stonehenge from being carved up and sent elsewhere!

How do you think they built Stonehenge?

____

____

____

____

____

September 22

September 22 was not a good day for the seven women and one man hung at Proctor's Ledge. It was particularly difficult, to the extent it could have gotten worse, for Martha Corey whose husband Giles had been "pressed" just three days before.

But it was a good day for love, perseverance, determination. It was a turning point day for Salem Town and Salem Village, both of which had suffered a grueling six months. While the twin communities would suffer more indignities over the next six months, the worst was in the rearview mirror.

Although to be fair, in 1692 the Puritans of Massachusetts didn't have cars.

In February of that year 9 year old Betty Parris and her 11 year old cousin Abigail Williams started having fits that mimicked epilepsy. They claimed there was the Devil about. This was particularly alarming to Betty's father Rev. Parris. He adhered to the Puritan belief that the Devil and his minions walked the earth and would sometimes possess a human.* Humans were in a battle with demons all the time and it looked like Betty and Abigail were on the front lines. It didn't take long for other girls to join in on the action and not much time after that before the Salem witch trials got rolling.

The twin communities combined had an estimated population of 2000. By the time it was over, 200 of their residents would be charged with witchcraft, including four year old Dorcas Good who immediately cracked under questioning.** The allegations of witchcraft were made largely against women from Salem Village. The Village was made up of farmers and the poor. But when the first wealthy church member was delivered up, all hell broke loose (lol!) and the merchant class and wealthy of portside Salem Town got their share of indictments. Salem Town and Salem Village were being run by a bunch of mean girls who would accuse anybody—and everybody who pleaded guilty or not guilty were doomed.

The last of the hangings—and there were 25***—was on the 22nd but the trials would continue until May 1693. Giles Corey, whose love of family propelled him to great courage, refused to plead either way. Giles (80) had only within the year married his third wife Martha (72) and when she was accused, he initially believed he was in a low rent version of Bewitched. After all, even besides the girls' accusations, there was the troubling aspect of her giving birth in 1677 to an illegitimate mixed race son Beroni. Puritans talked a good game about forgiveness and redemption but you gotta walk the walk.

Still, both Giles and Martha were covenanted which meant the Puritan church recognized that they were besties with the Lord. Giles began to defend his wife and promptly got himself charged with witchcraft. Giles was no dummy—he understood the odds of him being found guilty were high and he also understood that the odds of him forfeiting his property and being unable to protect his Martha were also grim. He refused to plead guilty or not guilty.

*They were teaching this stuff at Harvard! Prof. Increase Mather and his son Cotton put out treatises on such topics as "memorable providences relating to witchcraft and possessions".

**Four year old Dorcas was not hung, but her mother was and her brother died in prison.

***There are some historians who believe it was a mere 19.

Continued on Next Page

The court ordered that he be pressed until he pleaded one way or another and so on the nineteenth Giles, naked and shivering, was led out into the prison yard. He was ordered to lay down and heavy planks were put on top of him. And then rocks. And more rocks. Every once in a while the sheriff George Corwin would demand him to plead one way or another. Our plucky Giles had only one response—more weight.****

This went on for three days—the Puritans didn't want him to die quite yet, but they wanted him to join the witch trial party. At one point, Giles was in so much distress his tongue popped out of his mouth and corwin obligingly shoved it back in with a poker stick. Near the end of the third day, Giles died but his last words were the most loving he could have uttered.

"More weight."

I'm sure Giles understood Martha was going to be hung. But his property would not be forfeited to the local government. Corwin would shake Giles' daughters for 11 pounds 6 shillings but he couldn't legally take the land.

What made the accusing girls go so nutjob? Well, a recurring theory is that the lands surrounding Salem Village were largely growing rye and the fields were not rotated enough. A disease infected the crops called ergotism and the bread the girls were eating were infected with ergotism, the same disease that inspired the twentieth century filmmaker Alfred Hitchcock to film The Birds. The reason the girls were hit by this is that they were smaller than their fellow Salemites. A single piece of bread made from the crops would affect them more than others.

Gile's courage transformed his community.

Although the trials sputtered along until the following May, there were no more executions and folks had an "eeeeeuuuw" feel about it all. Salem Village went so far as to change its name to Danvers, while of course the more wealthy Salem Town made everything into a tourist attraction.

****Reminds me of St. Lawrence, a deacon of the early church. Emperor Valerian in 258 AD told the church elders y'all gotta die and I'm going to confiscate all your possessions. Our boy Larry said sure, boss, give me three days and I'll get stuff organized. He spent three days handing out church treasures to the poor. That didn't sit too well with Valerian who upped the ante by condemning him to die by being roasted on a spit. St. Lawrence repeatedly told those doing the slow roast "I'm done well on this side. Turn me over." Maybe that's where Giles got his inspiration.

September 23 is National Dogs in Politics Day, celebrating FDOTUSes (FODOTU-SI?) In the modern era, there's of course Liberty—Gerald and Betty Ford's golden retriever—who gave birth to nine puppies in the WH. There's Bo, the Portuguese water dog who figured prominently in Barack Obama's victory speech. Who can forget Buddy—the Clinton's dog—who was featured in one of Hillary's books but had the indignity of sharing top billing with a cat named Socks? Teddy Roosevelt's dog, Rollo, was largely forgotten by history because Roosevelt also had cats, horses, a parrot, a badger, and yes, a bear.* And then there's Biden's dog Commander who bit various Secret Service agents 24 times and was sent back to Delaware.

But there are two FDOTUS who transformed American politics on this day September 23.

The first was the irascible Scottish Terrier Fala (1940-1952) who was a bit of a prankster. Only four weeks after coming to the WH he was sent to the animal hospital for intestinal difficulties. Guess what? Our little boy had figured out how to sneak into the WH kitchen and beg for food. Franklin Delano Roosevelt himself went downstairs to admonish the staff against overfeeding Fala. Fala served his country well, being used at every possible photo op and mentioned frequently in speeches and broadcasts by the President. Fala was even named an honorary private of the US Army and he traveled with Roosevelt everywhere. But on a trip to the Aleutians there was a bit of kerfuffle. Fala ran off without notice, the Presidential ship sailed and then everyone's like "where's Fala?"

Roosevelt sent a Navy Destroyer to retrieve the mischievous imp.

And on September 23, 1944, at a dinner with the Teamsters Union, Roosevelt explained—

"These Republican leaders have not been content with attacks on me, or my wife, or on my sons. No, not content with that, they now include my little dog, Fala. Well, of course, I don't resent attacks, and my family don't resent attacks, but Fala does resent them. You know, Fala is Scotch, and being a Scottie, as soon as he learned that the Republican fiction writers in Congress had concocted a story that I'd left him behind on an Aleutian island and had sent a destroyer back to find him – at a cost to the taxpayers of two or three, or eight or twenty million dollars – his Scotch soul was furious. He has not been the same dog since. I am accustomed to hearing malicious falsehoods about myself.... But I think I have a right to resent, to object, to libelous statements about my dog."

That September 23 speech might have sealed the deal on this holiday, but there was a bigger, more explosive dogfight. A dog named Checkers changed everything about American politics in 1952 just because of a Texas man named Lou Carroll.

*Where do you think the term "teddy bear" came from?

Continued on Next Page

September 23

Richard Nixon was tenuously on the Republican ticket with war hero David Eisenhower. Most of those running for office up until then—Kennedy, Stevenson, Roosevelt— all had family money. Being raised by a family that ran a grocery store, the Nixon didn't have anything but friends** Still, those friends had put together $18K for Nixon's campaign expenses. Folks were pissed that someone's friends could "buy" a presidency and at a whistle stop Nixon was confronted by protesters many of whom referenced Pat Nixon owning a mink coat—as in "No Mink Coats for Nixon Just Cold Cash". Pat had no such coat but still the scandal had legs.

Eisenhower was expecting Nixon to do the gentlemanly thing and withdraw from the ticket with the de rigeur "I need to spend time with my family." Instead, Nixon got off that train and booked a flight to Los Angeles while the RNC worked feverishly to raise $75K to book a half hour directly after the Texaco Star Theater with Milton Berle. The broadcast would be from the El Capitan Theater instead of the studio's both because the lighting was better*** and because it was easier to sequester the press. Eisenhower had dinner on the night of the 23rd fully expecting to have Nixon give a speech that would conclude with him offering his resignation.

The speech started off pretty much as anyone would have expected. Nixon being a bit paranoid and Pat seated nearby gazing adoringly at him.**** There was even the famous reference to Pat wearing "Republican cloth coats" and no minks. Sixty million people were watching, the largest television audience at the time and every one was waiting for the "I withdraw" but then—

"One other thing I probably should tell you because if we don't they'll probably be saying this about me too, we did get something—a gift—after the election. A man down in Texas heard Pat on the radio mention the fact that our two youngsters would like to have a dog. And, believe it or not, the day before we left on this campaign trip we got a message from Union Station in Baltimore saying they had a package for us. We went down to get it. You know what it was? It was a little cocker spaniel dog in a crate that he'd sent all the way from Texas. Black and white spotted. And our little girl—Tricia, the 6-year-old—named it Checkers. And you know, the kids, like all kids, love the dog and I just want to say this right now, that regardless of what they say about it, we're gonna keep it."*****

**By friends I mean folks who had contributed to his senate campaign. When the vp nomination came up, a fund was set up and Nixon "didn't know" who contributed.

***Where were these advisors on the occasion of the Kennedy-Nixon debates of 1960? At least Kennedy's team knew about contouring.

****She would later say that she was staring so intently because she had no idea what he was going to say.

*****Thank you Texan Tom Carroll for the dog.

Nixon walked out of the speech on September 23rd convinced it was a disaster. He gave his secretary a resignation letter to send to Eisenhower which his campaign manager intercepted and ripped up. He didn't quite understand that Checkers had turned him from Nixon the vaguely reptilian politician into Nixon the dog lover.

Bring out the hankies and the ballot boxes. The phones at the RNC were jammed, telegrams started pouring in with letters to follow, and Eisenhower was trapped. The former general thought of himself as a master tactician and he had been completely undone. The ticket went on to victory but the two men were never really close after that.

Fala died several years after Roosevelt's death, is buried near Roosevelt, and has his own statue at the FDR memorial. Checkers died in 1964 before he could even lay his head down on the Oval Office rug or bite a Secret Service agent. He's buried at the Bide-a-Wee pet cemetery in New York.

I live by myself, my building doesn't allow dogs, I have such dog envy that I carry treats in my pocket in case I see an obliging dog/furparent couple. I have an intense relationship with Elvis the three legged lab who once dragged his fur mommy half a block because he knew I carry Pupperoni sticks. I can't walk in the 500 block of Chestnut

avenue without Mick the Dalmatian howling for his treat. If you have a pup, love them, give them treats, and if you get into trouble, drag them out for P.R. purposes.

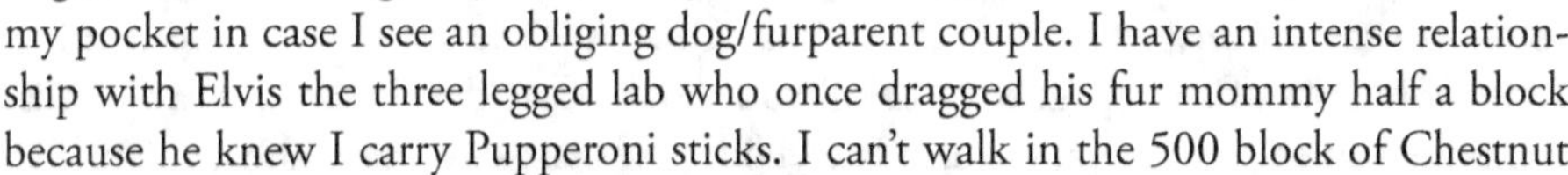

I thought it imperative that I write about September 24 because of course the end of the world is happening on the 24th. Yippee! I don't have to shave my legs or even put on mascara! I can binge watch Family Guy and eat cookies in bed. I can even flout Condo Association rules and adopt a dog for the End Times.

How do I know it's the end of the world? Nostradamus? No, he's been wrong so many times. A Mayan calendar? We already went through that. Q-Anon? Nah, too weird. Some Coptic or Aramaic text? Nope.

The Simpsons. The Simpsons have eerie portentous abilities. The show predicted the building of certain skyscrapers in London, the Trump presidency long before he announced he was running, the OJ trial, the ending of Game of Thrones, space tourism, the George Floyd episode and now this—in episode 9 of season 24 the Simpsons predicts ten days of darkness and then on the 24th of September kapowie! Solar flares figure in the story and frankly, we've had a lot of that going on lately. Flares can interfere with cellular and satellite transmissions and generally screw up everything. Spooky! to be fair, the Simpsons have predicted the end of the world a few other times but just to be on the safe side....

Enjoy September 23rd like it's your last day. Play candy crush all day if you want to. Go to the grocery store in your pajamas. Order two desserts if that's your thing. One more glass of champagne won't kill you. Look up at the clouds and say "gratias dominus vigiles." And since it's also everybody else's last day, make those reconciliation calls to old frenemies, reach out to relatives, and if you want to call me and say "I've always had a crush on you" I won't judge. I'll be flattered.

On September 25 we are reminded that the clothes make the man, clothes make the woman, and clothes make the social justice statement. And there are heroes like Emerald Holloway who know that and act on it!

In 1954, SCOTUS case Brown v. Board of Education ordered the integration of public schools. In Little Rock, black families were asked to volunteer to transfer their children to the all white Central High School. Over the course of three years of legal wrangling, the families would shift because kids would graduate, families would get cold feet, or maybe just move. None of the original volunteers actually started school. But in 1957 as the beginning of the school year approached, there were eight families—and Carlotta Walls.

Carlotta hadn't told her family that she had volunteered—the way her parents found out was a registration letter in the mail that came in July just before the beginning of classes. Carlotta, inspired by the story of Rosa Parks, had volunteered on her own. At fourteen, she was the youngest of what would become known as "Little Rock Nine".

News of Carlotta's registration spread fast and there were threats and even a bomb tossed towards the family home. In the face of anticipated protests, the National Guard and the Army had been called in and would escort her into home room. The Little Rock Nine would not be allowed to participate in extracurricular activities. Even beyond this indignation, the nine would be spat on, shoved, name-called. All nine were counseled to keep their cool.

But today is not just about legal wrangling, social justice and our painful past. It's about a hero who recognized the sartorial significance of the occasion and how we can obtain just enough confidence if we put on a brave outfit that might have to make up for a falteringly brave face. Ladies and Gentlemen, I humbly submit Civil Rights hero Emerald Holloway.

Mrs. Walls had always made clothes for Carlotta and her siblings. They were simple, functional, and cheap—if the only way you measure cheap is by dollars. I will wager the family didn't think too much about clothes as the school opening approached. Uncle Emerald did. He stopped by the house a few days before classes with a surprise gift of cash. He explained that this first day of school was no ordinary day and he wanted Carlotta to have a dress to match the occasion. He understood all eyes of the world would be on his beloved niece and she'd better represent.

Carlotta hightailed it to a downtown Little Rock department store and found a white blouse and dirndl skirt by Sportswear by Sheinberg. On that first day of class, September 25, 1957 the ensemble perfectly highlighted innocence, youth, and if you look very carefully you'll notice a subtle alphabet print which conveys her educational aspirations.

Continued on Next Page

____

____

____

____

September 25

That dress, her first store bought one, gave her just enough confidence to get through the door. And it made all of us, well most of us, sympathize with her in a way that not even a dress made by her mother would have. Thank you Emerald for your contribution to the cause of social justice!

I always wear the same uniform—black leggings, black T-shirts—that some might be forgiven for thinking I never change out of or that I never use my washing machine. But there's a good eighteen leggings and as many T-shirts in my closet. I'm starting to think about branching out like with a color. Maybe pink.

On September 26 1976 Ramses II, one of the world's longest reigning potentates, made the trip from Cairo to Paris in order to receive treatment for a fungoidal disease, a common medical problem for 3,000 year old mummies.

He was transported in a Transall-type military propeller plane that would promise the smoothest ride with no disruption to the Pharoah and his wood sarcophagus. Wish I had thought of that before making reservations with Southwest … Rames II was the first Egyptian jet setter.

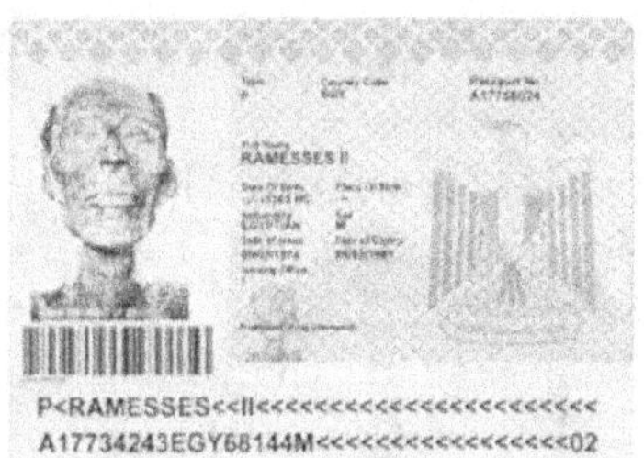

Ramses, er, Pharoah Ramses II was accorded full honors as befitted his rank. He was accompanied at all times by the French ambassador to Egypt and by Christiane Desroches-Noblecourt, then curator of the Antiquities Department of the Louvre. When the plane entered French air space it was escorted by two military jets. After all, Ramses was the greatest of all Egyptian emperors!

Upon landing, he was greeted by the head of the Universites Alice Saunier-Seite and a brigade of the French National Guard.

Ramses II ruled for nearly 70 years, built the temples at Abu Simbel and most folks believe he's the Pharoah who told Moses "Hell no, you can't go!" which Moses ignored.

While the head of the British royal family is allowed to travel without a passport, the French were not going to waive the requirement for the Ram. The Egyptian embassy issued him a passport. Under birthday it listed **/**/3000 and his occupation "king" (deceased).

He was remarkably well preserved, the fungoidal issues notwithstanding. Oddly, he had red hair and still a lot more of it than the average 3,000 year old man. He could have used some dental work—always floss even if you're a Pharoah.

One glitch in the treatments was that one of the lab workers decided to snip off a few strands of hair as a souvenir. Not cool. Otherwise, Ramses II was sent back to Cairo, passport in hand, pomp and honors and returned to the Cairo Museum where the rest of his relatives lived, er, were dead.

September 27 is significant because two amputees, separated by a sesquicentennia, taught the world about beauty, confidence, and elan!

In 1838 Mexico was a somewhat lawless place. A lot of looting was directed at foreign owned businesses. When business owners looked to the government for redress they were given a cold stare. M. Remontel, a French pastry chef in Tacubaya reported that Mexican officers had looted his store with damages of 60k pesos. After getting a Mexican hombro frio, he went to the French government which told the Mexicans "Sacre bleu! not only do you owe Remontel 60k but here's a list of other French citizens who got looted and you owe us altogether 600k." Mexico said "de ninguna manera" and thus began The Pastry War. Well, at least the first one.

In 1842 General Antonio Lopez de Santa Anna lost his leg in battle. Being a good Catholic, he was concerned about whether his leg would be restored to him in the Resurrection and the general practice of cremation revolted him. He sent word to the Archbishop of Mexico who, with some trepidation, organized the funeral for the leg on September 27, 1842. There was a military escort, Artillery Salvos, a te deum (fancy Latin hymn), flowers, and a eulogy. Then the leg was placed in a crystal case and lowered into the ground at Santa Paula cemetery in Guadalahara,* with an ornate stone monument to mark its location.

For the rest of his life, when Santa Anna was invited to parades, he would remove his cork leg and wave it at the crowd. Always a fan favorite. And a reminder that while many soldiers give up life and limb, Santa Anna just did it in a different order. What extraordinary confidence! What absolute elan!

One hundred fifty six years later, on September 27, 1998, Alexander McQueen held his spring/summer collection runway show in London. He named the show "13" because it was his thirteenth collection under his own label—he divided his time between his line and Givenchy, otherwise known as The House That Clothed The Hepburn, Audrey that is.**

After the crowd took their places and the celebrities preened a bit at their front row seats, a young woman sashayed down the runway. There was a collective gasp.

The woman was 24 year old athlete/model Aimee Mullins. Blonde, beautiful, poised, smoking hot body—she was the whole supermodel package. But pshaw! women like that are a dime a dozen at a show like McQueen's. The crowd was agog because Aimee was a double amputee.

Born with fibular hemimelia, Aimee's legs had been amputated when she was one. She grew up in Allentown, Pennsylvania and when she became attracted to track and field there were not yet Paralympic games opportunities. While she would go on to compete at the 1996 Paralympics in Atlanta. Within the NCAA she competed against able bodied athletes. And at McQueen's 13 show…

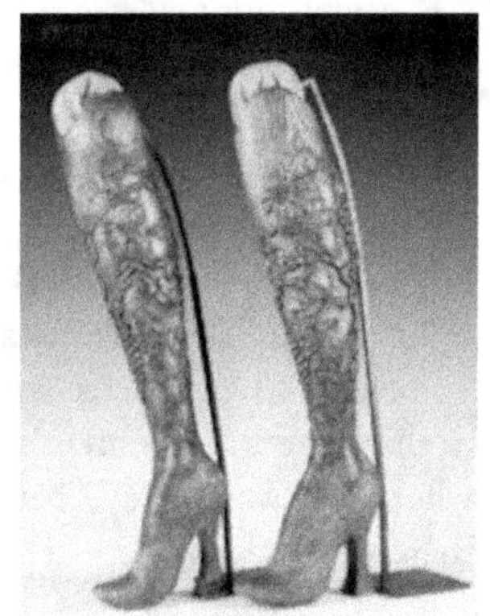

She strutted down the runway in a short white organza and tulle skirt. Her legs were made of elm and had been commissioned by McQueen and created by Bob Watts of the Dorset Orthopedic Institute. The hand carved grapevine and floral design perfectly meshed with the nineteenth century romanticism vibe of the show. Aimee had several other ensembles to walk with and McQueen had designed a Swarkovski crystal encrusted legs but they weren't ready in time for the show.

September 28

On September 28, 1597 a shrine was built in Kyoto, with a burial trove of over 126,000 pickled noses. It is the least visited, religious or tourist destination in Japan though it is just west of the popular Kyoto National Museum and Toyokuni Jinja, a shrine devoted to Toyotomi Hideyoshi, a Kami (divine) leader of Japan during the sixteenth century when the noses were, er, acquired.

In the late sixteenth century, Japan invaded the Korean peninsula and normally samurai would take entire heads as war trophies for which they would be paid by their leaders. Unfortunately, there were just so many Korean (and Ming Chinese mercenary) heads to transport during this invasion. To simplify matters, samurai were paid by the nose. Nose collection stations would count, record, salt the noses for preservation, pay the samurai and then pack the noses up to be buried in Kyoto.

A plaque, long since removed, read "one cannot say that cutting off noses was so atrocious by the standard of the time" ….

I'm not sure it's a good idea to compare atrocities and neither do the Koreans. There were in the late twentieth centuries plans to ship the noses back to Korea (tough call on what to do about Ming warriors' noses.) Instead, on September 28, 1997 there was a memorial service and funding for the shrine was pretty much pulled altogether. Today, local residents groom the grounds and while Korean tourist buses show up, most Japanese don't even know of its existence.

September 29

On September 29, 1829 Scotland Yard was formed. Originally designed to protect royalty it has become the investigation arm of London police. It also works with Interpol and is so dang glamorous!

The London Metropolitan Police were initially started with an act introduced by Prime Minister Robert Peele—hence the term "bobbies" in honor of his nickname Bobby—and it was housed originally in Whitehall which had an entrance through what was known as the Great Scotland Yard which was a guest house for visiting Scottish royalty. When the joint got taken over for this arm of the police, the nickname became more formalized as Scotland Yard. It was actually in the city of Westminster right on the River Thames at the Victoria Embankment.

Scotland Yard detectives were initially plain clothes and that led some Londoners to think there was something nefarious about them. They also got quite the reputation when there was an 1877 betting scheme with criminals. Uh, sorry about that. And then there was Jack the Ripper the dude (a woman maybe?) who cut the throats of prostitutes. They couldn't solve that one.

In late 1800s the original building was too crowded and the agency picked up and moved to the New Scotland Yard. In 2016 they settled in the Curtis Green Building.

September 30

September 30 is a particularly important day in military history—the anniversary of a recruitment effort which resulted in over 350,000 enthusiastic and devoted soldiers for the cause. All accomplished by a military hero who wielded needle and thread.

Chicago born Main Rousseau Bocher opened the Mainbocher* house at the swanky address 12 Avenue George V in Paris in 1929. He dressed socialites, royalty, and movie stars. He was perhaps best known for creating the dress for Wallis Simpson of Baltimore to wed that king who abdicated, er, stepped back from royal duties. Not Harry—instead, Edward VII. Mainbocher designed a deceptively simple dress in what he called Wallis Blue.**

In 1940 Bocher closed his Paris operations and returned to the USA.

*It's tempting to pronounce it Man-Boo-Shay like you're going all Frenchie. But no, it's Maine-Bocker.

**At the time, it was considered a faux pas to dress a previously married woman in white. Twice divorced Wallis definitely had to have an alternate color. To be fair, until the marriage of Victoria and Albert, women got out their best gown for their wedding, regardless of color, and it would be worn for special occasions not stored in the attic.

Modern warfare, and certainly World War II was all that, requires roughly ten percent of one's forces to be used in front line combat. The other ninety percent are involved in transport, logistics, communications—the sorts of things that can be done by soldiers of varying abilities. While women were definitely signing up for work in munitions factories a la Rosie the Riveter, the Pentagon figured women could also be recruited as soldiers. But there was a two part problem. Some old-fashioned parents and even some young potential recruits recoiled because being a soldier seemed unfeminine and even, dare I recount unblemished history, that women soldiers somehow put the L in the LGBTQ-plus community. Some soldiers and even officers believed that having women in uniform detracted from the manly man feel one wants in a young lad you're asking to rush into death's path. 

Still, Congress authorized the US Women's Naval Reserve, otherwise known as Women Accepted for Volunteer Emergency Service and on this day—September 30, 1942—the first class of 119 women graduated and they wore Mainbocher. A cinched waist, padded shoulders, shapely collar. Double breasted. Myself? I have the twins and when I wear double breasted I look like a low rent Winston Churchill.

The uniforms were an immediate hit and suddenly being a woman in uniform became glamorous, feminine and patriotic all at the same time. The New York Times Magazine declared women in uniform the best dressed woman of the year. Fashion editor Dorothy Roe wrote "Uncle Sam's sailor girls can now look the Duchess of Windsor in the eye and say: I believe we have the same dressmaker."

Mainbocher went on to design, again for free and as a patriotic duty, uniforms for the Coast Guard Reserves (SPARS), the Red Cross, and the Women Marines. All in all, 350K women put on a uniform and served their country.

We all have a uniform. What's yours?

October's poplars are flaming torches
lighting the way to winter

–Nova Beir

You might not be Facebook friends with John Howland. You might not follow him on Instagram. I can guarantee you that he doesn't do TikTok. But no one has possibly had more of an influence on you and on American history than Howland. And for him, October 1 is a day so pivotal that everything we know and cherish could have been destroyed if it weren't for the courage and tenacity he exhibited on this day even when he believed all had been lost.

In 1620 John Howland was a lowly indentured servant in the household of John Carver and his wife. The Carvers were of the separatist Pilgrim group in England and they had made plans to go to the New World. They took Howland who had been born to a Quaker family but had converted. An indentured servant was pretty much a slave so he didn't really have a choice on residence or religion and the servitude far outlasted the median age of death.

The Mayflower was overcrowded—a 100 foot ship with 102 passengers and a crew of thirty to forty—because another separatist Pilgrim ship The Speedwell had proved unseaworthy and its passengers were added to the already standing room only Mayflower. Within weeks of setting sail, everyone on the ship was sick, grumpy, hostile, crazed—and you thought the pandemic lockdown was tough!

But it gets worse, at least for Howland. On October first, during a violent thunderstorm, 29 year old Howland was washed overboard and left for dead. After all, he was just an indentured servant. Well, that's the end of the story....

Not quite. Somehow Howland grabbed hold of a topsail halyard rope that had come undone. As the ship forged forward Howland hung on and managed to climb that rope to safety on deck. I gotta say that when they did the rope climb in gym class I sucked—but it turns out to be a pretty valuable skill.

Howland, along with the other male separatist Pilgrims, signed the Mayflower Compact which laid out how everybody was going to live by the scripture in this Massachusetts. Kind of like they went all Hobbes, Locke and Montesquieu. Carver was named governor and Howland worked as his personal assistant until Carver's death. End of story.

Not so fast. After Carver's death (and the death of Mrs. Carver) Howland may have inherited the Carver money. In any event, he was a free man with money and he was one of eight men who agreed to pay off some of the Pilgrim debt in exchange for a monopoly on the fur trade. And this is when he began that influencin' history thang! He fathered ten children which would be somewhat average for the time. He had 88 grandchildren—which means he needed to have a gift wrap room in his home and a detailed day planner.

Continued on Next Page

October 01

Think on this: he is the direct ancestor to nearly two million present day Americans. There's some names you might recognize. All of the Roosevelts. The Presidents Bush. Ralph Waldo Emerson. Humphrey Bogart. Chevy Chase. The Baldwin brothers. Sarah Palin. And, of course, LDS (Mormon) founder Joseph Smith whose wives should get frequent flyer miles at the obstetrics ward.

When Howland grabbed that halyard he not only saved himself but he saved a country. So the next time you're feeling like you're a failure (me—guilty as charged) or that you haven't accomplished enough (guilty, guilty) or that you don't know what your purpose in life is (guilty, guilty, guilty) you just don't know. What you're supposed to accomplish might be unknown to you right now and might not be ten kids and a passel of grandkids in the future, but it might be something you don't realize will change the world!

October 02

October 2 is Gandhi Jayanti—the birthday of Mahatma Gandhi (b. 1896) who organized and engineered India's freedom from (you guessed it!) the Brits! Unlike the American colonials, he did it without a single musket firing and that's why this day is celebrated around the world as International Day of Nonviolence. This might be a good day to take a deep breath and figure out how to solve problems without smacking someone upside the head.

Oddly, he died in a most violent way. January 30, 1948 he was having a prayer service in his garden with family and friends. Around five in the afternoon, Hindu Nationalist Nathuram Godse forced himself into the garden, shooting Gandhi three times. Godse believed Gandhi had negotiated with the British in a manner which favored the Muslim population too much. Godse was put on trial for murder and sentenced to death. Gandhi's two sons pleaded for his life not because they liked Godse but because of their reverence for their father's beliefs. Godse was executed in 1949.

October 3, 2010 is when at long last World War I came to an end. It is a day of peace and bringing to a close any grudges or hostilities.

Now, I know what you're thinking. World I began with the June 28, 1914 assassination of the Archduke Franz Ferdinand* and concluded with the Armistice of November 11, 1918.** Or, if you want to get technical, the signing of the Treaty of Versailles on June 28, 1919, on the five year sapphire anniversary of the Archduke's demise.

But the Treaty had a kick out clause demanding reparations from Germany. The Allied Powers were asking for a lot and it took 92 years for Germany to pay up before war was officially over. I don't remember any parades or fireworks or celebrations. And some would say that the grudge the Allied Powers held against the Germans and expressed in the V.T. set the stage for crazy ass Hitler.

The Europeans have their Hundred Years War which was supposed to settle who ruled France—the English Plantagenets or the Lancasters, the Yorks or the French Valois family. The wars lurched on from 1337-1453 and included the show stopper Battle of Agincourt. You think my math is off but it really did last 116 years—maybe they didn't have calculators back then.

But nothing compares to the Reconquista otherwise known as the Iberian Religious War between the Catholic Spanish Empire and the Moors. Premiering in 711 a.d. this war saw the Moors at one point about to dip their foot in the Seine and at another the Spanish picking out summer homes in Morocco. The jam-packed epic ended with the fall of the Muslim Nasrid and the Kingdom of Granada in 1492. The Spanish had a clean house year, what with exiling Jews and Muslims and giving Columbus the greenlight on picking out new digs and trade routes across the ocean.

On this day, Germany made its last payment on WWI. There's a saying – always borrow form a pessiment. The won't expect you to repay the loan.

How about you—are you settled up on debts?

____

____

____

____

____

October 04

On October 4, 1963 Paul McCartney was the celebrity judge on a British television program called "Ready, Steady, Go!" Sort of like American Idol. Four girls competed with dance routines. McCartney awarded first prize to 14 year old Melanie Coe who received a signed Beatles album and had the opportunity to shake his hand.

When Melanie was 17 she ran away from home in the middle of the night and took a bus to London to a friend's flat. McCartney read about the runaway girl in the London Daily Mirror and from that wrote the song "She's Leaving Home" which is the sixth track on Sgt. Pepper's Lonely Hearts Club album. Many years later, McCartney made the connection between the two stories and on her fiftieth birthday the Rolling Stone magazine interviewed Coe. She hadn't actually run away with a man from the motor trade, as in the song, although her boyfriend had once worked as a mechanic. She returned home and discovered she was pregnant and had an abortion. The song is gorgeous and poignant and the entire album is a treasure.

October 05

October 5 is National Do Something Nice Day, a day for getting your Glenda the Good Witch goin' on. Maybe it's something small like the lady who said I could go ahead of her in line at the grocery store because I was only buying a few items and she looked like she was shopping to help her family survive the Apocalypse. I was tempted to tell her she had gotten her nice thing out of the way so early in the morning she could do anything she wanted for the rest of the day and karma would remain in balance but I didn't want her testing the theory by running me over in the parking lot.

Doing something nice does great things and not just for the person at the receiving end. Doing a nice thing lowers stress and blood pressure in a person—so throw out those pills and fire your therapist. Studies show that people who do nice things for others have greater energy and reduced risk of heart disease. They have a greater degree of the mood boosting hormones.

Here's some suggestions—call someone you think might be needing some propping, give a compliment AND mean it, hug somebody (well, not every random stranger), and even just SMILE. You don't know how much that might affect someone.

How will you celebrate?

October 06

October 6 is National Mad Hatter Day in honor of the eccentric habadashery/millinery enthusiast featured in the Lewis Carroll book Alice in Wonderland. The character is never referred to as the "Mad Hatter" in the book but he is quite mad, being perpetually stuck in a tea party with the March Hare.

The holiday is based on the political cartoonist John Tenniel's rendition of the illustrations for the book. The Hatter is depicted at tea wearing a tag reading 10/6, that being the cost of the hat—ten shillings and six pence. The holiday commemorates sixth day of tenth month. The holiday was first created in 1986 by a bunch of Boulder, Colorado computer technicians who were fans of the fantasy book. There might have been weed involved.

Ways to celebrate this auspicious day can be as simple as rereading the book, giving a tea party or as fun as wearing a hat all day. Perhaps with a tag 10/6. HOWEVER, if you're from across the pond, the holiday is the tenth of the sixth month (June). They do things backwards.

October 07

On October 7, 1916 one of the most lop-sided games in football history taught us the most about good sportsmanship (maybe), team loyalty (definitely) and a fundamental change in college football (yep).

Cumberland was a struggling college in Lebanon, Tennessee which had committed the previous year to a game to be played against powerhouse Georgia Tech on that day in 1916. But times were hard and Cumberland dismantled its football program that spring. Cumberland politely asked if it could pull out of the game and Georgia Tech refused. Forfeiting the game would have cost Cumberland $3k which would have shoved the school over the bankruptcy cliff.

Continued on Next Page

Continued from Previous Page

Georgia Tech was led by John Heisman. Yep, that one. He was ruthless on the field, brilliant and all that, but something of a softy at heart. But not enough of a softy to let Cumberland out of the commitment to play.

So Cumberland started recruiting. Fast. Any able bodied man or even not so able man was signed on and they knew in advance they were going to lose but they would save the school by showing up. Heisman was so determined for the match he put up the money for the men to travel to Atlanta (there's the softy part of him). Cumberland devised a team of English Literature majors, skinny dudes from the Chemistry Department, frat brothers who didn't listen to sports on the radio. All of them on the bus prepared to lay down their lives or at least their honor to save their school. Remember, this is during World War 1 when the manliest of men had been sent to the European front.

In each of the first and second quarters Georgia Tech scored 63 points. The third quarter didn't go so well for Georgia—they scored a measly 54 points against the Cumberland Bulldogs. The referees even reduced the time of the quarters from fifteen minutes to 12 just because it wasn't like the fourth quarter was going to give Cumberland a victory. The final score, after an extra 42 points for Georgia, was 222-0. Heisman, why didn't you follow the "slaughter" rule?

What an incredible debilitating humiliating loss for Cumberland.

Or was it?

Cumberland College was founded in 1842 and is one of the oldest private liberal arts university today with approximately 2-3k students. It's sent on their way two Supreme Court justices, gazillions of members of Congress, some social activists and army officers and all sorts of artists and leaders of education. Cumberland endures. I admire their football team of the season of 1916 which only played one game. But a pivotal game of sacrifice for the greater good. Those players getting off the bus back home (again, paid for by Heisman) were heroes.

So today if you have defeats or have endured defeats of the past, just try to remember what you might have endured or lost will transform you into a victor of another battle.

October 08

October 8, 1871 should be called Don't Play with Matches Day. As we all know, the great Chicago fire began that evening, most people of the opinion that it started when Mrs. O'Leary's cow tipped over a bucket in a barn at 137 Dekoven street. The bucket knocked over a kerosene lamp. Fire spread quickly. By the time it was all over, 300

Chicagoans had died and countless folk were homeless and buildings destroyed.

But there was another devastating fire in Wisconsin on that very night. Peshtigo was a town of 1700 about 45 miles northeast of Green Bay, Wisconsin. It had been settled in 1838, mostly in support of a lumber and woodworking factory. Everyone agrees that

the summer of 1871 had been unusually dry and hot and when the factory went up in flames, the conflagration moved fast. By the next morning, 800 Peshtigoians were confirmed dead, with another 1400-2000 people from the surrounding area. Many bodies were unidentifiable and so the cemetery has two mass graves, one for the children and one for the adults. Peshtigo had a hard time recovering but is now a town of 3000 and presumably lots of fire extinguishers.

Two towns, twin tragedies. We hear a lot about Chicago's rebuilding but not quite so much about Peshtigo. In any event, today is a good day to check your fire alarm batteries and make sure you don't go to sleep with a scented candle burning.

October 09

On October 9, 1984 scant years ago, Sean Lennon had his nine year birthday party hosted by parents Yoko Ono and John Lennon. His parents invited a passel of artists, including the very shy Andy Warhol.

One of Sean's birthday presents was a "macintosh" computer, fresh from the first production run. A mysterious stranger had brought the gift. Sean went to his bedroom with Warhol who was feeling a bit uncomfortable in his invisibility to other guests. But the computer was a draw and soon all the guests were crowding about. Warhol picked up a cigarette box sized contraption linked to the the screen which he

Continued on Next Page

October 09

was informed was a "mouse." He proceeded to wave over his head like a baton guided by the young stranger. The screen of the computer lit up.

"My God" Warhol exclaimed. "I just drew a circle."

The stranger introduced himself.

"I'm Steve Jobs."

October 10

On the morning of October 10,1995 economist Robert E. Lucas had just been awarded a Nobel Prize in Economics for his work in rational expectations in macro-economics. He shared a bottle of champagne—no judging—with colleagues in his department including his very young, very hot, wife Nancy Stokey who was no slouch in the brains department either. Her work on growth and public finance monetary theory was enough to make any man frisky.

The Lucases had everything—tenured positions at the University of Chicago and the Nobel committee was going to give him an 18k gold medal AND $1,000,000.

Robert Lucas knew that the tax man would be arriving shortly—Nobel winners at that time got to keep about half of their loot. If you're a professor at the U. of C. you made a salary in the mid-six figures. When Nobel winners get their winnings they tend to put it into charity—Barak Obama gave most of his to the Clinton Foundation. George Smoot (physics 2006) created a foundation to encourage youth in the sciences.

Once the check clears the charities pay them a salary. Some just put it in their bank accounts for mundane things like college tuition and retirement. There's some whimsy—Richard Roberts (physiology1993) built a croquet lawn for himself.

Lucas was looking, after taxes, at about $500k. But then there was a problem—the first Mrs. Lucas. Robert hadn't always had a younger, hotter wife. No disrespect to Rita Lucas, but she was in her fifties and had not gotten that much traction on her career in pharmacology as she raised two children and picked up stakes whenever it helped her husband's career. Botox and Cool Sculpting hadn't yet been invented.

They had separated in 1982 when Robert moved in with his colleague, Nancy. The divorce was finalized in 1988 and Robert and Nancy promptly married.

On that morning October 10, 1995 Robert Lucas remembered something that might have cut into his happiness. His first wife Rita had always believed in him and his work—so much so that she asked that a clause be added to their divorce agreement. If he received a Nobel prize within seven years of their divorce, she would receive half of the money awarded. At the time, he thought she was nuts and didn't mind signing off on it. If the committee had only held off three weeks…he would have been in the clear.

Before you think ill of Rita, please know that this is not the first time a Nobel Prize winner has had to take care of a discarded wife. When Albert Einstein got divorced from Meliva Maric in 1919, they agreed that if he won a Nobel Prize, Meliva would get ALL his winnings to be put in trust for their two sons, the interest from that trust to be given to Meliva.

October 11

October 11 is the fourth day of the five day celebration known as Cephalopod Awareness Week. I'm sure all of us have felt that October is a little, well, packed what with it being breast cancer, down syndrome, healthy lung, liver disease, and disability employment awareness month. To say nothing of Polish American, Italian American, and Hispanic Heritage month. Not to forget LGBTQ+ and Filipino history month. With this October holiday schedule, I'm not sure I've even seen a Cephalopod Awareness P.S.A. or a human interest story on CNN about it. So let me help your understanding of the week long (okay, five days) celebration that traditionally begins on the eighth day of the eighth month.

I know, I know, there are some of you that believe October is actually the tenth month even though the "octo" is a derivative for "eight" in Latin and heretics who created both the Julian and Gregorian calendars have kept the name even after they shoehorned two extra months—January and February—into the year. But pay them no mind! The Romulus calendar worked perfectly well without those two extra months which invariably include freezing temperatures, snow and that despicable holiday in February celebrating the 2% of the population that's all kissy face while reminding the other 98% that we're losers.

Cephalopod starts on the eighth and celebrates the wonders and achievements of Octopi everywhere. They are squishy and have eight arms (technically not tentacles). I celebrate the day with a look at Moby Dick, the Melville novel but upon realizing it is a snoozer I invariably honor Octopi everywhere by drinking a pint of Moby Dick Cervejaria Octopus. It's a stout. Nice taste to it and I think I have developed hair on my chest.

On the Cephalopod calendar, the Nautilus is referred to as the "sailor" of the Cephalopod world and is honored on the ninth day of October. Nautiluses are highly prized because their shells can be used as a pearl substitute.

Maybe just have some octopi at a nice Greek restaurant. Or sushi.

October 12

October 12 honors our first millennial saint of the internet and computer programmers.

I know, I know, the present patron saint is Isidore of Seville who died in 636 a.d. He never saw a computer, never trolled for pics of HOT nuns and there weren't no stinkin' computer programmers back in his day.

Nonetheless, John Paul II gave him that duty in 1997. Isidore's about to lose his job.

On this day, October 12, 2006 fifteen year old Carlo Acutis of Milan died of leukemia and almost immediately received the title "Servant of God" which is a first step towards sainthood. Although he had wanted to donate his organs to others, the leukemia's damage to his organs prohibited this. His heart was placed as a reliquary at the Basilica of St. Francis of Assisi. The rest of his corporeal body was buried at the nearby Church of Santa Maria Maggiore which happens to be the place where St. Francis tore off his rich clothes and declared that he had only one father—who art in heaven.

He had always been a devout kid. His parents were lapsed Catholics but agreed to send him to mass when he asked at the age of three. From then on, he pretty much went to mass every day. He gathered items for the poor and the homeless. He volunteered at his church, went to confession every week.

He developed a particular interest in Eucharistical miracles—miracles that occur at transubstantiation, the moment that the wafer and the wine have been transformed into flesh and blood. He created a website to celebrate, catalogue, and teach about these miracles. He extended his work to create websites for local churches and parochial schools.

When he was first diagnosed with leukemia he had scant months to live. He told his doctor "I offer all the suffering I will have to suffer for the Lord, the Pope and the Church." This sounds pompous at first glance, but no, it is simply the sort of words any of the early Christian martyrs would have said.

Knowing his time on earth was going to be brief, Carlo asked his parents to take him on pilgrimages to some of the places he had written about in his website. Unfortunately, his health deteriorated too rapidly. He never complained, never wavered in his belief, and was an inspiration to every person who had contact with him.

Carlo's body is displayed in the Sanctuary of the Spoliation at the Santa Maria Maggiore Church. He wears jeans, a sweater, and Nike sneakers.

He has one confirmed miracle attributed to him. Severely ill seven year old Mattheus Viana of Brazil was taken to church with his mom and at the moment of the Eurcharist he prayed that he might be able to eat and he asked for Carlo's intercession which is a fancy way of saying "could

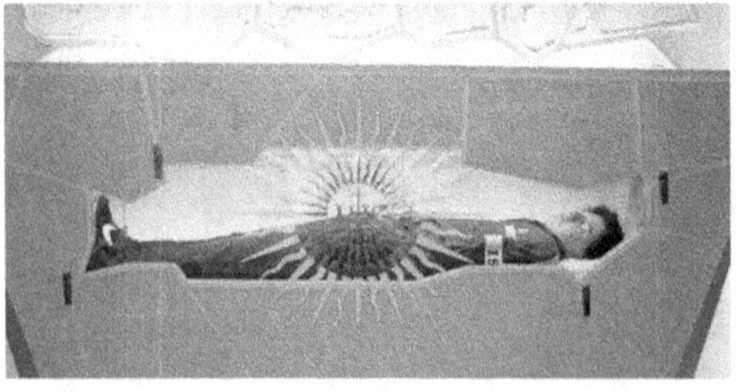

you please ask God for me?" At the service he touched a reliquary of Carlo, in this case a piece of cloth from one of his t-shirts. Mattheus had suffered since birth from a pancreatic illness that mandated a liquid diet. When mass was over he told his mother he was hungry and ate solid food for the first time since his diagnosis. The healing was in-

October 12

vestigated by the Congregation for the Causes of the Saints, which consists of priests and scientists. Carlo's intercession got him a gold star!

After beatification there's a few more hoops Carlo still has to jump through, but I am guessing he's going to get that all important ST honorific. That's going to get him an upgrade to first class with most airlines.

There is talk that he will supplant Isidore as the dude to pray to when you're being bullied on social media, when your computer crashes, when you are about to unleash the F-bomb because you forgot your password to your favorite website.

Still, even at fifteen, he won't be the youngest saint of the modern age—Francisco and Jacinto, two of the children who saw the Mary at Fatima, died of influenza in 1918 at ages 10 and 9 respectively. Carlo will, however, be the coolest saint—his Nikes are da bomb!

I'm no ecclesiastical scholar, but I would argue that his second miracle, easily confirmed, is his parents. Both returned to the Catholic faith and both agree it was their son who guided them there.

Be strong, courageous, be devoted and have faith with whatever belief gets you through the day. And if it's your birthday, blow out those candles and let all the usual sufferings of being human take a play hooky day!

October 13

October 13 is the 50th anniversary of Uruguayan Flight 571 in the Andes. It is a story of unbelievable tragedy, courage, painful choices, and determination.

The day started in Montevideo, Uruguay with the 19 member strong Old Christians Club, some family members and five crew members flying to Santiago, Chile. The O.C.C. were to play

futbol (soccer) against the Old Boys Club. Altogether 45 people were on the chartered Air Force 227-D. The pilot was experienced but the weather up in the mountains was hideous. The pilot thought he was heading into Curio airport, but actually he was about forty miles away. The control tower instructed him to descend for landing which he did—directly into the mountains. Many died on impact or in the next few days. Because South America's weather being generally mild nobody had thought to bring heavy coats and many simply died of exposure. Another eight died when an avalanche hit the plane.

Saved: Survivors of the crash wave to rescue helicopters after their 72-day ordeal in the Andes

Because the crew were dead or dying the survivors' only hope was rescue. They kept track of the search efforts by radio but were unable to communicate with the outside world. The plane was white and seemed to disappear into the snowy climes. They tried writing "HELP" in the snow with lipstick but ran out of the stuff. Then they arranged luggage into the shape of the cross. Nothing. They were eating snow and they took apart the seats of the plane so that they could huddle together for warmth. They were hungry, tired, cold, suffering from snow blindness and losing hope with every minute.

On the eleventh day of their ordeal, the radio announced that search efforts for Flight 571 had been called off. Gustava Nicolich relayed the news to the survivors this way:

Continued on Next Page

October 13

"Hey, boys, I have some good news! We just heard on the radio they've called off the search."

And why exactly was that good news?

"Because it means we're going to get out of here on our own," Nicholich said.

When they were down to 16 survivors they began to discuss cannibalism. Some were utterly opposed. But Nando Parrado suggested that it wasn't really cannibalism—no, no, it was a symbol of the Eucharist. After all, Christ didn't serve tacos and beer at the Last Supper. He gave his body and his blood. It was a difficult argument to make but the survivors settled on a pact that if they died they were willing to give their body up as Jesus had done.

Some fought through their revulsion and some held out for a while. Only a little while.

Nando Parrado and Roberto Canesso were chosen to look for help. They were relatively robust and were given extra rations and the warmest clothes available. They survived ten days of the grueling mission and found parts of an aircraft from an earlier unrelated plane accident. They scavenged frozen chocolates, meat patties, shared a bottle of rum, smoked cigarettes and read comic books for a few hours. And then they kept going until they found a river. Tip: if you follow a river you will eventually find civilization.

After grueling days, they saw a Chilean huasa (cowboy) across the river and while they couldn't be heard as they screamed for help, the cowboy arrived the next morning with reinforcements. Official rescue teams arrived and picked up Parrado and Canesso who helped with tracking down the plane and remaining survivors. A decision was made to bury the dead at the site, possibly to lessen the horror and grief their families might have experienced upon seeing their loved ones' bodies. The aspect of cannibalism was the subject of rumor which exploded when a news outlet featured a picture of a half-eaten leg. The survivors held a news conference to explain the ordeal and they all took confession where each was told that they were absolved because the cannibalism was in extremis.

There are other instances of groups using cannibalism to survive a seemingly hopeless ordeal. Donner Pass, the settlers at Jamestown, that sort of thing. It's shocking and always ends up in books, plays, movies—there are so many about Miracle Flight 571 (Tragedia de Los Andes 571 or Milagro de Los Andes 571.) I look at it this way—this a story of unbelievable teamwork and determination to overcome. Maybe today is a day to reach out to someone, friend or family, and say "I will always be here for you. You and I may face difficulties, tragedies, accidents, horrors that will abruptly turn our lives into a downward spiral, but I will always always always be here for you."

October 14

October 14 and you're way ahead of me on its significance.

"ArLynn," you'll say. "It's the day in 1066 when William, Duke of Normandy defeated King Harold II of England. Harry was the last English king. The Windsors changed their name from Hanover because they wanted to hide the fact that they were Krauts and they usually spoke German."

Or maybe you'll shake your head and sigh. "That was the day in 1980 when Ronald Reagan declared the War on Drugs. I was in my parents' basement doing something that's perfectly legal today. I even own a dispensary which gave me the financial freedom to move out."

Well, you're both wrong! The most important day in history event was the October 14, 2007 premiere of Keeping Up with The Kardashians. Kim and her sisters were united by their lack of accomplishment. Except for Kim's sex tape. And Kris, the mom, drooling over the potential windfall from said tape. At the time Gina Bellafante of the New York Times wrote of Kris Jenner "the only person in his household to have actually accomplished anything." Caitlin will be remembered not for his accomplishments in athletics but mostly for her gender change and her 1% of the vote in the California governor primaries.

That October 14th was history undressing in front of us. And quell derrieres!

On October 15, 1860, the Civil War became a foregone conclusion and all of American history was changed by a short letter written by eleven year old Grace Bedell of Westfield, New York. Abraham Lincoln was the Republican Party candidate for President* and the Republicans, while having a nice following in the New England states were truly despised elsewhere. And the candidate Lincoln? Skinnier than ever from stress of campaigning, he was an Ozempic mess.

Grace got the idea that if he got a beard and whiskers going, it would fill out his features. I quote without edits:

> Oct 15. 1860
>
> Hon A B Lincoln
>
> Dear Sir
>
> My father has just home from the fair and brought home your picture… I am a little girl only eleven years old, but want you should be President of the United States very much so I hope you wont think me very bold to write to such a great man as you are… I have got 4 brother's and part of them will vote for you any way and if you will let your whiskers grow I will try and get the rest of them to vote for you you would look a great deal better for your face is so thin. All the ladies like whiskers and they would tease their husband's to vote for you and then you would be President. My father is a going to vote for you and if I was a man I would vote for you to but I will try and get every one to vote for you that I can… I must not write any more answer this letter right off
>
> Good bye
>
> Grace Bedell

There was a quick response from the skinny dude.

> Springfield, Ill Oct 19, 1860
>
> Miss Grace Bedell
>
> My dear little Miss
>
> Your very agreeable letter of the 15th is received. I regret the necessity of saying I have no daughters. I have three sons—one seventeen, one nine, and one seven years of age. They, with their mother, constitute my whole family. As to the whiskers, having never worn any, do you not think

*The Republican Party's first convention was held in 1856 in Philadelphia. Delegates nominated John C. Fremont, under the slogan "free soil, free silver, free men, Fremont, and victory!" Well, that was a bust.

____

____

____

____

____

October 15

people would call it a silly affectation if I were to begin it now?

Your very sincere well wisher

A. Lincoln

On February 16, 1861 Lincoln was traveling by train and made a stop at Westfield. Gave a speech and at the end, asked if Grace were in attendance. Grace's father brought her forward and Lincoln kissed her on the forehead (not in a creepy Biden way) and chatted with the duo for a few minutes. A few years later, Grace wrote Lincoln again, asking for a letter of recommendation to get a job at the Treasury Department because her family had fallen on hard times. Before any response she got married and married women just didn't get jobs outside of the home.

Don't be afraid to make what others might think a ridiculous suggestion and don't be afraid to communicate with important folks. They're just like you!

October 16

October 16 is both the feast day of a 12th/13th century Polish saint named Hedwig and the anniversary of the coronation of King/Saint Hedwig of the late 14th century. These two gals have nothing to do with the 2001 movie Hedwig and the Angry Inch nor of botched sex change operations. Nonetheless there are some, er, salacious details of their lives that are necessary to understand the two of them. So if you're a lady of refined sensibilities or are easily excitable, you might want to skip this post and celebrate October 16 World Cat Day or shuffle off to October 17th's O. Henry Pun Off Day. Just fair warning.

Sometime in October 1373 Louis the Great of Hungary and Poland and his wife Elizabeth of Bosnia were blessed with a second daughter. They had already married off their first daughter Mary to the King of Luxembourg so you can imagine the couple's power, influence, and sovereignty over Europe. This new daughter Jadwiga (aka Hedwig) was promised in marriage at the tender age of one to William of Austria in what the church would term "sponsalia de future," a not terrifically uncommon practice in European royalty. William was 15 years her senior.

When Hedwig was eleven, Louis died and William of Austria wanted to cash in on his marriage. So did Mary's husband from Luxembourg. After all, it is a truth so well acknowledged that it hardly bears repeating—a country with two female heirs and a lot of real estate must be looking for a king. Er, devoted husband.

Continued on Next Page

October 16

Mary and her husband grabbed Hungary which was part of Louis' bequest, but Poland was still in play. The Poles quickly crowned eleven year old Hedwig KING on October 16, 1384, the title a clear signal that no dude was going to come in and rule the joint just by putting a ring on it.* William hightailed it to Krakow and obtained a special dispensation for the eleven year old King to marry him and there was some…consummatin'. A lot of it because it took until August of 1385 for Polish nobles to hustle William out of the country against Hedwig's wishes. She would not even be twelve but here's nineteenth century painter Jan Matejko's Dymitr of Gora depicting Hedwig attempting to break

out of the prison Grand Crown Marshall Dymitri had locked her in to keep her from William.

The Poles settled on Jogaila, Grand Duke of Lithuania who was a pagan. That's how desperate the Polish noblemen were for a second husband for Hedwig. They got Jogaila to agree to convert and recognize that Hedwig was King. Also, the age spread wasn't really as bad—he was a mere 26 and by the time they married she was twelve.

The couple appeared to have had a good marriage but she died at the age of twenty four and left no heirs. On her deathbed, she supposedly encouraged her husband to marry Anne of Cilli who would solidify Jogaila's claim to the throne. He would run through a number of wives before dying and leaving Poland in the hands of kiddy kings who weren't even Polish.

Hedwig was recognized as a woman of virtue and saintliness. In 1997 she was made a saint, a patron to Poland, queens, students, mothers, and a United Europe. Take that, Brexit! Within her iconography she is often pictured with an apron with roses in its pockets—a reference to when ole Jagaili discovered that she was smuggling food to rebels and when he went to inspect her apron, the food had turned into roses.

While her feast day is June 8, her birthday coincides with the feast day of Hedwig of Andechs who was also Polish royalty and also married just prior to her 12th birthday—in her case to Henry I the Bearded of Silesia. She was canonized in 1267.

Both Hedwigs were known for their devotion to the church, to the poor, to the infirm.

*Elizabeth I of England solved that problem by declaring that she was wed to her country. Elizabeth 2 solved it by getting Philip to abdicate his Greek crown.

On October 17, 1814 in St. Giles, London a vat of a million pints of beer burst open. A fifteen feet high wave of porter rushed through Bainbridge street, destroying two houses, crushing the local pub, and killing eight people.

A jury acquitted the brewers of wrongdoing, calling the episode "An Act of God".

There's no particular plaque or statue or memorial for the great London beer flood, but the pub Holborn Whippet brews a special anniversary porter each October 17th. If you haven't booked your tickets yet, aim for next year!

So pour yourself a pint. Not enough to drown,
but just enough to celebrate!

October 18

October 18 is known as St. Luke's Little Summer. Cute name for a day, the eighteenth day of the eighth month of the year. Even if October is the tenth month. The first Emperor Romulus (who got his crown by killing his twin brother Remus) created a ten month calendar in 753 b.c. October just happened to be the eighth month—octo means eight in Latin. In 713 b.c. Emporer Numa Pompilius decided to slip in two extra months and October got shoved into the ten spot.

Let's fast forward to St. Luke Evangelist who wrote one of the Gospels as well as the Acts of the Apostles. He went with St. Paul on some of his missionary trips and he hung out with Mary, even creating a portrait of her. His day of death was October 18 and therefore his "Saint's Day" is nestled into that wonderful teetering on the cliff moment of late summer early fall.

But why is his day a "little summer"? There is an Italian phrase "San Luca, el ton va te la zuca" which is to say "pumpkins go stale on St. Luke's Day"

Which I interpret as if you're not going to decorate for Halloween you've got an excuse in St. Luke—but please, would just a little pumpkin in the window really hurt you?

Around 1435, Rogier van der Weyden painted Saint Luke Drawing the Virgin. You can see it at the Museum of Fine Arts in Boston. I think he looks bored or maybe he's just politely averting his eyes.

How are you decorating?
Or not.

October 19

October 19, 2003 is a day to admire David Blaine the illusionist/magician. Sometimes he brings out the haters. Blaine had placed himself in a clear plastic box over the River Thames in London. He stayed there for 44 days, surviving on water. My question would be how did he, ya know, Number 1, but we'll leave that for a Depends commercial. Close to 250,000 Londoners came to gawk. Women showed their, uh,

twins. And men dropped their pants. People tossed eggs, tomatoes, paint-filled balloons. One man beat drums and another blew an air horn whenever it looked like Blaine was going to get a little shut eye. But on October 19 he was let out of the box, as it were.

October 19, 2004 is also a day to admire Curt Schilling who definitely put the red in Red Sox. It was game 6 of a league championship when Boston Red Sox pitcher Schilling was recovering from surgery on a right ankle tendon. The stitches busted on his right ankle and that white sock turned red. But he pitched on and the team won what would be called the Bloody Sock Game. The Red Sox ended up in the World Series for the first time since 1918. Schilling threw out the lucky red sock of game 6, but kept the bloodied socks he wore for game 2 of the World Series. They were later auctioned for $92,163.

Which brings us back to Blaine. He had lost 25 % of his body weight and his cardiologist was concerned about heart palpitations. He couldn't see straight. Just before he was taken to the hospital, he had words for those who had taunted him.

"I've learned how important it is to have a sense of humor and laugh at everything, because nothing makes sense anymore. I love all of you forever."

Might be babbling but he was babbling some real wisdom!

So today, go out there and keep your humor when all around you fail. You've got this one!

A story from October 20, 1968.

Mrs. Patrick was the second mother I had in my short life but by no means the last. On this day she was getting her hair done. We were staying at a motel in Pompano Beach which included luxuries such as a pool, a beach view, a restaurant where even the Shirley Temples came with umbrellas. And, in its lower bowels, a beauty salon. Mrs. Patrick had despaired of relying on this emporium because it wasn't as fine as one would find in New York or Los Angeles, but since we lived in Western Springs, Illinois, I couldn't really tell the difference.

I had been parked at one of two chairs beside a coffee table with stacks of magazines and papers. I was bored.

"She went off and married a black man!" Mrs. Patrick declared indignantly.

"It's horrible news," said the woman who was putting curlers into play. "Simply disgusting. And less than five years since her husband, her real husband, was shot!"

I picked up the paper.

"He's not black," I said. "Aristotle Onassis is Greek."

"Same thing," Mrs. Patrick snarled.

I decided to not pursue the matter because 1968 was not the first time that my opinions or comments about the Kennedys got me into trouble.

Mrs. Patrick woke me on the morning of June 5th to tell me that Robert F Kennedy had been shot. I sleepily opined that this would mean that Hubert Humphrey would get the nomination and Nixon would beat him easily. For that comment, I got the belt and had to endure three days of mandatory funeral coverage. On the other hand, I might have been seven, but I was right.

I put the paper on the coffee table and pretended that I was not in fact reading the account of the widow Kennedy flying off to a hastily arranged marriage in Greece. Her own mother was given just twenty four hours to stay for the celebrations. Her sister Lee Radziwell who had dated Onassis was given a generous forty eight hours. Aristotle was rich and claimed to be a mere 62. Her children John John and Caroline both looked a little shell-shocked. Perhaps even more so than Mrs. Patrick and the hair dresser in Pompano Beach.

Jackie's wedded bliss lasted until Ari's death in 1975. At his funeral she said "Aristotle Onassis rescued me at a moment when my life was engulfed with shadows. He brought me into a world where one could find both happiness and love. We lived through many beautiful experiences together which cannot be forgotten, and for which I will be eternally grateful."

Years later she was buried next to President Kennedy with her name engraved as Jacqueline Bouvier Kennedy Onassis. Strikingly, Onassis' name was not mentioned at the funeral or the burial service.

October 20 is a day of making choices that are right for you but might not be right in the eyes of others. Look at what you're doing, choose for you and not for others. Be courageous and be true. And if you're an October 20 birthday peep, courage is so much of a part of you!

October 21

October 21 is a great day to reflect on how you pick your relatives. Particularly your parents and grandparents. A wrong move and, well, you might regret your decision.

John Paul Getty 3rd managed to pick a terrible father and arguably a worse grandfather. And in 1973 JPG3 was kidnapped by the 'Ndrangheta mafia group in Italy. The kidnappers knew there was a deep pocket somewhere in the family line. After all, J. P. Getty One was one of the richest men in the world. He was estranged from his son JPG2 who had a lot of dough as well.

In 1975, the kidnappers politely asked for ransom from both grandfather and father. Both Gettys declined, with the younger Getty supposedly telling his mistress "do you realize that if I have to pay the ransom, I'd have to sell my entire library for that useless son."

So on October 21, 1975 sixteen year old JPG3 was given a few steaks as an extra special treat, then blindfolded. Before getting him fully restrained he asked if this was going to hurt.

"Of course it's going to hurt," one of his captors replied.

His ear was sliced, preserved in formaldehyde and sent to a newspaper in Rome with a warning that more body parts were on their way. That finally brought Grandpa JP1 to the bargaining table. He would pay only as much of the ransom as would be covered as an insur-

Continued on Next Page

October 21

ance loss. The rest he would loan to his son JP2 with a 4% interest rate. Talk about empathy, compassion, and love.

When the JPG3 was finally released,missing an ear, he telephoned his grandfather to thank him for his help. When told his grandson was on the line JP1 declined the call.

JP3 developed a drug and alcohol problem that resulted in a stroke and he was pretty much paralyzed until his death in 2011.

So today, think carefully about whether you've picked your relatives right. Sometimes they might not have money but they might love you awfully well.

October 22

On October 22, 2012 Lance Armstrong accomplished something quite extraordinary in the world of cycling. He managed to lose seven races in one single day—and all of them Tour De France!

Armstrong had won his first Tour in 1999 only 3 years after being diagnosed with testicular cancer which spread to his brain and his lungs. How brave and tenacious he is, the world cried out.

And then the rumors of performance enhancing drugs mounted even as he accrued endorsement deals and founded charities and even ditched a wife so he could get it on with musician Sheryl Crow.

The United States Anti-Doping Agency investigated and ultimately issued a 202 page report that slammed the cyclist and his teammates as well. The International Cycling Union did not appeal and Lance lost his seven titles.

"Lane Armstrong has no place in cycling," declared the president of the Union. "He deserves to be forgotten in cycling."

Exit Sheryl Crow although he has found happiness with Anna Hansen. Me? When I get on the treadmill I swear I don't use any performance drugs. Which is why I can read magazines and take phone calls and do my nails while I'm working out.

October 23

If October 23 is your birthday, fear not! Because it's actually not such a dis-mole day. My birthday wish is that you win the lottery and become a multi-mole-ionaire and that all your mountains of troubles become mole hills.

For, you see, in 1991, Wisconsin physics teacher Maurice Oehler came up with the holiday we commonly call mole day. They really don't have a lot of things to do in Wisconsin. The day—October 23 from the hours of 6:02 a.m. to 6:02 p.m.—commemorates Amadeo Avogadro's Number, an impossibly large one of

602,214,076,000,000,000,000,000

An easy way to remember this is to think of our most recent Illinois State tax hike proposal.

Another way to remember it is to think of

6.02214 x 10 to the 23rd power

Or, to be perfectly clear, a mole is a unit of mass which describes the number of particles—atoms, protons, electrons, whatnot. Water, for instance, has a mole mass of 18 while neon clocks in at a mole mass of 20.

My excuse for not really understanding moles is that I'm a high school dropout. Yours might be that you were asleep in class.

In any event the holiday itself works like this—

6:02 (get it) x the tenth month (get it) to the 23rd power (all right already). 6.02 x10 to the 23rd.

It's a lot easier to impress your friends by explaining mole day than by telling mole jokes so here's a few for you:

What do you get if you chop an avocado into 6.02 X 10 to the 23rd power? Ha, ha, guacamole!

What did the mole host say when people crashed his party? Ha, Ha, the mole the merrier!

The American Chemical Society decided the theme of the previous year's celebrations is Mole-zilla! I guess you would recycle your costume from last Halloween.

You can always find something to celebrate in a day, even if it's a dis-mole rainy cold afternoon. If geeky mathematicians and chemists can do it, you can too! I think it's the perfect day for a glass of champagne and a single piece of chocolate. I'll call it square root of negative one day because that's how many calories I'll be consuming!

Okay, okay, that wasn't even remole-tely funny!

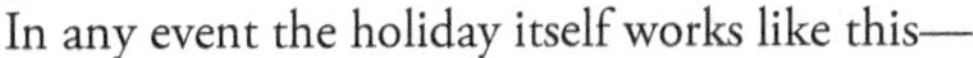

October 24

October 24 is both National Bologna Day and United Nations Day. Which I find very puzzling! Does this mean that I should bring sandwiches to the next Security Council meeting or that the United Nations is a bunch of....

October 25

I've got my holiday preps ready. A copy of The Economist. A selection of tourist maps. A bowl of oil down.* As an extra treat of verisimilitude I bought some firecrackers. All to celebrate the launch of one of America's greatest military victories! Maybe a party hat would be too precious?

On October 25, 1983, two battalions were up and ready to go. But at Fort Bragg, which would provide most of the invasion force, things were a titch chaotic because nobody had been told where we would invade. It would have to be Lebanon, non? After all, less than two days prior, terrorists bombed our marine barracks in Beirut, killing 241 American military and civilian personnel.

Deputy Commander Norman Schwarzkopf was infuriated by the lack of coordination between the two invasion battalions and the Fort Bragg marine battalion. Supposedly, a Bragg battalion commander entered his office to see that his subordinate had plastered the walls with maps of Lebanon.

*Oil downs is made with coconut, saffron, callaloo, chicken, crab, dumplings and breadfruit. Takes all day to make and it's Grenada's favorite dish.

"Tear all that shit down!" the Commander screamed. "We're invading Grenada!"

"Pardon me, sir, but why are we invading Spain?" was the response.**

Operation Urgent Fury invaded the tiny island country with 2,000 troops. They were sent to settle a bitchfest between two communist factions, one of which had cozied up to Cuba AND The Soviet Union. The troops were also sent to rescue medical students from the offsite St. George's Medical School. The prospect of Americans being held hostage kind of resonated given the recent lack of hospitality afforded Americans in Tehran.

Back at Fort Bragg, an officer was sent to purchase tourist maps of the island nation. Officers pored over back issues of The Economist magazine in order to figure out what the hell was going.

No worries. Within three days the New York Times was able to report that the American medical students were returned and how grateful they were. And deputy commander Norman Schwarzkopf took away a very important lesson:

Keep everyone in the loop and coordinate your efforts.

Schwarzkopf would later run the 1991 Persian Gulf war and became a national hero. He understood the lesson he had been given in Grenada.

So let's get on the phone. Keep your peeps close with zoom, text, email, and make sure everyone knows what's going on.

**Not such a stupid comment on the part of the soldier. After all, Grenada—that tiny little sliver of Andalusian Spain—was strategically important through many years, culminating in the ouster of Emir Muhammad XII (otherwise known as Boabill) in 1492 by the Catholic monarchs Ferdinand II and Isabella I.

October 26

October 26 is National Pumpkin Day, celebrating this "pepon"—that being the Greek word for the large melon.

Pumpkins can be traced back to the first known seeds cultivated in Mexico between 7,000 and 5,000 BC. The fruit and seeds are good for both people and animals. If your pet is having some stomach distress, give it a few cubes of pumpkin. On the other hand, if squirrels are going after your jack-o'-lanterns, spray it with hairspray. The pumpkin, not the squirrel.

Pumpkins are full of vitamin C which is particularly critical as citrus fruits go out of season in the fall.

How do you celebrate pumpkin day? Well, you could head over to Starbucks for a pumpkin latte or maybe buy a package of salty pumpkin seeds to snack on. Or maybe just pace yourself—pumpkin day really should stretch all the way until Christmas night when you eat the last of the pumpkin pie with your friends and family. Then and only then can you wash off the jack o lanterns and let the squirrels sink their teeth into them. Here's my jack-o'-lanterns!

October 27

October 27, 1966 is a day with treasures that will never be regained and a philosopher's quote that we should all live by.

On that day, Mrs. Patrick, the second of my many mothers, allowed as how we would watch television. Sitting on the floor in front of the screen, she admonished me repeatedly to scoot back or I would surely blind myself. Obviously, none of us knew about scrunching our eyes at a text message.

And there it was, the cartoon heretofore read and scanned in the papers—I was still a little shy of reading the front page because there was a war going on.

My hero Charlie Brown and all his friends were preparing for Halloween! A television event when there really were television events and not 279 channels each featuring a Kardashian family member.

There had been two specials before, one of them Christmas and the other not particularly tethered to a holiday. This 'It's The Great Pumpkin, Charlie Brown" would preempt an episode of the popular "My Three Sons" on CBS.

It would be followed with A Charlie Brown Thanksgiving in 1973. Many families considered the Peanuts Gang every bit as much of their holidays as Frosty the Snowman, visiting Santa at Marshall Field's (now Macey's) and a trip to Grandma's for a turkey dinner.

In the course of the Halloween special, Linus writes to the Great Pumpkin words of great wisdom that I hope to carry with me throughout this October 27:

"You must not get discouraged because more people believe in Santa Claus than you."

Truer, more prescient, words have never been delivered.

October 28

On October 28, 1811, the future King George IV (commonly referred to as "Prinny") purchased for 15 shillings* a book by a previously unpublished author referred to only as "a lady."** The booksellers at Becket & Porter in the fancy neighborhood of Pall Mall in London assured Prinny that the book Sense & Sensibility was divine. He was being given the opportunity to have the book two days before advertisements were to be sent out. Sneak peek, dontcha know?

Prinny loved the book and suddenly if you wanted to be part of le bon ton, you'd better be conversant in the romantic misadventures of Elinor and Marianne. And that you were so looking forward to reading coming novels of the anonymous

*About eighty bucks today and it didn't even have pictures!

**I had an English teacher who went all feminist about how women "weren't allowed" to publish under their own names because the patriarchy would be threatened by female intellect. I raised my hand and said plenty of men were in the same position. She asked me to name one man—I replied Common Sense later known to be by Thomas Paine; the Federalist Papers, later known to be the work of Hamilton, Madison, and Jay; Democracy by Anonymous, but really it was Henry Adams, Tamerlane by Edgar Allan Poe. She told me I could go to the principal's office. I said I wasn't finished with my answer. That's when she was so gracious as to keep me company on my way to his den.

Continued on Next Page

October 28

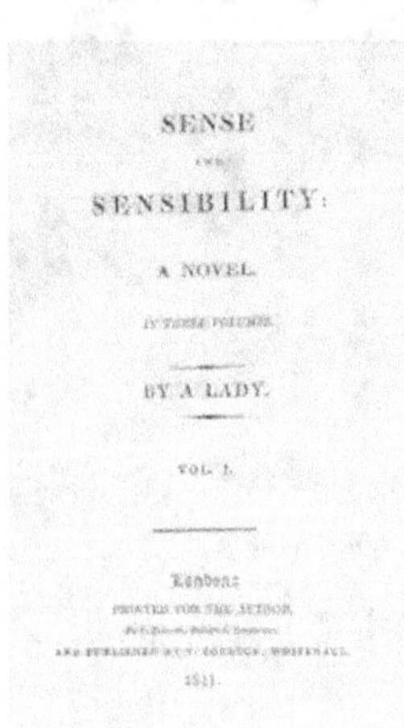

lady Pride & Prejudice,*** Mansfield Park, and Emma—particularly Emma since Alicia Silverstone has such perfect comic timing in Clueless and please not the Gwyneth Paltrow version where you think she's going to try to sell you face cream made out of yak urine or advise some weird self-care for your lady parts.

None of Jane Austen's works were published under her name while she lived. Two books, Persuasion and Northanger Abbey, came out soon after her death in 1817. A short piece—"Lady Susan"—wasn't published until 1871.

The Prince and Jane met but once, with Jane's reluctance because she didn't like his gambling, womanizing, and the general way he treated his wife Caroline of Brunswick. But Jane could have been a little more grateful—without Prinny's royal imprimatur, she never would have gotten any notice.

*About eighty bucks today and it didn't even have pictures!

**I had an English teacher who went all feminist about how women "weren't allowed" to publish under their own names because the patriarchy would be threatened by female intellect. I raised my hand and said plenty of men were in the same position. She asked me to name one man—I replied Common Sense later known to be by Thomas Paine; the Federalist Papers, later known to be the work of Hamilton, Madison, and Jay; Democracy by Anonymous, but really it was Henry Adams, Tamerlane by Edgar Allan Poe. She told me I could go to the Principal's office. I said I wasn't finished with my answer. That's when she was so gracious as to keep me company on my way to his den.

***Prinny had the advantage of growing up in the same era as depicted in Austen's novel. He didn't need an explanation of a brougham, a barouche, a morning dress, or whist. You might—and so take a look at any of W. W. Norton's annotated versions!

October 29

October 29, 1929 is commonly known as Black Tuesday, or The Great Crash. The stock market had been limping along since that August and there was even something known as Black Thursday before the weekend and then…whoops, the market was destroyed and the Roaring Twenties were over.

Here in my fair town of Winnetka a group of men "of means" had agreed to meet on that Tuesday night. The news was horrific. Some of their colleagues had thrown themselves off of New York skyscrapers based on their financial destruction. Many families were wiped out. The meeting was to solidify pledges to the Winnetka Community House, and each man at the meeting had every right to say "I can't make my pledge" but none did.

Every man kept his promise, though every family suffered. Winnetka is the better for it and survived the ensuing Great Depression. Difficult times call for difficult decisions. And these men represented their families' commitment. Today we have a place for art, community, theater, athletics.

Economic times are sometimes so tough. Hold out your hand and help the institutions you have espoused. Also make sure to hold your other hand out to the guy or gal.

October 30

On October 30, 1938 the earth suffered a devastating invasion by extraterrestrials which threatened the entire population. We nearly were exterminated, y'all!

Okay, maybe not. It was a regular Sunday night and families were gathered around their radios. Mom knitting. Dad snoozing over the papers. Kids playing quietly with their toys.

Urgent Alert! Martians had landed in New Jersey! Reporters "on the field" described glistening black serpentine characters emerging from metal "saucers" amidst green smoke and each invader was equipped with a heat ray gun! They annihilated a reporter corps!

Before you panic, I will give it all away—this was a radio adaptation of the H. G. Wells novel War of the Worlds meant as an opening of the '38 Halloween season. Orson Welles, a lad of just 23, masterminded this scare fest.

After the Martians emerged from their spacecraft, they grew to the size of trees and trotted through the New Jersey Palisades in search of hapless humans. Reporters interviewed folks who saw them. In Princeton Junction—just outside of Princeton University where you'd think smart people would prevail, terrified residents shot up the water tower thinking it might be a spaceship. Can't be too careful, eh?

After it was all over, one million of the twelve million radio listeners that night really believed the show. Emergency switchboards were inundated with calls from panicked Jerseyites wanting evacuation and safety procedures.

Welles apologized the next day and went on to make the movie Citizen Kane which some say is the best film of all time. But what if he had set the entire thing in Las Vegas? Nothing. Nobody would have noticed or cared. Martians? Just make sure to watch them at blackjack. Notorious cheats.

Drones have been sighted in NJ and elsewhere. Aliens? Foreign Adversaries? Government secret programs? Yeti?

October 31

October 31, 1977, an exhausted and disheveled Andy Warhol returned home from a Halloween party. Although to be fair, it could have been November 1 by that time. He recorded in his diary that his diamond choker caused him excruciating pain. "I hate jewelry," he declared. "How do ladies wear it? It's so uncomfortable." Andy—you have no idea how much the fair sex endures in pursuit of beauty. Try wearing stilettos.

What fashion trend has caused you the most pain?

November's thinnest yellow light is more warming and exhilarating than any wine they tell of.

–Henry David Thoreau

On November 1 and 2nd we visit our deceased loved ones. We bring food and the best wine and tequila. We clean up gravesites, we offer flowers, we chat and sing and in some larger cemeteries there are even mariachi bands to serenade our celebrations. We sleep overnight and dream of them. It IS a celebration of someone whom they loved. Happy Dia de Los Muertos. The first is also known as All Saints' Day celebrating the Church Triumphant.

November 02

November 2nd is All Souls' Day for which Pope Benedict XV in 1915 granted to all priests the right to hold three masses—one for the celebrant himself, one for the pope, and one for all the faithful dead.

I don't think anybody's going to visit my grave on a yearly basis, even with the lure of food, drinks and music. So I think it would be a waste of land space. I once asked one of my sons if he would be coming to my funeral. He said maybe. Does this mean I can ditch the idea of a funeral? You know, take what money I have left and go on a cruise?

Today and tomorrow think about someone you loved or loved you. Celebrate them, even if it's a pup that sauntered over the rainbow bridge, to join a bunch of playmates or a goldfish you flushed down the toilet.

November 3, 1970 actress and political activist Jane Fonda was on a speaking tour protesting the Vietnam War which would culminate in a 1972 visit to Hanoi at the invitation of the North Vietnamese government. After a rally in Canada, she reentered the USA at Cleveland and Customs Agents were mighty suspicious of a bag of pills in her baggage. Fonda explained they were vitamins but the Cleveland Police were having none of that. She was charged with drug smuggling and with kicking a police officer during her arrest. Her mug shot taken at the Cuyahoga County Sheriff's Office, with her fist raised defiantly became an iconic symbol of resistance. Her hair got most of the

attention—she had formerly dyed it blonde and kept it long for such star turns as Barefoot in the Park and Barbarella. But her stylist Paul McGregor persuaded her that she was more than a starlet, she was a serious person! He created an edgy haircut, a shag if you will, and brought her color back to her natural brunette.

Fonda's best film Klute came out later in the year with the haircut and it has taken fifty years for her to shake the nickname Hanoi Jane. All charges were dropped.

November 04

When pigs fly! Well, the first pig might well have been Icarus 2 named for the Greek mythological dude have got a little too close to the sun. On this day November 4, 1909 Brit aviator John Moore-Barbazon—first Baron Barbazon of Tara—attempted a "live cargo" plane flight. On a dare, he wrapped Icarus 2 in paper in a wicker basket (do you think Icarus 2 protested?). Then the Barron tied the basket to his French Voisin airplane and took to the skies. Probably no safety instructions nor a yellow vest in case of an aquatic landing. On the basket, he put a sign reading "I am the first pig to fly."

On this day, November 5, we celebrate the torment, the torture, ah, yes, that sweet death of the most hated man in history. We will burn his effigy in the streets, light bonfires, and do it all while wearing V for Vendetta masks to protect our identity. We will celebrate and give thanks that our dear King James I and IV* has been saved!

Oh, wait, I'm not talking about Trump. I'm talking about Guy "Guido" Fawkes of England. All of England celebrates his execution for his role in the failed Gunpowder

Plot to kill James 1-4 on November 5,1605 and replace him with the Catholic Princess Elizabeth of Bohemia (also known as the Winter Queen). Up until 1859 Guy Fawkes Day was a national Parliament sanctioned holiday but now it's just an excuse for mischief and fun.

Fawkes was born in 1570 in York, England and he had the misfortune to be borne into a Catholic family. The English are touchy about Catholicism, ever since that business about King Henry VIII and his one true love second wife Ann Boleyn. One true love might be an exaggeration—best to say one out of six true loves. Not including mistresses and gamed hens. Even today, a king or queen of England cannot be Catholic. Can't even marry a Catholic. Prince Michael of Kent had to give up his position in the line of succession to the throne under the Act of Settlement 1701 when he married in 1973 a double threat Catholic divorcee.

James was an ardent Protestant, Opposing legislation that would have allowed recusant** Catholics to, er, come out of the closet. Fawkes was so devoted to Catholicism that he went overseas to fight on behalf of the Spanish against just about everybody who wasn't Catholic. Spain's where Fawkes got the name Guido which is the name he "signed" on his confession. But that's later.

When he returned to England, Fawkes kind of, well, his mom would say he got in with the wrong crowd. A bunch of guys determined to kill James. They landed on the plan of setting off gunpowder at Parliament's opening session. To that end they rented an undercroft*** beneath the Palace of Westminster in order to set it all off on November 5, 1605 the day of the opening of the House of Lords.

They put Fawkes in charge of guarding the gunpowder. He got caught only a few hours before the fireworks were to begin. He was tortured and ultimately broke—divulging the names of all his co-conspirators. All of them were sentenced to be taken from the Tower in hurdles which would allow for them to be dragged through the crowded streets by their feet. Then to be hung. Then taken down from the gallows alive. Then have their genitals cut off and burned in front of them. Then... after a

____

____

____

____

____

few other niceties they would be quartered—at that point they'd die—and their body parts displayed in the four corners of the kingdom.

On the day of the execution, the torture weakened Fawkes headed up the ladder to the gallows. The public was cheering. King James and his family watched from behind a screen. Whether on purpose or by accident, Fawkes fell and broke his neck. Dead, he still was quartered and his body parts distributed for display along with his peeps. Parliament passed a law declaring November 5 a day to honor and give thanks to the Lord for the deliverance of James from this evil plot.

Thus the celebrations. Parades, effigy burnings, bonfires, etc. It used to be that children would create Fawkes effigies but now anybody's a target. Prime Minister Margaret Thatcher got her fair share of Fawkes Day burnings!

And the centerpiece of the holiday are the masks which bear a resemblance to the real Fawkes. Called the V for Vendetta masks, they have come to represent political action—particularly antiestablish protests as has seen in the London and around the world. You've seen the masks. They are based on the David Lloyd illustrations from Allan Moore's V for Vendetta comic series (1982-1986) and the 2005 film. But you couldn't identify anybody wearing them, except for Snowden's girlfriend but that's another story.

*James was both king of Scotland and England—the fourth as Scotland's ruler and the first of England. He was Protestant Queen Elizabeth's distant cousin. His mother, Mary Queen of Scots, was Catholic. There's some family issues there.

**Recusant meant that you were a Catholic but you did your best to hide it, because it was illegal to be a Catholic. Damn papists!

***A fancy term for a brick lined basement with a good sized pillar holding everything up. If you want to start calling your basement an undercroft I won't judge.

On this day November 6, 1973 record producer, road wrangler and tour manager Phil Kaufman was convicted of burning a casket at Joshua Tree National Park. The casket in fact contained the body of his friend Ingram Cecil Connor III, purloined as Ingram's estranged, adoptive, step-father was flying the body back from California to his home in Louisiana.

Ingram, otherwise known as Gram Parsons, was an exceptional songwriter and musician. Just twenty-six, he had already worked on one album with The Byrds, had collaborated with Emmylou Harris and was with the Flying Burrito Brothers. But he was a troubled guy who knew he would die young. He and Kaufman agreed, as tormented youth are wont to do, that whichever one lived the longest was obligated to arrange for the torching of the other's body at Joshua Tree.

The orphaned Parsons died of an overdose in September. His estranged, adoptive, step-father Robert made a fuss over returning his body to Louisiana. Interesting thing about Louisiana law—which runs by the Napoleonic Code—if you die without a will your closest surviving male relative gets everything. In addition to music royalties, Gram's grandfather had a fortune in agriculture which would also pass to Robert the Step-father. While the body was being transported to Los Angeles Airport to be flown to New Orleans, Kaufman and his assistant hired a hearse and signed Parsons' body out of the airport with the claim that the family had reconsidered arrangements. The duo torched the casket at Joshua Tree, just as Parsons had asked.

Their undoing was that the park had a strict rule against bonfires and the body snatchers were arrested. On November 6, 1973 Kaufman and his partner in crime were convicted of destroying a casket. At the time California had no law about stealing a body so the duo paid a three hundred dollar fine each for the destruction of the casket. It would have been Parsons' twenty seventh birthday.

Parsons might have squandered his vast talent and life on drugs. But he sure knew how to pick a good friend who would honor his wishes even after death.

I have asked my stepson, David, to arrange a Viking burial. He even researched the law on torching a boat with a dead body in it. Yet he's still willing to face the Coast Guard!

What's the most important and/or difficult promise
you've made to a friend?

____

____

____

____

____

France, long known for its devotion to the principles of freedom, equality, and brotherhood, passed a curious law on November 7, 1800. Women were no longer allowed to wear pants. Restricting women's clothing is a time honored way of designating women's status. Some countries do it by forcing the chador or hijab and have virtue police to ensure compliance, with strict penalties that might include whippings and whatnot. France seemed pretty lax with the penalties but in 1928, a track and field athlete, Violette Morris, who was best known for javelin and shotput was banned by her country's Olympic committee because of her pants wearing penchant. She was also a lesbian, but that was considered to be part of the reason she would WANT to wear pants. This particular athlete later killed a dude in a fight and she also collaborated with the enemy in World War II.

She was later executed by the French Resistance and never got to wear pants while participating in sports or just shopping the local boulangerie.

The anti-pants edict was rescinded in 2013—long after bell bottoms and Yves Saint Laurent's introduction of the feminine tuxedo ensemble.

Même pas un billet!
Or as the very French would say, go ahead and wear those pants!

____

____

____

____

____

On November 8 I'm reminded that you shouldn't count on winning until the game is over…and that the right pair of shoes is essential.

Nov 8, 1970 and the Detroit Lions were at Tulane Stadium playing the Saints. In the last 2 seconds of the fourth quarter, victory seemed assured to the Motor City. Just one last field goal attempt by the Saints. Tom Dempsey walked out onto the field. He had been born with no toes on his right foot and no fingers on his right hand and yet, somehow he had managed to secure a berth with the Saints.

Dempsey's kick was breathtaking and immediately put to an end the general high fiving and congratulatory hugs on the Lions sidelines. The ball glided across the field and closed a 19-17 Saints victory. It also secured Dempsey a place in football history with his 63 yard field goal setting a new record.

"I hit it sweet," he later recalled.

Immediately there were concerns that he had an unfair advantage. His custom constructed right shoe he wore gave him a wider and perhaps more solid surface area for the kick. When asked, he said—"unfair, eh? How about you try kickin' a 63 yard field goal to win it with 2 seconds left an' yer wearin' a square shoe, oh yeah, and no toes either."

Nonetheless, the League introduced the Tom Dempsey rule in 1977 stating that "any shoe that is worn by a player with an artificial limb on his kicking leg must have a kicking surface that conforms to that of a normal kicking shoe."

Dempsey went on to a 159/258 record before retiring. He had the usual health problems of a retired football player including brain damage from successive concussions. In 2010 he was diagnosed with dementia and was in a New Orleans facility when he developed Covid in 2024, which is listed as his official cause of death.

His record remained intact until 1980 when Denver Broncos' place kicker Matt Prater successfully kicked a 64 yard field goal against the Tennesses Titians.

But what a man, what a kick, what a shoe!

November 09

November 9 is national Chaos Never Dies Day which sort of feels like my entire life. So today is probably a good day to do something random to remind yourself that it's impossible to control everything and everything can be changed by something random and seemingly small.

Take a deep breath and do something small that just isn't your usual style.

If you always order the cheeseburger, take a chance on filet-o-fish. If you usually walk through a shortcut on your way to the grocery store, take a different path. Already this morning, I got on the treadmill as is my wont and aimed for 3.5 mph with an incline of 1.5. I settled in for a 60 minute workout. But as I was adjusting the controls, my hand slipped and I hit ten miles per hour. It didn't end well. But that's chaos for you—I learned that I can in fact run at ten miles an hour until I collide with the wall! Also, don't let chaos rule you. Flexibility is everything!

November 10

November 10 is a wonderful day of handshaking, particularly because it is the anniversary of the 1871 meeting of John Rowlands, aka Henry Morton Stanley* and David Livingstone which spawned the famous phrase....

"Dr. Livingston I presume?"

Dr. David Livingston was a Scottish doctor, missionary and celebrated author of the 1857 book Missionary Travels and Researches in South Africa. His work had captured the imaginations of Americans and Brits alike—but, alas, in 1870 he had gone missing during one of his travels along the Nile.

Meanwhile, Rowland, er, Stanley had been dispatched by the New York Herald to find the doctor. Not out of altruism but more like "The Kardasians have gone awol—find them and get pics!" In March 1871, Stanley took over a hundred porters on a 700 mile trek through the jungle to Ujiji, near Lake Tanganyika. The Herald reported in its July 1, 1872 issue—

"Preserving a calmness of exterior before the Arabs which was hard to simulate as he reached the group, Mr. Stanley said: – "Doctor Livingstone, I presume?"

Continued on Next Page

November 10

A smile lit up the features of the pale white man as he answered: "Yes, and I feel thankful that I am here to welcome you."

The full account would show up in Stanley's 1872 blockbuster "How I Found Livingstone." The meeting probably wasn't quite like that.

Remember that Stanley was born John Rowlands? Well, he was abandoned at birth and when he was 19 he emigrated to New Orleans from Wales. He promptly changed his name to Henry Morton Stanley, claiming that wealthy New Orleans trader Henry Hope Stanley was a relative. This was later found to be a, well, wishful thinking fabrication. But the name opened doors for Rowland, er, Stanley. He embarked on a life of adventure in journalism—ending up at The New York Herald was quite the coup!

Neither Livingston nor Stanley described the meeting as including the oft quoted "Dr. Livingston, I presume" at the time but both exploited the gullibility and eagerness of the public. Stanley even got himself knighted!

So today, don't settle for reality. Go out there and reinvent. Drop into a conversation with a friend a little anecdote about an aunt who is part of "the firm" or add the title Baroness to your driver's license. Have fun with your past and have even more fun with your future—both are yours to create and recreate!

In East Side Baltimore, the Armistice—the peace—came at 5:00 a.m. local time on November 11, 1918. Folks spilled out onto the streets, dancing and singing, hugging each other and popping open bottles of bubbly they had been saving for this day. Parents cried sweet tears of joy and told each other "our boy is coming home!" Wives and sweethearts let out the breath they had been holding for so very long, as they let themselves believe again in their True Love's return. Most folks were immigrants from Germany or perhaps just a generation removed. While their allegiance was to America, everyone had cousins and grandparents and other relatives back in the old country, those who had no doubt fought and died for the Kaiser.

The Gunther family was relieved their son Henry would be coming home. He had been drafted in 1917 and sent to the heart of the war in France. Because of his bank job, he was made a sergeant handling supplies for the 313rd infantry Division of the 79th Division of the American Expeditionary Forces. Cushy job, one might say, given that in late 1917 most of the German bunkers had been overrun and now France was hand to hand street combat. Gunther was horrified by what he saw that he wrote to a friend of his and implored him to do anything to avoid the draft.  The letter was intercepted by censors and Gunther was demoted to the front lines. His fellow soldiers considered him a traitor, the Germans though of him as a target just like any other.

On the tenth of November 1918, everyone knew that the Treaty of Versailles had been executed between the warring countries. But the French loved the palindrome created by 11th hour of the eleventh day of the eleventh month and wanted the ceasefire to begin precisely at that moment six hours from when it had been signed. If I was commanding a battalion, I'd want to hide my men and drink a nice glass of wine and wait it out. But some commanders thought this could be a ruse and, hoping to gain more land, pushed their men harder than ever. There were more casualties in those six hours of waiting than in any other day of the war.

And one of those was Henry Gunther, who had been caught in between lines and misinterpreted the German shouts of "Bitte! Bitte! Halt!" After first thinking they were saying "please, please, halt!" and then realizing his German was faulty. They were giving him a warning. Henry looked back at what should have been a line of American soldiers. But they had dispersed.

Henry was shot dead by the Germans at 10:59 a.m. and is widely acknowledged as the last American combat death of World War I. Every country has a similar story. All lives snuffed out are tragic and we never know if we'll laugh at our luck or leave a family to mourn. Gunther's family was not informed of his death until four months later. Make sure today your last words to your family are "I love you."

November 12, 1926 marks the first aerial bombing attack in the United States and it's also National Happy Hour Day. The two events may be celebrated together for reasons that will become clear.

I know, I know, you're thinking December 7, 1941 Pearl Harbor, Hawaii.

But no. This aerial attack was in 1926 and it was right here in my fair state of Illinois. Williamsburg county to be exact.

Let's go back to the beginning—Schachnai Itzik Birger, having emigrated from Russia as a young child—decided to go full tilt All American by changing his name to Charles and joining up with the Shelton brothers in 1920 to open an establishment called the Shady Rest. It provided customers with light refreshments—moonshine if you must know. The grounds included a guard post in case the feds showed up. Prohibition meant the government was most prejudiced against liquor sales. So, it seems, was the KKK. Charles Birger and the Shelton brothers (Carl, Earl and Bernie) found themselves fighting the KKK and the county government. Williamsburg got to be looking like a war zone, particularly when Birger and the Sheltons figured out how to build an aerial fighting force.

Unfortunately, these alliances sometimes don't work. In January 1925 Ora Thomas, a deputy for the county, shot a KKK leader who shot him right back. Then four other KKK members got involved and pretty soon the KKK got 15,000 rsvp's for a funeral for four members. Mighty tense in Williamburg, but it would get even worse when the Shelton brothers and Birger parted ways under mysterious circumstances.

No going away party, there was internecine war. On November 12, 1926 an aerial bombing of Birger's gem the Shady Rest. Luckily, the dynamite didn't go off but there were some fractured family relations!

Ultimately, Charles Birger was hung for the murder of Mayor Joe Adams in June 1927. Adams, a KKK sympathizer if not a member, was popular in town. Birger opted for a black hood instead of a white as he faced the gallows. His last words were "it's a beautiful world." I hope I look half as dapper or just as brave when I'm facing the gallows!

And don't forget! It's also Happy Hour Day so raise a toast to Mr. Bilger.

November 13, 1922, the Supreme Court declared in the case of Zucht v. King that public and private schools could require vaccinations EVEN if there was no public health crisis at the time. In San Antonio the Zucht family filed suit against the city for requiring smallpox vaccinations even though there wasn't a smidgen of smallpox go-ing around. High schooler Rosalyn Zucht was denied admission to both public and private schools and her parents were hopping mad.

Oddly, smallpox has come roaring back, along with polio—both diseases that were sup-posedly eradicated. Bubonic plague has even made a reappearance, mostly in the southwest along the border.

When I was working with Rotary Interna-tional which pledged itself to the job of elimi-nating polio, it was discovered that some Mus-lim fathers thought vaccination was just a ploy to sterilize their sons. Women Rotarians were encouraged to go on Vaccination Day missions where they would hopefully reassure Muslim moms and pops that if they as moms were willing to vaccinate their own kids it must be safe. I declined to pay my way for a trip to Pakistan or Iran to do so. I admit it I'm a scaredy cat.

I would have liked to avoid the Covid vaccine and booster because all three times I got violently ill, maybe even worse than the three times I actually did get the disease.

In any event, Rosalyn Zucht was told by Justice Brandeis and eight other Su-premes that it really didn't matter if San Antonio was having a smallpox crisis. And quarantining for those who declined to be vaccinated was not off the table.

November 14, 1920 marks the beginning of a strange variation of American baseball known as Pesapallo, or Finnish baseball. It was the brainchild of Finnish track and field athlete Lauri Pihkala who visited America in 1907 and must have gotten confused about some of the rules of American baseball. Or maybe she just thought the game was boring, which if you've ever been sat through a double header, yep!

In Pesapallo players run in zigzag base patterns, triples count as home runs and instead of sitting in the dugout chewing on tabacc-i, the opposing team stands in a semi-circle around the pitcher and heckles him. Coaches run the game with an intricate waving of fans being the means to communicate with players. Lordy!

Pesapallo was made an exhibition game in 1952 Olympics and while popular in Finland and some other Nordic countries, it really hasn't captured the imagination of the folks across the pond who play the desultory beer, nachos, hotdogs, and popcorn game we call baseball.

November 15

In the dimmest mists of history, sometimes things are a little confusing. And November 15, 1959 counts as a confusing day in history. For the second time in three years the Beatles—who had been known as The Quarrymen and then had in October changed their name to Johnny and The Moondogs—lost in the preliminary round Carroll Levis' TV Star Search (sort of like American Idol but veddy veddy lower key as Brits generally are).

The first time the boys competed was in October in Liverpool. They lost to a dwarf playing a tea chest bass and a woman playing the spoons. They carried on to compete with the same program in Manchester on this day in 1959. That darn spoon lady competed again and won. The disconsolate Beatles (Johnny and the Moondogs) had to make the last bus back to Liverpool that night and couldn't even stay for the curtain call. The historical mystery? Where is the dwarf with his tea chest bass and the woman playing the spoons now? Because we know what happened to the Quarrymen AKA The Beatles.

November 16

November 16th should be called Kinky Banker Day. On this day in 1979 that Pittsburgh area bank manager David Rhodes was sentenced to three years in the big house for spanking male customers who were late on bank payments.

"I didn't want to hurt the bank, yet I couldn't stop what had started," he said at the time. "I wanted to keep the bank's customers, to help the bank flourish, but it turned into a nightmare."

Uh, really dude? The 38 year-old father of two told U.S. District Court Judge Paul Simmons the spanking started as a joke—but spiraled out of control. He estimated that he spanked 50-odd people who were delinquent on loan payments. "I never had any trouble with them afterwards," he said.

Six of his customers had collaborated with each other to blackmail him to the tune of nearly $90,000. Ultimately, it wasn't the spanking that was his undoing. It was his embezzlement of funds to pay off the spank-ees. He served his time and the FBI concluded that he never personally profited from the spankings.

I wonder who organized the blackmail operation?

November 17

November 17, 1968 with just 61 seconds to go in the game between the Oakland Raiders and the New York Jets, NBC cut away for the beloved children's movie Heidi. The matchup was henchforth known as the Heidi Game.

As millions of viewers were happy to watch the frolics of an Alpine girl, others were like "what the… ?"

No worries. The untelevised Raiders scored two touchdowns in that final minute and won 43 to 32, in a stunnig reversal.

This is when streaming services come in handy.

I think all that matters in football is the last minute or tow of the fourth quarter. And I liked Heidi.

November 18

On November 18, 1993 Kurt Cobain of the grunge band Nirvana made a bold fashion statement by wearing an olive green "grandfather cardigan" at a taping of MTV's Unplugged.

Seattle pretty much had a fashion aesthetic of thrift shop finds layered together to protect from the soggy city climate. On the other hand, Seattle had the best music scene (Jimi Hendrix called it home and the bands Pearl Jam and Soundgarden originated in the city's music scene.)

Kurt committed suicide four months after the Unplugged appearnce. In 2015 the cardigan—shaggy acrylic and mohair and lycra with a decorative cigarette burn—sold for $137,500 at auction.

Moral of the story? Maybe don't go all Kon Mari and throw out all the not so joyful stuff. You don't know what that's going to sell for!

This is about the time of year I sell stuff to get money for Christmas gifting. How do you come up with your Christmas budget?

____

____

____

____

November 19,1925 was the premiere of a controversial movie about World War I. It didn't shy away from the brutalities of battle. It was ultimately a love story (isn't everything?) between an American soldier and a French farm girl. It was considered scandalous because it wasn't a typical propaganda piece and it paved the way for All Quiet on the Western Front. The Big Parade was a silent film but it contained a whopping 3 curse words—goddamn, helluva, and bitches in its title cards. Censors and critics were appalled but the slightly longer than two hour movie was a success.

Fast forward to 2013 and The Wolf of Wall Street which set a record for the most curse word ridden movie from Hollywood with 569 f-words alone. That's 3.16 per minute. It starred Leonardo DiCaprio whose girlfriends have a mandatory retirement age of 25.

I swear sometimes. Okay, a lot. But I don't think I could sit through Wolf of Wall Street without being just a titch distracted by the words.

Do you find swearing distracting or offensive? Or if you had a "swear jar" it would be full enough to finance your retirement?

On November 20, 1973, the career of drummer Scott Halpin of Muscatine, Iowa began and ended at the Cow Palace in San Francisco. So maybe today celebrate something YOU HAVE DONE with courage, determination and maybe not a lot of preparation.

It was the first stop in The Who's Quadrophenia North American tour. The first two songs went pretty okay but drummer Keith Moon had mixed ketamine (an anesthetic that is sometimes known as "horse tranquilizer") with brandy. Ew! That doesn't sound appetizing! He collapsed on top of his snare drum during Won't Get Fooled Again. He was carried offstage and revived with a backstage cold shower. He was brought back up onstage with Pete Townshend and Roger Daltry joking with the audience that Moon was just trying to get out of work. For the next song he started tapping wood blocks to begin his solo and collapsed again.

Townshend asked if anybody in the audience knew how to play the drums "good" and a friend held up Halpin's hand and said "he can!!!!!"

Halpin came up onstage, was ironically given a shot of brandy for courage and did a pretty damn good job on Smokestack Lightning. He hadn't played drums in a couple of years. There was no rehearsal. No clues as to which song was next. But he was enthusiastic. He finished the concert, joined the rest of the band for a curtain call, and was escorted to the VIP party (hope he remembered to take his friend!). He was given a commemorative jacket which was stolen later that night.

But, ah, the memories! And he received Rolling Stones "Best Pickup Player of the Year" award. He went on to a largely forgotten career in the San Francisco music and arts scene. In 1995 he moved to Bloomington Indiana where, in 2008, he died of a brain tumor. The Who's website posted a tribute to their once in a lifetime member.

And Keith Moon? He claimed his favorite drink was French Blues, which was a combination of sodium amobarbital and dextroamphetamine sulfite. The combo is no longer legally available but it kept him skinny and energetic. Then of course he would soften the hyper effect of French Blues with alcohol. As he used more alcohol to combat the French Blues, his weight ballooned and by 1978 he was self-conscious and somewhat reclusive. He rented flat 12, 9 Curzon Place from musician Harry Nilsson as a retreat. Nilsson was a bit superstitious because four years earlier Mama Cass Elliot of the Mama and the Papas had died there. (It was a heart attack, NOT a ham sandwich!) Moon said he was working on his recovery with the drug clomethiazole which suppressed alcohol craving—Ozempic users beware as that is now one of the many uses for the drug! Combined with alcohol, clomethiazole (no longer legal) was hazardous. Moon had consumed whiskey and thirty pills (the first four of which were quite enough to kill him the other twenty six just for good measure) at the time of death on September 7, 1978.

People remember Keith Moon. Few remember Scott Halpin. But I think it's Scott who had the better, more fulfilling life. Today is a good day to lay out a plan for your life. Where do you want it to go and how do you want to get there?

November 21

November 21 is an auspicious if somewhat hastily celebrated holiday of which cheechakos like me are generally unaware. And I always miss the parade. We're talking about Alascatallo Day and if you're not on Alaska Standard Time, you might still have a chance to celebrate properly!

Residents of Alaska are alternately amused, bewildered, and annoyed by cheechakos—people from anywhere else. First, cheechakos don't understand that when an Alaskan says you're going outside you're not just going to Starbucks. You're going outside the state. And cheechakos aka outsiders ask the stupidest questions like where do you find Alaskan penguins? An Alaskan will answer "go outside and look." Pretty witty if you think about it. BTW, you can find penguins in the Antarctic.

Sometime in the middle of the last century, miners (a lot of Alaskans are in the trade) started getting even more creative—goading outsiders with tales of the alascattalos. Part walrus, part moose. Some outsiders searched for the mysterious animal.

I've been to Alaska a few times, mostly spent in Homer and in Nome. I was never persuaded to go looking for an Alascattalo. Steven C. Levi, a business writer and amateur Alaskan historian wrote Alascatoola Tales (he spells it different but English is a living language.) You can order it on Amazon. And he settled on the November 21 as Alascatoola Day. In Anchorage, in the block long alley behind what was once called Club Paris owned in part by Levi himself, there is a parade. It starts PROMPTLY at noon and lasts about three or four minutes. A prize is awarded for the smallest and ugliest float (has to be both). Alaskans boast it is the longest running shortest parade in America.

So today be on the lookout. You never know what you might see if you're in Anchorage today——a penguin, an alascattalo or a native laughing at you! Just remember I warned you.

A little before noon on November 22, 1963 U.S. President John F. Kennedy took a thirteen minute morning flight on Air Force One to Dallas, Texas after finishing a speech in front of the Fort Worth Chamber of Commerce. The President and First Lady greeted well wishers and the First Lady was inundated with bouquets of Roses.

The couple joined Texas Governor John Connally and his wife Nellie in an oversized convertible. Vice President Lyndon Johnson and his wife affectionately known as "Lady Bird" were assigned a limousine behind the President's. Johnson and Kennedy loathed each other.

Just like today, the political geography has lots of feuding and vitriol. Many had thought that Texas democrats were splintered. But the crowd was so fine and inviting and enthusiastic that Nellie leaned forward to say to the President "now they can't make you believe there aren't some in Dallas who love and appreciate you, can they?"

The President replied, "No, they sure can't!"

Seconds later, John F. Kennedy was shot and as he slumped towards his wife Jackie, he looked puzzled.

"I love you, John," she said.

Just thirty minutes later, Kennedy was declared dead. Connally, who was also shot, survived. By two o'clock, the Johnsons and Mrs. Kennedy met the dead President's coffin. Within many royal families and heads of state, mourning clothing is automatically packed for unforeseen disasters. Mrs. Kennedy was offered a black dress. She declined, and wore her blood stained pink boucle suit and matching pillbox hat at the inauguration of LBJ on the plane as it flew back to Washington.

"I want them to see what they've done," she cryptically declared.

November 23

On November 23, 1991 the British band Queen's front man Freddie Mercury issued a statement to the press.

"Following the enormous conjecture in the Press over the last two weeks I wish to confirm that I have been tested HIV positive and have AIDS. However, the time has now come for my friends and fans around the world to know the truth and I hope everyone will join with me, my doctors and all those worldwide in the fight against this terrible disease. My privacy has always been very special to me and I am famous for my lack of interviews. Please understand this policy will continue."

Born in Zanzibar in 1946, Farrokh Bulsara was the supremely talented musician and an astonishing four octave vocal range, he moved with his family to England. There he formed Queen with guitarist Brian May and drummer Roger Taylor. Oh, the hits they made, all dependent on Freddie Mercury! Bohemian Rhapsody, We Are the Champions, Killer Queen …

AIDS was a death sentence. Now I think it's more of a chronic disease that can be managed by your doctor.

The day after his announcement, Mercury died. He left the bulk of his estate to the woman he claimed was his only friend (and former fiancee) Mary Austin.

____

____

____

____

____

On Wednesday, November 24, 1972 getting home for Thanksgiving was the last thing on Dan B. (D.B.) Cooper's mind. At three p.m. he walked into the crowded Portland, Oregon airport and bought from Northwest Orient Airlines a $20 one way ticket to Seattle, Washington.

He was slim, in his midforties, wore a nondescript suit, business shoes and a clip on tie. Over that he wore a trench coat. He carried a briefcase and a knapsack.

The flight was expected to hit heavy turbulence from the rain. He slipped a note to a flight attendant who put it into her pocket. Perhaps she was thinking it was a lovestruck come on, but she was shocked when she read it. She walked back to his seat and D.B. opened the briefcase, containing what appeared to be sticks of dynamite with wires attaching them to a detonator. She quietly entered the cockpit and gave the note to the pilot.

D.B. wanted $200,000 in twenty dollar bills to be placed in his knapsack. He wanted four parachutes. And he wanted the plane to fly to Mexico City. At Seattle's airport, he allowed 36 passengers to disembark but he kept the crewon board. Parachutes were delivered. Money too. The pilot aimed south for Mexico. The plane faced two hundred mile per hours wind, fog and heavy rain. Nonetheless, D.B. took two of the parachutes to the back of the plane and jumped. While one parachute was fully functional, the other—a military training parachute—had been sewn up. D.B. left behind his tie which would later prove useful to investigators.

Where D.B. went and what happened to the money was the cause of a long and cruel investigation. A break came in 1974 when a young boy found part of the knapsack alongside the Tena Bar off the Columbia River which runs through Oregon and Washington. Inside was some of the rotting money blackened with mud. Close to a thousand people in the area were investigated for air piracy but it only carried a 5 year statute of limitations. The FBI hung its hopes on the Hobbs Act for Extortion which has no

such statute of limitations. The clip on tie D.B. left behind was analyzed and amounts of "rare earth" elements were found on it—cerium, strontium, sulfide, and titanium. These chemicals were used in Boeing's research in developing airplanes so attention became more focused on men in the aeronautics industry.

Did D.B. survive his fall and bury the money in distinct locations? Did his dress shoes cripple his fall? Did he die immediately, having inadvertently used the training parachute? The mystery has never been solved. And if D.B. were 45 at the time of the heist, he might very well have since died of natural causes.

November 25, 1963 marked three funerals of men who we believe to be strangers to each other, but each was an integral part of American history.

President John F. Kennedy laid in state at the Capitol Rotunda for twenty four hours beginning Sunday the 24th. The line of 300k mourners anxious to pay their last respects stretched nine miles long and many had to be turned away as the funeral preparations proceeded. One hundred nations sent representatives, some of them heads of state . At ten thirty morning on Monday the casket was removed and taken to St. Matthew's Cathedral. After the service, the casket was transported to Arlington Cemetery. Few cannot feel an ache when they see the photograph of John F. Kennedy Jr. saluting his father as his casket was transported from the church. It was JFK Jr.'s third birthday.

At two o'clock that same day, thirty nine year old Dallas Police officer JD Tippit was given a goodbye at the Berkley Hills Baptist Church in Texas . Seven hundred Texas police and over 1,500 civilians crowded the church and the grounds around it. After the service, a fifteen man motorcycle escort led Laurel Land Memorial Park. Tippit had gone home for lunch on November 22, got the call on his radio about the Kennedy shooting. He was shot by Oswald as he questioned him on the corner of Tenth and Patton Streets. Some conspiracy theorists believe he was sent by CIA/MOB/LBJ to scratch out Oswald and he instead he took a bullet. Jacqueline Kennedy sent Tippit's widow a picture of JFK with wistful note. "There is another bond we share—we must remind our children all the time what brave men their fathers were."

In Fort Worth police guarded the Rose Hill Cemetery as Oswald's widow Marina, her two small children, Oswald's mother and his brother could attend a graveside service. There were five aluminum chairs and the casket was transported by news reporters as no one else wanted to be part of this. The newspaper reporters were ordered to back away as Oswald's brother had asked for the casket to be opened so that the family could pay their respects. The service was then conducted by Rev. Louis Saunders who filled in at the last minute when the assigned clergyman was a no show. Some witnesses recall there was a small bouquet of white carnations sent by a Virginia Leach. Nobody has ever been able to identify her. After the police left, onlookers clamored to dig up a piece of soil from Oswald's grave.

Three very different men in terms of their place in American history. Each finishing their journey on November 25, 1963 with very different styles of respect.

How will you be remembered? How will your loved ones say goodbye?

November 26

On November 26, 1922 archaeologist Howard Carter, his sponsor George Herbert 5th Earl of Carnavon and Carnavon's daughter Lady Evelyn Herbert dug a small hole into the door of a once forgotten burial site in the Valley of the Kings. The Valley of the Kings was the traditional burial place for Pharaohs and other royalty before and after the Amarna period in which King Akhenaten imposed the monotheistic worship of Aten the sun God. Akhenaten declared himself the physical embodiment of that Aten. But the people rose up against the loss of their traditional religion.

Carter was convinced that there was more to be found in the Valley of the Kings. With Lord Carnavon's money, he employed a host of excavators, both Egyptian and British, and had spent the better part of November, 1922 digging through debris tossed aside during the building of the giant pyramids of Ramesses V and Ramesses VII. Until they found it—a small door leading…where?

On the twenty sixth he and his sponsor and Lady Evelyn stood at the opening of the tomb. As Carter held up a torch, Carnavon asked him what he saw. "Wonderful things," Carter is said to have replied.

There were five main chambers. One was the burial chamber which would be found to contain the very young King Tutankhamun of the post-Amarna age. Later, two mummified bodies of infant girls presumed to be his daughters would be found. There were four other chambers containing jewelry, furniture, weapons, musical instruments. You know, the usual things one needs in the afterlife. Many years later, Nefrititi's grave would be found behind a false wall. She was King Tut's stepmother and mother-in-law. Yep, read that sentence twice.

For a pharaoh who had died quite young and not really accomplished much, King Tut sure got a lot of attention. Europeans flocked to the tomb and would end their days with parties at the nearby Winter Palace Hotel where they danced the Tutankhamun Rag. Even though Tut had died 3,300 years before, he was a star of silent movies and popular songs, most notably Vince Giordano's rendition of "Old King Tut" and much later, "King Tut" by Steve Martin. Tutmania swept the world and solidified Carter's place in history.

Too bad there was also within one of the chambers a stone tablet upon which was written (in hieroglyphics) "Death will slay with his wings whoever disturbs the pharaoh's peace." But one would think every pharaoh's resting place would have something like that!

November 27

On November 27, 1924 Macy's in New York held a parade they called the Christmas Parade. Of course, we know it now as the Thanksgiving Day Parade held on Thanksgiving from 9:00 a.m. to 12 noon. The first parade consisted mostly of costumed store employees who had organized the event to highlight that it was time to SHOP. There were also professional bands, and animals borrowed from the Central Park Zoo. The parade's grand finale was Santa's pulling up to Macy's Herald Square store and he was crowned "King of the Kiddies" on the balcony. The whole thing was meant to be something to do while mom was making a turkey but when Macy's realized 250,000 people had showed up on the parade route to observe the hoopla, they knew they had struck gold.

The parade began using giant balloons, starting with Felix the Cat in 1927. Mickey Mouse made his first appearance in 1934, the same year that the parade was featured on radio. Snoopy debuted as the Flying Ace in 1968 and there have been a total of 40 Snoopy balloons.

The parade was suspended for the years 1942, 1943 and 1944 because the rubber and helium were so expensive.

But in 1945, the Macy's Parade, er, paraded down Central Park West to 59th Street, turning east to 6th Avenue to W. 34th Street to Herald Square. Santa of course pulled up the rear and the Christmas shopping season began! By 1953 NBC was broadcasting the festivities and today an estimated 44 million watch some or all of the parade. A new Thanksgiving tradition even before you get to the turkey!

There have been a few speed bumps. My favorite is how in 1997 Barney, the giant tyrannosaurus rex blathering "I love you, you love me", got caught up in some sharp winds and a NYPD police officer stabbed him to death. Given how often I had to listen to Barney sing "I love you, you love me, we're a happy family…." I think of it as one of the finest moments in NYPD history.

Whether you go to the parade route, rent a hotel room overlooking the route, or if you sit on the couch and watch the parade while luxuriating in the smells of turkey and pumpkin pie, enjoy!

On November 28, 1582 eighteen year old William Shakespeare signed his marriage license. We only have six confirmed signatures of the Bard, and one of them is the license,

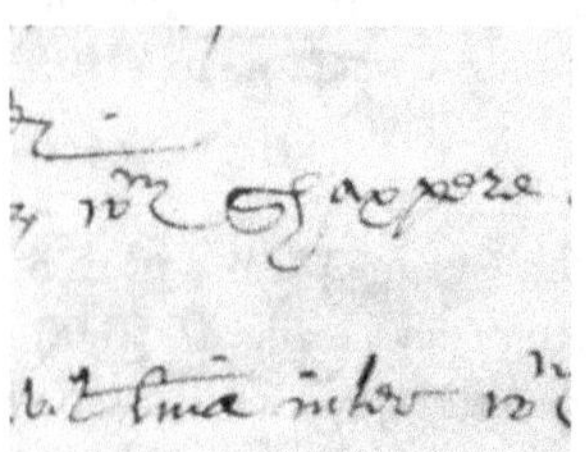

which he signed William Shagspeare, perhaps referencing the upcoming consummation of his bond. He had a habit of writing his name a few different ways and to be fair, spelling in the English language was not particularly standardized until well into the nineteenth century.

Me? I was born Arlynn Merrill Leiber. Three years later, my parents put me up for adoption and I was picked up by the Patrick family. The thinking at the time was that I wasn't old enough to formulate memory and all of the past three years of my life could be erased, the Patricks taught me my name was "Our Lynn" and eventually dropped the Our. They also switched out Merrill for Melody. My name was thus Lynn Melody Patrick.

My biological father justified the adoption as being an aspect of the divorce from my mother but also justified it because I was too young to have achieved "consciousness. He agreed with the adoption agency that my name, my family, every aspect of my prior life could be erased.

But I ALWAYS felt uncomfortable with my new name. I didn't remember my prior name but I knew this was different. And I was no Shakespeare playing with words, others were playing with them.

When I got married I changed my name to ArLynn Leiber Presser. ArLynn with an L capitalized in the middle to acknowledge the years I had been Lynn. Leiber for my biological parents' name (I had so many foster parents after the Patricks that if you strung together their patrynomics it would be several paragraphs). Lastly Presser for my husband and so that I would share the same last name as my children.

Well, you go tell that to the Social Security Administration when you're trying to change your name.

I have had my name spelled by others so many different ways. I've had it pronounced so many different ways. I draw the line at Ar-Leeeeeeene for reasons I can't explain. I once was rock climbing and the woman holding my safety line screamed encouragement—"You can do it Arleeeeeeeene!" I nearly took out my pocket knife and cut myself free from her. I had someone ask me if I minded if he pronounced my name the French way—Ar-Lynn with the emphasis on the second syllable. I told him I had never known he spoke French. He said he didn't. He just imagined it's how the French would pronounce my name. That one I was fine with. I have no idea why I have that distinction.

____

____

____

____

____

As for Leiber, most people pronounce it "leeeeee-ber" and it's actually "lie-ber."

Shakespeare used approximately 20k words in his works, 1,700 of which he made up, mostly by adding suffixes and prefixes to existing words.

My kindness to myself today is just let go and roll with it. I am blessed with a great name that is a mix of biology, memory, events. I've never had a nickname although I think it's the greatest honor a friend or family member can give you. What's yours?

Thanks William Shakespeare! Er, Shagspeare!

November 29

If you're of the right age, you probably get mail from AARP and say "I'm not THAT old!" But you also probably remember the joy of November 29, 1972 which means you ARE that old but in a good way. For it was on this day that Atari unveiled Pong. The game, for you young'uns, mimics ping pong. Back and forth, back and forth, until your eyeballs shrivel. But WOW! What a great leap forward for humankind.

Atari showed off the game at Andy Capp's Tavern in Sunnydale, California on this day as a test of whether it would be appealing and most importantly, profitable. Taverns, restaurants, and independent arcades were where people generally played pinball, pool, miniature golf and similar games. Oh, yes, EVERYBODY loved it!

Was Pong the first video game insofar as everything was onscreen? No, that would have happened in 1958 when engineer William Higinbottom's Tennis for Two was introduced as a novelty at the Brookhaven National Lab visitor's day in Long Island, New York. It was very popular with kids. For being such a genius at engineering, Higinbottom was a dope. Though he had over 20 patents he thought Tennis for Two was just a novelty and so the game was disassembled for parts the next year. Sanders Associates got the patent for it and they never so much as say thanks to Higinbottom.

Tennis for Two bears a striking resemblance to Pong, something I'm reminded of when I'm in hour three of a tennis tournament on a hot summer day. In 1975, Atari saw that video game arcades weren't the only places people wanted to play the highly successful Pong. That year, they released the first Home Pong in the Sears Catalogue (another thing you young'uns won't remember.)

So today, feel free to take the day off and waste time on Candy Crush or Call of Duty. Sometimes it can rejuvenate you for a productive tomorrow.

____

____

____

____

In 1968, Waterloo, Iowa housewife Marva Drew was forced to console her son who came home from school with the news that a heartless, ruthless, brutal teacher had told him that it was impossible to count to a million.

Mind you, this is before all the technology we have today. Google could count to a million in the time it would take you to articulate your Starbucks order. We didn't even have calculators in school back then. And there wasn't Starbucks.

Marva didn't like the notion of impossible and wasn't going to let her son learn that teacher's lesson. So she put a sheet of paper into her royal upright typewriter and commenced. 1, 2, 3,….

It took her six long years. She polished off 12 typewriter ribbons, five reams of paper and nearly destroyed her health what with the carriage returns and the insomnia caused by numbers crawling across her eyelids when she tried to sleep. On this day in history, November 30, 1974 Marva typed that last, magic, million number.

Nothing is impossible. I'M POSSIBLE. That's how it's spelled, that's what it means! The apostrophe is Marva Drew's present to you.

That's what your motto is for the day!

December 01

On December 1, 1916 as many fine men were enlisting and being shipped overseas to fight World War 1, Canada's 228 battalion's hockey team played its first game as an official member of the National Hockey Association. They were coached by Howard McNamara who, like his brother, was a professional hockey player. The team wore their khaki uniform sweaters and led the league in scoring. Alas, they had to hang up their skates and were shipped out in February and were not able to compete in the postseason. They're still champions in my book!

December 02

You really have to think how you're going to do it—suicide, that is. You mess it up and you either survive and have to explain yourself or you end up dying and having seriously messed up relatives who loved you and would have helped out if they had had any idea.

On December 2nd 1979 29 year old black single mom Elvita Adams had had quite enough. She thought the Empire State Building would do the trick. After all, others had been quite successful at it—so often that there were 24 hour a day guards to ensure that it didn't happen again.

But Elvita was determined. She went to the 86th story observatory and climbed over a 7 foot tall spiked fence specifically meant to thwart suicides. She jumped. A lot of people who jump to their deaths will have a heart attack long before they go splat! When I was in school I lived at a YMCA where lots of folk looked like a watermelon had been dropped on the sidewalk.

In Elvita's case, her body went down at about 20 feet before a strong wind gust shoved her onto a ledge on the building. One of those pesky guards retrieved her—just doing his job, ma'am. Elvita had a broken pelvis and claimed she might have just accidentally fell off the observatory deck. The 7 foot tall spiked fence she discounted.

When my marriage came apart at the seams, I fantasized about ways to off myself with it looking like an accident. One Christmas Day I sat on the pier at the forest preserve knowing all I had to do was just slip into the icy water. But I couldn't do it because of my children and how they would react if they doubted it was an accident.

Reach out if you're feeling blue. Make a list of five friends you can call in confidence. Or get on the suicide hotline. Life is a gift you've been given and you might not know what purpose you have right now, but there's somewhere a reason to live.

Worse comes to worse, call me.

December 03

December 3, 1967 is an auspicious day of heroism in the medical field. After all, on this day Dr. Christiaan Barnard, a celebrated cardiologist at the Groote Schuur Hospital near Cape Town, South Africa, performed the first successful human heart transplant.

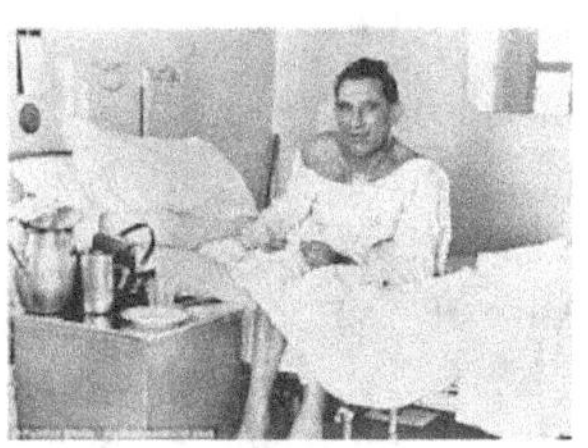

There had been a previous effort in 1964 with patient Boyd Rush who was given the heart of a chimpanzee. Rush lived for only one hour post-op and the chimp's family demanded justice.

In 1967 grocer Louis Joshua Washansky was willing to take his chances. Dr. Barnard described to his patient that the surgery was having a 80% success rate. Washansky was admitted to Groote Schuur Hospital to await a donor. The first was rejected because he was black, this being Apartheid. But then on December 2 fortunes changed.

Twenty five year old Denise Darvall was out with her mother for shopping and

a spot of tea when they were both hit by a drunk driver. Mother was dead on the spot, Denise was not quite. Denise's father Edward, who had witnessed the accident, was in shock. He sent his fourteen year old son home from the hospital and paced, as we all would, while he waited word on his daughter. Doctors appeared and gave him a hefty dose of sedatives—I would have opted for a line of vodka shots. The doctors told him that Denise had minimal brain function but should be considered brain dead.* As he processed grief over the death of his wife, nursing a cocktail of phenobarbital and the enormity of his daughter's condition—the doctors gently, oh so gently, mentioned that there was a desperately ill man in the hospital who needed a heart. Denise would be doing in her passing a great deed, a gift to humanity.

It took four minutes to persuade Edward and in that time he would later recall he simply thought about her birthday cake. The one that would never be sampled. He said if she's dead let her help someone who might live.

Minor problem: Denise wasn't dead. Sure, her brain was fluttering and floundering and without massive intervention wasn't going to improve. But her heart was beating like a twenty one year old looking forward to a birthday tea with her mum

---

*The generally accepted Harvard protocol on brain death had not yet been accepted. And for some people, it still hasn't.

Continued on Next Page

____

____

____

____

December 03

and friends. Beating like a 21 year old with a crush on that impossibly handsome rugby player. Beating like a gal who wanted a career, a wedding, kids.

As soon as Edward signed the papers, Barnard injected her heart with a lethal dose of potassium.

Her heart was installed in the body of Washansky and stabilized to beat. Washansky regained consciousness, talked with his wife lucidly, was interviewed by reporters, had a number of photo ops with his heroic surgeon. His wife asked him at one point how he felt and he said "I'm on top of the world." After all, the never before tried surgery had an 80% success rate, right? Except for that unfortunate episode that the chimpanzee community will never forget.

Unfortunately Washansky developed pneumonia and was given anti-rejection drugs (a protocol that has since been rejected in these circumstances). He died eighteen days after the surgery.

Barnard declared victory. He had paved the way for other transplants. He wrote two autobiographies—"One Life" and "The Second Life" and went on that talk show tour one does. He also created the luxe skin care creme "La Prairie" which if it shows up in my Xmas stocking I will ooze gratitude.

Edward Darvall testified at the trial of the drunk driver who had killed both his wife and daughter. He begged mercy, telling the judge his daughter's death "is not

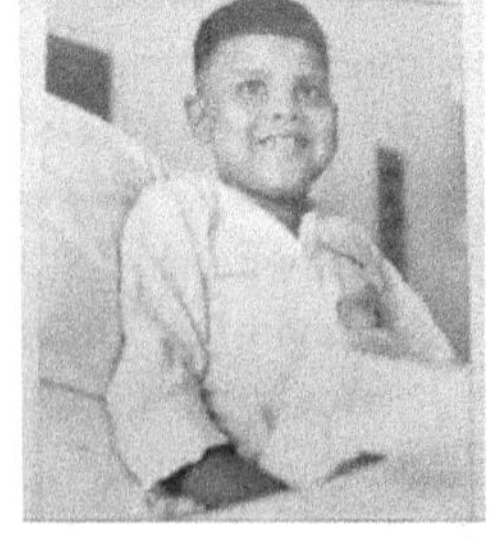

meaningless but benefited humanity." I think Darvall is the hero of this story.

But there is another hero in this story. As Denise Darvall's body was being scavenged and then ultimately tossed aside. Her kidneys were given to a 10-year old Khoekhoe boy Jonathan Van Wyk. Some controversy because the Khoekhoe were indigenous nomads and didn't speak the King's English or wear the King's skin color. Van Wyk appears to have made a full recovery.

A drama including Barnard, Edward Darvall, Denise Darvall, Van Wyk. pick your hero. Don't forget the chimpanzee and Washansky.

In October, 2021, Anthony Thomas Hoover II was declared dead and he was prepared for harvesting. During his walk of respect, he started to thrash about and tears streamed down his face. He wasn't dead and he wasn't an idiot. Two doctors refused to perform the harvesting. Ultimately, he was sent home to live with his sister.

It's December 4th so Happy Thanksgiving! Some of you are still having a turkey hangover from November's Thanksgiving—jeez, I had three different ones I went to this year! You likely think the first Thanksgiving took place in Massachusetts with Pilgrims and Native Americans sharing Stouffer's turkey TV dinners and pumpkin pie in front of the tellie.

But you're wrong! The first Thanksgiving in the North Americas took place on December 4, 1619 in Virginia, beating those self righteous, publicity hungry, Pilgrims by two years. The 38 Virginians didn't wait two years after their landing to make thanks—they did it the very day their boat the Margaret landed on the James River. I think just getting up in the morning is worth a "gratias ago tibi, dominae, quia eugilanas me"* But to get everybody safely to Virginia was definitely worth a feast. Just like Shackleton, they hadn't lost a man.

It seems like a feel good story but on March 22, 1622 Opechancanough, the leader of the Powhatan confederacy, led a slaughter of the newly minted colonists of the Virginia area. Warriors showed up unarmed, bearing game and other foods. Once everyone was in a conciliatory mood, the Powhatans grabbed Europeans' weapons and slaughtered them. Nine of the original colony brought over on the Margaret were among those killed.

The surviving Virginians who had that first Thanksgiving got right back on the Margaret and headed home, saying "quite enough of that, thank you very much." So give thanks, with or without turkey, every day because every day is a gift. No matter how it all turns out.

*Latin for thank you God for waking me up!" I try to say that every morning.

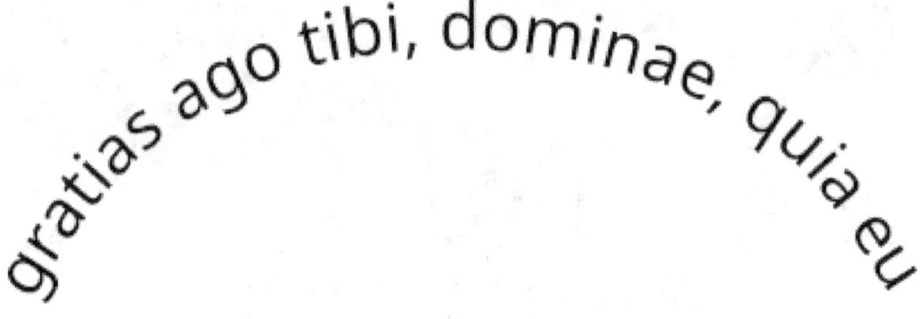

Do you give thanks for getting to your destination or reserve your thanks 'til after you've had a successful time of it?

____

____

____

____

____

December 5 is Krampusnacht when Alpine men drink a bunch of alcohol, run through the streets and frighten children. Not much different from a Family Guy night in Quahog, Rhode Island. Except on Krampusnacht, the men generally wear a mask, horns, leather or fur tunics, and cowbells around their waists. Not any weirder than anything I've seen Harry Styles wearing lately.

Santa is the guy we think of this time of year, the jolly fellow squeezing himself down the chimney, eating cookies and drinking milk, and leaving presents for the good boys and girls.

Ah, there's the rub. What do you do about "bad" kids? Well, about a thousand years ago or so, Europeans told their children Krampus was a demon who worked in concert with Santa, punishing those bad kids. Just so you know, there's still time to evade Krampus and get some love from the jolly old Santa.

However, as Vince Vaughan in the 2007 movie Fred Claus opined "there are no naughty kids."

So don't be like Krampus. Be forgiving. In particular of yourself.

And tonight might be a nice night to stay at home. Don't want to run into anybody with horns....

December 06

Happy Saint Nicholas Day! December 6 in the early fourth century is when this bishop of Myrna, Turkey had his Homegoing and in art he is depicted with three boys in a tub and three golden balls.

The story about the tub: a wicked butcher killed three boys and stuffed them in a tub with brine in order to pickle their bodies. Nicholas pulled the bodies out and brought the boys back to life. That's miracle number one.

The story about the balls—which, by the way, is the symbol of pawnbrokers everywhere. There was a poor man in Myrna who had three daughters and no money for a dowry for any of them. Bishop Nicholas snuck over to their house one night and threw a bag of gold coins (some people say it was just a baseball sized gold orb) over the family's fence. The eldest daughter was immediately inundated with suitors and married quickly. Then another bag of coins was thrown over the fence. That took care of the second daughter. And you guessed it, third daughter got married courtesy of the good Nicholas. The father said "now there's a second miracle."

Of course Nicholas performed the usual healings and whatnot that is the bread and butter of saints. He was particularly fond of bringing toys to children which is perhaps why he's morphed into Santa Claus.

He is depicted in art with his bishop's vestments with the three boys, the daughters and the golden orbs.

On this day of St. Nicholas, can you find a way to make a miracle for someone? Maybe not bring them back from the dead but perhaps finding time to have a coffee with someone lonely and listen to them. Maybe buy a gift card for someone at a store you know they like but can't afford. Or volunteer an evening of babysitting for a couple stressed by the demands of new parenthood.

In other words, be your own saint.

Today there is much to mourn—December 7, 1941 being the day of the attack on Pearl Harbor and the beginning of America's involvement in World War II. I don't want to take away from that.

But for the Scientology religion, it is a day of great celebration—Flag Land Base Day!

Ron Hubbard was a drifter who had been kicked out of college, kicked out of the Navy and found himself lounging about the home of mystic poet grifter Aleister Crowley. Hubbard had a dental procedure that went poorly and under medication, had a near death experience that allowed him to see what's REALLY going on and how this party we call the universe got started.

In 1950 he published "Dianetics" in Astounding Science Fiction magazine based on his enlightenment. It was a magazine that my own grandfather Fritz Leiber published in virtually every month. Although my grandfather never suggested he had founded a religion.

So here's how it goes. Seventy five million years ago, Xenu was the dictator of the galactic confederacy and he wanted to offload some Thetans (peeps.) He arrived at earth—he called it Teegeeack—in a spacecraft with some similarities to a DC-8. He stacked these Thetans around volcanoes and set off hydrogen bombs to kill them. But... There were survivors.

That's us. And we have within us the memories of all that and it just has to be accessed by pricey courses conducted by auditors of the faith. And the faith has its adherents—John Travolta, Tom Cruise, Kristi Alley (deceased), but not Leah Remini anymore.

Scientology has holidays like any other self-respecting religion. There's March 13 which is L. Ron Hubbard's birthday, May 9 Dianetics Day, June 6 Maiden Voyage Day (that's when we celebrate how we're going to travel to the next planet), and my favorite—Sea Org Day August 12, where lowly paid but highly evolved Scientologists travel to the beach to engage in group bonding exercises kind of like an episode of The Office.

Today, December 7 Flag Land Base Day commemorates the opening of the Scientology headquarters at Clearwater, Florida in 1975 after years of working on the top secret "Project Normandy" in order to take control of the city. I think they succeeded.

We're approaching the celebration of the birth of Jesus Christ to the Virgin Mary. But there's another, perhaps more intriguing, immaculate birth situation that occurred on this day December 8, 1726. Involving rabbits.

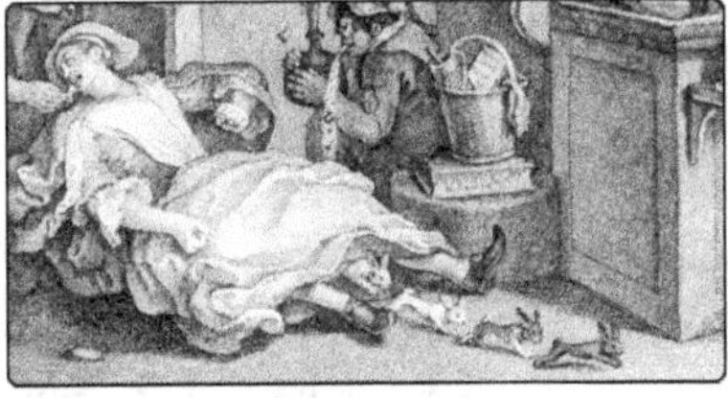

Twenty five year old Mary Toft was a peasant wife and mother of three from Surrey, England. She was all alone in her home and cried out in sudden labor pains. She didn't even know she was pregnant! A neighbor rushed over to help Mary. Lots of animal parts were, ahem, expectorated from Mary's body. A pig's bladder, a cat's paw, and a half dozen still born rabbits.

Over the next month, John Howard, the local obstetrician, delivered Mary of a dozen or so rabbits. The animals were not of good health and died almost upon birth—to be fair, some lived as long as a day after birth. Howard pickled their bodies in alcohol and invited doctors from all over the world to study the rabbits and the prolific Mary.

Mary became a celebrity with an aura of biblical importance about her births. When physicians put her under 'round the clock observation, the rabbit births stopped. A porter at the home where she was staying was caught trying to sneak a rabbit into Mary's room. Her husband was caught bringing in some leporine (fancy name for bunnies) as well.

Suspicions aroused, the police interrogated Mary for several days before she confessed on December 8, 1726 to inserting live animals into her, er, vagina. Rabbits being her favorite.

She was charged with being a "notorious and vile cheat" and sent to Bridewell Prison where the wardens allowed interested fans and haters to watch her in her prison cell. Then she was released, lived a regular life until her death at age 62.

I really don't have a moral to the story here. Do you?

On December 9, 1868 the world's first traffic light was installed in London outside the House of Parliament. I know what you're thinking—"ArLynn, you're crazy because the first car wasn't invented until 18 years later."

But this street light was intended to manage both pedestrian and carriage traffic at the busy intersection of Bridge, Parliament and Great George streets. The inventor John Peake Knight designed the gas lit lamp to be operated by a police constable who manually alternated colored lenses on the lamp with green for go and red for stop.

His marvel of modern life—presaging automobiles, airplanes and even cell phones—lasted three weeks. The gas line sprung a leak and there was an explosion. The constable on duty was badly burned and the newfangled stoplight was abandoned. It would be another 60 years before another was built in London.

December 10, 1937. Forty year old Bessie Wallis Warfield Spencer Simpson was a divorcee, awaiting her second divorce. She was American and, well, let's be blunt, not particularly attractive. She intended to marry forty-two year old Edward Albert Christian George Andrew Patrick David but everyone called him David. David's father, the King, had died on January 20, 1936 and David became King of England, taking on the regnal name Edward and his coronation was schedule for May, 1937. A coronation is a little more complicated than a children's birthday party—you can't just call Chuckie Cheese.

He had a nice life, ribbon cutting and giving speeches, keeping mistresses and swilling the really good stuff. But then one of his mistresses, Thelma Furness, introduced him to Wallis. Exit Thelma. I hope Thelma got some good jewelry out of the deal.

Under the Act of Success of 1701, King Edward would lose his crown if he married a divorcee or a Catholic. They could have (after that pesky second divorce) entered into a Morganatic wedding. It would be legal, and even recognized by the church but Wallis couldn't have the title Her Royal Highness and she couldn't inherit from her husband. Also, nobody had to go full tilt on the curtsey like the Duchess of Sussex on Oprah. Lastly, their children would have no claim on the throne. Seemed like a great solution—and then after a short period quietly make Wallis Duchess of, say, Winnetka. Oh, wait, that's my title!

The King wanted at least the title Duchess for Wallis, but his widowed mother the Dowager Queen and his younger brother Bertie, who was going to be King if David abdicated, wouldn't go for it. So on the tenth of December, the King signed his letter of abdication claiming he was doing this "for the woman he loved". All very romantic, but my theory is he never really wanted to be King. And I don't think our present day Harry wants to be the "spare". He'd like to be just an ordinary guy. But impossibly rich.

Ask yourself—do you love what you do and who you are in life? And if you could abdicate or withdraw from duties, would you?

On December 11, 1967 a ground breaking movie premiered in New York City. It was a rom-com, but not like a Jennifer Aniston thing. The movie answered the question "Guess Who's Coming to Dinner?" It boasted a stellar cast including Sidney Poitier, Katherine Hepburn, and Spencer Tracy. It would be the ninth cinematic pairing of Hepburn and Tracy although offscreen the married Tracy and the single Hepburn were publicly acknowledged paramours. Tracy was extremely ill and died only a few weeks after this, his last screen work. Hepburn never saw the completed movie because she claimed it would be too painful. For his part, Poitier—a very gifted and respected actor—was so intimidated by the couple that he did several scenes facing a couple of empty chairs.

The plot was pretty simple. Hepburn and Tracy, a married couple, are happy their daughter (in real life Hepburn's nepo niece) has returned home safely from a ten day trip to Hawaii. They aren't quite so pleased that she is bringing home the fiancé she met on the trip—he's a black doctor who plans to practice in Africa.

There's really only one reason to object to the wedding—after all, ten days? But the parents are also concerned about interracial marriage which, incidentally, was illegal in 17 states at the time. They aren't racists, it's more that they're realists of the time that an interracial marriage will face a lot of difficulties. Things REALLY get going when his parents show up and it turns out they are equally opposed and, well, I won't ruin the ending. Rent it yourself. Just PLEASE don't rent the Ashton Kutcher remake.*

The film was considered groundbreaking but these days we'd sort of just shrug at the premise. Except maybe the ten day courtship part. Amazing though, the forbidden nature of interracial marriage.

Our society changes so much and I hope we are more tolerant but of course some recent events have made me doubt we have left any prejudice and bigotry behind...

*Oddly, in the original release of 1967 there was a line in which a character replies to "guess who's coming to dinner?" With the sarcastic reply "Martin Luther King." That exchange was taken out after the Reverend's assassination but has been restored in some versions. I say you might as well see everything in its raw form.

December 12

I pity the fool!*

On December 12, 1982 Mr. T (born Laurence Turead) was quite frustrated. The A Team star had been invited to the White House by President Ronald Reagan and first lady Nancy to unveil the White House Christmas decorations. Mr. T was dressed in a Santa suit (pants cut off as shorts, natch), combat boots and his gold chains. But nobody wanted to sit on his lap at the Santa throne.

At the time he was living in Los Angeles, filming the popular ensemble action series The A Team. This trip to the White House was a cross country haul and he was in no mood to be snubbed.

And then the First Lady came over. Sat on his lap. Kissed him on the cheek. As Santa, he gave her a Mr. T doll and a bunch of air fresheners. I really don't understand the air fresheners.

The press went wild. Mr. T said "Burt Reynolds, eat your heart out!" Burt, at that point, was not dead and was in fact quite a sex symbol having posed nude for Cosmopolitan Magazine. Oh, and he was a movie star.

Mr. T had been invited by Nancy because she was spearheading the "just say no" to drugs campaign and oddly, Mr. T was in his spare time touring schools to deliver pretty much the same message.

Nancy's gesture mad a great photo op. EVERYBODY in the press corps covering the pre-Christmas event wanted to sit on Mr. T's lap. But the pic of him and Nancy? Kind of suggests she wasn't as uptight and stuffy as all that.

*"I Pity the Fool" was Mr. T's catch phrase when he was going to go off on someone.

December 13

On December 13, 1931 twenty six year old unemployed Yonkers mechanic Edward Contasino** nearly killed the Hon. Winston Churchill who would one day be Prime Minister of England. It was ten-thirty at night and New York was hopping even though there was of course Prohibition putting a damper on things.

But you couldn't keep Churchill away from the stuff. He was known to start his morning with a "whiskey mouthwash" and a bottle of claret, another bottle of cham-

**Often identified wrongly as having the first name Mario, perhaps reflecting some weird anti-eye-talian sentiment.

Continued on Next Page

December 13

pagne for lunch and after an afternoon nap he'd really get down to business with the drink and the cigars.**

On the evening in question, Churchill was midway through a forty lecture tour of America in order to get him and wife Clementine out of debt. He was getting out of a cab and as any good British gentleman, he looked to his left and seeing no southbound headlights, he sallied forth.

Right into Constasino's car which proceeded to drag Churchill several yards before Edward realized he had hit a Brit who didn't seem to understand that Americans drive on the "other" side of the street. Constasino put the dazed, drunk, and bloodied Churchill into his car and drove him to nearby Lenox Hospital.

Churchill was treated for cuts, bruises and a sprained shoulder. His body might, just might and I'm only an amateur pharmacologist, maybe have been a little more flexible and limber with the drinks in him and his injuries were minimal compared to what might have happened to a, ahem, sober man. Churchill owned up to the fact that the accident was entirely his fault. He was adamant in part because he worried that Constasino might suffer legal consequences. Constasino, meanwhile, said he was entirely to blame and he called the hospital repeatedly to inquire as to the health of the British statesman.

In the end, Constasino was allowed to visit with Churchill and his wife Clementine on the eve of Churchill's discharge. Clementine asked if they could help Constasino in a pecuniary sense. This is America, but the young man said no money, but thank you. Churchill gave him a copy of his most recent book The Unknown War. Just for a moment, imagine what momager Kris Kardashian Jenner would have done with such an offer on the table.

But Churchill definitely benefited from the experience—his physician Otto Pickhardt wrote him a note certifying that the post accident convalescence "necessitates the use of alcoholic spirits especially at meal times. The quantity is naturally indefinite."

And so, just like any self-respecting pet owner with access to the internet to order a blue vest and a friend with a degree in psychiatric services, Churchill got his service animal, er, bottle.

It is said that the Covid pandemic and resulting isolation will make one either a monk, a hunk, a drunk or a chunk. I don't think Churchill would have noticed.

**When the 2017 movie "The Darkest Hour" came out, the English version opened with a warning that second hand smoke, smoking in general, and heavy drinking could lead to an early demise. In 1965 when Churchill died, he was over ninety. Think how many more years he could have lived if he had ditched those habits in favor of lean cuisine, multivitamins and regular aerobic exercise!

December 14

Just five days after meeting Prince Albert of Saxe Coburg, Queen Victoria proposed.

They had a two year engagement. He was the love of her life and when he died on this day, December 14, 1861 after twenty one years of marriage the Queen and country were plunged into a period of mourning that would last until….

Seemingly forever. Or at least until she took up with her horseman John Brown. When he died she wrote "life for a second time has become most trying and sad to bear." Still, she was a mere whippersnapper of 68 years and she took up with her twenty four year old manservant Abdul Karim. When she died at the age of 81 in 1901, her love letters to Abdul were burned.

Damn, my life seems kind of boring!

December 15

On this day December 15, 1939 the movie "Gone with the Wind" premiered in Atlanta, Georgia where much of the action in both the movie and author Margaret Mitchell's novel took place. For the occasion, there were two very different outfits worn by two very different people.

Margaret wore a brocade evening coat from Rich's—an Atlanta department store founded in 1867. The book had been rejected over forty times by publishers before Random House offered her a contract. So the dress had sort of a "I'll show you vibe."

I know, I know—you're thinking ArLynn you're an idiot, the book was originally published in 1936 by MacMillan. You're right. Random House senior editors retracted the offer amid worries about how damn racist the book was. Disclaimer—I was introduced to the movie when I was at a group home as a teenager. It was a huge deal for us kids to get permission to watch television but even non-woke teenager me knew this movie was toxic.

Nonetheless, within a year of its publication, Margaret had sold the book's movie rights and there was the Atlanta premiere in 1939. Clark Gable, not normally known for his activism, initially threatened to boycott the premiere because the black actors would not be allowed to attend. Star Hattie McDaniel persuaded him to go. Later she would go on to get an Oscar for her performance, but was not allowed to be seated with her fellow actors.

So the night was glorious for Margaret, who would never again publish a novel. It was her peak. And it was the ground floor for another southern native ten year old Martin Luther King Jr.

MLK was part of a church choir which had been commissioned to sing at one of the many pre-screening charitable parties that evening. He was dressed as an antebellum slave and while I can't find a picture of him that evening, just imagine for a moment being ten years old and singing for white folk who won't let you sit down to dinner with them about how wonderful the Old South was. And while the choir brought home money to their church, I'm not sure as a mom I would have wanted my son up on that stage.

To give Margaret a smidgen of credit, she was a huge contributor in life and in her death to traditionally black Morehouse College.

I am of an age where I am aware that things that were perfectly unexceptional in my youth are now recognized as horrid. I'd like to believe we're better.

Brocade coat? Antebellum slave outfit? What was the better look?

____

____

____

____

____

December 16

On December 16, 1907 marked the start of a tremendous naval launch from Hampton Roads, Virginia that included 16 battleships divided into two squadrons with escorts.

President Teddy Roosevelt was onboard the presidential yacht The Mayflower as he waved goodbye to the ships. They were going on a year and a half long showcase of naval might that would circumnavigate the globe. The traditional song for naval launches—"the girl I left behind me"—was played. There are many variations on the lyrics, my favorite being…

> All the dames of France are fond and free
> And Flemish lips are really willing
> Very soft the maids of Italy
> And Spanish eyes are so thrilling
> Still, although I bask beneath their smile,
> Their charms will fail to bind me
> And my heart falls back to Erin's isle
> To the girl I left behind me.

So Beach Boys!

The tour was fraught with ceremony and pomp. No particular war was anticipated…er, sort of. In the 1880s the Naval fleet had consisted of 90 small ships, about a third of which were wooden. Hence, outdated. But Teddy, who had once been Assistant Secretary to the Navy, had commissioned steel ships. The ones on this voyage were painted white with ornate hull seals.

What in heaven's name possessed Teddy to do this circumnavigation of the globe that was pretty much just a show off?

Let's go back to very conservative, very bigoted San Francisco which had the previous year approved plans to segregate immigrant kids and "white" students in their school district. The immigrants included 93 Japanese children who were the ultimate targets of this policy—Anti-

Continued on Next Page

December 16

Japanese sentiment was high and the backlash was riots in Tokyo over the hideous Americans.*

At the last minute, Teddy managed to get the district to reverse the policy. But he had a sense that Japan would in time come after America. While the American government had fought battles over the Atlantic with various European and Berber governments, he could just as easily fight a war on the Pacific. And he wanted the Japanese to recognize that.

The voyage was called The Great White Fleet because of the colors on the ships and it lasted until late February of 1909. It might have put off a war over control of Asia but it didn't entirely eliminate it. The fleet was welcomed at Yokohama Japan in 1908 with great courtesy and a bit of wariness.

*Forty four of San Francisco's 125 present day schools, including Lincoln high school and Diane Feinstein school, are slated to be renamed because the honorees were or are racist. The city is definitely at the front end of political consciousness.

December 17

December 17, 1928 successful businessmen, er, conman, George C. Parker was sentenced to life in Sing Sing Prison in Ossington, New York. He immediately became a source of entertainment for his fellow prisoners, as he spun yarns about his thirty years of selling the Statue of Liberty, Grant's Tomb, The Metropolitan Museum of Art—mostly to naïve immigrants who had no idea he didn't own ANY of these properties. But his most important exploits involved selling the Brooklyn Bridge which he did almost 60 times. He didn't own the bridge. But he could spin a yarn and charm anybody with a wallet. The phrase "I have a bridge to sell you" was a popular way of teasing someone gullible. Today, nothing like that would happen. At least not with the Brooklyn Bridge.

On December 18,1843 I hope you will consider Marlowe, who—if we are to believe Charles Dickens—was dead as a doornail.

Yes, Jacob Marlowe was dead. Dead as a doornail, Dickens clarified in the opening of his novella Christmas Carol. Marlowe's passing influenced his former business partner Ebenezer Scrooge so much so that even the word "Scrooge' or the phrase "Bah Humbug" gives us a common experience of the joy, the redemption, the self-reflection and the reaching out of the holiday! And we think of the ghosts—Christmas Past, Christmas Present and Christmas Future—.

Dickens was in financial turmoil (he had a lot of children and a few mistresses) and he despaired of his literary career. But this novella was publishedon this day as A Christmas Carol, In Prose, Being a Ghost Story of Christmas. It was sold out immediately. Other editions were put out and Dickens even gave over a hundred public readings of the story right up until his death in 1870. He was rich, rich off of Christmas! God bless us everyone indeed! And though he wrote many other novels—Great Expectations, Oliver Twist, etc.—this is where his fortune was made.

If I were visited by three ghosts tonight, I would recall past, present and future Christmases with a mixture of regret, awe and joy. How about you?

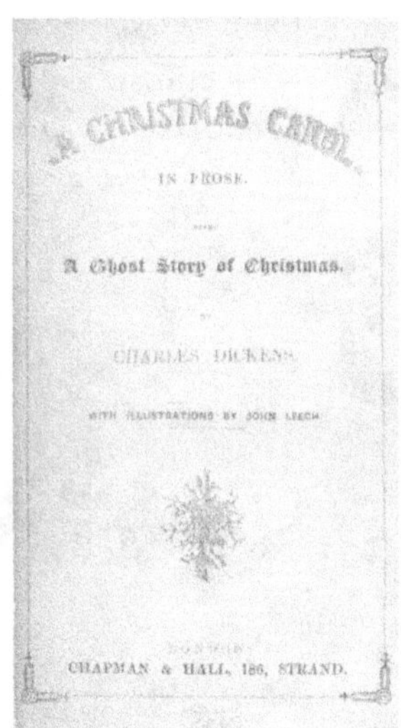

December 19

On this day, December 19, 1973 late night talk show host Johnny Carson ignited a crisis that will sound all too familiar to the alum of the COVID pandemic hysteria!

In his evening monologue opening the show Carson observed that people were tired of economic uncertainty, political unrest, and weird shortages. Oil, for instance, had been in short supply and American state legislatures had reacted by restricting gasoline sales on Sundays—resulting in long lines on Saturdays at every station. Every American could relate to Carson's words.

Carson followed up his comments about the oil shortage with his concerns about a report that wood pulp production had fallen in several Wisconsin paper mills and that there was a resulting toilet paper crisis coming.

There wasn't. It was just a joke. But the ensuing panic in America created a REAL toilet paper crisis. Folks cleared the shelves of grocery stores and it would take several months before the toilet paper industry righted itself.

When the Covid pandemic first got us locked down, it was impossible to find toilet paper, paper towels, and the so important hand sanitizer. I tracked down a recipe for homemade sanitizer and spent an afternoon making bottles of it for my local favorite diner. It required ethanol but Russian Vodka and glycerin wall all I had to work with.

I live across the street from the grocery store and there was a morning when I was pulled aside by the manager in charge of the paper goods and cleaning supplies aisle. "Shhhhhhhhh!" he said. "I have something to show you. I thought he was propositioning me—but no, he had set aside a bottle of Purell for me. Where he got it, I don't know and I didn't ask. I expressed my gratitude with the same enthusiasm as I would show if I had been presented with a bottle of Chanel No. 5.

____

____

____

____

____

December 20

December 20 is the feast or homegoing day of Katharina von Bora Luther who passed in 1552. She, as you might guess, is a Lutheran saint (I didn't even know the Lutherans had saints), who was also later included in the Episcopal list of saints. She was born sometime in 1499 in Saxony, Germany and it's unclear who her parents were. Back then lots of families didn't officially record the births of their daughters. But we do know that at the age of five she was sent to a Benedictine convent in the German town of Brehna. A couple of transitions later, she ended up at the Nimbschen Abbey or Mary's Throne if you want to use the English translation.

She was devout, as you can imagine, but she and some of her fellow sisters had started to think about the Reformation as described by Martin Luther. She wrote to him on behalf of herself and her fellow sisters. Luther responded by sending the guy who delivered herring to the abbey. The sisters hid under a cover on his wagon and he got them to Luther's home so they could be taught the "true" religion.

The sisters' families and the Abbey wouldn't take them back, largely because they didn't want the wrath of the Catholic Church.

Still, Luther wanted the best for these sisters. He found them jobs or husbands except for Katharina. He didn't want to marry her at first but then he considered… "it will please my Father, rile the Pope, cause the angels to laugh and the devils to weep."

Good enough reason to propose. She was 26, he was 41 when they tied the knot in 1525. It was a nontraditional, Protestant based marriage. She took care of the small stuff like their six children, four adopted children, their land and income, and when the plague rifled Germany she ran a hospital. He took care of the big things like writing and reading and teaching theology at Wittenberg University.

Martin died in 1546 and though he had written a will which left all his property to Katharina—including his home known as Black Cloister—Saxony law didn't recognize it as valid. In 1552 she was hit by a carriage and fell into a pit of mud. For three months she was pretty much unconscious. Her last words—"I will stick to Christ like a burr to cloth."

She may not be famous, certainly not in comparison to her husband, but together, and it could only have been together, they changed the nature of marriage and cemented the Lutheran faith.

December 21 is the winter solstice which on the Northern Hemisphere is the shortest day followed by the longest night. It's the beginning of winter and it's easy to look ahead with a twinge of dread. If you're in the Southern Hemisphere it's the beginning of summer and it's time to party!

Many Christian religions hold a Blue Christmas service which honors those who have lost a loved one or who have some other sort of grief. Many churches hold the service with some empty chairs to commemorate those we have lost and often participants are given an ornament on which they're encouraged to write the name of their loved ones.

There is a lot of pressure to be happy and joyful, to give thanks and see family. Oh, and presents! Don't forget the presents!

But sometimes there are some mixed emotions—maybe a divorce, an estrangement from a child or a dear friend, a financial disaster. And it doesn't help to be surrounded by unrelenting happiness. Every time I hear Andy Williams' song "It's the Most Wonderful Time of the Year" I want to punch the radio.

A Blue Christmas service is a good time to acknowledge that you're not the only one with mixed emotions about the holiday. In my fair town of Winnetka, I will go to a service and at first it will be a downer. But then as the service closes, I will know that there will be better days.

Or I might just put on Elvis Presley's rendition of Blue Christmas (released as a single in 1964, recorded in 1957) and I might just have a short pity party. The song clocks in at slightly more than two minutes. That's enough time to get my bearings.

____

____

____

____

December 22 is national Short Persons Day. Which originally started as "throw a short person" day. Don't even start with me about how politically incorrect this all is. When you're older, you'll say something and your grandkids will roll their eyes at how utterly horrible you are.

This is a great day to watch Bad Santa which I consider to be part of my foursome of Christmas movies and includes a semi-sketchy short person played by Tony Cox.

While you're on the couch with the remote in your hand this day you might think about how the movie Die Hard really should be considered a Christmas flick—I mean, jeez, there's Bruce Willis trying to save his family in time for a yuletide carol. And of course there's the 2010 Jalmari Helander film Rare Exports set in the Laplander territory of Finland.

On December 23, 1974 the ugly sweater was born.

President Gerald Ford was on vacation in Vail, Colorado with his family. He was photographed wearing a sweater with a WIN motif. The president was battling both to be elected (he had come into office after the resignation of his predecessor Richard Nixon) and he was fighting inflation and a sour economy.

Most people thought this truly wretched sweater was meant to suggest victory, as in winning the upcoming election. The WIN sweater was assumed to be a campaign poster in wool.

But it wasn't. WIN stood for Ford's motto to "whip inflation now". The push to bring inflation down failed miserably.

So wear YOUR ugly sweater proudly. The original is in the collection of the Gerald Ford presidential library in Grand Rapids, Michigan. That's where Ford was a high school and college football star. He would lose to Jimmy Carter the former peanut farmer and nuc-u-lar scientist—he couldn't pronounce nuclear.

____

____

____

____

____

December 24, 1931 might reasonably have been a bah humbug sort of day. The Great Depression had cost many a family their homes, their savings, their hopes for a prosperous future. Industrialist John D. Rockefeller was doing nicely. He was one year into building a 14 building complex in Manhattan that he intended to name The Rockefeller Center just in case anybody forgot who he was and how wealthy he was. The holiday might have been a good time to put a little something extra in the paychecks of his construction workers or maybe buy trees for the mostly Italian-American workers to put up in their tenement home.

But it was the workers who gifted Rockefeller. They pooled their available money to buy a 20 foot tall Balsam First which they erected in the Rockefeller Center. While they lined up to collect their paychecks, they decorated the tree with paper and cranberry garlands as well as festive tin cans, all of which were made by their wives and children.

It wasn't much of a hearty celebration but I sure hope they had a chance to share a few snorts from a flask and after a hearty Yuletide goodbye to their fellow workers and had enough wages to buy a nice dinner and give their tykes a toy or maybe a candy too!

Two years later, Rockefeller erected a 50-foot tall tree and had an elaborate tree lighting ceremony. In 1936 he constructed a skating rink. The tree and the skating rink make the season bright.

But I admire most of all the workers who took their own money to buy a tree. And their wives and families who made the decorations. God bless us everyone!

____

____

____

____

____

December 25

On December 25, 1914 World War I ended.

Well, it was just for one day, but what a day!

British and German soldiers climbed out of their bunkers and cautiously crossed the no man's land between them. There was hand shaking, exchange of gifts (cigarettes being a big one) and a sharing of whatever food they had available. There was a game of soccer organized. A German barber gave haircuts to several of the British soldiers who were looking a little shaggy. There might have been some liquor to be had.

And then when the day was over, the war resumed and it wouldn't be until 1918 that surviving soldiers could go home.

Today I have only one Christmas wish for you—ceasefire.

The gifts, the feasts, the merry making will just be a bonus!

December 26

December 26th is the feast day of Saint Stephen the patron saint of Britain. The day has come to be called Boxing Day. The name most likely came about because it was the day that servants celebrated their Christmas after their "betters" had been served on Christmas day. The meals for the "betters" were then put out in boxes for them to eat themselves almost like a picnic in the castle.

While I always think of Bridget Jones on Boxing Day it's also a day that traditionally has been reserved for fox hunting. On December 26, hunt clubs assemble in their "pinks" which is the term for the male traditional attire and women wear skirted riding habits and some still ride sidesaddle.

On this day in 2004 the Brits banned fox hunting with hounds who would track down the foxes. Now the custom is to "drag hunt" in which hounds are given an artificial scent rather than a live fox so they can participate but not spoil the experience.

December 27

December 27th is National Fruitcake Day. This much maligned dessert gets regifted and regifted again. But let's consider—fruitcakes were first made by the Romans around 500 B.C. and consisted of pomegranate seeds, pine nuts, raisins, pretty much anything you had lying around the house. Throw in some barley and some spirits and you've got fructus crustulam!

The dish became more and more complex, with the addition of sugar and butter. Almost criminal, well, actually it was outlawed in the eighteenth century in some parts of Europe because it was too rich and luxurious. Which means the upper class got to have it and the rest of us peasants just dreamt of it. When Marie Antoinette quipped "let them eat cake" maybe she was being egalitarian....

Dreaming of fruitcake probably is best commemorated in the 1956 Truman Capote short story A Christmas Memory. It tells of a poor dysfunctional aunt and young Truman making fruitcakes as presents for their wealthy relatives. I think it's Capote's best work and I hope you read it today. I mean, this is not the time of year for Truman's In Cold Blood.

Lest I fail to entice you to consider the fruitcake in a better light, just think of Manitou, Colorado which instituted Fruitcake Toss Day in the mid-1990s. That's when you take your fruitcake out to a public park and toss it out. Makes the pigeons happy. It's celebrated January 3. It's a diversion from the boredom of winter, and your relatives will love that you don't show up with one for twelfth night!

Ingredients

Fruit
- 1 1/2 cups (213g) dried pineapple, diced
- 1 1/2 cups (255g) raisins, golden or regular
- 1 cup (128g) dried apricots, diced
- 1 1/2 cups (223g) dates, chopped
- heaping 1 cup (170g) candied red cherries, plus additional for decoration,
- 1/3 cup (64g) crystallized ginger, diced, optional
- 3/4 cup (170g) rum, brandy, apple juice, or cranberry juice

Batter
- 16 tablespoons (227g) unsalted butter, at room temperature, at least 65°F

......

On December 28, 2008 in the 79th season in the NFL, after the 1966 merger of the AFL and NFL and the first after the expansion to a 16 game season, the Detroit Lions accomplished something remarkable in football history.

They finished the season undefeated.

Oh, wait no, ALWAYS defeated. Zero Sixteen. The Green Bay Packers (Lord, I hate that team) crushed them in that last one. Oddly, the Lions' preseason games had been okay and seemed to have presaged at least a passable season. As the defeats piled up, coaches and players alike were fired and the mood was sour.

I would have hated to have been in their locker room that last day. Actually, any of the days of the season. And not because they were losing. It's that they were losing morale by such insane job insecurity and shuffling of personnel. I frankly think they should have stuck with everyone on their team because they couldn't have done any worse.

The first year I coached soccer, I had a team of ten kindergarten boys—at least, I think they all self-identified as boys. You try explaining to five year olds that they shouldn't "honeycomb" the ball and should spread out and pass. Take control of the field. We had an undefeated, uh, completely defeated season of six games.

At the end of the last one, as I was assembling my equipment to take home, one mom came up to me and said "well, at least you're consistent." Winnetka is a brutal town.

By my ninth season, the boys I was coaching were undefeated. For real. And I usually had to invoke the slaughter rule at half time—as in "you can only score with your nondominant foot" or "we're going to voluntarily take one player off the field" or "just let them have one score for their pride."

Sometimes unremitting defeat can just wear you out. And it wears out other people who experience your defeats. Take today to count your victories and celebrate others' no matter how small or hard to find.

When my eldest was doing hockey, things didn't go so well at a particular game. Their coach assembled them in the locker room and said "the good news is we won the last period." They had scored one goal but it meant a lot. Find that third period goal in your life and build on it.

On December 29, 1566 a historical, magical, and memorable engagement party was held at the home of Professor Lucas Bachmeister of the University of Rostock in Germany. It was for his daughter and if the events of the day didn't create a bridezilla and a good one at that, I don't know what does.

In attendance at the party was Tycho Ottesen Brahe, a genius who was studying medicine, astronomy and astrology (at the time they were all considered the same thing), and alchemy (that's how you turn anything into gold or at least try). The Brahe family had an odd family trait—

They all dueled (or at least the men did, the women just said catty things about each other) and many of those duels were both mortal and familial. Tycho had four cousins who died in duels, two with each other. And you think your holiday dinners are contentious when the topic of dinner table conversation turns whatever happened to Aunt Maude's jewelry after her death.

At the party, twenty year old Tycho revived an argument with his third cousin Manderup Parsberg, a minor Danish nobleman over who was the better mathematician. It wasn't even an argument over a woman! They decided on a duel in the dark. I don't duel myself and it's illegal virtually everywhere in the United States, but I would advise dawn. Or at least lamps.

Parsberg was the better shot, nearly blowing Brahe's head off. Luckily, the best medical care was right there at the university. He ended up with a prosthetic nose with a sort of brace holding his forehead together. While the every day metalware was made of brass, his "dress up" or "formalware" was gold. He wore it for the rest of his life—he died at 55. I hope he was buried in the gold.

Tycho went on to make a number of discoveries, particularly in the field of astronomy that helped pre-telescope astronomers.

The two third cousins later reconciled. I suppose that's the point of this story in a weird convoluted way. In a family like the Brahes you really don't want to have enemies in your family. So now might be the time to consider—prosthetic nose or peace in the family?

December 30, 1854 celebrates James Garsden, the United States Minister of Mexico. On this day Garsden purchased from Mexico 29,670 acres of what would become sections of Arizona and New Mexico. Purchase price $10mil and the promise that the United States would protect Mexicans in other areas from Native American attacks (America's government sort of welched out on that second part of the deal but they at least showed up with the money).

The Garsden area wasn't all that large but it was a follow up to…

The Treaty of Guadalupe Hidalgo in which Mexico gave up California, Nevada, Utah, New Mexico, most of Arizona, some parts of Colorado, Oklahoma, Kansas and Wyoming. We ponied up $15 mil for 525k square miles. And gave the usual reassurances of protection from Native American attacks.

I say we give Mexico the land back, all of it certainly under the Garsden deal and let's throw in Guadalupe, Hidalgo. Mexico will get Vegas, the Hoover Dam, Angelina Jolie, Harry and Megs, In'n'Out Burgers and San Francisco. The only thing we ask is that any retirement communities be protected.

I'm going to get into trouble for this opinion aren't I? But what would you suggest?

Some years you have to look ahead. Very far ahead. Consider the foresightedness of Arthur Guinness who on December 31, 1759 signed a 9,000 year lease on a brewery in Dublin which had had the misfortune of going out of business. That's when he took to making stout.

The lease was only four pages long but it had one utterly fantastic aspect—it allowed Guiness free use of Dublin's water supply. All he had to get was some hops, yeast, and malted barley (most of which he would have to roast for that full-bodied flavor).

In 1775, the city fathers were getting a little miffed and demanded that Guiness pay for the water. Guiness relented and signed an agreement guaranteeing Dublin the sum of ten pounds per year for 8,795 years.

We'll all be dead when this story is over and negotiations for the renewal of the land lease and the water access are opened. I think there's two morals to the story. December 31 is a good day to plan big and it's also a day for great optimism.

What's your plan? Don't bother with trifles, get to a big one. Just making a decision is enough of a step for one day. And as for the optimism, smack that smile on your face—your future success deserves it!

____

____

____

____

____